SPORT IN THE GLOBAL SOCIETY
General Editor: J.A. Mangan

The interest in sports studies around the world is growing and will continue to do so. This unique series combines aspects of the expanding study of *sport in the global society*, providing comprehensiveness and comparison under one editorial umbrella. It is particularly timely, with studies in the cultural, economic, ethnographic, geographical, political, social, anthropological, sociological and aesthetic elements of sport proliferating in institutions of higher education.

Eric Hobsbawm once called sport one of the most significant practices of the late nineteenth century. Its significance was even more marked in the late twentieth century and will continue to grow in importance into the new millennium as the world develops into a 'global village' sharing the English language, technology and sport.

SPORT IN AUSTRALASIAN SOCIETY

Past and Present

Editors

J.A. MANGAN

University of Strathclyde

and

JOHN NAURIGHT

Charles Sturt University

FRANK CASS
LONDON • PORTLAND, OR

First published in 2000 in Great Britain by
FRANK CASS PUBLISHERS
Newbury House, 900 Eastern Avenue
London, IG2 7HH

and in the United States of America by
FRANK CASS PUBLISHERS
c/o ISBS, 5804 N.E. Hassalo Street
Portland, Oregon 97213-3644

Printed in Great Britain by
Antony Rowe Ltd., Chippenham, Wilts.

Contents

Series Editor's Foreword

J. A. MANGAN

In *The Decline and Fall of the Roman Empire*, Edward Gibbon was of the view that 'We imperceptibly advance from youth to age, without observing the gradual, but incessant, change of human affairs, and, even in our larger experience of history, the imagination is accustomed, by a perpetual series of causes and effects, to unite the most distant revolutions.'[1] It is doubtful whether followers of Australasian sport would agree. They have experienced a sporting sea-change and they are only too well aware of it.

Sea-change is defined by *The Oxford English Reference Dictionary* as 'a notable or unexpected transformation'.[2] In *Sport in Australasian Society: Past and Present* two polarities confront each other at the ends of a relatively short historical continuum spanning the period from the late nineteenth century to the late twentieth century. These polarities are reasonably well described by a cluster of concepts: corporatism and individualism, conformity and non-conformity, uniformity and pluralism. In general, in Australasian culture and in its sport which invariably mirrors culture, the last half of the nineteenth century was characterized more by conformity than non-conformity while the last half of the twentieth century witnessed saw more non-conformity and less conformity. These are generalities but they contain more than a kernel of the truth.

The truth inside the kernel is encapsulated in two period illustrations respectively from the late nineteenth century and the late twentieth century. Sport in the last decades of the nineteenth century was mostly, if not wholly, for men. It comprised a spoken and unspoken training in masculinity. It promoted, sanctioned and applauded the qualities of fitness, aggression, persistence and *esprit de corps*. Schools played a central and crucial part in this induction.

Of course, this was not the entirety of sport but it was a large part of it. By the late twentieth century, in contrast, sport was more and more for women as well as for men and historic masculine preserves gradually became also feminine territories. This was true, for example, of the most 'male' of sports – rugby football. The physical and psychological aggression traditionally required of men on rugby fields and viewed in the past, among other things, as an exemplary preparation for war, was now voluntarily embraced by women more as an extension of their freedom than of the extension of military training to both sexes. Some women, by their own frank admission, enjoyed the aggressive conflicts of the rugby field and wished to participate in them. It is foolishly naïve to see this *voluntary* participation as 'masculinization' into historical male brutality. It is the logical extension of the democratic freedom to choose any available attractive recreation. The fundamental difference between the past and the present is the past *compulsion* demanded of boys to take part; girls choose to take part in the present as a manifestation of their ever-increasing freedom. This is one sea-change. There are others caught in the essays in *Sport in Australasian Society* – sport as packaged commercial entertainment, as passive pleasure rather than active pleasure, as a celebration of hedonism rather than morality. In some one hundred years there have been momentous changes – some good and some perhaps not so good.

Thus to the final point – writing of the 'great principle of scepticism' and the immense part it has played in the history of European civilization, Henry Thomas Buckle wrote in his *History of Civilization in England*:

> ... it may be said, that to scepticism we owe that spirit of inquiry, which ... has gradually encroached on every possible subject: has reformed every department of practical and speculative knowledge; has weakened the authority of the privileged classes and thus placed liberty on a surer foundation; has chartered the despotism of princes; has restrained the arrogance of the nobles; and has even diminished the prejudices of the clergy. In a word, it is this which has the remedied three fundamental errors of the olden times; errors which have made the people, in politics too confiding; in science too credulous; in religion too intolerant.[3]

Prescient words.

In the year of the Sydney Olympics – the stimulus to this volume – it is surely time to exercise 'the great principle of scepticism' once again:

a sea-change is required in the spirit of Olympism and the morality of the Olympics! Now that would be unexpected. Advance Australia – *Fair*!

J. A. MANGAN
International Centre for Sport, Socialisation Society
University of Strathclyde
July 2000

NOTES

1. *The Oxford English Reference Dictionary* (Oxford, 1996, 2nd Edition), p.1305.
2. Quoted in H.A. Treble, *English Prose: Narrative, Descriptive and Dramatic* (Oxford, n.d.), p.197.
3. Henry Thomas Buckle, *History of Civilization in England* (Oxford, 1925 Edition), Vol.1, p. 271.

PROLOGUE

Sport and Past Australasian Culture

STUART MACINTYRE

In recent times, sport has become an ever larger business, both for those who do it and those who study it. Just a quarter-century ago, historians in Australia and New Zealand who were interested in sport pursued it as a fugitive enthusiasm. The Australians came out in 1977 with a conference on 'Making of Sporting Traditions', and published the proceedings of this and subsequent conferences. The fourth conference in 1983 established the Australian Society for Sports History, which in the following year commenced publication of the journal *Sporting Traditions*. Meanwhile in New Zealand, sport attracted the interests of academics through their involvement in the issue of sporting contacts with apartheid South Africa. The history of sport entered the university curriculum, theses were written and monographs published; a vigorous sub-discipline was established.

The academic practice of sports history coexists with other ways of recording sporting traditions and other ways of reflecting upon them. Long before university-based historians entered the field there was a substantial commemorative literature. Journalists and amateur historians produced chronicles and yearbooks for particular codes along with club and association histories. The increasing participation of the professional historian in the writing of commissioned histories lies at one end of the present spectrum of sports marketing and promotion. Similarly, there were avid collectors of sporting memorabilia well in advance of the creation of national museums and repositories. The growing employment of trained curators and archivists sits alongside the continued activity of other custodians and a vast industry in franchised sporting products.

History, moreover, is just one of the academic disciplines concerned with sport. The older departments of physical education have yielded to schools of human movement studies that draw on physiology and psychology, business studies and bioethics, to prepare their charges. Sports history and broader sports studies have been peripheral players in many of the new schools as they have rushed to embrace biological science models. However, several of these schools have also helped to preserve the embryonic discipline through the provision of academic positions for scholars interested in the social and cultural significance of sport.

The historians who pioneered the study of sport fostered a critical awareness of a seemingly innocent activity. They wanted to demonstrate that sport was a serious business, as amenable to rigorous analysis as other spheres of social life. They drew on the methodology of social history, with its attention to class, gender and ethnicity, to show how these social structures ran through play as well as work. Hence John Mulvaney's early study of the Aboriginal cricket team that toured England in the 1860s, and Leonie Sandercock and Ian Turner's pioneering account of Australian Rules football with its strong emphasis on the class composition of players and spectators.[1] Some sports historians subsequently followed the cultural turn and considered games as codes of meaning that work on their human subjects. Such holistic approaches are apparent in this collection and have had some effect on sports studies, but the stronger influence on that enterprise comes from the biological, human and social sciences. For the most part these other disciplines are ahistorical in their methodology; their practitioners display a correspondingly weak awareness of temporal change, contingency and contestation.

Nor, for that matter, has the work of sports historians entered fully into the ken of colleagues in their own discipline. Sport has a limited presence in the national histories of Australia and New Zealand. It appears fitfully as a marker of popular consciousness and serves as a counterpoint to the dominant political narrative. Hence Brian Fitzpatrick's conclusion to his survey of *The Australian Commonwealth* in 1956: 'The Australian people made heroes of none, and raised no idols, except perhaps Ned Kelly, an outlaw, and Carbine, a horse.'[2] Phar Lap plays a similar role in the final volume of Manning Clark's *A History of Australia* (except that he is credited with a second victory in the Melbourne Cup when in fact he finished eighth in 1931 after winning in 1930).[3] National sporting events figure as moments of contention (the Bodyline series in Australia, the Springbok tour of New Zealand in 1981,

Trevor Chappell's underarm delivery in the same year). Triumphs abroad mark the emergent national consciousness (the invention of the Ashes after Australia's first Test victory in England in 1882, the first All Black Tour of Great Britain in 1905, and the Australasian triumphs of Brookes and Wilding in the Davis Cup). But few of these general histories consider sport at the local level as a constituent of everyday life. Geoffrey Blainey's *A Shorter History of Australia* included a chapter on the close of association of sport and work in the second half of the nineteenth century as well as the rise of the sporting hero.[4] Jock Phillips investigated the cult of the hard man in rugby as part of his study of New Zealand masculinity, while Keith Sinclair discussed the role of sport in his historical study of the New Zealand national identity.[5] These were exceptional forays.

With the emergence in the second half the twentieth century of international sport as spectacle and industry carrying major implications for morale and economic benefit, sport becomes indisputably part of the national story. Thus most accounts of post-war Australia dwell on the Melbourne Olympics in 1956, while the America's Cup became a major preoccupation of both countries from the 1980s. But this is a story of planning and construction, tourism, sponsorship, mass entertainment and electronic media, in which national anxiety and celebration overshadows the games and yachting contests.

The transformation of sport has enlarged retrospective interest in its practitioners. With the transformation of the élite athlete into celebrity, sporting men and women have become far more prominent in reference works. The first 12 volumes of the *Australian Dictionary of Biography* appeared between 1966 and 1990. Covering the years 1788–1939, they made space for an impressive variety of sporting men and a small number of women: axeman and billiard players, bookmakers and dog racer, surfer and speleologist. But they number just 210 out of 7,200 entries.[6] The most recent volume of *The New Zealand Dictionary of Biography*, for the period 1920–1940, includes 61 in a total of 613 entries – more than three times as many.[7] The Australian biographical dictionary began in the 1960s, the New Zealand a quarter-century later, though certain preferences remain constant – the largest New Zealand category is rugby footballers (13 entries), the largest Australian one cricketers (54).

Sports historians have a tendency to normalize their subject, general historians to treat it as exceptional. The former show sport exemplifying broader historical themes: the transmission to the British colonies of leisure pursuits with their overtones of social hierarchy (exclusive fieldsports, popular pastimes); the investment of games with Arnoldian moral purpose; their enlistment in the martial project of the nation-state; the efficacy of sport as a social discipline; its capture by market forces. Hence a recent overview observes that 'Sport in Australia, as in many other nations, has been a prime means of gender-fixing; a way of socialising the populace into sex-based social roles; a method of informing, even dictating to both men and women how they should behave on and off the sports field'.[8] The obverse of this indictment is a conscious effort to retrieve the sporting achievement of minorities. Hence we have a celebratory account of *Sporting Immigrants*, a history of Indigenous Australians as *Proud Champions*, and a reminder that Australian sportswomen made up *Half the Race*.[9] Such emphases accord with the directions of recent historiography; they serve the desire to tie the sub-discipline of sports history to the work of other historians.

Those historians who create national narratives are slow to take up such findings. They take up the major themes of cultural transmission, social discipline, nation building and the operation of the market through other, more familiar forms of activity. They look for signal events as the pegs on which they arrange their plot. For sport to impinge on the story, it needs to spill beyond the confines of the playing field into public life and national consciousness. The historian thus draws on those aspects of sport that are somehow emblematic of a distinctive way of life. A recent *Concise History of Australia* suggests that sporting heroes occupied an exalted place in the country's imagination in the first half of the twentieth century because they signified betrayal of innocent virtue by unscrupulous foreign foes:

> Thus Les Darcy, the boy boxer forced to leave Australia in 1916 because he would not volunteer for the AIF, dead within six months; or the chestnut horse Phar Lap , who won the Melbourne Cup in 1930 but also died in America, 'poisoned by the Yanks'; or Don Bradman, the wonder batsman, against whose incomparable the English had to bend the rules during the 'Bodyline Tour' of 1932–3.[10]

That Phar Lap was a New Zealand horse is incidental to this usage, which follows in the footsteps of Fitzpatrick and others in making sport the apotheosis of Australian values.

Sports historians are understandably impatient with such attempts to make their subject serve these purposes. They see Australia and New Zealand as imitative rather than inventive. The only major sport that originated here is Australian Rules football and it remains restricted to its home country; though perhaps surf lifesaving has claims to recognition. They note that our sporting competitions remained localised throughout most of the nineteenth century, so that even national competitions were slow to emerge. They observe that the international games on which Australians and New Zealanders pride themselves on national prowess are pursued in a restricted number of countries. They recognize that other countries play and follow sport with an avidity equal to our own.[11]

Sport certainly flourished in the Australian and New Zealand colonial settlements. Immigrant groups quickly re-established a repertoire of leisure pursuits – from horse-racing and field sports to skittles and darts – and quickly institutionalized them. While the patterns of sport were shaped by class and ethnicity, there was a marked tendency towards broad participation in common pursuits. We might see this as a hallmark of the European settler societies that flourished during the nineteenth century as commodity producers for the home market. Australia and New Zealand, along with South Africa and Argentina, were located in temperate zones and possessed plentiful open spaces. Operating well above subsistence level and with the market controlling most aspects of material life, they were able to mark off the weekend from the working week and to afford discretionary expenditure. With large metropolitan centres endowed with modern public transport, they assembled crowds of spectators. With high levels of literacy, they enlarged awareness and interest in sporting achievement. As places of opportunity and improvement, they encouraged rational recreation. As new societies composed of newcomers, they were both inclusive and responsive to new pastimes.

All of this implies that sport was an activity set apart from the serious business of life. The Latin word for sport, *ludus*, is also the word for play and shades into amusement, frolic and trifle. Yet the Romans took their sport seriously, and so did the colonists. Commercial forces already operated on nineteenth-century sport through wagering, payments and promotion. There were close links between work and sport, with many competitions based on occupational skills such as horse-riding, rowing and cycling, stock management, ploughing, timber-cutting and other events still evident at agricultural shows. Sheep shearing sits on the border of the two categories. Sport channelled competition into formal and ritualized forms, both tamed and inflamed rivalries. It was a surrogate for war and a preparation for it.

Yet this understanding of sport is still restrictive. The idea that sport was transplanted in the settler societies, along with government, law, technology and culture, is premised on the disappearance of the institutions and practices of the original inhabitants. The recognition of Aboriginal and Maori aptitude in various European sports has stimulated a retrieval of their earlier achievements despite discrimination and disadvantage. It has not, to my knowledge, produced a consideration of the possibility that sport existed before the white occupation. The obstacles to such an exercise are partly methodological and partly conceptual. In the absence of written records, we have limited information from which to reconstitute practices that existed before they were disrupted. Those that continued and those preserved in memory and tradition suggest that playfulness entered into almost very aspect of life: that the differences between work and play, warfare and competition, religious belief and performance were distinctions on a continuum points on a continuum of social practice. It is not clear if our notion of sport, as an activity with its particular times, locations, rules, and precise measurement of outcomes, is appropriate in such a context. There have been attempts to suggest that Australian Rules football had its origins in an Aboriginal game, but this seems to stretch a putative resemblance to breaking point.

The settler societies took to games at a particular moment in the evolution of sport. The codification of games such as rugby, soccer, cricket and baseball allowed for their rapid spread within and beyond the English-speaking countries. Golf, rowing, athletics and swimming followed the same process of standardization. It is striking that these sports, which Australians and New Zealanders took up quickly and enthusiastically, retained their hold – and also that the only major sport to rival them, Australian Rules football, was itself codified at this time.

To be sure, they invested these games with distinctive local qualities. The early blurring of distinctions between the genteel amateur and the plebeian professional, better standards of nutrition and health, and the generous provision of facilities made for high standards of performance. In cricket, as Ian Harriss has suggested, the Australian batsman developed a calculated industrial efficiency that eclipsed the languid and free-flowing pastoral style of his English counterpart.[12] Similar qualities were attributed to the All Blacks of 1905, with an English journalist describing 'a complex, highly polished mechanism composed of a number of interchangeable units'.[13] Australians liked to think that their Davis Cup successes in the 1950s affirmed the superiority of the suburban church club over the grim professionalism of the Yanks; as Kevin Fewster has shown, it was the Americans who were the lilywhites and the Australians who created a production line of champions through sponsorship, coaching and fully-funded international tours.[14] A similar pattern is apparent in Australia's pioneering cricket academy: while complaining of the East German distortion of Olympic competition, the Commonwealth and State governments spend lavish sums on their sports institutes.

Sport is thus big business but it is something more. It serves an index of wellbeing and pride, which is of increasing significance in public policy. That function of sport is by no means new, nor is it restricted to the two countries – we may think of England's success in the World Cup for soccer back in the 1960s and its benefits for the Wilson Labour government. The dependence of a people and its polity on sporting triumphs might be taken as a sign of its immaturity. The smaller, more isolated and less resilient Australian states make more of their victories in national competitions than do the metropolitan states of New South Wales and Victoria, where there are other forms of self-assurance. But in the closing years of the twentieth century sporting spectacles have assumed an unprecedented significance. As the older manufacturing industries give way to the service sector, governments bid huge sums for special events. They enter into special relationships with providers, invest public money in the necessary infrastructure and suspend the normal planning and administrative procedures to maximize the economic benefits. Governments and their political leaders operate also as sponsors, exploiting all opportunities for association with the triumphs of sporting heroes. The Sydney Olympics display such strategies on an augmented scale, as well as the consequent interplay of popular enthusiasm and disenchantment.

NOTES

I am grateful to Martin Crotty and John Nauright for their comments and suggestions on this essay.

1. John Mulvaney, *Cricket Walkabout: The Australian Aboriginal Cricketers on Tour, 1867–8* (Melbourne, 1967); Leonie Sandercock and Ian Turner, *Up Where Cazaly? The Great Australian Game* (Sydney, 1981).
2. Brian Fitzpatrick, *The Australian Commonwealth: A Picture of the Community 1901–1955*, F.W. Cheshire (Melbourne, 1956), p.209.
3. C.M.H. Clark, *A History of Australia. Volume VI. 'The Old Dead Tree and the Young Tree Green'* (Melbourne, 1987), p.404.
4. Geoffrey Blainey, *A Shorter History of Australia* (Port Melbourne, 1994), ch.9.
5. Jock Phillips, *A Man's Country? The Image of the Pakeha Male* (Aucklands, 1987), ch.3; Keith Sinclair, *A Destiny Apart?: New Zealand's Search for a National Identity* (Wellington, NZ, 1986).
6. *Australian Dictionary of Biography* (Melbourne: Melbourne University Press, 1966–1990), and Hilary Kent (ed.), *Australian Dictionary of Biography. Index: Volumes 1 to 12* (Melbourne, 1991).
7. *The New Zealand Dictionary of Biography. Volume Four, 1921–1940* (Auckland and Wellington, 1998).
8. Wray Vamplew, 'Australians and Sport', in Wray Vamplew and Brian Stoddart (eds.), *Sport in Australia: A Social History* (Cambridge: Cambridge University Press, 1994), p.14.
9. Philip A. Mosely (ed.), *Sporting Immigrants: Sport and Ethnicity in Australia*, (Walla Walla, 1997); Bret Harris, *The Proud Champions* (Little Hills, 1989); Marion K. Stell, *Half the Race: A History of Australian Women in Sport* (North Ryde, 1991).
10. Stuart Macintyre, *A Concise History of Australia* (Cambridges, 1999), p.182.
11. See, for example, see also Daryl Adair and Wray Vamplew, *Sport in Australian History* (Oxford, 1997), Introduction.
12. Ian Harriss, 'Batting and Capital Accumulation', in June Senyard (ed.), *Polemics, Politics and Play: Essays in Nineteenth and Early Twentieth Century Sporting History* (Melbourne, 1997), pp.43–70.
13. Quoted in Phillips, *A Man's Country?*, p.115; see also John Nauright, 'Sport, Manhood and Empire: British Responses to the New Zealand Rugby Tour of 1905', *International Journal of the History of Sport*, 8, 1 (1991), 239–55.
14. Kevin Fewster, 'Advantage Australia: Davis Cup Tennis, 1950–1959', *Sporting Traditions*, 2, 1 (Nov. 1985).

PART 1

Sport in Earlier Antipodean Society

1

Manly and Moral:
The Making of Middle-Class Men in the
Australian Public School

MARTIN CROTTY

The rise of sport in Australia in the late nineteenth and early twentieth centuries was the result of a number of social, cultural and economic processes. The importation of the emerging English sporting tradition, the increase in leisure time available to working men and women, and the enthusiasm that greeted initial sporting triumphs over England all facilitated and fuelled widespread enthusiasm for sporting pursuits. Perhaps nowhere was this growth in the passion for athleticism more noticeable than in the élite corporate boys' schools (termed public schools for the purposes of this essay, in line with contemporary usage). Whereas in 1870 schoolboy sporting contests were relatively few and far between, and of little wider interest, athleticism had, by 1920, become one of the defining features of the élite schools and attracted an enormous following from spectators and the media. Estimates of the crowd at the Victorian public schools' Head of the River races in 1920, for example, were as high as 100,000, and the event dominated the front pages of the local press.[1] Other public school sporting contests, although not attracting quite such huge crowds, were of great public interest, in Melbourne and in other cities.

The aim of this essay is to show how the increasing importance and popularity of public school sport in Australia in the late nineteenth and early twentieth centuries was intimately bound up with changes in the Victorian ideal of 'manliness', and how games became a crucial element in the construction of a chivalric, patriotic, physical and militarist ideal. The gradual growth of a public school network, increases in enrolments, and the gradual acquisition and development by schools of the equipment and grounds essential to the dedicated pursuit of games were also important in the growth of public school athleticism, but changing constructions of manliness were the critical factor behind its official endorsement and encouragement, without which the cult of games could not have flourished as it did.

In examining the changing construction of an idealized public school masculinity and its relation to the games cult, we can turn to a variety of sources. I rely heavily upon the periodicals, prospectuses and annual reports produced by the schools, in which the views of the school on the purposes of a public school education, attitudes towards games, and the qualities a boy should seek to develop were delivered enthusiastically and incessantly. But we can also learn much by turning to the fictionalized public schoolboy. Robert Richardson in the 1870s, and Mary Grant Bruce, Lillian Pyke and others in the 1910s collectively wrote some 20 stories which either centred on school life or which used public schoolboys as central characters. Because of the didactic nature of such stories which meant that they reflected social mores with particular clarity, and because they offered to thousands of youngsters the opportunity for vicarious participation in public school life, these stories were as important in constructing an idealized public school manliness as pronouncements of headmasters and their assistants.[2]

Shifts in the public schools' construction of manliness in Australia closely mirror changes in England. The evolving educational ideologies of English public schools have been well documented. In broad terms, these changes amounted to a shift from what David Newsome has termed godliness and good learning in the middle of the nineteenth century, through athleticism, to militarism in the early years of the twentieth. Norman Vance has postulated a slightly more complex series of developments which included Hellenism and aestheticism, while J.A. Mangan has emphasized the strong undercurrent of social Darwinist thinking. Vance and Mangan have, however, tended to elaborate upon, rather than supplant, Newsome's original characterization, and most historians agree that the ideals of the English public schools became less focused on religion and intellectualism, and more on athleticism, muscularity, patriotism and military capability.[3] Much less has been written about the development of educational ideologies in Australia, but what work has been done tends to indicate a similar shift.[4]

Like their English counterparts until the 1850s, the Australian public schools which emerged in the middle of the century, and then at an increasing rate from the 1860s and 1870s, initially pursued intellectualism and Christian morality as their main goals. When

Geelong Grammar was first established in 1855 Bishop Charles Perry announced himself pleased that it would follow 'the plan of their good old English public schools' and 'would attract here all those who valued sound learning and religious education'.[5] The school's first headmaster was George Oakley Vance, an ordained minister uninterested in sport whose educational goals centred on intellectual knowledge and religious devotion. Under his watchful eye the school opened and closed with prayers, devoted a significant amount of time to religious instruction, and maintained a strict examination regime.[6]

The pattern was repeated elsewhere. Senior staff at Wesley College in the first 30 years after its opening in 1866, and particularly in the first 20 before the arrival of L.A. Adamson in 1887, were predominantly men of ascetic and religious backgrounds. Intolerant of 'boy culture', they imposed strict rules in an attempt to ensure that boys behaved in an orderly fashion and concentrated heavily upon academic pursuits.[7] Religion loomed large in the daily life of the school. Up to eight hours per week were devoted to religious instruction, demanding theological examinations were held at the end of every year, and from 1871 to 1888 the Methodist Theological Institute was a part of the school.[8] Similarly, the Act founding Sydney Grammar School in 1854 stated that it was established 'for the better advancement of religion and morality and for the promotion of useful knowledge'.[9]

Sport had little place in such an educational vision, for the rough and tumble of the games field sat uneasily with the steady endeavour of the class room and the quiet reflection of the chapel. Sport at most Australian public schools, although occasionally exploited or accepted because it helped to build school camaraderie and appeared to have positive effects for the health of students, remained in a rather disorganized and under-developed state. There appears to have been relatively little interest in games at Sydney Grammar and Geelong Grammar School until 1875, at St. Peter's College until the late 1870s, and at Wesley College until 1887. Facilities were poor, and what games there were tended to be organized by the students themselves for recreation, rather than by masters as an important part of the educational process. Wesley College, for example, later to become a bastion of public school athleticism, did not even boat a crew for three of the Head of the River contests in 1880s.[10] Similarly, in 1899 the headmaster, Thomas Palmer, referred to the interruptions games had caused to the normal work of the school as 'a source of annoyance'.[11] Games were a hindrance to training boys, not an aid.

Manliness was thus a feature of the mind and spirit, not of the body. A liberal education involved drawing boys into a state of moral and intellectual maturity by suppressing what was considered a natural instinct towards unruly and uncouth behaviour and impressing upon them the need for godliness and good learning. Such a project can be seen as one of de-masculinizing the boys, for the qualities of godliness and morality were culturally located within the feminine sphere. The middle-class mother, for example, was idealized as an 'angel in the house', guarding over the purity and innocence of her children.[12] Women were not 'naturally' or necessarily associated with religion, nor were they free from discrimination by the churches and their teachings. But they were culturally designated as keepers of the faith, the guardians of moral virtue.

The idealization of feminine morality and a feminine outlook as an appropriate aspiration for boys is more obvious in the public school stories from the period. Robert Richardson wrote a number of such stories in the 1870s which clearly reveal the feminine nature of the manly ideal promoted to boys. In rapid succession he produced *The Boys of Springdale* (1875), *Our Junior Mathematical Master* (1876), *A Perilous Errand* (1876), *The Cold Shoulder* (1876) and *The Boys of Willoughby School* (1877). Educated at Sydney Grammar in the years before athleticism had established itself, and a graduate in Arts at the University of Sydney, Richardson appears to have been a very devout man devoted to intellectual improvement.[13] His personal ideals closely matched those of headmasters devoted to godliness and good learning, and are mirrored in his pedagogical writings.

Richardson's stories all employ essentially the same narrative. One character, whether a boy or a master, is marginalized by the masculine boys, often partly because of his effeminate nature and refusal, or inability, to participate in the more masculine aspects of 'boy culture'. The marginalized figure, however, through deeds which display a mix of feminine selflessness and religious morality, becomes the hero and is lauded and admired by his peers. Feminine religiosity and sacrifice triumph over masculine bravado, muscles and selfishness.

Perhaps the best example is contained in Richardson's 1876 story *A Perilous Errand; Or, How Walter Harvey Proved His Courage*. Walter is immediately identified as an effeminate type of boy:

> Walter Harvey was a boy with bright blue eyes, a smooth red and white complexion, that many a young lady would have envied, and

that was almost too fine for a boy, and curly brown hair. He was stoutish, but this did not make him look any stronger, for it was a rather soft and flabby kind of stoutness. In fact, he did not look a strong boy, – neither sturdy nor wiry, but soft and loosely knit. His figure was nothing to boast of; his face was the best part about him. Besides the bright blue eyes and the fine complexion, its expression helped much to make it a pleasant one; it had a kind of sweetness that one sees more in girls' faces than boys'.[14]

Walter also possesses the feminine characteristics of being 'sweet tempered, and above all, affectionate'.[15] He is the son of a widow, and thus lacks masculine socialization. He is also not proficient at sports, and is described as 'little better than a muff' at shooting and at cricket, a game, we are told, 'that every urchin in Australia learns from the time he can first hold a bat a foot long'.[16] Other Richardson heroes are of a similar type – unable to take part in masculine pursuits such as games and fighting, and feminized through being the sons of widows, through their appearance, and through the morality acquired from selfless and holy mothers.

Richardson's villains, by contrast, are much more masculine. They are good at games, willing to engage in fisticuffs, play tricks on their fellows, and are built much more strongly. Will Bayliss, for example, the boy who most torments Walter, is described as 'a strong, sturdy fellow, with a frame like well-seasoned oak-wood, and muscles like whip-chord'.[17] However, in a series of crises the effeminate boys display their moral superiority over their masculine counterparts. Masculine muscularity is revealed as folly, and the masculine boys are either saved by, or come to appreciate, the qualities of selflessness and moral uprightness of those boys they have been persecuting. The qualities of femininity thus triumph over masculinity as part of Richardson's attempts to promote a religious, virtuous and effeminate conception of manliness.

Sport becomes intricately involved in Richardson's project in that it serves as a marker of an undesirable, somewhat savage, and amoral masculinity. A liking for and proficiency at games is one of the defining characteristics of anti-heroes such as Will Bayliss. Although the eventual heroes do on occasion perform feats which require a degree of physicality (such as Walter Harvey's courageous and desperate, but vain, ride to obtain much-needed medicine for Will Bayliss), these feats are always in service of a goal which is feminine in its selflessness. Masculine attributes of muscularity are only viable and desirable if in service of femininity.

Sports, moreover, are often a site for the initial marginalization of the hero figure in a conflict between masculine and feminine. Steven Kent, hero of *The Boys of Springdale*, is isolated over the purchase of a new cricket ball and Philip Freeling, hero of *The Cold Shoulder*, is teased for a lack of classical form when playing cricket. Will Bayliss and Walter Harvey also clash at a game of cricket after Walter has reprimanded Will for swearing. Far from being a developer of admirable character attributes, school games are associated with a brutish, immature and selfish masculinity which boys need to grow out of if they are to achieve a spiritual, moral and, ultimately, feminine conception of manliness.

The marginal place of sport in the public schools into the last quarter of the nineteenth century thus rested not only upon the difficulties posed by the lack of sizeable boarding communities and the poor games facilities, but also upon the gender identification of games. They were associated with a masculine hardiness, and a boyish rough and tumble quite antithetical to the educational ideals which posted religious piety and intellectualism as the ideals to be sought after. Games were masculine, whereas the ideal boy was defined by reference to feminine qualities.

This educational ideology, and consequently the place of sports, altered dramatically in the last quarter of the nineteenth century for a number of reasons. The first was that the educational ideal of godliness and good learning seemed to have little appeal to boys or to their parents. Fighting, bullying and vandalism were common problems, as were the often disappointing enrolments.[18] Geelong Grammar School, for example, struggled for survival in its early years after being founded in 1855, and actually closed down for several years from June 1860, due to poor enrolments, incompetent management and a recession in the colony.[19] Vance, the first headmaster, was reprimanded in 1859 by the trustees for his 'inability in securing the proper behaviour of the boys out of school, as evinced in the wanton destruction of all parts of the premises', and Wilson similarly had a number of discipline problems with his senior boys well into the 1870s.[20] Wesley College's enrolments were initially encouraging, before falling off. Numbers reached 271 in 1874, but plummeted in the depression of the 1890s, dropping to 128 pupils in September 1893, 93 in September 1895, and just 74 in July

1897.[21] Similarly, after encouraging early enrolments at Sydney Grammar School, numbers gradually fell away so that by 1866 only 127 boys were attending the school. Discipline appears also to have been lax, perhaps because of Stephens' dislike of corporal punishment, and he resigned amidst increasing dissatisfaction with his headmastership in 1866. When Albert Bythesea Weigall took over the headmastership at the start of 1867, there were only 39 boys in attendance and the school was in some danger of closing.[22] Vandalism of school property was also a major concern, and one that persisted into the 1880s, while fighting and bullying would appear to have been common in the early years of the school.[23]

Faced with such difficulties, the headmasters and administrators of these schools were receptive to new ideas, which duly arrived in the form of a new generation of headmasters devoted to instilling 'character' into boys, and a number of influential assistants who saw games as the best means of doing so. Australian public schools recruited their headmasters and other senior staff overwhelmingly from the English public schools and the Oxbridge universities, so the practices and ideologies of athleticism were diffused through the Australia schools in the latter half of the nineteenth century much as they were in England.[24]

Geelong Grammar School is a good example of this process. After being forced to close for several years because of severe financial difficulties, the school reopened in 1863 under the headmastership of John Bracebridge Wilson. He had received a private secondary education in England and had been an enthusiastic sportsman during his time at St. John's College, Oxford.[25] Although no champion of athleticism, Wilson did emphasize the role of the school in the formation of a boy's character, and not just his intellect and sense of piety. The scene was thus set for James Lister Cuthbertson, an old boy of Trinity College, Glenalmond, and a former student of Merton College, Oxford. Cuthbertson was a fervent believer in the benefits of an English public school education and set about transferring the ideology and practices of the English public schools to Geelong Grammar. With Wilson's support he re-instituted prefects, founded a school magazine and, most significantly, greatly expanded the role of games.[26] Cricket, rowing and football all soon improved. The school began achieving better results, facilities were rapidly upgraded and games moved from being a peripheral activity to being one of the central features of a Geelong Grammar School education.

Similar developments took place elsewhere. Albert Bythesea Weigall took over the headmastership of Sydney Grammar school at its nadir in 1867. He sought to instil character into his boys as much as scholastic knowledge, and thus introduced school colours, a school magazine, a prefect system and organized games. In doing so he was ably supported by a number of men who had received their education in élite educational institutions in England. Henry Anderson, for example, formed the school's cadet corps in 1870 and Edwin Bean and Charles Francis played an important role in expanding school sports. Weigall acknowledged the role of such men in giving Sydney Grammar the tone of an English public school when he reported to the board in 1883 that 'These men have brought with them the traditions, the discipline, and the spirit of the English Public Schools ... have added the intellectual training and associations of the Universities, and have thus assisted, as no other class of men could, in raising the mental and moral tone of the boys, who will soon be men.'[27]

Similarly, the games ethos flourished at Wesley after the arrival of L.A. Adamson in 1887, and especially after his appointment as headmaster from 1902, while games at St. Peter's were greatly boosted when the Reverend Henry Girdlestone took over the headmastership of the school in 1893. The development of the athletic ethos was not always smooth. In 1885 for example, the *Sydneian* lamented 'a woeful deficiency of unity and energy' in the school's cricket team, and complained of 'an utter want of sympathy and enthusiasm in the school at large for those who were selected to represent us in the all-important game of cricket'.[28] But by the early 1900s subscription to the games ethos was 'tediously uniform' through the public schools of Australia, more matches were being played, games facilities had been dramatically improved, and sport had moved to centre stage in teaching boys the chivalrous and noble qualities of leadership, obedience, team–work, loyalty and selflessness.[29]

To focus on the public schools alone, however, is to ignore the importance of the changing context within which the schools were operating. Despite the important role played by such influential men such as Adamson and Cuthbertson, their importation of athleticism would not have been successful had it not appeared to suit changing social, cultural and national imperatives in the construction of an idealized form of masculinity much different to the religious, moral and intellectual constructions which had dominated until the 1870s and 1880s. Three principal changes made athleticism appear desirable.

The first was an increased concern about the effects of physical degeneration in the colonies. An often crude environmental determinism suggested to many that 'we must be prepared for the inevitable deterioration of the Anglo-Saxon stock'.[30] The warm climate, it was widely believed, would produce languor and sap the energy of the race. In the late 1860s Sir Charles Dilke attributed the 'superior energy' of Victorians over New South Welshmen to their being of more recent British stock, and to Melbourne's climate being less tropical, and thus less debilitating and productive of lassitude, than Sydney's.[31] Spartan living, including a devotion to physical exercise in the form of games could, it was thought, overcome this natural tendency. The *Geelong Grammar School Quarterly* thus reported in July 1894 that 'without some hardy exercise like football boys [are] in danger of becoming effeminate. This is ... particularly true of boys in a climate like ours, where the tendency is to produce a tall, narrow-chested, thin-legged race without the "last" and stamina of the British pioneers who planted these Australian colonies.'[32] Games in the public schools would allegedly ensure that the rising generation maintained the vigour and power of their British forebears.[33]

The second was the moral threat posed by the increasing secularization of Australian society which took place in late nineteenth and early twentieth centuries and which 'seemed to push the churches into a corner reserved for the gullible and the unthinking'.[34] By 1900 Australian popular culture included a widespread indifference to religion, which lost much of its authority as a moral basis for society.[35] Many, ranging from intellectuals to larrikins, even adopted attitudes of open hostility towards religion.[36] Concern about the effects of secularism on the young crystallized in the debates over the question of the provision of secular education by the state. It was a conflict those in favour of denominational education lost, for between 1852 and 1895 state aid to denominational schools was abandoned throughout Australia.[37] The move towards increasingly secular education concerned many. One churchman, the Reverend James Hegarty, for example, argued that secular education would lead to 'a tendency to unbelief and to laxity of morals'.[38] Catholic Bishops in New South Wales described state schools established on secular principles as 'seed-plots of future immorality, infidelity and lawlessness' while another churchman warned in 1904: 'Sow the seeds of Secularism, and you secure a crop of the poisonous weed of juvenile delinquency'.[39] Numbers of non-churchmen also expressed concern, believing that morality without a religious base could not exist. George Higinbotham, for example, who chaired the Victorian Royal Commission charged with settling the education question in Victoria in 1866 and 1867, feared that a social order without religion would become social disorder 'unregulated by a single ascertained or unquestioned law'.[40]

The decline of religion demanded a new ethical framework as society made what Stuart Macintyre has called 'the transition from a society unified by faith to one joined in citizenship'.[41] Citizenship ideals were widely promulgated within the rubric of 'manliness'. Teaching boys the character attributes that would make them compliant and useful members of society became increasingly important. To achieve this, masters at the public schools employed sport as a vehicle for the dissemination of middle-class ideals of appropriate gendered civic behaviour. Sport, they argued, would teach a boy to be obedient, to be disciplined, to work for the greater good and devote himself to a cause. In short, the boy who played sport was to learn the ethics of how to 'play the game'.

The third major social trend which assisted in games coming to occupy a central role in the construction of manliness was the rise of nationalism in the late nineteenth and early twentieth centuries, and particularly a militarist nationalism from the 1900s. Boys needed to be educated to subsume their own interests to that of the greater body, to devote their lives to the service of the nation. Rowing, for example, was said to offer 'The discipline, mental, moral, ethical ... the voluntary submission to one master, the self-surrender to one aim, the conversion of self into part of a machine, devoid of free agency, the working and training for weeks and weeks, to uphold the honour of the school, college, or university, in the severest test of strength, wind and pluck which the whole range of athletics offers.'[42] Sport could thus be used to support the opinion espoused at St. Peter's that 'the truest freedom consists in willing and intelligent obedience to wise laws'.[43]

The most extreme example of sacrificing oneself for the nation was military service in the nation's defence. Loyalty to nation and empire, and the willingness and capability of fighting for them, became an increasingly important goal of character training in the early twentieth century as war seemed more likely. As well as fears that Britain's military supremacy was under threat from Germany, Australians were concerned about the prospect of invasion from the north. Nationalist magazines such as the *Lone Hand* pointed out the danger that Australia faced with its vast unpopulated and under-developed areas in the north. These were undefended while 'distant a few days' steam, cluster the myriads of Asia, threatening ever to swarm across the rich fields of a land, attractive in all respects to a frugal, industrious people, condemned at present to exist in a much poorer country'.[44] Japan was seen as a dangerously aggressive nation, and its large military forces and the problems of a growing population made it self-evident to such commentators that Japan had expansionist intentions.[45] Alfred Deakin, the principal architect of Australian defence policy in the new nation's first decade, believed that unless Australians were awake to the threats of Asiatic invasion, they would be 'only tenants' on the continent.[46]

The need for militarily trained and willing boys initially appeared as a threat to the reign of athleticism in the Australian public schools. Cadets boomed at all the schools and threatened to displace the athlete as the embodiment of manliness. At St. Peter's College, for example, 130 boys attended the first drill of the newly revived cadet corps in 1905.[47] They joined the Federal cadet scheme in 1906, a miniature firing range was constructed at the school in 1908, and by 1909 215 of the school's 340 boys were cadets. It was estimated that a further 100 were not eligible as they were not of the minimum age of 12 years or the minimum height of four and six inches, so cadet training was almost universal, and those who did not take part were the object of some scorn.[48] The cadets quickly became an important institution and were ceremoniously accorded a high status in the school, forming, for example, a guard of honour when the Governor visited in 1909.[49] The President of the Old Wesley Collegians Association, Major H.V. Champion, even looked forward to the day when military training would 'be considered the most important sport of any in the Public Schools' and told the boys 'I want you to believe … that the most important game is the military game'.[50]

Some critics within the schools and a number of commentators from outside alleged that games detracted both from the time available for military training, and from the intellectual work which was also of vital importance in the 'race of nations'. Leonard Hartford Lindon, for example, who took over at Geelong Grammar from Bracebridge Wilson in 1896, launched stinging attacks upon the games cult. It was under his headmastership that the *Quarterly* began to criticize games, including, in 1902, expressing some support for Kipling's comments about 'flannelled fools' and 'muddied oafs'. It considered that Kipling's criticisms of athleticism, if a little strong, were 'in the main just' since games, although essential to education of a boy, were liable to be accorded a wrongfully high place which left 'too little time and inclination for intellectual pursuits'.[51] In 1902 the *Quarterly* reported an address given by Lindon at a recent Church Congress in which he stated that he was humiliated that the spirit of athleticism 'permeated and saturated' the public schools. He described the games mania as an 'evil' before stating more specifically the problems he believed were associated with the over-concentration on sport. These included distracting men from the commercial race which the British Empire appeared to be losing, but also distraction from religion and refinement. Sport, Lindon seemed to suggest, was a brutalizing influence, and he thus implored the church to 'use all her efforts to put recreation back in its proper position', and to 'demonstrate to the people that ... recreation must ever be auxiliary to the true work of life, and not one of its leading motives'.[52] From outside the schools came similar attacks. Commentators argued that the schools' enthusiasm for games was interfering with both intellectual work and with military training, to the detriment of the nation.

To survive such attacks, the advocates of athleticism maintained that the pursuit of games was complementary to both a boy's intellectual work and his military preparedness. Adamson, for example, made the common argument at a dinner of the Old Wesley Collegians that 'If a student does not feed his brain with healthy blood, he will run the risk of petering out.'[53] Wesley also defended its devotion to games in a special supplement to the *Wesley College Chronicle* of June 1908 entitled 'Work and Play'. The supplement used examination and sporting results to show that Melbourne Grammar and Wesley College, the two most successful schools in sporting contests between the Victorian public schools, also attained the best academic results. The aim was to demonstrate that sporting and scholastic achievement were complementary rather than antithetical. Healthy boys, it was argued, could work more effectively.[54]

Sport was also more closely allied to the new imperative of military training. The idea that games would assist in developing the qualities of the soldier had existed for some time, but as a relatively minor part of the athletic ethos. From about 1900, however, the military applicability of qualities of discipline, courage, hardiness and physical fitness allegedly developed on the games field became one of the central planks of the ideology justifying the continued enthusiasm for sport. Dr Watkin, for example, a former president of Wesley College, stated at the 1908 speech day that just as boys 'strove on the football field or the river, so it might be that in the near future they would have to fight for the motherland, their king, and the Commonwealth', and that those boys who had played school games would be especially well-equipped to cope with the demands of the battle field.[55]

The language of games appears also betrays a more militarist purpose. Encounters on the games field were increasingly talked of as 'battles' in which the competing teams sought to 'conquer' their opponents. A good example is a Wesley College song by F. S. Williamson, a master at the school, entitled 'Before the Boat Race, 1907':

> There's a tumult in the distance, and a war-song in the air,
> Where the foemen in their galleys for another fight prepare,
> For they whisper in the country, and they noise it in the town,
> That the Wesley colours from the mast will soon be taken down.
>
> *Chorus*
> Then it's forward boys, to battle – hear the bugle's thrilling tone –
> With the Royal Standard borne ahead, march on to hold your own,
> With the Lion proudly ramping as the Ensign flutters free,
> Let the Lion keep the river, as the Lion keeps the sea.
>
> They have raised the Light Blue Pennon, and the Flag of the Maroon,
> See the Dark Blue Banner flaunting in the warm October noon.
> But who careth for the menace, for it only spurs the bold,
> And there are no boys that falter wearing Purple and the Gold.[56]

Similarly, a 1906 games song from Xavier College implicitly linked manliness, sport and battle in song which could easily have been written for or from the front lines of a war zone:

> Oh, when the battle sweeps along, fierce and strong,
> And when our luck for a moment is declining,
> Like heroes let us gaily meet our defeat –
> No wailing, no womanly repining.
> But raise again o'erhead our standard Black and Red,
> And if 'tis stained with gore, we'll love it all the more;
> As if our ranks we close, once more to face our foes,
> We fling them back defiance proud and strong.[57]

From about 1875 until 1900 sport had primarily meant fair play, loyalty, acceptance of victory and defeat, fortitude, discipline and obedience. It did not lose these meanings after 1900, but the meanings themselves were more allied to militarist purposes. As the demands of the nation shifted from disciplined and ordered peacetime citizens to soldiers prepared to die for their country and empire, so too did the purpose of sports change.

Sport thus bore a completely different relationship to the ideal boy of the 1900s than it had to the ideal of the 1870s. Whereas muscularity had in the 1870s served as an indication of a masculine barbarity at odds with a feminine conception of manliness, by the 1900s it served to distinguish manliness from effeminacy. The gender identification of muscularity and physicality had not changed, but games became more acceptable and desirable as the ideal of manliness within the public schools became a more masculine, and even anti-feminine, construct. 'Effeminate' games such as tennis and marbles were scorned by men such as Cuthbertson, while the *Wesley College Chronicle*, even before Adamson's arrival, advocated the more rugged boarding life over the feminine home, which threatened to make a boy 'weak, reliant on others, thoroughly un-Spartan-like'.[58]

Again, the role of sport as a marker of a distinct masculinity emerges even more clearly if we turn to fictional depictions of the Australian public schoolboy in the early twentieth century, and in particular if we examine two of the main heroes produced by Mary Grant Bruce and Lillian Pyke. Bruce, author of the famous series of 'Billabong' stories for children, so-named because they are set on Billabong Station, used Jim Linton as her main male hero figure. Although only a small portion of her Billabong stories concern school life, Jim is a Melbourne Grammar school boy, and later old boy, who is clearly meant to represent the public school 'type'.

Jim is immediately discernible from earlier public school heroes because of his physique and his liking for sport. He is described in *Mates at Billabong* (1911) as

> a big, quiet fellow, very like his father; not over-brilliant at books, but a first-rate sport, and without a trace of meanness in his nature. At school he was worshipped by the boys – was he not captain of the football team, stroke of the eight, and best all-round athlete? – and liked by the masters, who found him to be careless over work,

but absolutely reliable in every other way. Such a fellow does not win scholarships, but he is a tower of strength to his school.[59]

Jim, who is also a lieutenant in the school's cadet corps, wins the school prize for best all-round athlete, the prefect's prize, and, to show that he is not completely incapable academically, the French prize. In subsequent stories he joins the British Army out of a sense of chivalric obligation, and performs with distinction in the Great War.

Lillian Pyke's heroes are similarly drawn, particularly Max Charlton, hero of *Max the Sport* (1916):

> Broad of shoulder and deep of chest, he stood quite six feet, and though he had no superabundance of flesh, his bones were well-covered, and he turned the scale at about twelve stone. His face was well browned from exposure to sun and wind, but beneath the tan, there was a healthy glow in his cheeks. His dark eyes were alight with intelligence and his square chin showed a determined, not to say obstinate, nature. Surely a son of whom any parent might be proud.[60]

Like Jim Linton, Max excels at football, cricket, rowing and athletics, and serves bravely in the Great War.

The ideology of games as a developer of a militarist manliness is often evident in these stories. It is partly honour he has learnt on the sports field that makes Jim determined to 'do the square thing' and enlist, while the strength and courage acquired through a combination of bush life and games help make him an excellent soldier.[61] Similarly, the ethics of the games field are likened by Pyke to the sense of fair play which motivates Britain and her empire to fight the Germans:

> the way the Kaiser regarded the 'scrap of paper' in which he had guaranteed the neutrality of Belgium, aroused warlike feelings in the most peaceful ... It was as if the big bully, in his desire to get at a declared enemy, should say to an onlooker, 'Now, you stand on one side while I knock this little chap down ... Oh, yes, I know I did put my name to a scrap of paper saying I wouldn't touch him...but the little beggar's in the way, so I'm going to give him a lesson. I won't harm you so long as you don't interfere.
>
> What college boy with sporting blood in his veins would listen for a moment to such reasoning? What 'sport' that had played for the honour of the school could hear such sophistry without

doubling up his fist and striking the bully? What use all the talk about 'playing the game if it only applied to the small things of life and was not incorporated into the nation's body politic?[62]

Honourable public schoolboys are so outraged by German aggression and the atrocities in Belgium that they rush to enlist.

In contrast to Richardson's stories, it is the effeminate boys who provide the villains. Cecil Linton, a cousin from town visited upon the Linton family at Billabong, is described by Bruce in terms that in many ways make him comparable with Walter Harvey, Richardson's effeminate hero. Cecil is a 'slim' and 'pale' youth whom Jim Linton's father refers to as 'neither one thing nor the other'.[63] He is city-bred, spends a lot of time with his mother, is not proficient at manly sports, can not ride, detests the Australian bush, and is affected and aloof. He is an effeminate 'other' to the manliness of boys such as Jim. Worst of all for Mary Grant Bruce are those men who do not volunteer for the war effort, and a number of references are made to their lack of manliness. Jim, for example, angrily states at one point that any man 'who wants to stay out of the game and do women's work...ought to have some sort of brand put on him, so that people will be able to tell him from a man in the future!'.[64] Lillian Pyke also has her anti-heroes, including 'the habitual Stewer, that contemptible person with a dull preoccupied look', and those 'who engage in the foolish occupation of introspection, which in some people, amounts almost to a disease'.[65] Neither type, of course, plays manly sports or leaps to the defence of the nation and empire.

Feminine influence is presented as a threat to manliness. Jim has no mother, while Max has to attend a boarding school because his father's death has made the home environment too feminine. It is stated that although Max's mother has tried to 'take a man's view' of Max's upbringing, it is inevitable that she should 'be to some extent hampered by the difference in outlook peculiar to her sex'.[66] Max's mother is thus relieved when he wins a scholarship to St. Virgil's College as she fears that he has had enough 'petticoat government'.[67] In another Mary Grant Bruce story about the adventures of Dick Lester, Dick's absent father writes to Dick's mother that it is time Dick went to boarding school and was cut from his mother's apron strings: 'he must learn things that you cannot teach him, and it's time he began'.[68] Dick's mother is initially reluctant to give up her son, but realizes that 'he knows best, Dick'. Dick replies: 'Oh, of course ... He's a man. Of course he'd understand about a boy.'[69] Raising adolescent boys is thus clearly a matter for men. Women are likely to make them soft and effeminate, to instil qualities which by the 1900s were no longer associated with an ideal manliness.

To explain the values which attached to sport in the Australian public schools and to understand the rise of the cult of athleticism, we thus need to look beyond factors such as the inevitable time it took to develop adequate games facilities, or the influence of masters who had been educated in the élite English schools and the Oxbridge universities. Necessary as such factors were, they were only able to influence Australian educational ideals because of changing constructions of manliness in wider Australian society in response to the perceived problems and needs of the Australian nation. In the 1870s masculinity appeared as a threat to an effeminate ideal of manliness, offering a lapse from Christian piety and intellectual devotion into a muscular, unholy and uncultivated beastliness in a rugged new land far from the civility of England. The schools thus pursued an ideal of godliness and good learning, to which the activities of the games field appeared as antithetical. But social Darwinism, the fear of racial decline in Australia, the growing interest in post-Christian secular ethics and the rise of a militarist nationalism all worked to create an ideal of manliness far more physical, masculine and anti-feminine over the next 50 years. Games flourished precisely because the values which the games field appeared to inculcate coincided far more closely with this new ideal than with the old one.

NOTES

1. *Geelong Grammar School Quarterly*, 45, 1 (May 1920), 78. Crowd figures from the period are, however, notoriously unreliable, and the *Wesley College Chronicle* gave a much more conservative estimate of between 60,000 and 70,000. See *Wesley College Chronicle*, 158 (May 1920), 38–40.
2. A.S.W. Rosenbach, *Early American Children's Books* (New York, 1966), pp. xxvi–xxvii. Quoted in Margaret Ingham, 'Young Australia Reads, 1800–1900', in Guy Featherstone (ed.), *The Colonial Child: Papers Presented at the 8th Biennial Conference of the Royal Historical Society of Victoria, Melbourne, 12–13 Oct. 1979* (Melbourne, 1981), p.24; Brenda Niall, *Australia Through the Looking-Glass: Children's Fiction 1830–1980* (Melbourne, 1984), p.5; Claudia Nelson, *Boys Will Be Girls: The Feminine Ethic and British Children's Fiction, 1857–1917* (New Brunswick, 1991), p.1. See also Terry Eagleton, *Literary Theory: An Introduction* (Oxford, 1983), pp.23–4. Eagleton suggests that literature became a much more important ideological force in the second half of the nineteenth century as religion progressively ceased to function as a 'social cement' naturalizing social realities.
3. David Newsome, *Godliness and Good Learning: Four Studies on a Victorian Ideal* (London, 1961), *passim*; Norman Vance, *The Sinews of the Spirit: The Ideal of Christian Manliness in Victorian Literature and Religious Thought* (London: Cambridge University Press, 1985), pp.185–8; Vance, 'The Ideal of Manliness', in B. Simon and I. Bradley (eds.), *The Victorian*

Public School: Studies in the Development of an Educational Institution (Dublin, 1975), p.128; J.A. Mangan, *Athleticism in the Victorian and Edwardian Public School: The Emergence and Consolidation of an Educational Ideology* (Cambridge, 1981), pp.142–3.

4. See, for example, Ian Brice, 'Australian Boys' Schools and the Construction of Masculinity: An Exploratory Excursion' (unpublished paper, May 1996), *passim*; Geoffrey Sherington, R.C. Petersen and Ian Brice, *Learning to Lead: A History of Girls' and Boys' Corporate Secondary Schools in Australia* (Sydney, 1987), *passim*; Martin Crotty, 'Making English Gentlemen from Australian Boys?: The Manly Ideal in Two Elite Protestant Schools of Victoria, 1875–1920', *Australian Studies*, 13 (1998), 44–67.

5. Quoted in Bob Bessant, *Schooling in the Colony and State of Victoria*, Centre for Comparative and International Studies in Education (Melbourne, 1983), p.6.

6. Weston Bate, *Light Blue Down Under: The History of Geelong Grammar School* (Melbourne, 1990), pp.6, 18.

7. Geoffrey Blainey, James Morrissey and S.E.K. Hulme, *Wesley College: The First Hundred Years*, Robertson and Mullens, Melbourne, 1967, pp.35–8, 62–3; Felix Meyer, *The History of Wesley College, 1865–1919* (Melbourne, 1921), pp.14, 29.

8. Blainey, Morrissey and Hulme, *Wesley College*, pp.30–40, 65.

9. Quoted in C.E.W. Bean, *Here, My Son: An Account of the Independent and Other Corporate Boys Schools of Australia* (Sydney, 1950), p.107.

10. Blainey, Morrissey and Hulme, *Wesley College*, pp.74–5.

11. Wesley College, *Prospectus for 1900, Summary of Reports and Honor Lists for 1899*, p.15.

12. Kociumbas, *Australian Childhood: A History* (Sydney, 1997), p.92. See also, for example, Peggy Pascoe, *Relations of Rescue: The Search for Female Moral Authority in the American West, 1874–1939* (New York, 1990), pp.xiii–xvi. Pascoe has shown how nineteenth-century missionary women in the American west used gender differences to assert their moral superiority over males, associating femininity with piety and purity.

13. E. Morris Miller, *Australian Literature: From its Beginnings to 1935*, Vol.1 (Sydney, 1973 (1940)), p.45; Victor Crittenden, 'Robert Richardson: First Australian Born Writer for Children', *Lu Rees Archives: Notes, Books and Authors*, 7 (1986), 39–41.

14. Robert Richardson, *A Perilous Errand; Or, How Walter Harvey Proved His Courage* (Edinburgh, 1876), pp.55–6.

15. Ibid., p.57.

16. Richardson, *A Perilous Errand*, pp.58–9.

17. Ibid., pp.63–4.

18. Geelong Grammar School, *Church of England Grammar School, Geelong: History and Register, Jubilee 1907* (Geelong), ch.6; Michael Collins Persse, *Well-Ordered Liberty: A Portrait of Geelong Grammar School, 1855–1955* (Melbourne, 1995), p.2.

19. Geelong Grammar School, *Church of England Grammar School, Geelong*, ch.6; Marles, 'An Evaluation of the First Thirteen Years of the Headmastership of John Bracebridge Wilson at Geelong Grammar School, 1863 to 1875' (MA Thesis, University of Melbourne, 1974), 15–16.

20. *The First Annual Report of the Geelong Grammar School, April 8th 1859 and Extracts from the Minute Book of the Lay Trustees of the Geelong Grammar School Aug. 1856 to Sept. 1861 and Correspondence with the Lord Bishop of Melbourne*, Geelong, the Lay Trustees, 1861, p.33. Quoted in Marles, 'An Evaluation of the First Thirteen Years...', p.56. See also Bate, *Light Blue Down Under*, p.16, Marles, 'An Evaluation of the First Thirteen Years...', pp.175–8.

21. Meyer, *The History of Wesley College*, pp.16, 20, 32. The school had opened with 80 boys in 1866.

22. Clifford Turney, *Grammar: A History of Sydney Grammar School, 1819–1988* (Sydney, 1989), pp.49–69.

23. Ibid., p.60; *Sydneian*, 90 (Aug. 1890), 6–7.

24. T.J.L. Chandler, 'Games at Oxbridge and the Public Schools: The Diffusion of an Innovation', *International Journal of the History of Sport*, 8, 2 (April 1991), 171–204.

25. Bate, *Light Blue Down Under*, p.66, Marles, pp.34, 44–7.

26. *Geelong Grammar School Quarterly*, 34, 1 (April 1910), 2.

27. Quoted in Turney, *Grammar*, p.72.

28. *Sydneian*, 56 (April 1885), 9; (Sept. 1885), 7–8.

29. David W. Brown, 'The Legacy of British Victorian Social Thought: Some Prominent Views on Sport, Physical Exercise and Society in Colonial Australia' in *Sport and Colonialism in 19th Century Australasia*, ASSH Studies in Sports History, no. 1 (Sydney, 1986), p.26.
30. Anon., 'Will the Anglo-Australian Race Degenerate?', *Victorian Review*, 1 (Nov. 1879), 122.
31. David Walker, 'War, Women and the Bush: The Novels of Mary Grant Bruce and Ethel Turner', *Historical Studies*, 18, 71 (Oct. 1978) 279–315. See also Lynette Finch, 'Introduction', in Lynette Finch (ed.), *Young in a Warm Climate: Essays in Queensland Childhood* (Brisbane: University of Queensland Press, 1998), pp.xiii–xiv, special issue of *Queensland Review* (1998). Later in the nineteenth century and well into the twentieth, concerns remained about the effects of the northern climate upon Europeans even after fears of climatic degeneration in the rest of Australia had faded.
32. *Geelong Grammar School Quarterly*, 18, 2 (July 1894), 20.
33. See, for example, *St. Peter's School Magazine*, 4, 19 (Oct. 1894), 301.
34. Hilary Carey, *Believing in Australia: A Cultural History of Religions* (Sydney, 1996), p.88; Michael Hogan, *The Sectarian Strand: Religion in Australian History* (Melbourne, 1987), p.96.
35. Ibid., pp.154–5.
36. Carey, *Believing in Australia*, p.105.
37. Alan Barcan, *A History of Australian Education* (Melbourne, 1980), pp.132–44.
38. Rev. James L. Hegarty, 'Primary Instruction in Victoria', *Victorian Review*, 2 (Dec. 1879), 208–10. See also H.B. Macartney, 'The Education Question', *Victorian Review*, 3 (Jan. 1880), 374–83.
39. Ian Breward, *A History of the Australian Churches* (Sydney, 1993), p.80; Thos. Rhodes, 'The State Boy', *The Boy Problem* (Adelaide, 1904), p.14.
40. George Higinbotham, *Science and Religion, Or the Relations of Modern Science With the Christian Churches: A Lecture by George Higinbotham* (Melbourne, 1883). Quoted in Stuart Macintyre, *A Colonial Liberalism: The Lost World of Three Victorian Visionaries* (Melbourne, 1991), p.126.
41. Macintyre, *A Colonial Liberalism*, p.154.
42. *St. Peter's School Magazine*, 2, 11 (Dec. 1885), 9.
43. Ibid., 2, 17 (Dec. 1886), 12.
44. J.C. Watson, 'Our Empty North', *Lone Hand*, 1, 4 (Aug. 1907), 420.
45. See, for example, frequent articles in the *Lone Hand*.
46. Robert Dixon, *Writing the Colonial Adventure: Race, Gender and Nation in Anglo-Australian Popular Fiction, 1875–1914* (Melbourne, 1995), pp.136–7. See also Thomas W. Tanner, *Compulsory Citizen Soldiers* (Sydney, 1980), p.71.
47. *St. Peter's School Magazine*, 9, 5 (Dec. 1902), 441; 60 (Aug. 1905), 2, 7–8; 60 (Dec. 1905), 10. In 1905 the Debating Society was addressed by Col. Reade who impressed upon those present the duty of everyone to take part in the defence of the empire. It is perhaps indicative of the militarist and almost authoritarian attitude of the public schools on this question by early in the twentieth century that the motion 'That this House would favour the adoption of some scheme of compulsory military service throughout the Commonwealth' was carried by 20 votes to four.
48. Ibid., 62 (Aug. 1906), 25; 69 (Dec. 1908), 1;. 70 (May 1909), 47.
49. Ibid., 71 (Aug. 1909), 1.
50. *Wesley College Chronicle*, 122 (July 1909), 21.
51. *Geelong Grammar School Quarterly*, 26, 1 (April 1902), 2.
52. Ibid., 26, 4 (Dec. 1902), 25–6.
53. Quoted in Felix Meyer (ed.), *Adamson of Wesley: The Story of a Great Headmaster* (Melbourne, 1932), pp.16–17.
54. 'Work and Play', p.1. Special supplement to *Wesley College Chronicle*, 118 (June 1908).
55. *Wesley College Chronicle*, 119 (Oct. 1908), 5.
56. Ibid., 115 (Oct. 1907), 3.
57. Geoffrey Sherington *et al.*, *Learning to Lead: A History of Girls' and Boys' Corporate Secondary Schools in Australia*, p.138.
58. Bate, *Light Blue Down Under*, p.123; *St. Peter's School Magazine*, 57 (Dec. 1904), 2; *Wesley College Chronicle*, 26 (Oct. 1884), 461.
59. Mary Grant Bruce, *Mates at Billabong* (Sydney: Angus and Robertson, 1992; Melbourne,

1911), p.16.
60. Lillian Pyke, *Max the Sport* (Melbourne, 1916), p.219.
61. Mary Grant Bruce, *From Billabong to London* (Sydney, 1992; Melbourne, 1915), p.19.
62. Pyke, *Max the Sport*, p.235.
63. Bruce, *Mates at Billabong*, pp.33, 38.
64. Mary Grant Bruce, *Jim and Wally* (Sydney, 1992; Melbourne, 1916), p.55.
65. Pyke, *Max the Sport*, pp.95, 121.
66. Ibid., p.59.
67. Ibid., p.59.
68. Mary Grant Bruce, *Dick* (Melbourne, 1918), pp.18–19.
69. Ibid., p.24.

2

A Pioneer of the Proletariat:
Herbert Milnes and the Games Cult
in New Zealand

J.A. MANGAN and COLM HICKEY

On 4 October 1917 during the battle of Passchendaele Ridge, 'A' Company of the 3rd Auckland Battalion of the Royal New Zealand Expeditionary Force were ordered to attack a position known as Abraham Heights. During the attack a German shell exploded at the feet of the Company commander who was killed instantly, oddly without any visible sign of injury. He thus became another statistic in the long roll of New Zealand's fallen of the Great War. As such he might have remained yet one more forgotten figure among so many. This would have been unfortunate. Herbert Albert Edwin Milnes, originally from Beeston Hill in Yorkshire prior to the Great War, arguably, was one of New Zealand's foremost educationalists. His career merits examination. It links two influential period ideologies – athleticism and imperialism with elementary education in metropolis and empire; an association as yet barely explored, yet well worth exploration.

The global influence of the late nineteenth-century English public school phenomenon known as athleticism[1] is now unquestioned as is its impact in Britain's imperial possessions.[2] In his introduction to *The Games Ethic and Imperialism: Aspects of the Diffusion of an Ideal* J.A. Mangan reminds us that team games were the medium through which the concept of imperial 'manliness' was mostly developed. It was widely believed that they transmitted values such as perseverance, stoicism, self-reliance, loyalty and obedience. Among other things they were considered, therefore, a useful instrument of colonial purpose. At one and the same time it was thought, 'they helped create the confidence to lead and the compulsion to follow'.[3] Consequently Mangan notes: 'In the guise of educator, many late-Victorian and Edwardian Imperial missionaries and some administrators from public school and ancient university, and sometimes from more *humble* (emphasis added) institutions, clung tenaciously to these...values...with sincerity and self confidence...'[4]

This essay examines for the first time the ways in which these influential beliefs were inculcated initially in an English teacher training college, and then, subsequently, in a New Zealand teacher training college, and the consequences for both elementary education and society in that distant antipodean outpost of empire.

In Britain, by the 1890s, teacher-training colleges had become a major feature of elementary education. There were no less than 47 colleges in England and Wales and all had been subjected to examination by the Royal Commission set up in 1886 under the Chairmanship of Viscount Richard Assheton Cross to enquire into elementary education. The Cross Commission report, as it became known, was published in 1888, had some scathing things to say about the colleges in general: they were too small, their standards too low, their teaching second rate, their staffing poor, their facilities inadequate. Many, if not all, these criticisms could be laid at the door of each and every college including the nation's oldest, Borough Road[5] located in a then extremely insalubrious part of south-east London. It responded to the Cross report first with embarrassment and then with energy. It relocated from the 'black gaunt jail-like building ... cheek by jowl with that festering slum of misery on which great ground landlords batten, Kell Street...'[6] to a semi-rural site in Isleworth, Middlesex, and it recruited for the first time, a young Oxbridge games-playing graduate, P.A. Barnett, to be principal of the college.

P.A. Barnett, who was only 30 at the time of his appointment, revolutionized life at Borough Road. He had been educated at the City of London School and Trinity College, Oxford, where he had taken a First in Classical Greats, and he had been Professor of English Literature at Firth College, Sheffield, before taking up his post at Borough Road in 1888. A firm believer in team games and their virtues, one of his first actions was to ensure that every weekday afternoon was now given over to compulsory games. In short, Barnett, was an energetic proponent of the powerful educational ideology of athleticism as part of a wider commitment to good health – moral, mental and physical. In a chapter in *Common Sense in Education*,[7] which he published in 1899, and which he dedicated to his former headmaster, Abbott Abbott,[8] he set out his views concerning exercise, health and the body. He was 'Almondian'[9] in his insistence that children be weighed three or four times a year, and in a passage that could easily have come from the pen of Hely Hutchinson Almond himself, the famous Headmaster (from 1862 to 1903) of Loretto School in Musselburgh, near Edinburgh,[10] he asserted that:

> It is a teacher's obvious duty to be in good health ... One of the first considerations of cheerfulness of soul is soundness of body. And it is useless to attend to one set of rules if we habitually disregard others. The daily outdoor exercise – preferably a game; – the morning tub; carefulness in food; the spare use of strong drinks, alcoholic or other; these are excellent things to bear in mind.[11]

For Barnett, as for many at the time, sport was a moral medium. In a book on etiquette for children, *The Little Book of Health and Courtesy* published in 1905, he declared:

> Englishmen pride themselves on 'playing the game,' that is, on being fair to every one. Take a beating in your games just as you would behave after a victory – quietly. If a point is disputed, hear everything that the other side has to say; and if there is no umpire or referee, consider it carefully. But always uphold an umpire, and play a losing game as cheerfully and as hard as if you were winning.[12]

Barnett practised what he preached at Borough Road. He set a new tone that was both muscular and moral. He rode the wave of the educational fashion of the time shrewdly. In this he was uncompromising in his commitment. Although youthful in appearance, he was mature in judgement. P.B. Ballard, later to become Chief Inspector for Schools at the London County Council and a student at Borough Road from 1884 to 1886, recalled: 'The new Principal looked a mere boy, but ... in the wisdom with which he reformed the system of education at the College, lifting it to a higher level and fitting it better to the tastes and talents of the students – in all this he proved himself a man, and a man of insight and courage,'[13] while F.H. Spencer, a Borough Road student from 1892 to 1894, was of the opinion, that one of Barnett's 'greatest reforms ... was to abolish work in the afternoon, to concentrate all lectures and private-study periods in the morning and evening, and leave us free in the afternoons. One result of this was that we rapidly became the best

Training College at games and athletics as we already were at the business of passing examinations.'[14]

Barnett's re-organization of the timetable was part of a quite deliberate emulation of the upper and middle class educational system in which athleticism was then prevalent. He knew what he was doing. His appointment was to be a turning point in the fortunes of the college. If the 1880s had witnessed, as some thought, the nadir in the fortunes of Borough Road, according to Ballard, in the 1890s Barnett's period was a 'golden age … The College received a new life and a new milieu. The spirit of the elementary school and the grammar school was replaced by the richer and freer spirit of the university….'[15]

To develop Borough Road along university lines Barnett initiated a policy which had served the public school system well[16] and now was to serve the College well for the next 30 years, namely appointing young games playing graduates as junior staff. As F.H. Spencer explained, Barnett

> introduced a new element into the College staff. Before his day it had been recruited exclusively from old students … Barnett, whilst retaining openings in the junior staff for men of mind and character produced by the College itself, originated the practice of recruiting also from Oxford and Cambridge … The junior tutors, recruited from the most brilliant of the students, were not expected to remain on the staff for more than some two or three years, when they moved on to all sorts of openings in the system of public education at home and abroad; some of them to positions of considerable responsibility.[17]

In 1893 Barnett left Borough Road to take up a position in the Inspectorate and was replaced by H.L. Withers. Withers had been educated at Balliol College, Oxford, where he too had gained a First in Classical Greats. After Oxford he had taught in a number of public schools, including Clifton, where he had been a House Master.[18] Although he subsequently had reservations about organized team games,[19] while he was at Borough Road, he fully subscribed to the games culture that Barnett had successfully established.[20] In 1900 Withers left to become Professor of Education at Manchester University. The man who replaced him, Arthur Burrell, was one of the most vigorous apologists for athleticism in the history of the College. Like Barnett and Withers, Burrell was an 'Oxbridge' graduate from Wadham College,

Oxford, and had taught for over twenty years at Bradford Grammar School.[21] His subscription to an Almondian-type programme of institutional athleticism was total. And he led from the front. He was, it was remarked by the college historian,

> probably the only Principal who has personally supervised a weekly remedial class for physically underdeveloped students. He formed a special gymnastic squad, engaged a boxing instructor, founded an annual boxing championship and pressed the College committee to provide funds so that every student had an opportunity of learning to swim at Brentford baths. He encouraged early morning runs and afternoon paper chases, whatever the weather. 'We shall not do our duty by the students', he wrote in one of his Reports 'until we see every single member of the College taking daily exercise.'[22]

This triumvirate of public school and Oxbridge-educated Principals transformed Borough Road from a narrow non-denominational, inward-looking institution with a strong emphasis on probity and piety into something more akin to an ancient university, or rather a public school with a house system, prefects, and compulsory participation in team games for both staff and students alike.

With its history of missionary zeal and overseas work, the British and Foreign School Society,[23] responsible for Borough Road, had established a tradition of sending men all over the world. Thus, the College was ideally placed to continue this missionary role now with an emphasis on the physical as well as the spiritual! Herbert Milnes was to take full advantage of this propitious development. Milnes arrived at Borough Road in January 1893. His love of games perfectly matched the now prevailing ethos of the College. Spencer has described the enthusiasm for games at the time: 'Every afternoon and from Saturday midday until Sunday night we were our own masters. We played hard at football and ran very successful Soccer and Rugger teams, four of them altogether, and anyone could, and most of us did, kick about at large to our great physical benefit.'[24]

Spencer continued, proudly if immodestly:

> Our ideal was the man who was clever, but not too industrious, who worked hard but not long, and was a good fellow and a good athlete. And, indeed, a good half of those in the football and cricket teams

were men of brains who did well in the pervading world of examinations, which surrounded but did not dominate most of us. Our soccer team was perhaps, by the accident of its possessing one future international player, and at least three or four of League standard, a first rate one. Not only did it never lose a match, but it emulsified the other training colleges and the local teams. I remember their winning one match by 17 to O.[25]

Almondian athleticism was now alive and thriving in the College. Milnes fully exemplified its virtues. Arthur Burrell, the author of a memoir on Milnes, recalled:

> He was clean, healthy, virile; he had an air of a person who was going to do what he thought right whether you liked it or not ... There was not an ounce of superfluous flesh upon him, and from the beginning he kept fit ... When he took to football he had found his métier, and he was never out of the rugby game. His cold baths, in a day when the love of them in College was not universal, were proverbial; and the lightness of his bedclothes ('the fewer the bedclothes, the harder you get') made other people who believed only in the theory shiver.[26]

Influenced by external forces directly by the Cross Commission and indirectly by the public schools and Oxbridge – in the 1890s the College went through an educational transformation. Games, which formerly had been frowned upon, were now both valued and compulsory. In consequence, many of the students who graduated from the College did so imbued with a sporting missionary zeal. They took it literally into hundreds of elementary schools throughout England and Wales *and* the Empire. Borough Road thus played a vital part in the dissemination of the ideology of athleticism, albeit in adapted Almondian form.[27]

The College, a fact hitherto little known, became outstandingly good at sport and it produced outstanding sporting heroes. Apart from Milnes who was to win county caps at rugby for Yorkshire, there was J.G. Gettins who played football for a number of league sides including Middlesbrough, Reading and Millwall, and James Haydock. Haydock played 79 games for Blackburn and was picked for England in *1895* although injury prevented him getting his cap. He was to die at the tragically early age of 27 in 1900.[28]

Milnes left Borough Road in 1895. He returned to teach in the school where he had been both a pupil and pupil teacher, Beeston Hill, elementary school in Yorkshire. He wasted no time: 'he formed a football club for the boys, and trained them so well that they won the Shield open to … all the Leeds schools'.[29]

He was not forgotten at Borough Road. And successes in the North did not go unnoticed. In 1899 he was appointed to the staff of Borough Road by Withers. By this time the College was even more completely run along the lines of Almond's Loretto, due to the arrival Allan Ramsay Smith who joined the staff in 1900. Smith, who had been Head Boy at Loretto and a student at Trinity College, Oxford was an outstanding rugby player, and captained both Oxford in the 'varsity match, and Scotland'.[30] As was the custom at Borough Road, he played for the College in what was an extremely strong XV containing not only Milnes but also R.T. Gabe, a Welsh international centre. Indeed, as Spencer with caustic gentleness observed, 'How many Oxford or Cambridge Colleges, may I mildly ask, could put two internationals in the field at one and the same time? For, remember, we were only 130 all told.'[31] As professionals who shared the same educational philosophy, as colleagues who worked in the same college, as men who enjoyed sport, and as team mates who played the same games, it is wholly reasonable to suggest that Smith and Milnes inspired each other, reinforced each other's enthusiasms and demonstrated, above all for all to see, admire and imitate, ideological imperatives in action. Milnes, who trained daily, made a strong impact on many within the college with his dedication to physical fitness. 'It is difficult,' recalled Burrell, 'to say what are the outstanding recollections round which all others group to make his memory. But this is what I seem to see. He swings, a burly close-knit figure, clad in a minimum of garments, on his way to the fives courts; or returns, past my study window, from the football field, a mass of mud and health; or he trots heavily … passed by me on my bicycle, on some foggy or drizzly morning at seven o'clock, when…the grumblers are mouching in overcoats.'[32]

One aspect of Almond's 'Lorettonianism'[33] that would doubtless have appealed to Milnes was the fact that intelligence was the third, not the first aspect of education that Almond valued. For Milnes was far from being an intellectual. Although he was awarded a geography prize reputedly owing 'to his complete [if idiosyncratic] acquaintance with the names of minor Siberian rivers',[34] he repeatedly failed his degree. When he did eventually pass, such was his popularity however, that this was greeted with great enthusiasm: 'I shall never forget,' recalled Burrell, 'when, after speaking of those in the body of the hall who had been successful, I came to the announcement of his success. Men had seen him fail while students succeeded, and yet he was their House Tutor. Nothing daunted, he had continued his studies in the intervals of time that he could get; and when most men would have given up in disgust, he persevered. A thrill went through us all as we recognized the worth of the man in connection with this fight for his degree.'[35]

Clearly he was loved at Borough Road and in turn loved Borough Road, but in 1905 he reluctantly tendered his resignation. His fiancée was seriously ill and he had successfully applied for the post of Principal of a teacher training college in Auckland, New Zealand believing that the climate there would be better for her. When he left the College, Burrell wrote, typically, that 'he refused any testimonial from the men except a football on which their names were written; and with this record of the way he had fostered all manliness, he left us'.[36] Milnes retained happy memories of Borough Road. When a former student visited Milnes in Auckland: 'He spoke with enthusiasm of the College at Isleworth, and I still recall the little traits that showed how much he loved the place, its association, its students and their sports.'[37] Milnes was delighted to discover that on reaching Auckland there were three more Old B's 'so we shall have our Old B's Club after all and will forward our annual subscription to the Whitunside sports like all real members. We are all enthusiastic about the Shield…'[38]

When Milnes arrived in Auckland no training college had yet been built. It was his job to build it. It was a challenge to which he responded with enthusiasm. As a colleague remarked 'there are undoubted advantages in building on his own foundations, and he will have the satisfaction, as his College grows and prospers of knowing that it is entirely his own creation'.[39] Eventually it was. Milnes first met his student teachers one Saturday morning after Easter in 1906. His college in number was little more than one small school class of the time – only 19 women and 9 men. Immediately he had a galvanising effect on those present as one recalled:

'He emphasised again and again that the teacher was a key figure in the New Zealand economy. We had just come out of the depression of the 1880s and the country needed teachers capable of providing the education needed to rebuild a sound and healthy nation … We began to take on something of this enthusiasm for education and to realize that we too must accept his motto *"Totis Viribus"*.'[40] Another remarked, 'If

Milnes' philosophy could be summed up in two words they would be his oft repeated motto *Totis Viribus* – with all their strength.' What this actually meant in practice was: 'the amount of strength one could put into any effort – physical, mental or social – would depend largely on one's physical fitness. To achieve this end one should devote oneself wholeheartedly, and with almost religious fervour'.[41]

From the outset Milnes insisted on the importance of good health and ample exercise. He set an example. He went for a run every morning before breakfast, and insisted on every student doing likewise. While Milnes was careful to emphasize that the stress placed on physical fitness was to be applied equally to studies, he was emphatic that applying oneself wholly to study to the neglect of physical needs, was likely to lead to disaster.[42] Mangan has written of Hely Hutchison Almond that: 'The physical care of his boys was the main work of his life and "Lorettonianism" was "the informing principle of the community". It constituted an elaborate and systematic programme of health education covering food, clothes, physical exercise, sleep, fresh air and cold baths.'[43] Almond's philosophy and more importantly his methods, were faithfully copied by Milnes. At his drill sessions, for example, he made the students change into loose clothing. Drilling in everyday clothes, with a stand-up collar on, he insisted (like Almond) 'was an absurdity'.[44] In his Report to the Board of Education in 1907, at the end of his first year, Milnes was at pains to point out the importance of physical exercise. Milnes made it absolutely clear that he did not see physical fitness as an adjunct to successful education, he saw it as its core.

> I want to emphasise the importance of this branch of work. Good health means better work all round, – it means happier lives, and happier teachers mean happier scholars. Anyone not engaged in active exercise deteriorates mentally and physically; and if I can only involve the students with the love of hygienic exercise and cold bathing I shall have done much to brighten the lot of the students, and indirectly of those whom they will teach in due course.[45]

As Principal of Auckland Teacher Training College and zealous 'advocate of bodily training and physical fitness', Milnes was in the vanguard of a new games playing movement in New Zealand elementary education at a time when there was a sea change in attitudes concerning the value of games. Brian Sutton-Smith in his, *A History of Children's*

Play in New Zealand 1840-1950, states that by the late 1890s 'a new generation of teachers had arrived – teachers who as boys had themselves played in the sporadic inter-school fixtures of the preceding 20 years and who now gave their time voluntarily to coaching and organising school teams'.[46] Milnes had timed his arrival well. It was an environment made for him. Furthermore, with his conviction that physical exercise was not only desirable in the development of the child, but also a prerequisite for the intending teacher, he was in the right place at the right time!

Milnes once wrote:

> The longer I live the more I am convinced of the need for active sweating exercises followed by cold baths for young people – it clears them physically and mentally … A student unable to take part in a game is not, in my opinion, suited for school teaching. Playing with your children is the surest help to influencing them I know, and if the teacher is unable to do this he loses a help he cannot get in any other way.[47]

Sutton-Smith appreciates the period novelty of this categorical assertion stating that it was 'a comparatively new view in 1910. Today it is commonplace, the wise tip of every headmaster to every young teaching student on the problem of discipline.'[48] Whether Sutton-Smith is right about the modern headmaster, and there are some who would argue with him, the fact remains that Milnes firmly believed in the value of exercise in education *and* the value of games in building character. In the *Journal of Education* in May 1912 he asserted:

> As character training is admitted to be our goal, it is interesting to see what effect the play of school games has on it … Games undoubtedly have a great effect on character, summed up in the one word 'sportsmanlike'… they promote social growth and in many and other ways improve one's powers, but when all is said and done, it is learning 'to play the game' and never to hit 'below the belt' that constitute the 'great values'.[49]

If Milnes was dismayed by the fact that there was no actual training college in Auckland when he arrived, as already noted he at least had the advantage of being 'a painter with a blank canvas'. Whatever Milnes was, he certainly was not an academic. Ideas had little appeal for him. He was a man of action. He immediately set about filling in his Auckland 'canvas'. He 'painted the college in his own primary colours' giving priority to provision for boxing, drill, tennis, rugby, hockey and basketball:

> The three tennis courts were in great demand and everybody played as opportunity arose. Though voluntary, the playing of tennis was made an adjunct to the physical drill class. Matches were played with the *Otahuhi* and Papatoioi teams and a college championship was held at the end of the year...Photos of these two winners are to be hung in the respective common rooms. A hockey team for the men was begun and a promising start was made. On the opening day the college team took part in a Knock-out Competition, and ... won the final, and a finely embroidered banner which now graces the common room ... Boxing classes were held twice a week by the Principal for the men. All attended.[50]

Just as he had done at Borough Road, Milnes, by now in his mid-thirties, joined the students in their games and played in the front row of the University College, Auckland XV. He also threw himself wholeheartedly into the national 'Varsity Tournament held every Easter. The competition covered athletics, tennis and debating 'with a shield for the winners.' The Tournament proved rather expensive for the students, owing to the distances to be travelled. Wellington College for example was 426 miles by rail. Milnes, therefore, organized socials to raise funds and preliminary contests in order to select suitable representatives.[51]

Milnes also took every opportunity by other means to reinforce his message of the importance of exercise. Photographs, shields cups and banners of sporting success acted as symbols of achievement and statements of belief. And there was yet another way in which the message could be transmitted. Mangan has observed that 'students of society too often discuss ritual having in mind behaviour of a non-verbal kind, speech is often a form of ritual and non-verbal ritual merely a signal system of a less specialised kind'.[52] Milnes certainly appreciated the fact. The students at Borough Road had borrowed Edward Bowen's famous Harrovian anthem 'Forty Years On'. Milnes took it to New Zealand.[53] Auckland Training College also celebrated sports successes with the singing of the famous Maori Haka

> Kamate Kainate Ka ora Ka ora
> Tene te tangata
> Puhuru hururu

Nana i tiki mai
Whakawhiti te ra
Upane Kaupane
Upane Kaupane
Whiti te ra!

It was death! It was death
Now it is life Now it is life
Behold the man, the hairy man who
has caused the sun to shine
Up this step, then up that step
Into the blazing sun[54]

Milnes thus deliberately took the same songs he had no doubt sung many times, from his old institution to his new institution with the intention of producing the same responses of loyalty, affection and *esprit de corps* but he also chose those of traditional Maori Life, particularly those that celebrate the warrior. In doing so he endorsed period manliness in its militaristic essentials: comradeship, courage and self-sacrifice.[55]

As already noted, Milnes was in step with new trends in education in New Zealand. His concern with the moral development of the young mirrored that of other educationalists. Cohn McGeorge has remarked of the period moral curriculum in New Zealand elementary schools: 'I take the moral curriculum ... to include practices and activities meant to shape character and conduct.'[56] At this time understandably there was a close relationship between moral education in New Zealand and British elementary school. Milnes in effect, was an influential synthesist. There was a good reason for this:

> Although the New Zealand moral curriculum came to vary from its British counterpart ... it was, originally, very much the British moral curriculum transplanted. Like other settlement colonies of the Empire New Zealand inherited two models of the school as character factory: one based on the British common or Board school and the other with an obvious debt to Arnold and the British public schools.[57]

It is clear that elementary education in New Zealand followed the British pattern.[58] It is unremarkable therefore that the introduction of games into elementary schools, in New Zealand followed a similar pattern to that of Britain. Firstly, the development of the curriculum was based on British practice. Secondly, several major educational diffusionists came from the mother country. Milnes for example, clearly had strong convictions about the moral value of organized games and was able to shape a college for the training of New Zealand teachers to his convictions.

In this era of New Zealand elementary school and training college creation and expansion Milnes must have been an impressive figure. He radiated energy, he glowed with conviction, he led by example. In Auckland inspired by the arguments of Herbert Spencer, the ideals of Hely Hutchinson Almond and the fashions of the English public school, he created a training college in his own (and their) image. With his subscription to active bodies, cold baths, character training, courage, unselfishness, and leadership, he personified ideological purity. In a world of Edwardian certainty he was among the most certain. He was Kipling's 'Muddied Oaf'. If Kipling would not have appreciated him, New Zealanders did. This should cause little surprise, Scott A.G.M. Crawford has written that from the start New Zealanders' 'values ... reflected the influence of their parent society'.[59] This was equally true of education, on and off the games field.

In New Zealand as in Britain in the late nineteenth century militarism, imperialism and games became significant aspects of middle-class culture. In particular, rugby-playing was a 'soldier-making game'. Milnes must have been in his element. He would have appreciated and welcomed the perceived relationship between masculinity, sport and war.[60] It should come as no surprise, therefore, that when the First World War broke out Milnes now in early middle age, immediately enlisted. He was rapidly promoted from corporal, to sergeant, and then to second lieutenant. Once again his physical energy, his strength of character and his love of games served him well. As at Borough Road and Auckland College he rapidly won the affection of his men. 'Of course he buys them a football; of course they come to him with their troubles; he has any number of heart affairs on his mind, and is a sort of a father confessor; the men, he says aren't shy at all.'[61] Milnes arrived in France in December 1916. Less than a year later he was killed at Passchendaele.

Milnes's death had a profound effect on those who had known him both in Auckland and at Borough Road. The wholehearted, burly, almost 'superhuman' Milnes had proved to be as mortal as everyone else. In life he was inspirational; in death he became iconic. In a memorial service held in Auckland, Professor Dettmann of University College, Auckland offered the following eulogy:

> We should all say of him that he was, above all else, simple, single-minded, straight, honest, sincere, a clear, sane thinker, in action forcible, fearless, direct ... we should apply to him Shakespeare's description of Brutus...
>
> > His life was gentle, and the elements
> > So mixed in him that Nature might stand up
> > And say to all the world: 'This was a man!'
>
> That is surely his real epitaph: This was a man. In our day and generation has there been any man in our city, anyone we have known, in whom Nature had so perfectly mixed and combined all the elements of manhood?[62]

In death Milnes became the athlete-warrior incarnate. Burrell captures in his memoir a passage that demonstrates the hold that chivalric notions of duty, death and glory had on contemporary consciousness:

> It was for a fairer object far, than even the country he loved that Milnes went cheerfully and gallantly to his death. Death must come to us all in any case some day, come it soon or come it late: happy is the man who, with work well done that was given him to do, with clean hands and a pure heart, meets death on the field of battle, in the cause that he knows to be the most sacred man may die for.[63]

For the purposes of this volume, this essay and antipodean social history, however, Milnes offers early evidence that the ideology of athleticism was *not* confined to the public schools of Britain and Empire, but in adapted form, was carried successfully into elementary schools and teacher-training colleges in both Britain and its Empire. He also offers evidence of the appeal of the ideology at this level when embraced and introduced by forceful adherents.[64] Milnes was a man of admitted limited intellectual attainments, but such was his personality, determination and, without exaggeration, undoubted charisma that he was able to overcome social disadvantage and educational handicaps that would have defeated many others – from elementary schoolboy to college student; from school teacher to college principal; from enlisted corporal to commissioned officer. Milnes, of course, was a man of his time and for his time in his firm belief in physical fitness and the value of games in the formation of character. In holding this belief he was doing no more or believing no less than thousands of public school and university educated men involved in imperial school teaching, educational administration and government.[65]

Burrell recalled that although Milnes' knowledge of the classics was limited, the 'Lampadephoria' was one of the few works he knew. He continued:

> Indeed, writers have always understood the race as a parable of life, and the Roman, Lucretius, in an unforgettable line, has immortalised it: 'Et quasi cursores vitaï lampada tradunt' (And like runners in the ancient race they hand on the torches of life). A writer of our own day has again seized on two of the words in this line, and has written a poem, Vitaï Lampada, which is known in every English school; to him the passing on of the torches means what it did to the man of whom I have been writing:

> Play up, play up and play the game.[66]

The tribute had an element of truth, however foolishly romantic and sentimentally exaggerated it may seem to modern ears and eyes.

At a time when games playing, and especially rugby football, has never been more popular, when the total numbers involved in playing, coaching, administrating or merely watching runs into billions, it is appropriate to reflect on Milnes' contribution to the games cult in New Zealand. Once in New Zealand, Milnes transformed teacher training to such an extent that 'soon the influence of the College became apparent throughout the province. Indeed, it would be difficult to estimate the influence of Milnes in education in the Auckland Education district and probably throughout New Zealand.'[67]

Inspirational in life Milnes in death remained an inspiration for New Zealand educators. A life-sized photograph of him was hung in the College hall and the New Zealand Board of Education put up an inscribed brass shield. It read:

> In Memory of Herbert A.E. Milnes (B.Sc.Lond.)
> Who lies buried at Otto Farm, Zonnebeke, Flanders
> As Principal of this College (1906–17), devoting himself to the welfare of his students, he inspired in them great enthusiasm and laid a broad foundation for their professional life.

In the hour of his Country's need, he gave up the work he loved, to enlist in the N.Z.E.F., and as Corporal, Sergeant and Lieutenant (A Coy., 3rd Auck. Batt.), carried the enthusiasm and skill, which had marked his educational work, into the service of the Empire. A Gallant Soldier and a true friend to his men, he fell fighting in the great attack on Passchendaele Ridge, 4 October, 1917, to the last the worthiest exponent of his College Motto: '*Totis Viribus*'.[68]

As we enter the third millennium, when the success and status of Australasian sport is at a high point it is perhaps timely to recall the early influence of Herbert Albert Edwin Milnes, 'Pioneer of the Proletariat'.

NOTES

1. See J.A. Mangan, *Athleticism in the Victorian and Edwardian Public School: The Emergence and Consolidation of an Educational Ideology* (Cambridge, 1981).
2. See J.A. Mangan, *The Games Ethic and Imperialism: Aspects of the Diffusion of an Ideal* (London, 1988).
3. Ibid., p.18.
4. Ibid.
5. Borough Road dates back to 1798 when a young 21-year-old Quaker, Joseph Lancaster, established a school in Southwark, London. The school rapidly became both successful (Lancaster had invented a system whereby over 100 children could be taught by a single teacher) and famous when it attracted the patronage of George III in 1805. From that moment it became the pre-eminent non-denominational teacher-training college in the country, although constantly bedevilled by lack of funds. The site was by 1888 cramped, overcrowded and utterly unsuitable as a training college. For a full account see G.F. Bartle, *A History of Borough Road College* (Kettering, 1976).
6. T.J. Macnamara, 'Training College Student Days', *The New Liberal Review*, VI, 32 (1903), 228.
7. P.A. Barnett, *Common Sense in Education: An Introduction to Practice* (London, 1899), p.74.
8. Edwin Abbott Abbott D.D. was educated at the City of London School and St John's College, Cambridge, 1861. He was ordained in 1862. On leaving Cambridge he became Assistant Master at King Edward's, Birmingham, and was later Second Master at Clifton and then Headmaster of City of London School from 1865 to 1889. He was an author of numerous books on education. See A.E. Douglas-Smith, *The City of London School* (Oxford, 1965), pp.531–3, and T. Hinde, *Carpenter's Children. The Story of the City of London School* (London, 1995), pp.46–66.
9. Hely Hutchinson Almond was Headmaster of Loretto School, Musselburgh near Edinburgh from 1862 to 1903. Almond was one of the first public school headmasters to make physical education an integral part of the school curriculum. Frank Stewart, author of the school history, has written, 'The five essentials he prescribed for good health were: Fresh air, personal cleanliness, diet, physical exercise and dress.' F. Stewart, *Loretto One Fifty* (Edinburgh, 1981), p.52.
10. For a more detailed analysis of Almond, his life, work and impact on education see J.A. Mangan 'Almond of Loretto: Scottish Educational Visionary and Reformer', *Scottish Educational Review*, 11, 2 (Nov. 1979), 97–106, and Mangan *Athleticism*, see especially pp.48–58.
11. Barnett, *Common Sense*, p.309.
12. P.A. Barnett, *The Little Book of Health and Courtesy* (London, 1905), pp.23–4.
13. P.B. Ballard, *Things I Cannot Forget* (London, 1937), p.47.
14. F.H. Spencer, *An Inspector's Testament* (London, 1938), p.129.
15. Ballard, *Things I Cannot Forget*, p.47.
16. See Mangan, *Athleticism*, p.122.

17. Spencer, *An Inspector's Testament*, pp.129–30. For a more detailed examination of this policy in action, see G.F. Bartle, 'Staffing Policy at a Victorian Training College', *Victorian Education*, Occasional Publication, 2 (Summer 1976), 14–23.
18. Clifton, of course, was brought to prominence by its famous headmaster Percival.
19. In 1901 he gave a paper to the Frobel Society on the distinction between work and play. He argued that 'the prevalence of some half a dozen great games in English schools to the destruction of all other pastimes, hobbies and amusements has had some deplorable results.' J.A. Fowler (ed.), *The Teaching of History and Other Papers by H. L. Withers, Clifton College* (Manchester, 1904), pp.225–6. Fowler, however, did point out that Withers liked spectating 'A good match at either cricket or football he would watch with keen interest. But it was perhaps in long walks that he took the most pleasure.' Ibid., p.12.
20. Withers expressed reservations about the role and value of team games in 1901 after he left Borough Road. While he was Principal of the College the expansion of games playing continued apace. Indeed Withers himself was a member of a staff crew which was only narrowly defeated by a student crew in a challenge match in 1897. See Bartle, *A History*, p.57.
21. Arthur Burrell was Principal of Borough Road from 1900 to 1912. A graduate of Wadham College, Oxford, Burrell had extensive experience of public school education including twenty years in charge of the junior department at Bradford Grammar School prior to his appointment. See Bartle, *A History*, pp.54–63.
22. G.F. Bartle, *A History*, p.58.
23. The British and Foreign School Society was established in 1808 to run the affairs of Borough Road and to co-ordinate the development of non-denominational Christian elementary education both in Britain and overseas. The society became heavily involved in the anti-slavery campaign and soon had a presence in West Africa, India and the West Indies. Foreign and overseas work became very important from the society's earliest days. Many distinguished visitors from the continent visited Borough Road to see the monitorial system of education in operation. This resulted in Monitorial schools on 'British' (as in British and Foreign) lines being established in France, Belgium, Scandinavia, Spain and Russia. See Bartle, *A History*, p.13, and H.B. Binns, *A Century of Education 1808–1908* (London, 1908).
24. Spencer, *An Inspector's Testament*, p.138.
25. Ibid., p.138.
26. A. Burrell, *Bert Milnes. A Brief Memoir* (Letchworth, 1922), pp.12–13.
27. See J. A. Mangan and Colm Hickey, 'English Elementary Education Revisited and Revised: Drill and Athleticism in Tandem', in J.A. Mangan (ed.), *Sport in Europe: Politics, Class, Gender* (London, 1999), pp.63–91.
28. James Haydock (1873–1900). Haydock was born in Blackburn and attended Furthergate Congregational School before going to Borough Road in 1892. After College he returned to Blackburn to teach at his old school. He played a total of 79 games for Blackburn Rovers. He was selected to play for England in 1895, but was unable to play due to an injury. Illness forced him to retire from football in 1897 and prevented him from remaining a teacher and he died in March 1900 aged 27.
29. Burrell, *Bert Milnes*, p.16.
30. Allan Ramsey Smith (1875–1926). Smith had been a pupil at Loretto School from 1884 to 94 and had been Head of School. He represented Loretto at rugby, football, hockey and fives. He attended Trinity College, Oxford and won four 'blues' and captained Oxford in 1897. He was also a Scottish rugby international winning caps in 1895, 6, 7, 8 and 1900 when he was captain. He graduated from Oxford in 1898 and spent two years travelling before being appointed as House Tutor at Borough Road in 1900. After leaving Borough Road in 1901 he became a Junior Inspector of Schools and from 1903 to 1908 Inspector of Schools in Liverpool. In 1908 at the age of 35 he was appointed Headmaster of Loretto where he remained until his death in 1926. See Stewart, *Loretto One Fifty*, pp.157–206.
31. Spencer, *An Inspector's Testament*, pp.138–9.
32. Burrell, *Bert Milnes*, p.17.
33. 'Lorettonianism' was Hely Hutchinson's philosophy of education, see Mangan, *Athleticism*, p.54.
34. Burrell, *Bert Milnes*, pp.14–15.
35. Ibid., p.15.
36. Ibid., p.20.

37. E. Walker, 'An Interview with M. Milnes in New Zealand', *B's Hum*, XVIII, 130 (Oct. 1906), p.18.
38. B. Milnes, 'Through the Suez' in *B's Hum*, XVII, 128 (May, 1906), 6.
39. Walker, 'An Interview', p.18.
40. 'Totis Viribus' (With all thy strength). This was the motto that Milnes chose for the College.
41. Auckland College of Education (ACE) 13/2/1.
42. Ibid., p.7.
43. Mangan, *Athleticism*, p.54.
44. Report for the year 1907 on the work of the Auckland Training College ... to the Secretary of Board of Education, Auckland, ACE 9/2/27, p.10.
45. Ibid., pp.10–11.
46. B. Sutton-Smith, *A History of Children's Play. New Zealand 1840-1950* (Philadelphia, 1981), p.193.
47. D. Baird, 'History of Physical Education in New Zealand' (unpublished MA thesis, Victoria University, Wellington, 1942), 42, quoted in Sutton-Smith, *A History*, p.197.
48. Sutton-Smith, *A History*, p.197.
49. *Journal of Education* (Sept. 1912), quoted in Sutton-Smith, *A History*, p.198.
50. Report for the Year 1907, ACE 9/2/27, p.13.
51. Burrell, *Bert Milnes*, p.29.
52. Mangan, *Athleticism*, p.161.
53. ACE AKTC 13/2/1 p.8.
54. Ibid., p.8.
55. See J.A. Mangan, 'Duty unto Death. English Masculinity and Militarism in the Age of the New Imperialism', in J.A. Mangan (ed.), *Tribal Identities: Nationalism, Europe, Sport* (London, 1998), pp.10–38.
56. Colin McGeorge, 'The Moral Commitment: Forming the Kiwi Character', in Gary McCulloch (ed.), *The School Curriculum in New Zealand: History, Theory, Policy and Practice* (Palmerston, New Zealand, 1993), p.40.
57. Ibid., pp.41–2.
58. See Sutton-Smith, pp.176–200. The curriculum of primary schools was thoroughly revised by George Hogben. Hogben was a Cambridge graduate and had served as a teacher, headmaster and inspector of primary schools when he was made Inspector General of Education in 1899. 'Under his leadership there began a movement for reform that has left its mark upon the character of New Zealand education', J.C. Dalkin, *Education in New Zealand* (1973), pp.26–27. Hogben's revised syllabus was very much influenced by British developments specially in the aftermath of the Cross Commission. See also J.L. Ewing, *The Development of the New Zealand Primary School Curriculum*, 1877–1970 (Wellington, New Zealand), pp.87–150.
59. Scott A.G.M. Crawford, 'Muscles and Character are There. The First Object of Necessity': An Overview of Sport and Recreation in a Colonial Setting - Otago Province New Zealand', *British Journal of Sports History*, 2, 2 (Sept. 1985), 109.
60. See J.A. Mangan, 'Duty unto Death', *passim.*
61. Burrell, *Bert Milnes*, p.39.
62. Ibid., pp.30–1.
63. Ibid., p.33.
64. Milnes was only one of a number of athletically-minded Training College graduates who had a significant impact upon the development of games playing in elementary education in empire. Others involved L.G. Gruchy and A.A.B. Macfarlane, both former students of St John's College, Battersea who were joint principals of Mico Training College in Jamaica from 1884 to 1919, John Adamson, Director of Education for the Transvaal and first Principal of Rhodes University who was knighted for his services to education in 1924 was trained at St Marks College from 1889 to 91. For a fuller list, see C.F. Hickey, 'Athleticism and the Training Colleges' (Ph.D. University of Strathclyde, forthcoming).
65. See, for example, Mangan, *The Games Ethic and Imperialism*, *passim.*
66. Burrell, *Bert Milnes*, pp.46–7.
67. ACE AKTC 9/2/6 p.2.
68. Burrell, *Bert Milnes*, p.45.

3

Gender Associations: Sport, State Schools and Australian Culture

DAVID KIRK

The physical culture of government schools in Australia was shaped by the practices of sport, physical recreation and exercise and by the institutional imperatives of the school. With only a few exceptions, state schools were co-educational, in contrast to schools serving the privileged classes, which were almost entirely single sex. The single sex institutions' explicit uses of physical cultural practices to construct the gendered identities of girls and boys have been well documented by historians.[1] Less well understood are the co-educational government schools' uses of physical cultural practices to construct gendered identities. This is in part due to the delimited range of ways in which the majority of Australians were able to experience sport, physical recreation and exercise during the first 50 years of the twentieth century. It is also due in part to the narrow and pragmatic uses of physical activity to meet the schools' institutional requirements for social order.

Although sport was a prominent dimension of popular culture for working-class Australians in the first half of the century, their experiences were generally confined to spectatorship and gambling rather than active participation. Even so, sport provided a set of cultural values and norms for making sense of everyday life, though as the work of Michael McKernan and others has shown these values were disputed across and within sections of Australian society.[2] The institutional imperatives of the school in terms of the need for social order determined to a large extent the form that physical culture could take. From the beginning of the twentieth century until the 1940s, the common experience of physical culture in schools across the government education systems was drilling and exercising, a mixture of military marching and squad manoeuvres done in unison, and exercises borrowed from Dano-Swedish gymnastics.

The practicalities of dealing with large numbers of potentially truculent children within relatively small spaces produced a need for bodies that were compliant. The economics of government investment in mass education within a capitalist economy produced a need for productive bodies. Fears for the safety of the realm and its racial integrity produced a need for healthy bodies that might be able to defend Australia and propagate a sound Anglo-Celtic race in the Antipodes. In attempting to respond to these imperatives of mass compulsory public schooling, educators drew on particular aspects of physical culture to manipulate the coordinates of space and time on and around children's bodies.

In this context, this essay explores the social production of femininity and masculinity through the physical cultural practices of government schools in Australia. The study begins with a brief overview of the concepts of physical culture and the social production of gender. These concepts are then located within a discussion of government schooling and the social regulation of children's bodies through physical training. Following this discussion, number of syllabuses and texts are analysed. The texts contained for teachers key information on physical training and a narrative on the androgynous child who was to be constructed through a regime of formal physical training. The essay concludes with a discussion of the demise of physical training and with it the narrative of the androgynous child, and their replacement with the explicitly gendered practices of sport-based physical education after the Second World War.

PHYSICAL CULTURE

Physical culture refers to a range of practices concerned with the maintenance, representation and regulation of the body centred on three highly codified, institutionalized forms of physical activity – sport, physical recreation and exercise. Physical culture is one source of the production and reproduction of corporeal discourse, a series of interconnecting symbol systems concerned with meaning making centred on the human body.[3] This definition of physical culture proposes that sport, recreation and exercise are a specific dimension of the broader category of corporeal practices ranging, for example, from surgery to personal hygiene to cosmetics and fashion, all of which are concerned with embodiment and meaning.

These three key dimensions of physical culture require some preliminary consideration. Sport is by far the largest set of practices, and indeed provides resources upon which both physical recreation and exercise draw. P. Bourdieu has suggested that one of the central tasks of a social history of sport is to identify from what set of conditions and at what moment it became possible to speak of sport in its contemporary sense.[4] He argues that modern sport emerged from the practices of the British public schools of the nineteenth century, a proposal that is strongly supported by much subsequent historical research by Mangan and others.[5] Understood historically, the term sport refers to a complex set of practices that feature highly developed techniques and strategies, organized competition and specialized facilities.

The concept of physical recreation has a long lineage, but it was not until the 1930s in Australia that its meaning began to resemble contemporary use, as changing conditions of work and play began to make it possible for the masses to engage in physical recreational activity. Recreation refers to our ability to re-create or re-generate through activities that are alternatives to work, whether this be the domestic work of running the home or wage labour. The first national campaign to promote recreational physical activity in Australia occurred in 1938 and 1939, and lead to the successful passage through federal parliament of the National Fitness Act in 1941. Recreation shares some of the features of sport, particularly at non-elite levels of participation where sport can be a medium for recreation. However, organized competition is not an essential element of physical recreation as it is with sport, since many informal, non-competitive or 'pick-up' games and physical activities have had recreational uses.

The notion of exercise has also had a long lineage. However, it was only towards the end of the 1940s, following developments in the use of progressive resistance activity, that exercise began to acquire relatively more specific and precise associations with physical fitness and health.[6] During the first half of the twentieth century exercise was most commonly associated with the many systems of formal gymnastic activities such as the Lingian system. Such exercise activities could be a medium of physical recreation. Sport could also be an exercise activity for some people.

Following this very brief consideration of the notions of sport, recreation and exercise as components of physical culture, these terms can be viewed as labels for sets of discursive practices that are complex and overlapping. This interweaving of practices is important because it points to a discursive structure with components that are interdependent and that are constantly reworking themselves. Since physical culture is centrally concerned with embodiment and meaning making, it is a fundamental concept in understanding the social production of gender.

THE SOCIAL PRODUCTION OF GENDER

It is not possible to understand gender without some consideration of physical culture and, in particular, the social construction of the body. Within a naturalistic perspective on the body, matters of gender, involving social values, are invariably reduced to matters of biology. A social constructionist view of the body, in contrast, suggests that biology and social values interact to produce forms of femininity and masculinity.[7] Neither femininity nor masculinity can be reduced to the other. In other words, femaleness and maleness do not determine gender; it is possible for females to display masculine characteristics and males to display feminine characteristics. These characteristics are themselves socially produced and vary across cultures.

In the social production of gender, physical culture is of central importance.[8] This is because the codified, institutionalized practices of sport, recreation and exercise are key sites in which social values – such as caring, co-operation, competitiveness, aggression, and so on – are conjoined with particular physical activities and their performance. An individual need not actively participate in sport, recreation or exercise for the social production of gender to impact upon them. This is because physical cultural practices such as sport acquire symbolic properties over time. In Australia from the 1940s, the Bronzed Aussie became a powerful cultural icon, superseding the Bushman and the Digger as symbols of Anglo-Celtic Australian identity.[9] No individual Australian could remain untouched by the symbolic power of the Bronzed Aussie, even though their relationship to it may have involved defining their own gender identity in contrast or opposition to the icon's hypermasculinity, heterosexuality and mesomorphism.

The team games that emerged in the late nineteenth century from the schools serving the privileged classes were firmly and explicitly designed to emphasize the social characteristics of femininity and masculinity valued by those social groups at that time. Throughout its modern history sport has been an important means of emphasizing differences between men and women and of maintaining those differences.

A good example is netball. Netball was developed as a modification of basketball and was for many years known as 'women's basketball' until women began to play the male version of basketball. This development forced the name to be changed.[10] Middle-class women in Australia, Britain, New Zealand and North America developed rules and styles of play that clearly demonstrated their beliefs about appropriate behaviour for 'young ladies', such as the absolute prohibition on physical contact.

Netball stands in stark contrast to a game such as rugby union where rough physical contact, including knocking other players over, is accommodated within and actually required by the rules of the game. Historians such as J.A. Mangan have noted the explicit educational goals for games like rugby union.[11] These were the development of 'character', where a boy who had been knocked down would get up and rejoin the fray, and 'manliness', which required that players show appropriate levels of controlled aggression and competitiveness. While games such as netball emphasized physical dexterity over strength, speed and force, the rules of rugby and other football codes often advantage the fast and strong over the skilful player.

As the dominant category of bodily practices within physical culture, sport exerted a profound influence on the social production of gender. Indeed, it is not possible to separate one process from the other, since the emergence of the practices we now call sport, from the mid to late 1800s, were from the beginning gendered. Sport comprises bodily practices fused to preferred definitions of femininity and masculinity. It is significant too that many of these sports took shape in educational institutions, specifically in the schools serving Australia's social élite. So sport and schooling were during the latter part of the nineteenth century and the first half of the twentieth century interlocked with the social production of gender.

PHYSICAL CULTURE AND STATE SCHOOLING

Given the strength of these relationships between sport, schools and the production of gender, it is significant to note that opportunities for children attending government schools to participate in sport were limited until after the Second World War. Until the 1910s most working-class women would not have played any organized sport, while the extent of most men's experience of sport was spontaneous participation in ad hoc games and spectatorship. As K. Reiger has shown, attempts by reformers to 'rationalize' working class domestic life from the 1880s to the 1940s met with stiff resistance from within the working classes.[12] While this reform movement had a profound impact on such matters as provision for infant and maternal health, notions about proper female and male contributions to domestic economy, family life and wage labour proved to be much harder to change. When working–class people did become involved in sport within the context of traditional conventions of femininity and masculinity, it was something men for the most part watched or betted on for fun, as a form of entertainment. This working-class, predominantly male, involvement contrasts with the way in which sport was represented within the ideology of the privileged schools, as an educationally valuable and ennobling experience.[13]

Following the First World War, this situation began to change, but only gradually. Sport became available to working class children in schools primarily as an extra-curricular pursuit.[14] It was only after the Second World War that sport gradually began to become accessible to all children as part of their regular, timetabled school physical education experience. Sports historian John Daly has suggested that 'Australian sport has always catered for the masses. Community sport is available to anybody and everybody. Few sports are class orientated and the climate and natural facilities encourage most to participate from an early age.'[15] McKernan's study of social class conflict surrounding sport during the First World War, supported by the work of other researchers, suggests otherwise. From the late eighteen hundreds and for much of the twentieth century, sport has remained a highly visible marker of deep social class division in Australia, where opportunities to participate have been limited to all but a privileged section of the community.[16]

Between 1900 and 1950 physical culture was represented in the schooling of working class children by Dano–Swedish or Lingian gymnastics and military drill. This choice of activity was in part prompted by the need to support through the school system the military training of junior cadets (boys aged 12–14) and in part by the need to meet the institutional imperatives of the school for social order. As I have argued at length elsewhere, schools in Australia and in many other western countries have been centrally concerned with the social regulation of young people's behaviour by working on their bodies.[17] This work has involved the organization and manipulation of two principle coordinates, space and time, in an attempt to impose order on the body of pupils and, at the same time, produce bodies for an orderly society. Schooling, in Foucault's terms, 'produces subjected and practised bodies, docile bodies. Discipline increases the forces of the body (in economic terms of utility) and diminishes the same forces (in political terms of obedience).'[18] The school constructs bodies that meet its own institutional imperatives. The school as an institutional form requires a particular kind of body, and social regulation and normalisation of young people's bodies has been a central concern of the school as an institution.

It is within this context of concerns for corporeal regulation that policy-makers considered Lingian gymnastics to form an appropriate basis for the physical training of children in government schools. Physical culture was represented in schools in the form of a system of formal exercises carried out, in aspiration at least, with precision and absolute 'correctness of performance'.[19] This system of physical training was encoded in a number of syllabuses and other texts that produced a narrative on the embodied, but androgynous, child.

SYLLABUSES, TEXTS AND THE NARRATIVE OF THE ANDROGYNOUS CHILD

A series of syllabuses and other guidelines for teaching physical training were in widespread use in Australian schools between the 1910s and the 1940s. These texts legitimated particular ways of moving that collectively made up physical training. The texts contained a narrative that described the schooled child and, more specifically, the embodied pupil. This narrative was not seamless, but there was a high degree of continuity between the various syllabuses. Later texts borrowed heavily from earlier versions in the process of updating and adapting them to meet new needs and circumstances.

Continuity derived, first and foremost, from the central place of Dano–Swedish or Lingian gymnastics in physical training from the 1910s to the late 1940s. The militaristic delivery of physical training lessons diminished somewhat during this period, as too the precise attention to detail that characterized earlier forms of physical training. But even in the less regimented forms that were in place in government schools by the 1930s and 1940s, the practices of Lingian gymnastics sought to construct a particular kind of child. A good example of this construction of the schooled, embodied child can be seen in the 1933 Board of Education *Syllabus of Physical Exercise* advocacy of good posture as one of the major outcomes of physical training.[20] Another example is the repeated insistence that the schooled child is obedient, alert, and cheerful and that the installation of these qualities is the special province of physical training.[21]

The earlier versions of the narrative of the embodied pupil were curiously and somewhat surprisingly gender-blind, given the strong coupling of physical culture with the social production of gender. This narrative was inscribed in the 1916, 1922 and 1925 *Junior Cadet Training Textbooks*, each of which consisted of substantial and only minimally amended borrowings from the 1909 Board of Education's *Syllabus of Physical Exercises*.[22] The child who was the subject of this narrative is androgynous. One reason for this may have been based in biology. Few children would have been pubescent by the time they were due to finish compulsory schooling at age 13 or 14. Children's bodies could be treated for the purposes of physical training as 'sex-less' in the absence of the secondary sexual characteristics that marked them as obviously female and male. Another reason, argued explicitly in the 1925 *Junior Cadet Training Textbook*, was that children must be treated differently from adults.

> A scheme of exercises designed for men undergoing training is not suitable for young boys and girls. To meet the special circumstances of continuous growth and development, a course of graduated exercises has been framed to suit children of all ages and both sexes, which aims at training every part of the body harmoniously.[23]

On the one hand, this statement was intended to correct the common but ill-conceived practice of subjecting children to inappropriate, adult forms of physical training. On the other, the statement made explicit a belief that it was possible, indeed desirable, to treat elementary school-age children as if their sex was irrelevant to the form of physical training they experienced.

But, paradoxically, this androgynous child of the physical training texts was a masculine construction. The commonplace practice of referring to all children as 'he' is perhaps too obvious a sign that this form of physical culture was created by men for men and boys. More telling is the substance of the physical training itself. The Australian syllabuses borrowed heavily from the Board of Education texts. The Board of Education texts had been carefully sanitized of overt military practices.[24] Nevertheless, the prevalence of military language such as 'squad' and 'drill', 'rank' and 'file', the persistent use of words of command, and the practices of exercising and marching in the mass leave no room for doubt. This version of Lingian gymnastics was designed to develop forms of social regulation that had their home as much in the barracks and parade grounds of the military as in the school.

So the texts of this period contained a narrative of the schooled body that is androgynous, on the one hand, but which is embedded in militarism and a particular, associated form of masculinity, on the other. This paradox sits oddly beside the realities of physical culture in Australian society more broadly. Educational policy-makers and teachers themselves were highly attuned to questions of gender and appropriate physical cultural practices. For instance, participants in the 1909 and 1910 Melbourne Conferences on Physical Training strongly recommended that any syllabus of physical training to be used in schools in conjunction with the national junior cadet training scheme for 12–14 year old boys must also be suitable for girls and younger boys.[25] Very early in the implementation of this new scheme of junior cadet training, state governments and the Defence Department together proposed that it was more appropriate for women teachers to be trained by other women rather than male physical training instructors.

Moreover, the ways in which men and women were expected to participate in Dano-Swedish gymnastics were firmly shaped by prevailing notions of masculinity and femininity. Reporting on training courses for teachers during the summer vacation of 1912, the *Argus*'s Donald Macdonald provided a glimpse of these prevailing expectations.[26] At the camp held in Geelong, 140 men were drilled with 'military discipline', though according to Macdonald, not without humour and tact: 'the man who drilled them on routine lines, making it pure drudgery, would have them resentful in next to no time'. Harvey Sutton, director of the school medical service in Victoria, supplemented the physical and military drill with lectures on hygiene, physiology and body mechanics, while the champion swimmer Frank Beaurepaire took morning and evening classes. The women, on the other hand, were drilled 'just enough', reported Macdonald, 'to facilitate falling in and forming squads'. Billeted three miles from the men at Osborne House, 130 female teachers were instructed by Gertrude Anderson in the 'arts' of physical exercise and folk dancing. Meanwhile May Cox, the female Organiser of Swimming in Victoria, taught dry-land swimming in a tree-lined sunken garden, since the beach at Osborne House was unsuitable for bathing. Macdonald was moved to record that the women's 'physical culture costumes, in which they spend the greater part of the day, are decidedly dainty, and rational, but not at all in a weird way. They wear short tunics and knickers, dark blue, and white rubber shoes.'

Macdonald's description tells us much about his assumptions concerning men's and women's participation in organized physical activities. As a reporter for a popular daily newspaper, he clearly expected his contemporary readers to accept without question the matters he chose to draw their attention; the men were 'drilled with military discipline', while the women wore 'dainty' costumes. The structure and content of the courses themselves betray an acute sense of gender difference within physical culture, with the men being lectured on the sciences of physiology and body mechanics while the women experienced the arts of physical exercise and folk-dancing.

The persistence of the notion of the androgynous child in the physical training texts of this period is clearly inconsistent with prevailing practices of physical culture within and beyond the education systems. However, we must not make the mistake of assuming that the text in itself and the practice of the text coincided. For example, by the early 1920s, Rosalie Virtue, the first female Organiser of Physical Training in Victoria, was recommending the use of modified exercises and methods of training for infants, including greater use of games and rhythmic activities performed to music.[27] Adapting material issued earlier by the Board of Education in London, Virtue argued that 'anything in the way of formal gymnastics is, of course, out of place'. She proposed instead that organized play experiences could foster alertness, joint flexibility, health and well being and self-control, and prepare small children for more formal exercising in the upper elementary school. These instructions for infants represent one of the first acknowledgements in the official discourse of physical training that the aspiration of the junior cadet training textbooks to design a scheme of work 'to suit children of all ages and both sexes' had been unsuccessful.

It was not until the early 1930s that the narrative of the androgynous pupil began to change as government schools were faced with the need to cater for older, pubescent boys and girls. Once again, Rosalie Virtue was to the fore in advocating alternative methods to the masculine, military form of physical training. In 1933 and on the subject of physical exercises for girls in the senior school, Virtue was emphatic that 'quick and informal methods of organization should be employed. Drill has no place in the daily physical training lesson for schoolgirls'.[28] Virtue was especially keen to utilize music to enhance the rhythmic qualities of movement and was a strong advocate of folk dancing as a key part of both primary and secondary school physical education.

In 1934 the Victorian government published the General Course of Study for Elementary Schools. For the first time in official government discourse on physical training, there was separate provision made for girls and boys. However, this applied only to grades five to eight. For the earlier grades, boys and girls continued to receive the same physical training, though Virtue's influence was clearly in evidence in the statement that 'physical education ... should be informal (and) ... the play spirit should dominate all movements'.[29] While there were separate sections for the physical training of older boys and girls, much of the work remained common to both sexes. The Tables of Exercises, a characteristic of systems of physical training such as Ling's, continued to be the central organising structure of the curriculum. Only a very close reading of the descriptions of the exercises reveals that those for girls appear to require less vigorous and dynamic movement, with slightly greater emphasis placed on flexibility work. More obvious differences appear in the section of the Course of Study dealing with sport, which was separate from physical training. All children were to participate in athletics and swimming, but while the girls played basketball (netball) and rounders, the boys' played football and cricket.[30]

Acknowledgement of the need to cater for older girls and boys in physical education became established practice in Victoria and other states during the 1930s and 1940s, though younger children in grades one to four continued to be constructed within the official texts as androgynous. The Queensland government's *Physical Education Handbook for Primary Schools*, published as a supplement to the *Education Office Gazette* in 1947 and 1948, illustrates the trend towards softening the militaristic character of physical exercises for both girls and boys.[31] In similar fashion to the 1934 Victorian Course of Study, the scheme of work for girls required less dynamic and vigorous activity than the scheme for boys. The Queensland Handbook also displayed the trend towards incorporating sport skill practices in lessons, and this was a further factor in differentiating physical education provision according to the gender of the older children. While the boys 'take passes from the base of the scrum' and practice 'drop kicks', the girls 'throw a vigoro ball 20 yards' and practise the 'one hand shoulder pass with basketball (netball)'.[32]

The trend away from Lingian physical training towards sport-based physical education was clearly signalled in the Victorian Grey Book, a 1946 publication that was intended to replace the 1933 Board of Education *Syllabus of Physical Exercises* (the 'Green Book').[33] The Grey Book was the first physical education text in Australia to incorporate this fundamental and enduring shift from gymnastic exercises to sport. Along with the shift in subject matter, the Grey Book heralded a more sharply focused concern for gender differentiation. Although children up to the age of nine continued to be treated as androgynous, the emphasis on major games as the core component of physical education resulted in explicitly different practices for girls and boys. In similar fashion to the Queensland *Physical Education Handbook*, the boys' programme of work was firmly centred on games such as cricket and football, while the girls' physical education experience revolved around games such as netball and hockey.

CONCLUSION

This essay has argued that the discursive practices of sport, recreation and exercise that together form the physical culture of Australian society were of central importance in the social production of gender during the first half of the twentieth century. Sport in particular played a central role in both shaping and legitimating dominant versions of masculinity and femininity and of positioning each of these dimensions of gender as opposites. The team games that emerged from the schools for boys serving the socially privileged sections of Australian society were from the beginning gendered practices, explicitly designed to promote physical strength, aggression, competitiveness, courage and loyalty as defining characteristics of masculinity. The schools for girls developed their own versions of these games, but always in tension with dominant notions of femininity that contrasted strongly with favoured constructions of masculinity, and positioned women and girls as fragile, co-operative, loyal and dexterous.[34]

Sport did not play a prominent part in the school experience of working class children until at least the end of the Second World War.

Instead, as seen above, physical culture was represented predominantly by Dano-Swedish gymnastics. In the various syllabuses and texts produced for the guidance of teachers in government schools between the 1900s and the 1940s, the child, particularly in the infant grades, was constructed as androgynous. This construct was explicit and intentional. Within a 'scientific' system of rational exercises aimed at the harmonious development of the entire body, the sex of the individual appeared to be irrelevant. But reality contrasted markedly with this aspiration. Both teacher trainers and teachers implemented the narrative of the androgynous child differentially according to prevailing, dominant definitions of femininity and masculinity. These differential practices themselves came to be inscribed in the texts of the 1930s and 1940s as state government education departments responded to the need to provide what they considered to be gender appropriate physical education to older, pubescent, pupils in the upper elementary and secondary schools.

The narrative of the androgynous child was, in any case, embedded in broader masculine discourses of militarism and disciplinary practice that resonated with governments' views on the relationship of compulsory mass schooling to social order and economic productivity. Dano-Swedish exercising and military drilling accorded with the institutional imperatives of the school because this system of physical training provided excellent opportunities for the regulation and normalisation of children's bodies in space and in time. There was criticism of the national system of physical training associated with the Junior Cadet Training Scheme within a decade of its commencement.[35] Yet in the face of its apparent unpopularity with teachers, pupils, and sections of the general public, governments persisted with drilling and exercising because it appeared to be ideally suited to meeting the goals of social order and economic productivity. Systematic work on children's bodies seemed to politicians and government officials to be central to the achievement of these goals. Drilling and exercising was believed to produce disciplined, healthy bodies capable of reproducing a race that was thought earlier in the century to be deteriorating and of contributing to the prosperity of the owners of the means of production and to the wealth of the nation.

It can only be concluded that formal physical training was unsuccessful in achieving most of the goals its advocates set for it. It is doubtful that teachers had the expertise or commitment to extract from children the precision in movement that the system required for the goals of social order and economic productivity to be met).[36] Nor was the goal of providing an appropriate physical training for children of all ages and both sexes met to any satisfactory degree. Leading figures such as Rosalie Virtue carefully but actively worked against the official discourse of government texts as she advocated modifications to suit young children and older girls. Physical training did contribute to the social production of gender, but at times in contradictory fashion to the prevailing orthodoxy of the time. It was only as sport began to appear in the physical education programmes of government schools after the Second World War that there was a closer fit between that the orthodox gender order and the practices of physical training. This was due to sports' central role in the social production of gender.

Perhaps the narrative of the androgynous child in physical training had the potential to challenge some aspects of the gender order. Certainly, as it was practised in the British middle class women's physical training colleges of the period, Dano–Swedish gymnastics was a key component of women's emancipation.[37] But two features of physical training's use in government schools in Australia fatally undermined this potential. The first of these was its embedding in militarist, masculine practices and the second was its role in the social regulation of children's bodies to meet the institutional imperatives of the school. Further to this and in contrast to Britain, there was no 'female tradition' in physical training in Australia to foster the educational dimensions of Lingian gymnastics. This work was left to individuals such as Rosalie Virtue and her few colleagues spread thin around the states of Australia. Indeed, it is in many ways remarkable that formal physical training lasted as long as it did in government schools. The embryonic Australian physical education profession's embrace of sport-based physical education in the post-war period brought an end to the narrative of the androgynous child, but heralded instead an era of practice in which school practice reproduced and legitimated the dominant gender order of Australian society. The ideological power of this 'new physical education' of the 1940s becomes apparent when we realize that it has taken physical educators some 40 years to begin to question the relationship of their practices to the social production of gender.[38]

NOTES

1. For example, J.A. Mangan and R.J. Park (eds.), *From 'Fair Sex' to Feminism: Sport and the Socialisation of Women in the Industrial and Post-Industrial Eras* (London, 1987); J.A. Hargreaves, *Sporting Females: Critical Issues in the History and Sociology of Womens' Sport* (London, 1994); K.E. McCrone, *Playing the Game: Sport and the Physical Emancipation of English Women, 1870–1914* (London, 1988); M.A. Hall, *Feminism and Sporting Bodies: Essays on Theory and Practice* (Champaign, IL, 1996).
2. M. McKernan, *Sport, War and Society: Australia 1914–18*, in R. Cashman and M. McKernan (eds.), *Sport in History* (St Lucia, 1979), pp. 1–20.
3. D. Kirk, *The Body, Schooling and Culture* (Geelong, 1993), p.34.
4. P. Bourdieu, 'Sport and Social Class', *Social Science Information*, 17, 6 (1978), 819–840.
5. J.A. Mangan, *Athleticism in the Victorian and Edwardian Public School: The Emergence and Consolidation of an Ideology* (Cambridge, 1981). For a review, see D. Kirk, 'School Sport and Physical Education in History: An Overview and Discussion of Published English Language Studies, 1986–1998', *International Journal of Physical Education* 35, 2 (1998), 44–55.
6. D. Kirk, *Defining Physical Education: The Social Construction of a School Subject in Postwar Britain* (London, 1992).
7. C. Shilling, *The Body and Social Theory* (London, 1993).
8. Hall, *Feminism and Sporting Bodies*.
9. J. McKay, *No Pain, No Gain. Sport and Australian Culture* (Sydney, 1991).
10. J. Nauright and J. Broomhall, 'A Woman's Game: The Development of Netball and a Female Sporting Culture in New Zealand 1906–1970', *International Journal of the History of Sport*, 11, 3 (1994), 387–407.
11. J.A. Mangan, *The Games Ethic and Imperialism: Aspects of the Diffusion of an Ideal* (Harmondsworth, 1985).
12. K. Reiger, *The Disenchantment of the Home: Modernising the Australian Family 1880–1940* (Melbourne, 1985).
13. McKernan, *Sport, War and Society*.
14. D. Kirk and K. Twigg, 'Civilising Australian Bodies: The Games Ethic and Sport in Australian Government Schools, 1904–1945', *Sporting Traditions: Journal of the Australian Society for Sport History*, 11, 2 (1995), 3–34.
15. J.A. Daly, 'Structure', in *Australian Sport: A Profile* (Canberra, 1985), p.15.
16. McKay, *No Pain, No Gain*; R. Crawford, 'A History of Physical Education in Victoria and NSW 1872–1939: With Particular Reference to English Precedent' (unpublished Ph.D. thesis, La Trobe University, 1981).
17. D. Kirk, *Schooling Bodies: School Practice and Public Discourse 1880–1950* (London: Leicester University Press, 1998); D. Kirk, 'Embodying the School/Schooling Bodies: Physical Education as Disciplinary Technology', in C. Symes, and D. Meadmore (eds.), *The Extraordinary School: A Moral Technology for Postmodern Times* (New York, forthcoming).
18. M. Foucault, *Discipline and Punish* (New York: Allen and Unwin, 1977), p.138.
19. On the question of 'correctness of performance' in relation to Dano-Swedish gymnastics, see, for example, H.C. Bjelke-Petersen in Australian Archives Victoria, MP84–1, 1832/13/573, 17 June 1912, internal minute paper to Adjutant General, and R. Virtue, 'Physical Training for Children of the Infants' School', *Education Gazette and Teachers' Aid* (Victoria), 24 Jan. 1922, 18.
20. Board of Education, *Syllabus of Physical Exercises for Schools* (London, 1933).
21. On the question of the repeated insistence that physical training had a key role to play in relation to the obedient, alert, and cheerful child, see Kirk, *Schooling Bodies*, ch.1.
22. Australian Military Forces, *Junior Cadet Training* (Melbourne, 1916); Department of Defence, *Junior Cadet Training Textbook* (Melbourne, 1922); Department of Defence, *Junior Cadet Training Textbook* (Melbourne, 1925).
23. Department of Defence *Junior Cadet Training Textbook* (1925), p. 8.
24. Thomson overviews the collapse of the militarist lobby in Britain by the end of the beginning of the first decade of the twentieth century, in I. Thompson, 'Militarism and Scottish Schools in the Boer War Era', *Physical Education Review*, 8, 2 (1986), 110–19.

25. AAV, MP 84/1, 1832/1/220, Report of the 1909 & 1910 Melbourne Conferences on Physical Training.
26. Donald Macdonald in the *Argus*, 10 Jan. 1912.
27. *Education Gazette and Teachers' Aid* (Victoria), 24 Jan. 1922, 18.
28. *Education Gazette and Teachers' Aid* (Victoria), 16 May 1933, 119.
29. *Education Gazette and Teachers' Aid* (Victoria), 22 Nov. 1933, 493.
30. *Education Gazette and Teachers' Aid* (Victoria), 498.
31. Physical Education Handbook for Primary Schools, Grades 1–4, Supplement to the *Education Office Gazette* (Aug. 1947); *Physical Education Handbook for Primary Schools*, Girls, Grades 5–7, Supplement to the *Education Office Gazette* (July 1948); *Physical Education Handbook for Primary Schools*, Boys, Grades 5–7, Supplement to the *Education Office Gazette*, Sept.–Oct. 1948.
32. *Physical Education Handbook for Girls*, pp.9, 19; *Physical Education Handbook for Boys*, pp.7,9.
33. Education Department, Victoria Physical Education for Victorian Schools (Melbourne, 1946).
34. R. Crawford, 'Sport for young ladies: The Victorian independent schools 1875–1925', *Sporting Traditions: The Journal of the Australian Society for Sports History* 1(1984), 61–82; R. Crawford, (1987) Moral and Manly: Girls and Games in Early Twentieth Century Melbourne, pp. 182–107 in Mangan and Park (eds.) *From 'Fair Sex' to Feminism*.
35. Kirk, *Schooling Bodies*.
36. See H.C. Bjelke-Petersen in AAV, MP 367, 629/22/97, Reports on Physical Training 1918–1920, Interim Report of Inspections made in the Second Military District, December 1919.
37. S. Fletcher, *Women First: The Female Tradition in English Physical Education, 1880–1980* (London, 1984).
38. J. Wright, 'Mapping the Discourses in Physical Education, *Journal of Curriculum Studies*, 28, 3 (1996), 331–51.

The 'Green' and the 'Gold':
The Irish-Australians and their Role
in the Emergence of the Australian
Sports Culture

PETER A. HORTON

From the very moment the penal colonies in Australia were established, a culture of sport, dichotomized, 'classed' and 'gendered' began to evolve. The colonies immediately formed societies based upon power and position. On one side were the prisoners, the lower ranking garrison troops and ex-convicts (the aboriginal Australians were, of course, outside of all European society in the earliest times); and on the other were the officers, government officials, free-settlers and traders. The environment and climate encouraged recreation, and sporting activities offered distraction, recreation and even sustenance. The officers, once they acquired sufficient suitable stock assumed their equestrian pursuits whilst the lower echelons sought excitement in ways familiar to them, such as bare-knuckle prize-fights and various blood sports all of which were platforms for strenuous gambling and the enthusiastic consumption of alcohol. Troops played cricket and football, while swimming, or at least 'bathing', and fishing became popular with the lower classes. The better off took up yachting and the 'sport of kings', horse-racing.[1] Women in the settlement were subjected to absolute levels of marginalization consistent with the social norms and attitudes of the time. In the earliest years of Australia, sport was not a domain contested by women.[2] The history of Australian sport as a feature of popular cultural activity was and remains a central component of the overall cultural struggle.

If the land proved to be an eventual 'paradise for sport',[3] then it was the settlers that made it so, for truly it was in many ways a torrid place to play. In time the land, the climate and the water were tamed to a degree and an avidly sport inclined society emerged. By the second half of the nineteenth century the obsession Australians had for sport brought continual critical, and at times, amazed comment. In 1873 Anthony Trollope argued that because of the nation's preoccupation with sport, particularly horse-racing, and gambling and beer, Australia was a paradise for the working class.[4] Mark Twain was astonished that the Melbourne Cup had such an appeal that it could bring the whole nation to a standstill.[5] Other luminaries believed Australians were so obsessed with sport it subsumed all other cultural pursuits making this hedonistic paradise a 'cultural desert'. In the twentieth century D.H. Lawrence believed Australia to be a vast land devoid of speech and inhabited by sport-obsessed barbarians. This impression was formed after just a few days of research for his novel *Kangaroo*.[6] Henry Lawson, quintessential of all Australian colonialists, viewed the linkage between sport, the working man and his heroes with concern. He cast serious doubts as to the efficacy of sport's central and prominent identity in Australian society. Lawson in a verse from *A Son of Southern Writers* implies that sport had become somewhat of a stigma, an embarrassment:

> In a land where sport is sacred,
> Where the labourer is God,
> You must pander to the people,
> Make a hero of a clod.[7]

Whatever the views of the critical, sardonic and defensive, for Australia sport was, and is, a wonderfully potent expression of the nation's soul. Australia, and many other ex-British imperial territories, adopted the cultural heritage bequeathed by the British and to varying degrees absorbed various aspects of an imposed culture. In Australia settlers of all hues, origins and classes found the antipodean environment a fertile 'field' for sporting pursuits and institutionalized competitive sport was avidly and enthusiastically embraced by all communities in Australia. Sport was central to the process of constructing a 'community identity'[8] with issues of class and status always apparent and central to such issues were the Irish. Paradoxically, sport was a medium for ensuring overall cultural unity and individual, sectarian and class difference.[9]

LESS THAN PROPER AUSTRALIANS

All Australian history, including the history of its sport, is the history of dissonance between the classes. Every aspect of Australian social life resonates with the politics of inequality; indeed there is not a single history of Australia but a dual history that of the majority and that of the minority.[10] All such 'histories' were for the first 150 years were also essentially only about men. Though, not a 'minority', as such, women were certainly a grossly marginalized and underrepresented social group in colonial Australia. For the first 150 years or so of Australia's modern history the English Protestants were the dominant social group whilst the Irish Catholic migrants formed, initially at least, a significant part of the Australian lower classes. And a vociferous, irksome and insubordinate minority they proved to be for the English. Their very existence, as Patrick O'Farrell states, 'deflated and confused the English majority'.[11]

By 1850 the Irish who came, willingly or otherwise, to this antipodean land became the single largest group, save for the English and, collectively, they were to make an enduring impact upon the cultural future of this new outpost of the Empire. In this essay the extent and nature of their contribution in the making of the Australian sporting culture will be shown to be as significant, if no more significant, than any other ethnic group.

The initial Irish 'migrants', who were convict-settlers, gravitated to the rural areas of New South Wales, Victoria and Queensland. The 1860s and 1870s were periods of agricultural boom and the Irish migrants swarmed to the rural regions. As the agricultural boom waned an urban drift occurred and the population of the cities of Australia began to swell dramatically. Sydney's population in the forty years from 1860 to 1900 grew by over 500 per cent[12] with similar trends being recorded in Brisbane,[13] Adelaide, Perth and Melbourne.[14] In the 1880s workers and new immigrants were drawn to the colonial capitals and to the industrial and mining cities of Newcastle and Wollongong. Here they sought work in the docks, the emerging manufacturing industries, coal mines and the building and service industries associated with urbanization. Migrants, many of whom were Irish Catholics, came to these cities to establish new lives and, as marginal as these lives often became, they still offered hope for a life with some element of self-determination and a chance of prosperity which previously had been an impossibility. As in all other industrialized cities the cities in Australia became the major sites for the institutions of organized sport.[15] It was in the cities that the sport culture of Australia first began to gain its definitive character. By the 1880s sport was to become an integral and pervasive aspect of the Australian way of life. Australian culture was not merely an outcome of the process of cultural diffusion associated with British imperialism. Conflict and interaction between all elements within the social structure contributed to its development. The Irish added a quintessential ingredient to this process, as they were particularly influential in the characterization of urban sport. Thus the impact of the Catholic Irish-Australians upon the development of Australia's sports culture requires a careful and thorough consideration. This contribution was far-reaching. It was also very complex. The essence of history, and *raison d'être*, of Australia require that all discussion of its early cultural development has to focus upon its settlers, all of its settlers, both men and women from all ethnic groups. The nature of the roles of the English as the majority and the Irish as the largest minority migrant groups cast them as critical predetermining elements in the creation of the nation. Their interrelation was not only the earliest but also the most dynamic inter-migrant relationship in this whole process.[16] The English as the initial controllers of society in their imperial territories established all major institutional structures through the imposition of their culture as well as through governance. The uniqueness of the Australian way of life emerged from the interrelation of a host of contributive factors and the immanent dynamics that emerged from their interactions.[17] The process of cultural development has not ceased and today Australia's culture is still evolving. Recent migrant groups, the influence of regional political and economic influences and the now ever-attendant forces of globalization, all continually impact upon Australian society and its culture.

O'Farrell suggests that it was the particularity of the cultural input of the Irish, coming as it did at the critical time in the emergence of the nation of Australia that contributed to Australia's uniqueness. He contends that it was the resistance of the Irish minority to the institutional attitudes and conservatism of the English that gave Australia its distinct national identity.[18] With regard to sport Irish activity certainly played a major contributive and formative role. In the earliest years of settlement Australia did not offer an overly hospitable environment and although it was an 'unlikely sporting paradise',[19] sport became one of the major vehicles for the expression of an Australian identity. This was first demonstrated dramatically by the nationalistic sentiments that erupted following the Australian cricket team's victories over an English representative team in the late 1870s. From these victories a great wave of jingoistic and parochial pride arose and it appeared as if the collective decision to settle in Australia had been somehow vindicated. Tremendous symbolic significance, going far beyond the sporting arena, was attached to these historic victories. A sense of independence and national pride rapidly spread from the sporting context to become a feature of the political context and it is now accepted that sport facilitated and reinforced the process of uniting the previously 'separate' colonies of Australia.[20]

'THE DIFFERENCE THAT UNITED'[21]

The dominant attitudes, ideologies and cultural institutions upon which the new nation was to be founded had been established long before Federation in 1901. O'Farrell suggests that the most important influence in this process emanated from the conflict between the Irish-Australian Catholics and the English Australians.[22] Sport, as with all other social institutions and cultural activities, as mentioned above, has always been demarcated along class and gender lines.[23] The emergence of institutionalized sport in Australia coincided with what were to become the two most significant movements in the country's development: the rise of Labour and the drive to nationhood. The Irish Australians provided much of the energy and vitriol for both movements.[24] They were also prominent in sport, particularly in boxing and football, sports that have universally been identified with the working classes. It was thus not surprising to see political, social and sectarian messages being expressed in the sporting arena; sport as a vital and passionate undertaking was enlisted to promote many social and political causes. Class divided sporting foundations both within sports and between various sports. The bifurcation of rugby football in the 1900s graphically demonstrated one such split, with rugby league representing the working class whilst rugby union could be said to have been the game of the 'silvertails'.[25] Such cleavages were about ownership and control as much as the much-proclaimed issues of match payments and compensation.[26, 27]

By the end of the First World War Australia and its people had acquired a distinct cultural identity.[28] Many of the most contentious issues in this process, such as Catholic education, religion in politics, access to freehold land, conscription, immigration policy and of course sectarianism, centred on the Irish-Catholic migrants.[29] Running through the entire course of Australian history, is the ongoing conflict of 'labour versus capital' and this preoccupied the majority of the Irish Catholic working class as it did, and still does, all Australian workers.[30]

The Irish Catholics in Australia were, in the main, anti-English, yet there was no apparent desire to create a definitively Irish society in Australia. A life in Australia was their chance to create a free, prosperous and utterly different life, in a world that was not dominated by the English. In many ways it was the Irish Catholics who thus provided the cultural resistance and distinctions that prevented the establishment of a totally English cultural hegemony. However they did not completely resist. The Irish-Catholic Australians' involvement in sport did exhibit a collective pragmatism, for example, by not exclusively supporting Gaelic sports to the exclusion of English sports.[31]

In the late nineteenth century it appears that support for Gaelic sports came largely from new migrant males whilst Australian-born Irish men and women tended to support and play the mainstream sports.[32] This inclination was enhanced by the fact that the Catholic parish schools and the leading Catholic boys' colleges, such as St. Joseph's College in Sydney, St Joseph's, Gregory Terrace in Brisbane and (St. Francis) Xavier's in Melbourne, had all become powers in their respective sporting competitions. This transpired because, when considering the 'important matters, such as sport, ... (they had to) Australianise or perish'.[33] In such important matters in terms of integration and acceptance, the schools could not be seen to be flagrantly asserting either Irish nationalist sentiments or any great degree of individuality.[34] Thus, the leading Catholic schools, which were supported by the wealthier Irish-Australian families, became a feature of the dominant hegemony. Nevertheless, even though the élite Catholic schools became part of the dominant system, sectarianism and bigotry abounded within the Australian public school system during the Victorian and Edwardian eras.[35]

ROLE, EFFECT, VALUE

The collective impact of the Catholic Irish Australians on the development of Australian sport was so marked that many of what may be called typically 'Irish' behavioural traits have become part of the sporting personality of Australia. Consider, as O'Farrell points out, the Irish-type traits that are now universally associated with the Australian national psyche: 'independence, lawlessness, stereo-types that were (are) easy-going, anti-hierarchy and authority, generous, fun-loving, boozy, and game as Ned Kelly'.[36] It was such traits coupled with talent, enthusiasm and the motivations that drove them that the Catholic Irish Australians brought to sport in Australia.

The emergence and development of Australia's sport did not take a logical or direct course. Whilst Australians were 'very much inspired by the Anglo-Celtic notions of sport'[37] a large and idiosyncratic collection of forces was at work in this process. Such factors as the origins and enthusiasms of the people, the country's geography and climate, strategic, political and economic influences, all contrived to produce a uniquely Australian model of sport. Obviously, a central element in the construction of this model was the people, both indigenous and immigrant, and their various individual and collective contributions.[38] Though not the sole minority involved in the cultural conflict that spawned the Australian way of life, the Catholic Irish Australians were, however, an aggressive and most assertive group, refusing to accept that the English model was the one upon which the new nation would be exclusively founded.[39]

In Australian history the Irish are seen to be the major catalyst in the general move to nationhood and this was particularly apparent in sport. The folk-heroes of the working-class Catholic Irish Australians were boxers and footballers as well as bishops and bushrangers and their exploits provided much of the intensity and energy that surrounded Australia's primary sporting passion: beating the English.[40] It could be said that this passionate preoccupation was a major driving force that energized Australia's efforts to assert its identity. In this quest, however, the Catholic Irish Australians, at no stage, attempted to construct a *de facto* neo-Hibernian reality. Patriotism in Australia was dual construct. The loyalty of the Irish to Ireland was nostalgic and not greatly concerned with any Irish political activism. Support for the 'rebels' and the more fanatical Home Rule activists, for example, who came to drum up support in Australia was minimal.[41] Furthermore, Irish nationalism was soon subsumed by the Australian variety as the Irish, of all descriptions, spread over the continent and began to establish their new lives and loyalties.[42] Antagonism to Metropolitan England was channelled, in part, into sport as a gesture of retribution, defiance and dissimilarity.

SPORT, CITIES AND THE IRISH-AUSTRALIANS

Australia, for all its vastness has always been, predominantly, an urban society. A massive influx of migrant workers prompted the rapid growth of all the major cities in the second half of the nineteenth century. By 1911, 55 per cent of all Australians lived in the major cities on the eastern seaboard.[43] It was in the colonial capitals of Perth, Adelaide, Sydney, Melbourne and Brisbane that the sport culture of Australia was born as a function of urbanization. Thus from the earliest days of the colonies sport had long been a feature of urban and suburban life in Australia. By the time a more advanced level of urbanization/industrialization became established the notion of sport was well entrenched.[44] Sport was part of the social fabric by the time the gold rush hit Melbourne in the 1850s whilst Sydney, as the first settlement, had long reverberated to the sounds of sporting activity. The space and wealth available in the City of Melbourne gave rise to expansive sporting facilities such as the Melbourne Cricket Ground. The planned city of Adelaide boasted the grand Adelaide Oval by the time the first English cricket team played there in 1874.[45] Sydney boasted a splendid harbour and the sports fields of Hyde Park and later (1870) the expanse of Moore Park beckoned. In the heart of these growing cities the workers resided centrally so as to provide a workforce for the burgeoning industries and docks. The central areas of the capitals were to become the urban slums,[46] and consequently, the heartland of the Labour movement in Australia. In Sydney, the inner suburbs of Surry Hills, Redfern and Paddington being the major Irish-Catholic centres. The Irish also claimed the Melbourne suburb of Richmond, which by the 1900s was called 'Struggletown'.[47]

These centres became symbolic locations of the Australian working class sub-culture and geographical bastions of the workers' struggle in Australia. Consequently, they emerged as major centres of influence in the development of an Australian sport culture. The class and race struggles associated with such sports clubs as South Sydney rugby league club are central to much of the symbolism that is attached, perhaps mythically, to the nation's sporting heritage.[48] In Melbourne the history of early Richmond, the definitive working class suburb of Melbourne, is closely linked with the Irish, their religion, politics and sport. Richmond at the start of the twentieth century was, according to O'Farrell, almost exclusively Irish.

Around the name and place of Richmond, the shared and sacred symbols of the local variant of Irish Australia were grouped, bidding in their vigour, stridency and clannishness to claim a pre-eminence in the shaping of the image. The municipal council, a Labour Party branch, a football club (Australian Rules) which in 1920 had seventeen Irish-Australians among 37 players, a Catholic Church, a common work (and unemployment) pattern, fierce friendships, tolerance of hard drinking and larrikinism – all of these things were conditioned by and, flavoured by Irishness, but still remained true to their Australian selves.[49]

In such sites of urban struggle sport was a central and unifying form of expression for the working class. Consequently, the sports played and supported assumed a symbolic representation of the working class struggle.[50] Rugby league became the working-class form of rugby football, while the inner-city suburban Australian Rules teams of Melbourne assumed the mantle of the champions of the working class in the south. Sport became institutionalized, part of the process of urbanization. It adopted a new character and function. It acquired class allegiances and political agendas and assumed a male identity because along with Irish proletarian urbanization and the industrialization of Australian society, gender roles were still defined.[51]

Cricket is generally considered to be Australia's national summer sport. Many of the spectators, therefore, who attended early Australian cricket matches would have been Irish-Australians. However, from an analysis of the birthplaces of Australian First Class Cricketers from 1850/1 to 1940/41,[52] it can be seen that cricket during this period was very much the game of Australian-born nationals. Eighty-two per cent of all first class players during this period were Australian-born; the number of Irish-born was just eight. The game in Ireland had always been viewed by working-class Irish Catholics as being a 'big house game'[53] and, as Richard Cashman points out, 'it was not until the second and third generation that they (Irish Catholics) gravitated to the élite ranks.'[54] Cashman indicates that although few leading Australian Test cricketers up to 1930 were Irish-born many, 'were of Irish descent – Lindsay Hassett, Chuck Fleetwood, Leo O'Brien, Bill O'Reilly and Stan McCabe'.[55] Cricket appeared to be able to accommodate all levels of society just as horse-racing had done in early Australia and it gained its universal acceptance in Australia because, initially, it formed part of the dominant British imperial ideology and was thus viewed as an 'integrative' social agency.[56] Following the first tour made to Australia by an English representative team, albeit an unofficial 'professional' outfit in 1862, a further 14 English teams toured Australia before the turn of the century. Australia won the first official Test, played in 1877, by 45 runs.[57] The eleven included Thomas Horan an Irish-born 23-year-old who played his club cricket for East Melbourne.[58] Horan thus, obviously, became the first Irish-born Catholic to represent Australia in international sport. Strangely, despite the historic victory in the inaugural Test match Horan, along with two others, was dropped for the second Test, yet ironically one of the replacements was another Irish-born player from Victoria, Tom Kelly.[59] Horan was to play 15 Tests whilst Kelly's career was limited to just two Test matches, however, both must have been very positive role models and inspirations to young Irish Catholic Australians.

The Australians were to make ten official tours to England before 1900 cricket thus became a major vehicle for the expression of an Australian identity. Cricket assumed the mantle of the national summer sport without opposition. The Ashes Test series of 1882, in which Australia claimed its first victory in a Test against England on English soil, was to become a defining moment in Australian history *per se*, and a momentous one in its sporting history![60] Captained by English-born Charles Bannerman, eight of the team were Australian-born, most notable being the 'Demon' Fred Spofforth, who took 14 wickets for 90 runs, the team once again included all-rounder Thomas Horan.[61]

Cricket had become not only the leading sport, but also one of the most potent unifying forces of the burgeoning nation. Test matches against England were accompanied by a special intensity and passion. The cricket ovals of Sydney, Melbourne, and later Adelaide, Perth and Brisbane were readily accessible to the people. The crowds that attended were enormous and with beer in good supply the English were, as they still are, the target for the collective animus of the 'outer'.[62] For the Catholic Irish-Australians the situation would have provided them with an ideal opportunity to pour bile upon the symbols of the English establishment, to emphasize their separateness from it while demonstrating their fealty to Australia. As 'unifying' as the national game may have been, Richard Cashman suggests that in its earliest days Test cricket was beset with sectarian issues. He points out that there was a gap of 60 years between the first Catholic captain, Percy McDonnell in 1888 to the second Lindsay Hassett in 1948.[63]

A central component of the sports culture of Australia is the cult of football. All the states, in both urban and rural areas were compliant in the establishment of the Australian obsession with football. Whatever the code, football is an enormously important vehicle for cultural expression throughout Australia.

The Australian Rules football of Melbourne was an invention of two establishment English-Australian cousins, Thomas Wentworth Wills and Henry Harrison and any suggestion that it was a direct descendant or bastardized form of Gaelic football is incorrect.[64] It was obviously an offspring of the British village football games but the uniqueness of its encoded rules is indisputable.[65] The game was first played in Melbourne in 1858 and the game has never been seriously rivalled there by any other code of football.[66] Less than two years later in Adelaide John Acraman, also a noted cricketer, convened a meeting to form South Australia's first 'Rules' football club, the club was to become the Adelaide Football Club.[67] The game was to be later adopted as the off-season athletic distraction for the more athletic males of the upper echelons of Adelaide society.[68, 69] In New South Wales[70] and Queensland,[71] competition to be the premier football code was a far more complex process being significantly influenced by factors of class and ethnicity. In Melbourne, however, the fact that the status of 'Rules' football was never in question meant that it was the location and socio-economic complexion of the suburb from which the various clubs came that became the arbitrating factor in the class dynamic. From the late 1880s to the 1920s the inner suburbs of Richmond and Collingwood were very much working-class enclaves and both had large Irish Catholic populations.[72] Thus, support for the associated football clubs of these suburbs came to carry overtones of race, religion and class. The clubs from the richer suburbs became the focus of vilification from the supporters of the 'battler' clubs. Competitive intensity increased, as team allegiance became an agent of parochialism and community pride: 'To defeat the silvertails of Melbourne ... was a source of great community satisfaction.'[73] Thus, it could be reasonably argued that the nature and intensity of the parochial support axiomatically associated with Australian rules football, has its origins in the dynamic that emerged from the ethnical class conflict O'Farrell described as being central in 'determining the character of Australian life and institutions'.[74] Today the demographics and socio-cultural identity of such clubs has changed but the obsession and intensity of the fans' support persists. Indeed, for the majority of

Melburnians it is what makes Melbourne tick and today this sporting fanaticism and the energy generated is an entrenched and essential feature of the culture of the city, which claims to be the 'sporting capital of Australia'.

George Parsons in his brilliantly scathing critical analysis of rugby league argues that 'class consciousness produced Rugby League'[75] and the history of rugby league in Australia resonates with the class conflict to which the Irish-Australians, who lived in the inner suburbs of Sydney and later Brisbane, heavily contributed. Towards the end of the nineteenth century rugby union football had assumed the status of the premier code in Sydney. By the 1870s rugby union football had fast become the accepted form of football in the leading schools of New South Wales. By this time the game was also well entrenched at the University of Sydney and with the founding of what was, in essence, the old boys' club of the King's School, Parramatta, the Wallaroos, the game had become the winter team sport of the dominant classes in New South Wales,[76] and, thus tended by definition and probably a deal of intent, to become an element of social division. Considering the origins of the foundation clubs of the New South Wales Rugby Union, few, if any, of the players would have been working class 'lads'. In fact the game did not spread to the lower echelons of New South Wales's society until the Sydney suburban clubs, such as Toxteth and St. Leonard's,[77] and clubs in the country districts like Newcastle, Maitland, Bathurst and Mittagong, became established. The reformation of the Sydney competition in 1900 based clubs according to the electoral roll and created what was essentially, a district competition in Sydney. This move, theoretically, spread the talent from the traditional clubs. It may have marginally achieved this but in terms of control it only served to re-confirm the power of the middle-class administrators of the game. Parsons suggests that this reform was a predetermining factor in the creation of a social climate that seven years later provided the stimulus for defection to League:

> The new club system, introduced in 1900, did not really change the face of Rugby … The 'gentlemen' remained in charge and those new clubs from the working-class suburbs were controlled by the capitalists without roots in the communities they pretended to represent…League was the game for those fighting for economic justice, for some alleviation of the appalling social conditions

resulting from an unskilled unemployment rate of 9 percent, for better housing, for reform, dignity and decency.[78]

When rugby league became established in Sydney a nexus was formed between sport and the social justice movement. It could be said that for working-class lads the match payments on offer to the top players, as meagre as they were by current standards, offered hope of some form of social advancement. If not, they were at least compensated for loss of earnings through playing or as a consequence of time lost due to injuries gained in the course of a match. In 1907 the 'defection' to Rugby League was supposedly precipitated by a single incident over compensation for loss of earnings following an injury to the Australian representative and Sydney grade player, Alex 'Bluey' Burdon.[79] The creation of the concept of amateurism and the bifurcation of rugby football were both outcomes of the efforts of the establishment to protect their hegemony. Amateurism became a class-distancing mechanism by which social division could be maintained and control retained. In the North of England as was the case in the eastern states of Australia, the move to 'professional' rugby was merely the façade that hid the real issue, class struggle.[80] In Britain the issue centred upon the question of 'broken-time' payments for the players who had to lose wages whilst they played rugby. As Tony Collins reflects, this represented a deeper schism in English society of the late nineteenth century.[81] The issue attached to professionalization became a rallying point for the marginalized groups of the nation. In Sydney rugby union football had become the game of the ruling classes even though, its surrounding ethos and the manner of play was utterly different to the game in Britain.[82] In 1908 the First Wallabies, during the inaugural tour to United Kingdom, received a frosty and patronizing reception from the administrators of the game, the press and particularly the spectators. This attitude and personal criticism of the individual players, the Australian team's tactics, intensity and determination to win, their obvious physical superiority, invariably accompanied by sneering and largely incorrect references to the players' 'convict' origins, marred the tour.[83]

The anti-establishment spirit of rugby league, the financial potential it held and, even the less complicated nature of the game itself attracted the working class of Sydney. The working-class Irish Catholics were particularly enamoured by the professional code and its administration as it definitively represented an anti-English establishment activity;

hordes of working class Irish-Australians gravitated to it for the solidarity it offered.[84] Rugby League became the people's game in Sydney, Newcastle and the bush and as 'it was a game of class and community' it became the iconic symbol of the working class in New South Wales and Queensland.[85]

CHURCH, COLLEGE AND SPORT

Major vehicles for cultural diffusion in the territories of the British Empire were the schools. As J.A. Mangan has commented, 'Once the Empire was established, the public schools sustained it.'[86] The public schools of Britain provided the men and ideology that were to become the basis of the hegemony that became established in colonial Australia.[87] The leading boys schools in New South Wales such as The King's School, Parramatta, Newington College and Sydney Grammar School in the city and Scots, Bathurst and The Armidale School in the country regions soon assumed the guise of English public schools. Similarly, in Victoria, at Melbourne Grammar, Scotch College, Geelong Grammar and Geelong College and in Queensland at Brisbane, Ipswich and Toowoomba Grammar Schools and The Southport School, the conduits of imperialism, muscular Christianity and athleticism were formed. In South Australia, that 'essentially English'[88] of all the colonies in Australia, all church leaders applauded sport as 'a moral pastime'.[89] In Adelaide Saint Peter's College, which was established in 1847, became the epitome of English Public School under the leadership of the Reverend George Farr.[90]

The educational sub-culture that emerged had an intense association with team sports, athletics and swimming, and this dynamic supported the diffusion of athleticism into the leading schools of the various colonies, including those that serviced the burgeoning Catholic middle classes.[91] Schools such as St Joseph's College, Hunters Hill, St. Ignatius, Riverview in Sydney, Nudgee College and St Joseph's College, Gregory Terrace in Brisbane and Assumption and Xavier's Colleges in Melbourne gradually became the colleges for the male children of the Catholic élite. They were not only protectors of Roman Catholicism but also proselytisers of muscular Christianity and the cult of athleticism.[92]

As the new century began the schools and colleges that serviced the children of Irish-Catholic Australians had not become the bastions of

Irish culture.[93] They were very much Australian in terms of both their professed Catholicism and certainly in respect of their adherence to the cult of games, particularly in cricket, rugby football and of course, Australian rules football.[94] A major contributing element to the status of sport in Catholic schools was the establishment of the Australian Marist order in 1872. Their presence in the Marist Colleges elevated the status of sport.[95] The French brothers at colleges such as St. Joseph's (Joey's) in Sydney were clearly not *au fait* with the moral dimensions of sport or its educational potential unlike the Jesuit fathers at their rival, St. Ignatius, Riverview.[96] For the Jesuits games had, as Mark Connellan pointed out, long been part of the ethos and curriculum of their British schools, such as Stonyhurst.[97] In Victoria the Jesuits had also instilled this ethos into Xavier's College, Kew following its establishment in 1878. Xavier's fiercely adopted the cult of athleticism with participation in team sport being compulsory for all students.[98]

The long-standing debate over the form of Australian Catholicism and the direction the educational system should take had been a contentious on-going issue, since Archbishop Polding established Australia's first Catholic secondary school in Sydney, in 1838.[99] The split between the Anglo-centric Benedictines and the superficially 'Irish' oriented Australian Catholic laity and priests saw the decline of the Benedictines. The movement led by Polding, to increase the influence of the Marists, particularly that of the Australian Marists precipitated many structural as well as doctrinal and pedagogical changes in the teaching orders.[100] One such change was the elevation of competitive sport and all its trappings to a central position in the élite Catholic boys' schools in Australia. This was also further facilitated by the diminishing influence of the French brothers. This move was not restricted to élite Catholic schools, as sport soon figured as a significant feature of the parish primary schools and the secondary schools and colleges that served the working-class Catholics.[101]

Colleges such as St. Joseph's College, St. Ignatius and Loretto – Normahurst had become the schools of the élite Sydney Catholics whilst in the inner suburbs of Sydney the children of the working-class Catholic Irish-Australians were being schooled in far less pretentious and less Anglo-centric institutions.[102] Nevertheless, by 1900 most Catholic parish schools (co-educational primary) had adopted robust sporting and physical education programmes. The support and encouragement the teachers at the humbler primary schools gave to the sporting endeavours of their charges was unquestionably a major influence in the development of the wider Australian sports culture.

The private school system in Australia expanded at a tremendous rate in both the cities and in the rural regions. Several tiers of private education emerged and the various Catholic orders established schools that were enthusiastically supported. In Sydney, the now Combined Associated School (CAS), football giant, Christian Brothers College, Waverley rose to sporting and academic prominence soon after its establishment in 1903. Waverley College's rugby history and tradition are at the very heart of the birth of Australian rugby's heritage.[103] It was founded as a denominational day school to service a clientele that came largely from the families of the emerging Catholic lower-middle class of the inner eastern suburbs of Waverley, Paddington, Woollahra, Randwick and Bondi. The school's heritage is enshrined in the memory of Brother Conlon, headmaster and great advocate of muscular Christianity. In his 1917 annual report, he demonstrated this support when he stated that 'a rational indulgence in manly sports forms a very essential part of a boy's education. Sport develops the judgement, makes the boy self-reliant, teaches him to think and act at a critical moment, and helps in the physical development in a most pleasant, natural and effective manner.'[104]

Waverley's more specific legacy to Australian sport could be said to be the contribution of the 'running game' to Australian rugby union football. This cult, sweepingly, can be said to have been the creation of their first 1st XV coach Arthur Hennessey, who instituted a 'no-kick' rule that soon became synonymous with Waverley College rugby.[105]

The host of second and third level Catholic schools that emerged after the turn of the century played their part in the creation of Australia's passion for sport. This contribution was to be, arguably, the most expansive source of the dynamic that O'Farrell considers central to the creation of the Australian national identity and culture.[106] By the 1920s virtually every major centre of population, suburb, provincial city or country town was endowed with its Catholic college, convent school or parish primary school. Few, if any, of these schools did not have sport as a pillar of its curriculum and in most cases, its dogma!

The contribution of the multitude of minor colleges and schools was immense. The dynamic social energy produced by their sporting community and academic rivalry with the grammar schools and other denominational institutions was the life-blood that energized the body of the growing nation's culture. Sport was to become a voice for social change and rallying point for the various communities, including schools. The place of sport in Australian schools, the centrality of the competitive sporting ethos, the parochialism and the fanaticism is enthusiastically expressed through the pleasure Australian parents got and get, from the sporting achievements of their children. Junior sport, both school and club, was and is, a major area of family activity and often a tremendous source of pride. It was and is, at the very heart of Australian sport. In the wider sense sport can, and does, communicate a sense of identity and belonging and the relationship between family and junior sporting achievement was and is a major socializing force that emanated, and emanates, from the process of sport in Australia. The competitive intensity of junior sport and the nature of its support are, and have been, two of the most significant characteristics of the Australian sport culture that have assured sport its pre-eminence in post and present Australian society.

A NATION DIVIDED: SPORT AND WAR

The élite Catholic colleges throughout Australia became part of the establishment system and thus as a corollary gained more influence and power. They did so by essentially becoming part of the hegemony and clearly this was what the parents of the boys and girls at leading schools demanded. For the schools and the graduates to become accepted, socially, professionally and, of course in sport, they had to conform to the dominant ideology.[107] Appropriate association with the élite offered access to scholarships, certain professions and marriage. The merit and viability of the various public schools in Victorian and Edwardian Australia was earned as it was in England through the 'slavish emulation'[108] of the rhetoric that supported athleticism and the concomitant elitism. Adherence to the dominant ideology meant that such institutions and their clientele were, as a consequence, enmeshed in the imperial ideological foundations and thus assumed an Anglo-Australian identity.[109] This loyalty gained seriousness far beyond the sports oval and the professional domain when the call to arms sounded in 1914. The conflict dynamic that O'Farrell believes had such an influence on the development of the nation had many manifestations, some quite trivial, some deadly serious. To Australians war and sport are serious and when they intersect, passions run high, but add to this the complexities of sectarianism and loyalty, we have the stuff of explosive history. The war further divided Australia into two 'nations' as it split into pro- and anti-conscription lobbies these were, in essence, based on levels of emotional and cultural allegiance to Britain. The First World War focussed many of Australia's social, political, spiritual and philosophical energies that were to eventually fix its cultural identity.[110]

At the time sport, as made clear above, had become an endemic feature of both the image and the reality of Australia. However, to what extent the middle-class ethos of sport was a totally entrenched characteristic of Australian society at this time is debatable. Superficially, it may appear that the recruitment propaganda used during the First World War, such as the Victorian Sportsmen's Recruiting Committee's campaign and their call to the young sportsmen of Victoria to 'join the Sportsmen's 1000', demonstrates that it was universally accepted.[111] The use of the bourgeois sporting credo as a means of positively satisfying the Australian government's pro-British policies apparently demonstrates how the continuing dominance of such values as loyalty, honour and duty could be enlisted to support the British Empire. However, how successful such campaigns actually were and to what extent they worked, is debatable. Michael McKernan has long maintained that the sportsmen recruitment campaigns used during the First World War were only marginally successful. They failed, he suggests, because of the complete misreading of the extent to which the amateur sporting ethos had penetrated Australian society.[112]

The extent of any significant loyalty to the King or Empire is difficult to assess; most enlisted or not, as the case may be, for reasons of loyalty to associated ideals, loyalty to friends, family or even school. The attempt to recruit on the basis of sporting involvement and the use of sporting events to garner favour and hard cash often collapsed as they met resistance based along class and ethnic lines.[113] Ironically, the recruitment campaigns embracing sporting themes soon assumed an element of class and thus aroused antagonism and resentment. Furthermore, sports and the various administrative bodies became embroiled in the question of whether or not to continue to play. Turmoil existed in Victoria with the Victorian Football Association (VFA) and the Victorian Football League (VFL) clashing whilst in New South Wales and Queensland arguments arose between the internal administrations of both rugby league and rugby union. Other sports, such as the 'sport of the workers', boxing, also became embroiled in this dispute as they identified with various levels of society and their constituent ethnic groups and, thus, their loyalties. The intrusion into the nation's sport as a jingoistic tactic was met with a variety of reactions and most were quite predictable. The majority of the responses and sentiments regarding the war effort were dogmatic and as a consequence opinion polarized. It was patriotic to attend a race meeting and donate to the war effort, yet unpatriotic to play a game of rugby league or an interstate cricket match. Those who attended the Les Darcy v. Eddie McGoorty (USA) boxing clash, in August 1915, in what appeared to be an all-Gaelic affair, were vilified. Critics of the audience were particularly vexed as the crowd had unceremoniously 'booed down' the Premier of New South Wales and Labour politician, W.A. Holman, as he attempted to make a recruitment speech. The large, predominantly Irish audience, of some 16,000, was expressing more than their preference in fighting.[114]

Across Australia, in Queensland, New South Wales, Victoria, South Australia and in Western Australia both factions exploited the issue of the continuance of sport to promote their relative positions. The continuance of sport bore, in the main, a direct relationship to the prevalence of the Catholic working class in the administration and of course the playing ranks of the games involved. In Brisbane and Sydney rugby league was played throughout the war whilst in the Melbourne, working-class-oriented Victorian Football League clubs of Richmond, Collingwood, Fitzroy and Carlton played a modified round in 1916.[115] Attempts by both the Southern Australian (1915) and Western Australian (1916) Football Leagues (Australian Rules Football) to abandon their respective competitions failed to stop play despite considerable government and journalistic pressure. In 1916 the *Bulletin* vociferously came out against 'football' of all kinds when it questioned the morality of continuing to play rather than taking part in the 'greatest game of all'. 'War and football are rivals, and there is no room for both of them ... Every footballer is a possible soldier, so the winter game will have no excuse this year for showing itself in public.'[116]

The sporting manifestations of the trauma of identity that beset Australia at the time of the First World War represented but one characterization of the division in society. The conscription issue led to what is often considered to have been a sectarian fight, with the supporters being led by William Hughes and its opponents following the Roman Catholic Bishop of Melbourne, the Most Reverend Doctor Mannix.[117] However, in this, at times extremely hostile campaign, the battle lines were not so simply drawn, for as many Catholics voted for conscription as against it. (Remembering of course that not all Catholics were Irish by decent. Though most were.) Obviously many 'loyal' Catholic Irish-Australians had volunteered, many making the ultimate sacrifice. Mannix's openly anti-English stance and his support of the Irish, which had intensified following the 1916 Easter rebellion and massacres in Dublin, would have undoubtedly alienated the establishment Catholics.[118]

The opinion of Herbert Moran, the captain of the first Wallabies, the Australian Rugby Union team that toured the United Kingdom in 1908, illustrates the feelings of middle-class Catholic Irish-Australians to the involvement of Cardinal Mannix in the conscription issue.

> It was a painful epoch for Catholic citizens; they became now the scapegoats for every social evil. In both the laity and the clergy a great gulf divided two sections. Lukewarm Catholics publicly denied their faith. Many, who didn't, became bitterly anti-clerical, speaking of some of their own priests with crude offensiveness. Doctor Mannix achieved nothing more than notoriety that seemed strangely gratifying to his austere mind. It is doubtful if he induced one single person to vote NO who had not already for personal motives decided to vote that way. On the contrary, he must have provoked many into voting YES who had thought that there was an excellent case for opposing Conscription on economic grounds. He severely penalized the poorer Catholics and the little Catholic tradesmen. He caused social ostracism of the professional Catholics.[119]

This view illustrates that complexity of Australian society at this time. The impression is further evinced by other examples drawn from the autobiographical work of Herbert Moran, who as the first Wallaby captain holds a very special place in the history of Australian sport. His career and his expression of his personal thoughts and feelings are in themselves a vital key to what was the reality for Australians, and obviously élite Australian sportsmen, at the time of the emergence of modern sport in the young nation. The insights give us a picture of the nature of the 'young' Australia and caution us from being too sweeping in our pronouncements on the nature and extent of any hegemony we believe may have been in place at the time. Consider Moran's statements regarding loyalty following the death of Queen Victoria:

The death of the Queen marked an important change in Irish sentiment towards the Throne. The new generation of Irish-Australians ardently desired to be loyal. They wished to escape the bleak moorland of perpetual resentment ... For us in Australia, of every race and of all religions, there is one symbol, only, our unity within the nation of nations. It is the monarchy. During the Victorian period the subject of republicanism was always being discussed ... An Australian will often express himself rudely about a visiting Englishman who behaves superciliously. That is common. He will frequently hurl angry criticisms at the British Government. That, he considers his right. He will even in a pet be disrespectful to a British Governor, though this is rare. But to the King no man with impunity may offer insult.[120]

The paradoxes and complexities of Edwardian Australian society can be further illustrated from the rugby union scene of the time. In Moran's autobiography *Viewless Winds* he deals with his rugby career in a wonderfully evocative chapter entitled 'Men, Rough Men, and Rugby'. In this classic of Australian rugby narrative, written some 30 years on, Moran talks of his experiences in Britain as captain of the first Wallabies. The autobiographical work was penned whilst he was living as an 'English' and very conservative medical practitioner; even so, he still reflected sadly on the attitude of the English rugby establishment. He noted how disappointed and upset the Australians became as a consequence of the treatment they received from officials of the Rugby Football Union, some spectators and a predominantly hostile and vexatious press. The players' resentment became so intense and as a result of the continuous barrage,

> ... their British patriotism wilted. Most of them developed a dislike for everything British... Had they not heard innumerable speeches about their 'brothers over the seas' and the 'kinship of sport'? Instead, they were now finding nothing but cautionary sermons and Public rebukes ...

The significance of it all can be seen from what happened six years later. When war broke out those thirty-one men were still in the flower of their physical vigour, yet only seven took part in the war.[121]

HEROES OR VILLAINS?

Moran was a hero of the middle classes, captain of his nation's rugby union team, a medical doctor, an icon and on the surface an inspiration to middle-class Irish-Australians.[122] The working-class Irish-Australians also sought and found heroes, who invariably attracted the reprobation of the establishment. Throughout the years of the First World War the sporting heroes of the working class became their champions. They carried their hopes and were symbols of their collective angst and feelings of alienation, particularly for the urban Irish-Catholic working class. The establishment sought to retain control by limiting their effectiveness to the deep antagonism of the 'ordinary little people'. When Les Darcy, an Irish-Catholic working-class lad, apparently refused to enlist in the nation's war effort he immediately became a target of patriotic resentment.[123]

After a series of sensational local victories in the Hunter Valley, the 19-year-old Darcy fought and won his first 'big' bout in Sydney in 1914. He immediately became a favourite of the boxing crowd in Sydney and was adopted by the working-class Irish Catholics as a symbol of their struggle. Darcy's career in Australia and in the United States following his illegal departure from his homeland was full of controversy and shrouded in a mist of allegations of cheating and foul play.[124] His surreptitious flight to America was, on the surface, at least prompted by a desire to fight for the world title although his detractors believed he was simply fleeing from the 'greater' challenge offered by the war. However, to his supporters he was still 'a pure and simple hero, a good boy who loved and looked after his mother, went to daily Mass, said the rosary – and won: "the power in his fists came straight from God"'.[125] As an individual who bucked the system and attracted popular support he was in a very exposed and dangerous position. He was Irish, a Catholic and to his critics a 'traitor' but much to the chagrin of the establishment, he was also a working-class hero.[126] He had to be discredited. Darcy represented the dark side of the 'conflict' whilst the other 'fighters', those in France and Belgium, were held up to represent the side of righteousness. In absentia he was vilified by the Australian press and even 'crucified by his own countrymen, Irish included'.[127] His death through complications, ironically precipitated by injuries to his front teeth received in 1916 in a bout with the definitive 'Aussie' hero Harold Hardwick, only further polarized opinions as to his place in Australian history. Peter Corris maintains that Darcy was wrongly accused of cowardice because he had made at least three attempts to enlist and to stake guarantees upon his returning to serve.[128] The forces of the right, in the guise of the Council for Civic and Moral Advancement set Darcy in its sights as representing the unpatriotic sport of boxing and some would argue that they hit their target.

An analysis of Darcy's life and his death neither emphatically establishes him as a martyr nor as a villain. However, the enduring myths that surround him illustrate a predominant feature of the Australian national psyche, the support, if not the cult, of the 'underdog'. This also stands as a definitive characteristic of the nation's sport culture. Darcy's life, his struggles with the establishment and the nature and circumstance of his death, 'poisoned, by those rich and greedy Yanks, dying in his fiancée's arms in American exile',[129] are, indeed, the 'stuff of legends'. The propensity for Australians to create heroic myths to express the sense that they are much-prevailed upon and oppressed is particularly expressed through their support of the tragic sporting icons: it is the substance of their dreams and aspirations being played out on the sporting stage. Given the history of Australia it is perhaps no accident that Darcy was an Irish-Australian Catholic.

EPILOGUE

It is impossible to attempt to capture, in literary form, a 'culture' for as one writes the sands shift, the tide changes and all life and the culture moves on. We are constantly being moulded by global forces so powerful that they can bring political and economic systems down within moments. At best only an attempt can be made to list the forces that collectively spiralled together and interacted to produce the dynamics that created both the concept of Australia and its reality. The reality of Australia is represented by a collection of ideas, beliefs, values, passions and memories as much by its physical and institutional form. Australians, reflecting nostalgically from afar upon the soul of their home, seek to feel the essence of the country as much as they yearn for the sandy beaches, the thronging city streets or the 'footy' crowds. They long for the honesty; they want desperately, once again, to simply be 'direct' with their comments and opinions; they miss the unpretentiousness of it all. The nation has bred a people who have achieved much. The land nurtured and acted as the humus in which its migrant peoples planted their hopes and built their realities. The British came and claimed the land for political and economic exploitation and then to complete the imperial process, imposed their culture. Subsequently, waves of migrants combined with a host of situational forces all contributed to the culture and immutably changed it.

The Irish Catholics who came to Australia were drawn from all parts of British society and were cast around the land by the winds of power, providence and necessity. During the Victorian and Edwardian era the Irish and their descendants represented over 30 per cent of all people in the land. Clearly, they had a considerable effect, by sheer weight of numbers, upon the development of the nation and upon the emergence of a national identity. Collectively, the Irish had an impact matched only by that of the English. Similarly, the contribution of individual Irish-Australians to the history of Australia was immense. Their efforts ranged from the anti-establishment impact of outlaws such as Ned Kelly, to the achievements of such ultra-establishment figures as the Queensland squatter, Sir Joshua Bell. In sport, not all were rebels or working-class heroes like the tragic Les Darcy, as demonstrated by the efforts of the eminent rugby men, Herbert Moran and Arthur Hennessey. Their fame and success, however, were achieved as Australians. Sport not only gave a religion and a class the opportunity to assert its identity, claim distinctiveness and seek status, but also gave a neophyte nation a chance to express its identity and its people a medium through which to express their patriotism as well as their physical talents. In addition sport provided a tap-root for the migrant peoples to establish new lives and new identities. In Australia it became a central feature of the national culture which now defines Australia and its people.

Australian sport has its roots in fields and arenas far from Australian shores. The sports ethic was part of that now much referred to cultural baggage. This baggage was soon unpacked, items disposed of, others added and then repackaged in its new home. The whole social and physical environment wrought massive changes on the residual British sports and within 100 years an Australian sporting identity emerged. The nature of Australian sport, its shape and colour and all its societal implications evolved from the convergence of a host of forces. It would be far too simplistic to attribute all credit for the emergence of the Australian sport culture to the contribution of the Irish and their role in the conflict between the Catholic Irish-Australians and the English-

Australians. Indeed, it would be naïve and wrong. However, the tension between the two groups was directly responsible for many of the traits now viewed as being definitively Australian.

As globalization continues its rationalizing process, the nature of Australian sport may well become more boringly global but this is most unlikely. The legacy of our truculent origins will always emerge especially when a ball is bowled, a football is passed, a goal is scored or a race is run. Somehow it will always be different; somehow it will always be the 'Green' *and* the 'Gold' against the Rest.

NOTES

1. R. Cashman, *The Paradise of Sport: The Rise of Organised Sport in Australia* (Sydney, 1995), pp.15–21.
2. B. Stoddart, *Saturday Afternoon Fever: Sport in Australian Culture* (Sydney, 1986), pp.137–9.
3. Cashman, *The Paradise of Sport*, pp.15–21.
4. A. Trollope, 'Australia and New Zealand' (1871), in K. Dunstan, *Sports* (Melbourne, 1981), p.14.
5. Mark Twain (Samuel L. Clemens), *Following the Equator*, pp.161–3, in J.A. Daly, *Elysian Fields: Sport, Class and Community in Colonial South Australia 1836–1890* (Adelaide, 1982), p.102.
6. D.H. Lawrence, *Kangaroo*, in Dunstan, *Sports*, p.19.
7. Henry Lawson, in Dunstan, p.2.
8. B. Stoddart, 'The Hidden Influence of Sport', in V. Burgmann and J. Lee (eds.), *Constructing a Culture: a People's History of Australia since 1788* (Ringwood, 1988), p.135.
9. See S. Bennett, 'Regional Sentiment and Australian Sport', *Sporting Traditions*, 5, 1 (Nov. 1988), 97–111.
10. P. O'Farrell, *The Irish in Australia* (Sydney, 1993), p.11.
11. Ibid.
12. Ibid., p.155.
13. R. Lawson, *Brisbane in the 1890s: A Study of an Australian Urban Society* (Brisbane, 1973), p.19.
14. L. Frost, *Australian Cities in Comparative View* (Melbourne, 1990), pp.15–17, in Cashman, p.35.
15. Ibid., pp.34–53.
16. O'Farrell, *The Irish in Australia*, pp.8–13.
17. N. Elias, *What is Sociology?* (London, 1978). E. Dunning, 'The Figurational Approach to Leisure and Sport', in C. Rojek (ed.), *Leisure for Leisure: Critical Essays* (London, 1989), pp.36–52.
18. O'Farrell, *passim*.
19. Cashman, p.33.
20. W.F. Mandle, 'Cricket and Australian Nationalism in the Nineteenth Century', *Journal of the Royal Australian Historical Society*, 59, Pt. 4 (Dec. 1973), 225–45.
21. O'Farrell, pp.9–17.
22. O'Farrell, *passim*.
23. See Cashman, pp.72–91.
24. P.A. Mosely, 'Australian Sport and Ethnicity', in P.A. Mosely, R. Cashman, J. O'Hara, and H. Wetherburn (eds.), *Sporting Immigrants: Sport and Ethnicity in Australia* (Sydney, 1997), p.28.
25. Stoddart, *Saturday Afternoon Fever: Sport in Australian Culture*, pp.33–55.
26. C. Cuneen, 'Men, Money, Market, Match', in D. Headon and L. Marinos (eds.), *League of a Nation* (Sydney: ABC Books, 1996), pp.24–7.

27. M.L. Howell, '1909: The Great Defection', in, ibid., pp.33–7.
28. C.M.H. Clark, *The History of Australia VI: 'The Old Tree and the Young Tree Green' 1916–1935* (Melbourne, 1987), pp.136–7.
29. O'Farrell, p.12.
30. Ibid.
31. O'Farrell, pp.185–7.
32. A. Hughes, 'The Irish Community', in Mosely *et al.* (eds.), *Sporting Immigrants*, pp.76–9.
33. O'Farrell, p.186.
34. Ibid.
35. See, M. Connellan, 'The Ideology of Athleticism, Its Antipodean Impact and its Manifestation in Two Elite Catholic Schools', ASSH Studies in Sports History Series: No.5, 1988.
36. O'Farrell, p.19.
37. Cashman, p.53.
38. P.A. Horton, ' "Padang or Paddock": A Comparative View of Colonial Sport in Two Imperial Territories', *International Journal of the History of Sport*, 14, 1 (April 1997) (London and Portland, OR), pp.1–20.
39. O'Farrell, p.10.
40. For an excellent review of many of the heroic Irish ballads of the period see, Bill Wannan's, *The Folklore of the Irish in Australia* (Melbourne, 1980), pp.194–224.
41. O'Farrell, pp.252–88.
42. Ibid, p.155.
43. L. Frost, *Australian Cities in Comparative View* (Melbourne, 1990), pp.15–17, in Cashman, p.35.
44. See Cashman, pp.34–53.
45. Daly, p.69.
46. S. Fitzgerald, *Rising Damp: Sydney 1870–90* (Melbourne, 1987).
47. J. McCalman, *Struggletown: Public and Private Life in Richmond 1900–1965* (Melbourne 1984), cited in O'Farrell, p.156.
48. G. Parsons, 'Capitalism, Class and Community: Civilising and Sanitising The People's Game', in Headon and Marinos (eds.), *League of a Nation*, p.9.
49. Ibid.
50. Cashman, p.95.
51. J. Hargreaves, 'Playing Like Gentlemen While Behaving Like Ladies', *British Journal of Sport History*, 2, 1 (May 1985).
52. R. Webster and A. Miller, *First Class Cricket in Australia, vol.1, 1850/51 to 19441–42* (Melbourne: Globe Press, 1991), in R. Cashman, 'Cricket', in Mosely *et al.* (eds.), pp.174–84.
53. O'Farrell, p.123.
54. Cashman, pp.177–8.
55. Ibid., p.178.
56. Daly, p.68.
57. See Richard Cashman, 'Cricket' in Vamplew *et al.* (eds.), *The Oxford Companion to Australian Sport*, 2nd Edition (Melbourne, 1994), pp.115–22.
58. C. Harte, *A History of Australian Cricket* (London, 1993), p.86.
59. See ibid. for a full outline of player biographies and match statistics as well as an excellent socio-historical analysis of the game in Australia.
60. Mandle, 'Cricket and Australian Nationalism in the Nineteenth Century'.
61. Harte, p.125.
62. See R. Cashman, *Ave a Go, Yer Mug! Australian Cricket Crowds from Larrikin to Ocker* (Sydney, 1984), pp.38–68.
63. Cashman, p.178.
64. See Colden Harrison's autobiography, *The Story of an Athlete: A Picture of the Past* for a full account of Tom Wills' tragic life, in, A. Mancini and G Hibbins, *Running with the Ball: Football's Foster Father* (Melbourne, 1987).
65. See G. Blaney, *A Game of Our Own: the Origins of Australian Football* (Melbourne, 1990), and Mancini and Hibbins, *Running with the Ball.*

66. Ibid.
67. Daly, pp.58–60.
68. Ibid., p.60.
69. It is rather ironic that some 20 years before one of the first colonial references to football was made in the *Southern Australian*, 17 March 1843, from what would have been the other end of the social continuum. It was a game of *Caid*, an Irish form of the traditional village mob-style football games that were the precursors of Public School games and all codified British football games. Obviously, the game was played as part of the traditional St. Patrick's Day celebrations, by '…A few colonisers from the Emerald isle' (Daly, p.58).
70. T.V. Hickie, *They Ran with the Ball: How Rugby Football began in Australia* (Melbourne, 1993).
71. P.A. Horton, 'A History of Rugby Union Football in Queensland 1882–1891' (Ph.D. thesis, University of Queensland, 1989).
72. O'Farrell, pp.155–6.
73. Cashman, p.94.
74. O'Farrell, p.10.
75. Parsons, p.9.
76. Hickie, *passim*.
77. Ibid., pp.179–81.
78. Parsons, p.9.
79. M.L. and R. Howell, 'The Great Defection', a paper presented at ACHPER, Jan. 1984.
80. Horton, '"Padang or Paddock": A Comparative View of Colonial Sport in Two Imperial Territories', pp.6–7.
81. T. Collins, '"Noa Mutton, Noa Laaking": The Origins of Payment of Play in Rugby Football, 1877–86', *International Journal of the History of Sport*, 12, 1 (April 1995), 33–50.
82. E. Dunning and K. Sheard, *Barbarians, Gentlemen and Players* (Canberra, 1979), pp.145–65.
83. See H.M. Moran, *Viewless Winds* (London, 1939). Moran was captain of the first Wallabies that toured in 1908. His chapter outlining the tour is outstanding.
84. Parsons, p.10.
85. Ibid.
86. J.A. Mangan, *The Games Ethic and Imperialism* (London, 1986), p.21 and *The Games Ethic and Imperialism* (London, 1999), p.21. *The Games Ethic* was reprinted by Cass in 1999.
87. The hegemony was not merely educational but also external, see J.A. Mangan, 'The Noble Specimens of Manhood: Schoolboy Literature and the Creation of a Colonial Chivalric Code', in J. Richards, *Imperialism in Juvenile Literature* (Manchester 1989), pp.173–94.
88. Daly, p.14.
89. Ibid., p.71.
90. Ibid., pp.71–2.
91. Connellan, pp.36–8.
92. See C.E.W. Bean, *Here, My Son* (Sydney, 1950).
93. O'Farrell, p.187.
94. R. Crawford, 'Athleticism, Gentlemen and Empire in Australian Public Schools: L.A. Adamson and Wesley College, Melbourne', *Sport and Colonialism in Nineteenth Century Australasia*, ASSH Studies in Sports History: No. 1 (1986), pp.47–8.
95. Connellan, p.37.
96. Ibid. pp.41–60.
97. Ibid., p.52.
98. G. Dening, *Xavier: A Centenary Portrait* (Melbourne, ?date), pp.1–46.
99. Bean, p.29, in Connellan, p.34.
100. Connellan, pp.34–40.
101. O'Farrell, pp.185–7.
102. Cashman, p.95.
103. T.V. Hickie, *The Game for the Game Itself: The Development of Sub-District Rugby in Sydney* (Sydney, 1980).
104. Brother Conlon, Annual Report Christian Brothers College, Waverley, 1917, in, T.V. Hickie, ibid., p.101.

105. Ibid., *passim*.
106. O'Farrell, *passim*.
107. This is the force that drove the diffusion of Athleticism in the colonies and territories of the British Empire. See J.A. Mangan, *Athleticism in the Victorian and Edwardian Public School: The Emergence and Consolidation of an Educational Ideology* (Cambridge, 1981).
108. Connellan, p.38.
109. Daly, pp.178–93.
110. Clark, pp.1–46.
111. M.G. Phillips, 'Sport, War and Gender Images: The Australian Sportsmen's Battalions and the First World War', *International Journal of the History of Sport*, 14, 1 (April 1997), 78–96.
112. M. McKernan, 'Sport, War, and Society', in R. Cashman and McKernan (eds.), *Sport in History: The Making of Modern Sporting History* (Brisbane, 1979), pp 17–18. See also Mangan, *Athleticism* for a fuller discussion of the origins and evolution of athleticism at Stonyhurst.
113. M.G. Phillips and K. Moore, 'The Champion Boxer Les Darcy: A Victim of Class Conflict and Sectarian Bitterness in Australia during the First World War', *International Journal of the History of Sport*, 11, 1 (April 1994), 108.
114. P. Corris, 'The Trials of Les Darcy', in *Lords of the Ring* (Sydney, 1980), pp.60–74.
115. M. McKernan, 'War', in W. Vamplew *et al.* (eds.), p.375.
116. *Bulletin*, 27 Jan. 1916, in McKernan, 'Sport, War, and Society', p.10.
117. O'Farrell, pp.271–3.
118. Ibid., p.253.
119. Moran, pp.158–9.
120. Ibid., pp.29–30.
121. Ibid., pp.69–70.
122. Dr Moran's autobiographical work, *Viewless Winds*, was not, as O'Farrell points out, well received by some of the wealthier members of Irish Catholic society in NSW. In his chapter on the Irish Catholics in NSW in the1890s he portrays them as a 'breed apart' and he referred to the 'Irish priest' as 'constantly belching forth a windy hatred'. An attempt was actually made to buy up and burn all copies of the text! See, O'Farrell, p.171.
123. Phillips and Moore, *passim*.
124. Corris, 'The Trials of Les Darcy', pp.60–74.
125. O'Farrell, p.262.
126. Phillips and Moore, pp.109–11.
127. Ibid.
128. Corris.
129. O'Farrell, pp.262–3.

5

'They Play in Your Home': Cricket, Media and Modernity in Pre-war Australia

FRAZER ANDREWES

TUNING IN

To say that cricket was an obsession for many Australians in the 1930s, and that every summer the mental world of Australia was structured and defined by the vicissitudes of national and international cricket, is probably not stretching the truth too far. For a sport that originally had been considered to be the most 'English of English Games', Australians rapidly championed it as their own and developed it into a national and distinctively Australian game.[1] For many fans, commentators and historians the early 1930s were the apotheosis of Australian cricket; the striding colossus of Don Bradman, the infamy of the 'bodyline' test series against the visiting Marylebone Cricket Club (MCC) team in 1932–33, and the subsequent retrieval of the Ashes when Australia toured England in 1934, all helped to prioritize this period in the mythology of Australian test cricket.[2] The national fascination with cricket, and the amount of feeling that both the playing of the game and the controversies it generated could stir up, were even patently evident to those who had not been embroiled in them since an early age. Egon Kisch, the radical Czech journalist whose attempts to enter Australia to speak at an anti-war congress in 1934 had been the cause of much comment in the Australian press, found the time between his leg-breaking, pier-head jump in Melbourne and his subsequent departure from Australia in 1935 to fully appreciate the position of cricket (and bodyline) in the Australian psyche. 'Bodyline is connected with sport,' he wrote, 'but it also has a profound political significance. To write about Australia and to omit the bodyline affair would be like describing the Vatican without the Pope, or – but there is no end to such comparisons if we are to describe the significance of cricket for Australia.'[3]

What Kisch so observantly noted was that cricket in Australia assumed a cultural and political importance out of all proportion to its actual position as a sporting code; it is partly for this reason that I have chosen to focus this essay on the 1930s. I have also chosen this period because of its importance in the way the representation of cricket was technologized and commercialized. As other writers have noted, the radio broadcasting of cricket matches became a national event in the 1930s, at first for matches played locally only, but from 1934 for matches played abroad as well.[4] Richard Cashman has observed that cricket dominated the radio airwaves by the 1932–33 season, and in doing so capitalized on a rapidly growing radio audience.[5] It was particularly serendipitous for the Australian Broadcasting Corporation (ABC) that the first broadcast national ball-by-ball broadcasts coincided with the Bodyline tour, as it has been suggested that these broadcasts both enlarged the wireless audience, and whetted the appetites of those listening for live attendance of the matches.[6] What the introduction of match broadcasts did create, however, was a new focus for the commercialization of cricket, a commercialization, it must be said, which had put down solid roots long before the 1930s.[7] The advertisements and articles that swept in on the coat-tails of match broadcasting made it their business to sell modernity and in doing so lift Australia from the mire of the Depression on the strings of technological progress. As Rita Barnard has suggested, the 1930s were a decade of contradictions and sometimes jarring juxtapositions. 'They were certainly "hard times",' she writes. 'but as other histories suggest, the years of the Great Depression were also self-consciously "modern times" and modernity ... was generally understood as having to do with the comfort, mobility, and pleasure promised by the "dime-store dream parade" of commodities.'[8] This study seeks to explore the promises of modernity and the way in which cricket provided a national vehicle for the dissemination of its messages. It will also explore the specifically gendered way in which this message was delivered, and comment on the effective marginalization of women from the cricket mainstream and, in effect, from the modernising process.

'WIRELESS GAVE THE WHOLE COUNTRY A PART
IN THE GAME'

The 1932–33 test series was a watershed in the broadcasting of cricket matches, and has been represented as the moment when the nation was brought together for the first time as a listening public. Bodyline, Ken Inglis states, enlarged the listening audience and gave the people the unprecedented feeling of being close to the action and involved in the controversy. 'When a ball from Larwood felled Woodfull on a Saturday afternoon in Adelaide and Jardine set a "bodyline" field for Larwood's next over against the injured Australian captain, listeners all over Australia could hear spectators hooting, share their outrage and ask their neighbours to listen.'[9] In a country struggling to come to terms with the social and economic dislocations of the Depression, broadcasting enabled the people to come together and commune in a national obsession; isolated from the world, and in many cases from each other, the wireless annihilated distance.

At least that is what some perceived. Commenting on the test match played in Sydney in early December 1932, a Melbourne newspaper, the *Argus*, assured its readers that 'Broadcasting came into its own' in relaying the excitement to listeners so many miles from the action. 'The single voice which told the story of the day's play from the Sydney Cricket-ground poured a tale of woe and ecstasy into the ears of tens of thousands of adults and countless children in every State of the Commonwealth. Everybody interested in cricket – and everybody is now – envied the crowd which watched the struggle between Larwood and the Australian batsmen in Sydney; but wireless gave the whole country a part in the game.'[10] According to the newspaper account, the city of Melbourne was festooned with 'a thousand scoreboards', outside shops and cafés and on bridges, which 'told the story of Australia's changing fortunes to a thousand separate crowds'.[11] The streets became congested with enthusiasts gathering under the scoreboards and the police, still wary of any mass gathering of the unemployed or indigent, had many of the boards removed.

The belief that the wireless had succeeded in bringing the nation together was infectious. Where many had blamed the ills of the modern world and its devices for the current period of want and uncertainty, technology seemed to provide them at last with the possibility of entertainment and relief, for a moment, from the stresses of daily life. A correspondent to the *Sydney Morning Herald* was most fulsome in his praise of the efforts of a cricket broadcaster, one who, indeed, deserved to 'receive the hearty commendation of his hundreds of thousands of listeners'. Unable to attend the match, the correspondent was still able to fully partake in and enjoy the unfolding spectacle. 'It was a delightful afternoon's pleasure to listen to his vivid description and witty comments. I can remember during my long experience of the game no more thrilling moments than those wherein he described the tense situation and seething excitement of the 70,000 people present while Bradman was pluckily struggling for his well-deserved century.'[12] Without knowing the context it could almost be assumed that he had witnessed these events in person. Another correspondent to the *Argus* neatly captured the air of excitement, tension and expectation that the wireless broadcasts brought to people all over the nation. 'What a wonderful thing is a Test match! Who cares, for the moment, if Britain pays America in gold? Who cares if Gandhi starves to death to gain his point? Who cares if a wool clip averages 6d. or if wheat brings less than 2/? All we want to know is "What's the score?" And yet our nerves are shattered by everlasting fears of the unknown. We tremble for the voice of the radio announcer, fearing the worst when he says, "A telegram from Sydney has just come –." We can do no work while the slow hands of the clock creep to the magic moment of the crossover.'[13]

Advertisers were quick to capitalize on the depth of such sentiment, and radio manufacturers sought not only to fill this gap, but even attempted to convince potential customers that listening to broadcast cricket would be just like, perhaps even better, than being at the real thing. Healing Golden-Voiced Radio purported to do just this. Their advertisement pictured a man literally on the edge of his seat, face intent and arm slightly raised while the spectral figures of cricketers in action hovered above him and his radio set. 'Unfortunately,' the copy declared, 'many people do not get the opportunity to actually see the games, but they do the next best thing, and that is to listen to them – faithfully reproduced on their Healing Golden-Voiced Radio. If you are not able to see a Test Match, you will not want to miss any of the thrills, so why not take a grandstand seat de luxe – in your own armchair and enjoy every moment of the game.'[14] The fruits of modernity offered the Australian people not only the chance to engage with their favourite sport anywhere in Australia, but also suggested that now anyone could also avail themselves of the best seat in the stands, an egalitarian dream at a time when the inequities of society were proving all too obvious.

It must be said, however, that not everyone embraced the introduction of cricket broadcasts or the way in which the rapid spread of news and controversy was facilitated, nor yet the increasing commercialism of the game and the desire for thrilling copy. The poet and humorist C.J. Dennis bemoaned in verse the evils the advent of cricket broadcasts had wrought on the farmer in the country.

I reckon (said Dad) that the country's pests
Is this here wireless an' these here Tests.
Up to the house and around the door,
Stretchin' their ears for to catch the score,
Leavin' the horses down in the crop,
Can you wonder a farmer goes off pop? ...
There's a standing crop an' the rain's not far,
An' the price is rotten, but there you are:
As soon as these cricketin' games begin
The farm goes dilly on listening in.[15]

Other protests were not framed in such a humorous (or tongue-in-cheek) way as this. A common complaint was not that the matches were broadcast at all, but that what the ABC broadcast was insufficient. 'Fed-Up Listener', writing to the *Sydney Morning Herald*, railed at the 'niggardly' action of the ABC in only broadcasting short descriptions of the test matches, and refused to accept the ABC's explanation that during the day the Post Office could not spare trunk lines which were required for business. In an early example of consumer activism, 'Fed-Up Listener' urged all fellow listeners to work together for the reform of a system which took 'thousands of pounds ... from listeners as licence fees' but which still held the consumers at 'the mercy of the commission'.[16] Still other authorities pondered whether the modern turn of cricket was really warranted at all, and didn't instead spoil the essential character of the game. At the height of the bodyline fiasco, the *Argus* editorialized on the current direction of the game and what appeared to be going wrong.

The field of the spectator is now nation-wide. Passions are inflamed and partisanship is accentuated by publicity in its many modern forms; and when partisanship flies in at the door judgment leaves by the window. 'Stunting' has been indulged in to such an extent as could not eventually fail to produce bitterness upon some issue or other. Comment upon every phase of the game has been broadcast so continuously that the public mind has become obsessed by the controversy. From every point of view these developments are bad.[17]

The *Argus* and other newspapers were, however, not strangers to the lure of publicity and the commercial possibilities inherent in a popular and controversial story. Just two days before the publication of the editorial quoted above, the *Sydney Morning Herald* had published an article headed 'Opinions exchanged by wireless telephone', detailing an argument between several prominent players over the rights and wrongs of bodyline and its aftermath, which had previously been broadcast on radio in Sydney, Melbourne and Adelaide.[18] It was actions such as these, and the co-manager of the English team's comment early in the tour that 'too much publicity was the fault of modern cricket',[19] that led the *Argus* to point the finger at all the 'modern' problems of the game, including 'players, publicists and partisans'. 'All have assisted in distilling in the alembic of ultra-modernity an essence which has in it the rarefied elements of cricket, but it is not cricket as the world used to know it.'[20]

GLIMPSES OF TECHNOLOGICAL MARVELS

The 1932–33 test series proved so popular with cricket-loving Australians for several obvious reasons. Firstly, the nature of the bodyline bowling and the ensuing furore focused unprecedented attention on the game and brought it centre-stage in the domestic politics and imperial relations of both Australia and the Great Britain. Secondly, the technological revelation of test match broadcasts captured the imagination of the populace and budding media entrepreneurs alike. The listening public quickly developed a taste for the ready access to scores, match reports and complete match relays anywhere in the country, regardless of where the game was played, the ABC realized the boost this could mean for radio licences, wireless manufacturers grasped what this could mean in terms of the sales of equipment, and other advertisers came to understand the growing nexus of cricket and cash. The *Argus* neatly summed up this attitude when commenting on the entrepreneurial spirit (excusing the pun) shown by those hoteliers who placed a radio and scoreboard in their establishments 'in the hope of stimulating trade by offering beer and cricket'. '"Give the public what it wants" is a good slogan; and every shrewd businessman gave it cricket news.'[21] The third factor, of course, was that everyone wanted to see, or hear, Don Bradman in action.[22] The 1934 return test series, in which Australia travelled to England, was, if anything even more eagerly anticipated than the bodyline series. Originally in doubt because of continuing wrangles between the MCC and the Australian Board of Control over bodyline, its eventual clearance was greeted with joy by the Australian public who saw in it a chance to avenge past grievances. The ABC, other broadcasters, and advertisers saw the possibility of furthering their revenue by exploiting a cricket- and technology-hungry population.

The main innovation of the 1934 test series, as most histories of the period have discussed, was the development of 'reconstructed', or what were later termed 'synthetic', broadcasts. Direct relays of the matches from England were, at this time, not able to be broadcast with any degree of reliability or quality. Instead, cables with the account of each over bowled were sent to Sydney from whence they were telephoned through to the ABC. At the studio these messages were turned into notes for the commentators. A scoreboard and chart with up-to-date field placings were also kept in the studio. Sound effects could be added to the commentaries from pre-recorded material, and from the commentator tapping one of three hemispherical pieces of wood to imitate the sound of bat on ball.[23] The fact that these broadcasts were immensely popular, and that the nation rapidly embraced wireless technology and the new techniques associated with it, can be deduced from the amount of air time the ABC was willing to spend on match commentaries. Inglis compared the coverage adopted by the BBC and the ABC during the test series, and found that while the BBC gave their listeners two ten-minute commentaries and an occasional half-hour description of particularly exciting play per day, the ABC offered continuous reporting through the night and into the small hours of the morning.[24] This 'fever' of test match excitement, as the *Argus* at one point chose to term it, was also manifested in both the sale of wireless sets and the number of licences issued. According to one report, the number of licences issued per month increased from 8,288 in April 1934 to 13,708 in May.[25] Wireless manufacturers also reported a 'remarkable increase' in their business and claimed that 'most manufacturers were working at high pressure to meet the demand'.[26] Neither the licencers nor the manufacturers had any doubt that the impending test series in England was the cause of the increase.[27]

The point that needs to be stressed is that such figures and descriptions not only attest to the keenness, bordering on fanaticism, which many Australian followed cricket, they also show that the populace was as caught up with the technology, the means of delivery, as with the game. Cricket was a game, as the newspaper editorials never tired of reiterating, bound up with tradition, empire, codes of conduct, honour and manliness, but it was also now, and again editorials grudgingly acknowledged this, a modern game and was increasingly subject to modern production and reception.[28] Australian society, by and large, embraced this with vigour. A report published to coincide with a large radio and electrical fair provided listeners with a tantalizing glimpse of the technological marvels due to be employed during the test broadcasts. Not only would the 'synthetic' broadcasts be heard, but

> Beam wireless and cable messages dealing in detail with every stroke played will be received during the earlier part of each day's play in the Tests. The radio-telephone will be employed at the luncheon and tea intervals and immediately after the drawing of stumps to enable [the commentators] to give [their] impressions of the play. Whenever it is possible to receive short-wave signals at sufficient strength, the actual running commentary which is to be transmitted from the British Broadcasting Company's Empire station will be broadcast.[29]

Such a growing passion for technology was seen to dovetail neatly into the already extant love of cricket. The *Sydney Morning Herald* editorialized that 'the drama, the colour, and the atmosphere of cricket, lend themselves far better to description than the movement and vicissitudes of most other sports, with the result that cricket has readers and listeners who far outnumber those who have opportunity to be spectators'.[30] Fortunately, then, cricket seemed to be well adapted to the demands of the modern fan.

'NOT SO MUCH CRICKET AS DRAMA'

As mentioned above, the main innovation of the 1934 test series was the use of 'synthetic' broadcasts, and it appears that these enthralled and puzzled listeners in equal amount. Those who were not alert to the methods employed in creating the ball-by-ball broadcasts seemed sure that the descriptions came directly from the ground; even some of those who did know of the procedure expressed doubt that what they had been told was true.[31] The broadcaster most credited with developing the technique, Charles Moses, even went to the length of exploiting another modern and rapidly expanding medium, the motion picture, by having a film made of the entire process of the commentary from receiving the cable to the announcer's reconstruction.[32] The Sydney-based broadcasting magazine *Wireless Weekly* also went to great pains in describing for its readers the process of the match broadcast, including publishing facsimile copies of the original cables, the messages as they were then transcribed, and even a photograph of one of the gramophone records which contained the recorded sound effects.[33] What makes this extensive article most interesting is the sense of delight it evinced in the construction of an entirely simulated environment. In some ways the fact that the broadcasts sought to present a version of an actual game of cricket was irrelevant. As the article revealingly states, 'what follows is not so much cricket as drama'.[34] While sport, in the best traditions of journalistic hyperbole, has often been described in the terms of a human drama, the representation of ball-by-ball broadcasts *was* shaped as fiction or drama and not as merely facsimile. Perhaps this is most adequately displayed in the semantic difference between the original term for the broadcasts, 'reconstruction', and its replacement, 'synthetic'. 'Reconstruction' implies an act of creation from the former constituent parts of an entity, whereas 'synthetic' suggests that which has been made to *imitate* a real event. In the 1930s 'synthetic' was also a very modern-sounding word, associated with man-made fibres and plastics, including, possibly, the Bakelite from which many of the listeners' radio sets were produced, and technological progress.

Perhaps it was no accident that cricket broadcasts were described in such a way. By 1934 radio dramas were a fast developing and increasingly popular form of entertainment for radio listeners, and their pattern and formula were no doubt familiar to radio habitués.[35] Indeed, it seems the drama genre had become so much a recognizable part of radio broadcasting that by 1935 the ABC were even not averse to providing dramatized re-creations of news items.[36] Describing the accoutrements of the recording studio, the *Wireless Weekly* termed them 'stage properties', used for creating a 'show'.[37] The magazine went as far as claiming that really what the listeners tuned in for at the dead of night was not the cricket *per se*, but rather the wonderful flights of invention the commentators brought forth. 'It is as a reconstruction that the broadcasts appeal to listeners. Very few listeners would be much the wiser if the cabled message were read out exactly as they were received; and such messages gain in interest as they are amplified.'[38] It was the imagination and the creation of a feeling of 'atmosphere' by the commentators and the assembled group of experts and technicians which was thought particularly worthy of mention and praise.

> It is worth while listening, just for the fine points of their descriptions, to hear how they simulate the shock of Bradman being out. Suppose he was out third ball of the over, they would see this from a glance at the message, yet they would have to describe two balls and the bowling of a third in a quiet way before they could say 'He's out. Bradman's out,' as though such a thing had not till that moment occurred to them. They must not seem too surprised. They must not work up to it in the manner of a playwright reaching up to his catharsis; it must all come suddenly, and take them by surprise, and it must sound quite natural.[39]

Finally, it asserted, 'If you listen to a description in a critical mood,' as no doubt a drama critic would, 'you cannot but be struck with the brilliance of the acting.'[40]

While the ABC seemed content to emphasize the dramatic qualities of their match descriptions, one commercial broadcaster fell back on another time-honoured tradition of popular entertainment to endear itself with its cricket audience. The Sydney station 2UW eschewed ball-to-ball descriptions, and instead offered a service that they assured listeners was an improvement on previous broadcasting techniques. What they instituted was 'not so much a cricket broadcast as a very entertaining vaudeville, with cricket scores and comments thrown in'.[41] While cricket was obviously still the main *raison d'être* of the broadcast, it appeared that as far as the broadcaster was concerned, providing a comedic and entertaining context was just as important.

> The chief vaudevillian is a Mr. Charlie Vaude, who romps around in the red-nosed comedian manner very effectively, and is assisted by Charlie Lawrence … and Renn Millar, and various other well-known Melbourne artists. They have what you might call a theme song: 'Who's afraid of the Big Bad Bear,' which they sing when an Australian bowls out an Englishman, and so on, and they make jokes on the state of the game, or on telegrams and 'phone calls received from listeners, and ask silly questions of the commentator, Mr. Vic Richardson.[42]

Maybe to leaven concerns about undue frivolity being associated with its broadcasts, 2UW emphasized that the distinguishing feature of its cricket service was that it announced the latest scores a few minutes before the other stations, and thus held the edge in actual cricket service if not in the dramatic description of play. What dramatic devices such as these sought to achieve was a sense of closeness and familiarity with a game which was being played 12,000 miles and (for eastern Australia) ten hours' time difference away. In an effort to maintain ratings and popular support, both networks and advertisers strove to present the immediacy and action of the game, at once bridging distance and bringing a sense of the visual where there was none.

'THEY PLAY IN YOUR HOME'

Lesley Johnson has written of the impact radio had in the 1930s in instituting structures and regimented notions of time through the use of time calls and the predictable occurrence of programmes.[43] She quotes a *Wireless Weekly* editorial of 1931 which declared that radio's development of time-consciousness was beginning to affect the population: 'The outcome is an observed quickening of our pace, better scheduling of all our movements and actions to a standard and accurate time.'[44] The broadcasting of the cricket matches from England in 1934 certainly seem to bear out this confident assertion. The *Wireless Weekly*, among others, prominently displayed the time of play, including lunch and tea intervals, in both English and eastern Australian time, and alerted listeners when to tune in to the broadcasts of all the different stations. It could be assumed, therefore, that thousands of Australians were doing exactly the same thing at exactly the same time through the mediation of their radio sets. As the *Argus* wrote, 'There are more than 1,000,000 wireless receivers licensed in Australia, and few are idle on Test match nights.'[45] But while the radio broadcasts encouraged temporal regimentation, they also suppressed distance and whittled time down to smaller and smaller increments. 'On Friday night, and all other Test Match nights, we in Australia, at a distance of 12,000 miles, will be in possession of minute details of the game ... The time required for collecting the particulars of the occurrences relating to an individual ball, the passage of those particulars over the distance between England and Australia, and furnishing them to a listener in any part of any State, will occupy only a minute or two. Every effort is being made to keep the actual time down nearly as possible to one minute.'[46] Similarly, the same magazine's editorial pondered the speed at which the descriptions could be broadcast and the diminution of time and distance this entailed. 'One service claims that, after the first few nights ... it will be putting a description on the air only three-quarters of a minute behind the game in progress in England; thus you will see the services considerably speeded up, and for those interested in the technique of broadcasting it will be interesting to observe whether the usual atmosphere of the cricket ground can be maintained at such a high speed.'[47] Like much else in the modern world, cricket was now also accelerating into the future.

To endeavour to create a feeling of presence and participation in the matches, wireless guides and advertisers, in collaboration with the broadcasters, provided listeners with scoring cards and field diagrams which they were supposed to consult and amend as the games advanced. It was suggested that those listeners not versed in the finer points of the game would benefit from keeping the *Wireless Weekly* score sheet beside them: 'To keep the score in detail imparts an added interest in the game, and this course alone provides the means for reflection, and settles the ever-present "post-mortem" during the regular adjournments of the game.'[48] One company developed a special 'radio cricket scoreboard' which, it claimed, had been adopted by the broadcasting stations for official use. The advertisement expressed the belief that not only was the 'Astor Radio Cricket Score Board' a novel and useful addition to broadcasting pleasure, but that it was a 'new thrill in Test Match Broadcasting', and the 'craze of 1934' which, by the time the matches started, very few homes would be without.[49] While avoiding the grand pretensions of the Astor scoreboard, *Wireless Weekly*'s chart of fielding positions and list of the cricket terms the announcers would use, promised to provide an almost cinematic experience for the listening public. 'For those not well acquainted with the field positions, this Chart could be cut out and pasted on cardboard, and so placed conveniently when listening. You will soon pick the positions, and at once visualize the ball speeding away in its true direction.'[50]

Advertisements for wireless sets also offered the tantalizing fiction of attending all the matches and seeing the action. The Stromberg-Carlson Receiver invited the listener to 'Imagine turning the dial and listening in direct to the lunch-time resumes by England's leading cricket authorities', and to envisage the even greater thrills of being able to pass from country to country and 'listen-in' to the world.[51] A Philips company advertisement was even more evocative of the rich possibilities of cricket broadcasts.

They play in your home ... A flick of the switch and the set merges into the background – surely this can be no radio receiver, but a pulsing, living thing. Let us close our eyes and listen – we have skipped twelve thousand miles, our cushioned armchair gives place to the grandstand. Who is that bowler? Ah! a voice at our elbow announces that the speed merchant is none other than Tim Wall. Again the bowler comes pounding down – a wicket falls – this is cricket.[52]

Such advertisements and scoring paraphernalia asked listeners to suspend belief for a while and immerse themselves in a world of cricket, one played many thousands of miles away but one which had been artificially re-created and disseminated for them through the radio. Distance and time became variables which could be schematized, diminished and controlled through the mechanism of the wireless, and cricket was modernized and repackaged for an increasing and hungry audience. It could be argued that radio had aided in democratizing cricket, and had turned what was an already strong passion into a truly mass-cultural event. Yet however democratic the appeal of cricket might have been, in terms of gender it was still packaged as being essentially a man's game.

'THE TROUBLE WITH MEN IS THAT THEY TAKE THEIR CRICKET TOO SERIOUSLY'

It is not to be doubted that many women listened in with as much eagerness as men to cricket broadcasts in the 1930s. As C.J. Dennis bemoaned in the poem previously cited, when the farm stopped working to listen in to the tests, it was 'Not only the boys and the harvester crew, But Mum and the girls gits dotty too.'[53] Issues of technological control and representation, however, could serve to render the position of women marginal. While women were specifically targeted as listeners and consumers of radio in the 1930s, it was presumed that real control of the technology would lie in the hands of men, whether those in the household or those who controlled the broadcasting. As cricket was taken to be a man's game (albeit with a significant female following), advertising, and newspaper and magazine copy, represented it as such.[54] Almost universally men were the only sex to appear in advertisements featuring the cricket tests as a marketing pitch. The Philips Radioplayer advertisement from 1934 featured the stylized figures of two men listening to the cricket on one of the company's products.[55] Ads for Diamond Batteries and ESM Radio both featured men, at ease in armchairs, soaking up the action from nearby radio receivers.[56] In one radio advertisement a man is depicted nonchalantly speaking into the telephone, 'The cricket? Yes, come right over – ours is a Raycophone.'[57] Men are the ones who figuratively controlled access to the cricket and the radio, reinforcing the male privileges in matters relating to both. In one of the few advertising images to include women, Ever Ready Batteries depicted a farming household engrossed in listening to a test match commentary. But here, too, men dominated. Those closest to the radio set are men, and the two women, mother and daughter, stand up against the wall while almost all the men sit or lounge around. The only figure more marginalized than the women is one at the very edge of the picture, an Aboriginal stock-hand who stands not only outside the door, but down a level from his white employers.[58]

Only too often were women pushed to the figurative margins in such ways. Women were clearly interested in cricket and were, in reality, just as likely to be consumers of the radio broadcasts. Richard Cashman makes the point that in the inter-war period women were as keen as men to exercise their right to leisure. He writes that while there are no accurate figures for the number of women attending test matches, some test players of the 1930s estimated that between 30 and 40 per cent of the crowds were women.[59] The English cricket journalist William Pollock, writing on the crowds during the 1936–37 English tour of Australia, asserted that tens of thousands of women would turn out to watch the test matches. In Adelaide, he wrote, 'They were on the ground hours before play began, and one morning a lady brought the domestic hearth to cricket: she arrived with the family green peas and conscientiously proceeded to shell them while she waited for the heroes.'[60] In Melbourne he was told that about 60 per cent of the huge crowds were women. 'To many of these women, Test cricketers are more thrilling than film stars ... If they have the mind to, women can save cricket.'[61] Yet it was despite such evidence that suggested that women as much as men were passionately interested in the game that the dominant representations figured and appealed to men. Women were routinely the butt of jokes predicated on their supposed lack of knowledge about the game's finer points, and chided for their inability to take cricket matches for the serious business they were.[62] Even when their presence at the great communion of cricket was acknowledged they were still casually sidelined. During the 1934 test series the *Argus* commented on the deleterious effects the cricket broadcasts were having on everyday life. Not only was the 'march of science' increasing the lethargy of retail staff and helping the coffers of the electricity company, alcohol wholesalers and tobacconists, it was also to blame for an absence of shoppers, the majority of whom would have presumably been women.[63] The same article also hinted that women along with men stayed up into the small hours listening to the unfolding match on the radio, but found the time most useful in attending to domestic and feminine pastimes. 'The family man has not been left out. Long-sought buttons have been sewn on, pockets have been patched, and socks have been darned in quantity while the Australians were batting at Manchester.'[64] Yet women could and did see through the carefully constructed façade of male control. The captain of the English women's cricket team, touring Australia in late 1934, pointed out that while Australian crowds had a great sense of humour, by-and-large men's greatest failing was that they 'took their cricket too seriously'.[65] Cricket was, after all, only a game, but to men, it seemed, this was a truth that should not be expressed; cricket represented for them a mastery they were reluctant to relinquish.

FADING OUT

Cricket broadcasting in the 1930s opened new horizons for all associated with the sport, and its fusion with Bradman, bodyline and the Ashes served to consolidate it as the most popular sport in inter-war Australian society. Cricket could stand as the metaphor for many things: perhaps the strongest of these, at least amongst the more conservative and traditional, were the tie of Empire and the blood bonds of the Anglo-Saxon people. In 1934 the editor of the *Argus* wrote, 'It is a game which embodies many of the virtues which people of British stock cherish … It is a game which demands the surrender of individual glory to the common good; its vicissitudes cannot be resisted without good temper and self-control; and it is a game which requires moral and physical courage.'[66] Perhaps it was because of the perception that these intrinsic qualities bound the disparate Empire together that made the Bodyline debacle all the harder to take. But cricket also had appeal at a simpler, more personal level. In the dislocation of the early 1930s cricket was a comforting, comprehensible, supposedly unchangeable, link to happier times. Beneath a picture of young boys choosing sides before the start of a backyard cricket match, Exide wireless batteries placed this copy. 'Where is the man who can study this picture for a few minutes without experiencing a flood of happy recollections, carried back in memory to those carefree days when panics, depressions, strikes, or other national calamities meant nothing to our boyish minds.'[67] Cricket was safe, part of a lived experience. Yet cricket was also modernizing along with the rest of Australian society; that this advertisement was used to sell batteries for wireless sets used to listen to the broadcast matches asserts this.

Cricket became modern and helped disseminate modernity. No longer was it only the game of nostalgia and hoary imperial rhetoric. It had became a part of modern culture and new media. Radio drew cricket into its own web of progress and in doing so made the game just one of the many forms of mass entertainment which began to flourish in the 1920s and 1930s. Cricket also became part of a new formation of consumerism and commodification, and was 'sold' along with radios, razors, batteries, cigarettes and numerous other consumer goods. In this sense the game truly became a symbol of modern life in the 1930s. As one newspaper editor wrote, 'Cricket, like many other things in the British scheme of life, means far more than is apparent on the surface.'[68] It is unlikely that he meant this in the way this essay has suggested, but he, like Egon Kisch, realized that cricket could mean so much to Australian society. What match broadcasting and advertising in the 1930s did show, however, was how mutable this game could be to the demands of a nation intent on making their culture and society modern.

NOTES

1. R. Cashman, 'Australia', in B. Stoddart and K.A.P. Sandiford (eds.), *The Imperial Game: Cricket, Culture and Society* (Manchester, 1998), pp. 34, 47.
2. The literature, scholarly and popular, on both Bradman and bodyline is voluminous and varied. The latest works published on Bradman are C. Williams, *Bradman: An Australian Hero* (London, 1996), and Roland Perry, *The Don* (Sydney, 1995). Perhaps the most thorough treatment of the bodyline controversy can be found in R. Sissons and B. Stoddart, *Cricket and Empire: The 1932–33 Bodyline Tour of Australia* (Sydney, 1984).
3. E. Kisch, *Australian Landfall*, trans. by J. Fisher, I. Fitzgerald and K. Fitzgerald (Australasian Book Society, 1969 [1937]), p.303. Kisch was famously refused entry to Australia because of supposed Communist affiliations. In defiance of this order he jumped from the ship onto the dock at Melbourne, breaking his leg in the process. The work from which this quote is taken is the description of his time in Australia and a commentary on Australian society as he perceived it.
4. B. Stoddart, *Saturday Afternoon Fever: Sport in the Australian Culture* (Sydney, 1986), pp.92–3; R. Cashman, *'Ave a Go, Yer Mug! Australian Cricket Crowds from Larrikin to Ocker* (Sydney, 1984), pp.92–4.
5. Cashman, *'Ave a Go, Yer Mug!*, p.93.

6. Ibid., p.94; K. Inglis, *This is the ABC: The Australian Broadcasting Commission 1933–1983* (Victoria, 1983), p.36.

7. 'Commercialisation', in R. Cashman *et al.* (eds.), *The Oxford Companion to Australian Cricket* (Melbourne, 1996), pp.115–17, provides a useful potted history of commercial involvement in Australian cricket.

8. R. Barnard, *The Great Depression and the Culture of Abundance: Kenneth Fearing, Nathanael West, and Mass Culture in the 1930s* (Cambridge, 1995), p.21.

9. Inglis, *This is The ABC*, p.36.

10. *Argus*, 3 Dec. 1932, 24.

11. Ibid.

12. *Sydney Morning Herald* (*SMH*), 6 Jan. 1933, 4.

13. *Argus*, 5 Dec. 1932, 10.

14. *Bulletin*, 2 Nov. 1932, 5.

15. Quoted in *The ABC Cricket Book: The First 60 Years*, compiled by J. Maxwell (Sydney, 1994), p.8.

16. *SMH*, 3 Jan. 1933, 5.

17. *Argus*, 21 Jan. 1933, 22.

18. *SMH*, 19 Jan. 1933, 9.

19. *SMH*, 17 Nov. 1932, 11. The co-manager, P.F. 'Plum' Warner, went further to state that 'Every feature of the private lives of the team was recorded on the journey of the Orient liner Orontes … That one player was adept at dancing, that another paraded the deck in short pants, or that another bathed in the morning or played deck tennis well had all been given prominence.' The *Argus* also reported Warner's speech, but seemed less inclined to heed his subtle hint. Under the article an advertisement advised Warner would speak to the *Argus* luncheon club that day, and that his address would be simultaneously broadcast through station 3UZ in Melbourne. 17 Nov. 1932, 9.

20. *Argus*, 2 Jan. 1933, 6.

21. Ibid., 3 Dec. 1932, 24.

22. Sissons and Stoddart, *Cricket and Empire*, p.111.

23. Inglis, *This is the ABC*, p.37; Cashman, *'Ave a Go, Yer Mug!*, pp.101–3.

24. Inglis, *This is the ABC*, pp.36–7.

25. *Argus*, 25 May 1934, 12

26. Ibid., 9 June 1934, 19.

27. Also see the *Wireless Weekly*, 8 June 1934, 32, which makes the same claim.

28. The editor of the *Sydney Morning Herald* tried to impart a sense of both the traditional and the modern in cricket in one of his editorials. 'The people who to-day rush to read cabled reports of the test matches in England before the news of the Disarmament Conference are of the same stock as the men who, when the Spanish Armada was approaching to attack them, insisted on finishing their game of bowls before getting ready for the defence.' 16 June 1934, 14.

29. *Argus*, 2 June 1934, 15.

30. *SMH*, 2 July 1934, 8.

31. Inglis writes that despite the fact that listeners were told before the start of play that the broadcasts were not actually coming from England, people would still lay bets as to whether it was. *This is the ABC*, p.37.

32. Maxwell, *The ABC Cricket Book*, p.11.

33. *Wireless Weekly*, 22 June 1934, 11–15.

34. Ibid., 12.

35. See R. Lane, *The Golden Age of Australian Radio Drama, 1923–1960: A History Through Biography* (Carlton South, 1994); also see Inglis, *This is the ABC*, ch.2.Cricket could also literally appear in radio drama. In an ongoing series, 'We Await Your Verdict', broadcast on the Sydney station 2BL, one of the hypothetical situations was a manslaughter charge brought against a bodyline bowler who struck a batsman in the head with a fast, rising leg-side ball. *Wireless Weekly*, 16 March 1934, 7.

36. L. Johnson, The *Unseen Voice: A Cultural Study of Early Australian Radio* (London, 1988), p.166.

37. *Wireless Weekly*, 22 June 1934, 12.

38. Ibid., 13.
39. Ibid.
40. Ibid.
41. Ibid., 14.
42. Ibid.
43. Johnson, *The Unseen Voice*, pp.107–110.
44. Ibid., p.108.
45. *Argus*, 11 July 1934, 6.
46. *Wireless Weekly*, 8 June 1934, 17.
47. Ibid, p.32.
48. Ibid. p.18.
49. Ibid., 1 June 1934, 62.
50. Ibid., 8 June 1934, 20.
51. Ibid., 17 Aug. 1934, 18.
52. Ibid., 27 July 1934, 11.
53. Maxwell, *The ABC Cricket Book*, p.8.
54. For a comprehensive survey of women's relationship with cricket in all its forms, see Richard Cashman and Amanda Weaver, *Wicket Women: Cricket and Women in Australia* (Sydney, 1991).
55. *Wireless Weekly*, 27 July 1934, 11
56. Ibid., 17 Aug. 1934, 20; 18 May 1934, 40.
57. Ibid., 1 June 1934, 5.
58. Ibid., 27 July 1934, 46.
59. Cashman, *'Ave a Go, Yer Mug!*, pp.69–70.
60. W. Pollock, *So This Is Australia* (London, 1937), p.104.
61. Ibid., pp.104–5.
62. The *Bulletin*, Australia's largest selling weekly in the 1930s, regularly featured in their sporting section the comic strip adventures of Bert and Gert. Throughout the bodyline series of 1932–33 readers could amuse themselves with Gert's constant cricketing gaffes and non sequiturs and Bert's continued bemusement at them.
63. *Argus*, 11 July 1934, 6.
64. Ibid.
65. *SMH*, 21 Dec. 1934, 11.
66. *Argus*, 9 June 1934, 20.
67. *Wireless Weekly*, 15 June 1934, 35.
68. *Argus*, 21 Jan. 1933, 22.

6

'Ladies are Specially Invited': Women in the Culture of Australian Rules Football

ROB HESS

Within a few decades of the first recorded game of football in Melbourne in 1858, the sport had become a passionate, locally based, collective involvement which expressed values of great importance for its participants and its supporters. In fact, it was an organic interaction between particular communities and their football clubs during the long economic boom between 1860 and 1890 that underpinned not only the success of the code, but the structure of its first administrative body, the Victorian Football Association (VFA), which was established in 1877.[1] The boom also precipitated an increase in population which spawned a multitude of social, civic and sporting associations, and the growth of Melbourne as a city meant that new suburban clubs and societies built on membership fees formed across the metropolitan area, with the activities of football and cricket soon establishing themselves as the pre-eminent winter and summer pastimes respectively. Furthermore, it is evident that the hierarchies within these clubs were the natural expression of status and power distinctions within the community.[2] Concomitantly, according to Leonie Sandercock and Ian Turner, 'a close and often fanatical identification of the football clubs and their local communities' quickly developed and nowhere was this symbiotic relationship more evident than in the inner working class suburbs of the city.[3]

While such a relationship is almost axiomatic, it should be noted that a number of football club histories have strongly emphasized the links between club and community in describing the genesis of local teams. For instance, Gerard Dowling relates how the interests of civic authorities, local businessmen, and supporters converged at the annual meeting of the Hotham (later North Melbourne) club in 1877. After a short-lived amalgamation with the Albert Park team, 'These supporters hoped that the re-formed club would maintain the honour of the district in the football arena and come to share a leading position among the senior football clubs.'[4] In a similar manner, John Lack *et al.* also outline the way in which the local press became an agent through which the affairs of the community and the club coalesced. The intensely parochial *Independent* newspaper, for example, actively proclaimed the interests of supporters, sponsors and patrons and 'continually thrust the club into the limelight by reporting club business, matches, and players'. In this case, not only did the Footscray Football Club assume the role of progenitor and promoter of football in the municipality, but its adoption of the tri-colours worn by the successful Footscray Rowing Club confirmed its role in boosting local pride.[5] Other suburban newspapers also saw the value of featuring sport in their columns and by the early 1870s the local press regularly printed reports devoted to parochial football matters. As Robin Grow notes, football 'gossip' columns were also common, and players would often be referred to by nicknames, with feuds, romances and other 'in the know' information revealed for local consumption.[6] Even more significantly, in those suburbs such as Footscray and Collingwood, which were comparatively isolated and had underprivileged beginnings, community involvement and support, manifestly fostered by the local press, was essential if local teams were to participate in organized contests against wealthier and more powerful neighbours.[7]

Against this background of inter-suburban rivalry, it is not surprising that soon after the game originated teams and clubs became increasingly aware that a central body was needed to control the code. This was especially the case following the introduction of 'Challenge Cups' in the 1860s, and, according to newspaper sources, speculation that an organization would be formed to regulate competition between the growing number of clubs was rife among the sporting fraternity of Melbourne.[8] Throughout May 1877 the press reported on proceedings which proposed that an association be instituted, and in the same month a meeting of the senior metropolitan clubs was provided with a draft constitution and a set of by-laws. The VFA was to consist of one delegate (later increased to two) from each of the senior clubs, and country teams were to be represented by proxy, with other junior clubs to be taken 'under its sheltering wing'.[9] After just one year of operation, the VFA was applauded in the press for a range of much-needed initiatives, including the revision of the rules, a reduction in the number of disputes, the commencement of inter-colonial matches, improvements in on-field play, and the continued development of a number of grounds.[10]

The initial office bearers were largely men from the professions who had considerable expertise in administration and had strong links to other sporting bodies. This coterie remained in office for the crucial formative years of the VFA, providing not only a stable administration, but establishing the Association as a key sporting body in Victoria.[11] Given the rapid urban growth of Melbourne during this period, it is not surprising that the new Association soon expanded from its original base of senior clubs (Albert Park, Carlton, Hotham, Melbourne, East Melbourne and St Kilda) to include promising junior teams from suburbs such as Essendon, Fitzroy, Footscray, Williamstown, Richmond, Prahran and Port Melbourne. Geelong, one of the oldest clubs in the colony, regained its senior status in 1878 after a temporary slump in form, and Melbourne University, which had fielded a side since 1866, entered a team in the VFA in 1885.[12] Numerous football associations and leagues were formed throughout the colony, as the number of junior sides, church teams and country clubs continued to increase. Most of these organizations became affiliated to the VFA, which acted as adviser and arbiter of disputes and provided umpires for important matches. The Association also adopted an evangelical approach to the promotion of the game and its member clubs received every encouragement to play matches in provincial centres and other colonies.[13] When three Ballarat teams joined the Association in 1887, however, the senior competition had grown to such a large and unwieldy number that its unchecked expansion eventually led to a series of administrative crises and widespread discontent with the operations of the VFA.[14] It was these rumblings which eventually led to a major schism in the competition in 1896, resulting in the formation of the rival Victorian Football League (VFL), and it is within this structural framework that gender dimensions of the game during the late nineteenth and early twentieth century can be considered.

WOMEN AND FOOTBALL

In a football world dominated by men, perhaps the most remarkable feature of the Australian code is the consistently large number of females who support the game in various ways. At face value, this observation might seem extravagant, for the notion that Australian Rules football is exclusively a male domain, with no place or function for women has been regularly espoused in the media, helping to reinforce the strongly masculinist nature of the sport. After all, as Beverley Poynton and John Hartley confirm, it seems only 'natural' that it is men who play, coach, umpire, promote, administer, provide commentary on, and follow the game.[15] Even when the role of women as spectators is acknowledged, female football fans are often marginalized, for as one journalist has noted: 'Despite the presence of women, it's a male chauvinist show ... on Saturday afternoons. The atmosphere is heavily masculine. Women are mere appendages to the game, extras in an all-male saga, tolerated but not taken seriously.'[16]

Academic literature on the game has also added weight to such exclusive and narrow perspectives. Sandercock and Turner, for example, admit that in their book material on women was relegated to an appendix and they note apologetically that 'It somehow seemed out of place in the body of this work to say anything much about the role of women in Aussie Rules.'[17] Similarly, Robert Pascoe makes little mention of women's involvement in the history of the game and there are no specific entries in his index devoted to the role of females as fans.[18] Indeed, his somewhat vague observation that 'Women are far more numerous in a Rules crowd because the game belongs to an era of greater participation by women in the struggle between the haves and the have-nots' is only offered in the context of a discussion concerning cultural and sporting differences between Melbourne and Sydney, and no empirical evidence whatsoever is provided to support his view.[19] While perceptions of women as peripheral to the game support and reflect the traditional paradigm of hegemonic masculinity in sport, a more thorough historical survey of the development of football in Melbourne reveals more contradictory perspectives.[20]

New research has demonstrated that since the origins of the game in the late 1850s women have usually made up a greater proportion of the crowd at Australian Rules games than at any other football code in the world.[21] While the exact percentage of female spectators attending Australian Rules football has never been accurately measured over an extended period of time, estimates in various secondary sources give some indication of the phenomenon. For example, Mary Brady, in an Appendix to Sandercock and Turner's pioneering study, claims that women make up 'half the crowd each week'.[22] More recently, and more conservatively, Stephen Alomes has asserted that the fraction of female spectators in a typical football crowd is somewhere between one quarter and one third.[23] Whatever the precise percentage might be, the figure is certainly far above all other major football codes in the world, as demonstrated initially by the following brief discussion of soccer, and, later, by analysis of the two rugby codes.

At British soccer games, for example, female support has traditionally been very low, with 'Women ... now up to between 12 and 13% of fans'.[24] Allen Guttmann supports this observation by suggesting that soccer in Britain has never attracted large numbers of female fans due to its working-class origins, although occasionally young women accompanied their male friends to the terraces, and large numbers of female spectators attended some games in the late 1920s.[25] More recent scholarship confirms that soccer crowds have been predominantly male, but anecdotal evidence suggests that some of the leading clubs did attract female supporters in the past. Tony Mason, for instance, claims that in the 1880s middle class sections of the crowd were marked by the presence of the 'fair sex' and 'slim-waisted girls as fresh as daisies'.[26] As he explains, women were usually offered free admission to soccer games during this decade, and half price ladies' season tickets allowed them to sit in the reserved stands. With the advent of professionalism, however, such conventions were abolished. Mason is coy about the impact of these developments on overall female attendance, but he does suggest that as soccer crowds increased in size and watching the game became less comfortable in the 1890s, it was understandable that the proportion of women spectators would fall.[27] The aspect of comfort was important, for as Derek Birley points out, in some places soccer clubs provided footwarmers for those ladies who sat in the somewhat primitive grandstands.[28] Guttmann and W.J. Murray also cite evidence for isolated pockets of female support for soccer outside Britain, but these are exceptional cases that do not reflect long-term historical trends.[29] The problem is that while the phenomenon of females attending at Australian Rules football has frequently been commented upon, it has rarely been discussed critically, subjected to comparative analysis with other codes, or placed in a broader historical context.

In part, then, this essay aims specifically to address these problems. Moreover, given that the role of women in football has virtually been ignored in the literature of the game, a detailed discussion of the gender dimensions of Australian Rules football seems not only relevant, but appropriate. Such a discussion also provides a much needed historical context for more recent contemporary analyses of women and football that have been expressed in public forums by academics such as Margaret Lindley, a self-confessed football fanatic.[30] At such events, the subject matter has often been trivialized and important debates have, in the end, been reduced to a discussion of the delights of male bodies in tight shorts.[31] To guard against this possibility, a variety of sources, including photographs, poetry, illustrations, annual reports and newspaper accounts has been analysed, so that a greater appreciation of the role and influence of women in football can be gained. While this essay deals largely with various categories of women as spectators, the neglected involvement of women as auxiliaries and players is also highlighted as an area requiring more detailed research.

By way of introduction, it should be also be explained that although the typology of female fans presented below does have a loose chronological structure, the categorizations are largely used as an artificial organizing tool rather than as a rigid framework limited to discrete periods of time. While the categories of female spectators may at first glance appear to be reductive, in the absence of any substantial analysis of the issue by football historians they serve as a useful starting point for further discussion.[32] As other sports historians have noted, an understanding of crowd behaviour in any sport is usually difficult given the often transitory and scarce resources available, and this study of female Australian Rules football spectators is no exception.

WOMEN AS PASSIVE ONLOOKERS

In July 1859, less than 12 months after the first recorded game of football in Melbourne, the *Herald* reported that 'a large contingent of the fair sex' were in a crowd of 2,000 people who had gathered on a Saturday afternoon to watch a match of the fledgling code.[33] A few years later, in September 1866, not long after a meeting of delegates had adopted the official 'Victorian Rules' of the code, the Melbourne journal, *Bell's Life*, noted in the report of a match that a 'numerous assemblage of spectators (including many of the fair sex) honoured the game by their presence'.[34] During this period the game was played on unfenced grounds, and there were often no clear demarcations of the playing field. Few facilities were provided for spectators or participants, and observers of the game were inclined to creep over the arbitrary boundary line during matches, often interfering with the movements of the players. Some spectators even preferred to watch matches from the middle of the playing arena, despite the dangers involved.[35]

As Grow notes, 'By the end of the 1860s women were not only attending in large numbers but were joining the men in encroaching on the playing field.'[36] But it was the type of descriptive phrases noted above that characterized the early accounts of women at the football: they were the fair sex, they honoured the game by their presence and they tended to be middle- and upper-class women who helped to give the game status and prestige just by their attendance, which was usually fairly passive in nature. As noted, football games were played in open parkland, so some spectators, including women, were perhaps just passers-by, attracted by the shouts of the crowd. There were no dressing rooms in these areas of public domain, so players would use nearby pubs and hotels for changing purposes.[37] It should be recognized that Victorian football, like many other codes at this time, was initially a game for the participants rather than the spectators. However, although many of the early games of Victorian Rules in Melbourne were initially played on an *ad hoc* basis in the parks and gardens of that city, it was not long before the distinctive code attracted such large crowds that a move to enclosed cricket grounds was inevitable.[38]

In terms of other codes of football in Australia during this period, it is important to note that the history of rugby in this country does provide something of a contrast to the development of football in Melbourne. For even from its earliest years the rugby code in Sydney exhibited a much more exclusivist ethic, both in terms of spectators and participants.[39] Indeed, according to John Nauright and Timothy Chandler, rugby union in general has always been a highly gendered activity. In their strident view, it is a sport controlled by males 'that denigrates females, is underpinned by female domestic service and child-minding and promotes violence against "others" particularly against females'.[40] This overtly hostile attitude to women was clearly not a feature of the Victorian game and although women did attend rugby matches in Australia and other countries, it seems that their role and significance in the game never matched the welcome acceptance accorded to females spectators at football games in the southern states of Australia, particularly in the city of Melbourne.

In this context, it is also worth acknowledging that in Australia (noting that there was a bifurcation of the code in 1907), Rugby League failed to attract female spectators and in Sydney, according to Murray Phillips, 'relatively few women were present at games', helping to confirm the masculine hegemony of the new professional code.[41] The role of women as auxiliaries in Australian Rules football, as distinct from spectators, is later contrasted with the rugby codes, but to conclude this section it is clear that something about the nature of the Australian game, as well as the social and cultural context in which the code developed, made the sport particularly open to female involvement and support. A number of these distinctive elements are explored in the remaining categories of the typology.

WOMEN AS VOYEURS

A precise explanation as to why the game should be so attractive to female supporters seems elusive. Although the sexual attraction of athletic men in tight shorts should be rejected as too simplistic an exegesis of the issue, it must be acknowledged that this notion is supported by some historical evidence. In 1873 the *Australasian* published a poem extolling the athleticism of the players, the opening lines of which read as follows:

> Around the boundaries hundreds of spectators stand,
> The scene presented to us is strikingly beautiful and grand,
> Our men are as tough as trees with deeply earthed roots
> And the ladies quite mutually pronounced them really
> 'Killing' in their new knickerbocker suits.[42]

In this context, it ought to be noted that the very early uniforms covered up the bodies of the participants in a fairly modest way. By 1873, however, the streamlined knickerbocker suit, with lace up breeches down to the knee and sometimes bare arms, exposed flesh in the same daring fashion that tight-fitting shorts are viewed today. Towards the end of the nineteenth century, as Jennifer Pullman points out, the presentation of sportsmen in press photography and art also reflected and contributed to the dominant masculine culture of the time.[43] Many non-action photographs of footballers, for example, emphasized the attractiveness of their knickerbocker suits, while the exposed flesh of bare arms was clearly evident.[44] Sport, and particularly football, during the sexually repressive reign of Queen Victoria, thus enabled women to appreciate male bodies in a socially acceptable way, hence the recognition by the poet that women at the football were admiring the participants for the way they looked as well as the way they might play the game.

Other evidence also indicates that particular players held voyeuristic appeal for female fans. Early in the new century the *Argus* conducted a contest to determine the most popular player in the VFA. Brunswick captain 'Dookie' McKenzie easily won the poll with 17,884 votes, and at one game during the 1909 season the newspaper had noted that 'a great many lady supporters of Brunswick ... were loud in their cheers for McKenzie', causing one supporter to break into song during the match.[45] Whether the approbation was for his clever play or his athleticism is not clear, but it is obvious that women took a special interest in the performance of League and Association footballers, and were not afraid to admire and show their appreciation of them in a public manner.

WOMEN AS SOCIALITES

But neither the players nor the game itself were necessarily the focus of attention by female spectators. By time the Victorian Football Association had been formed, attendance at matches reflected not only the public's growing confidence in the status of the competition, but the importance of the social occasion. By the early 1870s it had become fashionable for women to 'promenade' at the football on Saturday afternoons. The intent of the outing was not meant solely for the display of female fashions, for football matches also offered women the opportunity to meet young men in 'an approved social setting'.[46] In such circumstances, the sporting spectacle seemed less important than the social occasion, a fact that was clearly depicted in a sketch that appeared on the front page of the *Australasian Sketcher* in July 1877. In this instance the entire front page is devoted to a detailed illustration of a section of the crowd on their way to a football game. Several extremely well-dressed women in long skirts are prominent in the scene, along with male companions in top hats and children of both sexes. As the caption explains, 'The winter fashions displayed by ladies always find their full exemplification here.'[47] It is only on close inspection that one notices the actual game in progress *behind* the throng of spectators, with the ball just visible above the heads of the crowd. In the artist's view, therefore, spectators had now become more worthy of attention than the game itself.

The social nature of matches is also exemplified in an illustration depicting the first football game under lights at the Melbourne Cricket

Ground in August, 1879. More than ten thousand spectators were in attendance, and from the artist's perspective, a good proportion of those watching 'the novel entertainment' were women and children. Adding to the attraction were tug-of-war contests at the half-time interval, and the presence of the Engineer and Collingwood Rifles' bands, who 'played a varied selection of popular music, and contributed greatly to the success of the evening'.[48]

Women, more so than men, were often viewed by the press as more interested in the social aspects surrounding the game than the athletic nature of the contest itself. The interest in who attended and what they wearing at the football also reflected the growth of Melbourne's social scene, and football, as the town's major winter sport, was now firmly part of this experience. In this context, it is worthwhile to note that Michael Oriard makes some similar observations about the early involvement of women in American college football prior to the turn of the century. As he says, 'Women played a crucial part in football-as-social-event' and observations on their presence was an important part of the narrative of the game constructed by the press.[49] Descriptions of their dress and behaviour, for instance, imply much about female cultural power, about standards of female decorum and about gender relations. As Oriard indicates, though, 'The writer's conscious intentions were most likely simpler: by commenting on women's presence at the game he confirmed for readers that watching football was a suitable pastime for both sexes.'[50]

To carry the comparisons further, a few decades later, according to Andrew Doyle, the role of women in American football, particularly in the southern states, had altered considerably. It had become the custom for small numbers of female supporters, including mothers of the players, to be feted by the team, leading parades in colourfully decorated horse-drawn carriages and being presented as important 'sponsors' during matches of special significance. For Doyle, these activities seemed to have had a strong medieval overtone, harking back to an age of chivalry and pageantry, where young men vied on the 'field of honour' for the attention and affection of young women.[51] Whilst such rituals never became part of the Australian football experience, the essential point remains, though, that newspaper accounts of the game which specifically commented on the presence of women helped to soften the masculine nature of the narrative of the game, and by so doing challenged the perceived male hegemony of the code itself, albeit unwittingly.

WOMEN AS BARRACKERS

In a somewhat lighthearted vein, a report on Melbourne's winter sports, by 'an Outsider', noted that:

> So deep is the interest taken in the struggle of the respective clubs by the ladies of Melbourne and Carlton that it is not difficult to tell from the expression of their countenance which side is winning. Five goals to one, and the damsels of Carlton fairly bristled with smiles, while, on the other hand, the brows of the Melbourne ladies were wreathed with frowns.[52]

Comments such as these reflect the view that women did not simply attend matches as ornamental figures, socialites or voyeurs, but as interested, passionate observers of the game, with knowledge of how the code was played and an interest in the fortunes of particular teams. Perhaps in some ways they were beginning to adopt and support the more tribal culture of their male family members. As June Senyard reveals in her study of sport and community in Fitzroy, even though wives might not attend games with their husbands, some oral evidence indicates that fathers and daughters would travel to nearby home games together. Family ties to a team and a suburb were thus an important factor in the formation of allegiances and underpinned the widespread practice of barracking at Australian Rules football.[53]

There is also other anecdotal evidence that women of all classes were beginning to watch the game in large numbers during this period. Richard Stremski illustrates quite well how the involvement and interest of female spectators at a club level is reflected in the sale of season tickets during this period. According to his evidence, drawn from club records, it is reasonable to assume that women attended matches at Collingwood's home ground, Victoria Park, in numbers at least proportionate to their purchase of season tickets. He claims that one-eighth of season tickets in 1893 were held by women, and this percentage eventually peaked at almost one-quarter in 1900, declining to one-sixth by the First World War.[54] Stremski also astutely points out that since season tickets for women were available at half price from 1892 to 1922, few women would have bothered to become members, since the requirement for membership was the purchase of a full price season ticket.[55]

In the context of women as active supporters, one of the more infamous examples of the antics and language of female barrackers occurred at a match between North Melbourne and Collingwood in July 1896. Although the general standard of umpiring was usually a matter of concern to newspaper commentators, the response of spectators to poor umpiring was also highlighted by the press on this occasion. In this particular game, the behaviour of female spectators came under special scrutiny and, in contrast to the observations of the *Australasian Sketcher*, noted above, it seems that working-class women were also capable of 'active support'. The extensive coverage of incidents arising from the match by the *Melbourne Punch* is especially noteworthy, for it provides us with not only an artist's illustration of the fracas at the end of the game, but also with examples of the type of language used by female spectators.[56]

Commenting on the same match, a writer from the *Argus* noted that:

> The woman 'barracker', indeed, has become one the most objectionable of football surroundings. On some grounds they actually spit in the faces of players as they come to the dressing-rooms, or wreak their spite much more maliciously with long hat pins. In the heights of this melee some of the women screamed with fear. Others screamed 'Kill him'. One of these gentle maidens at the close of the struggle remarked regretfully that it was a pity they 'let off' the umpire in the Geelong match, as they should have killed him. Yet these women consider themselves respectable, and they 'support' football, which is *consequently* in a serious decline.[57] [emphasis added]

Thus female spectators were seen in some quarters as having a deleterious effect on the tone of football matches. They took their barracking too seriously, and were, as a consequence, blamed for at least some of the social ills surrounding the game in Melbourne. Significantly for the arguments developed in this essay, it is clear from this instance that female spectators were not peripheral to the game and their actions and attitudes are worthy of comment in the press. Importantly, it should also be noted that appropriate social behaviour in a more general sense was a matter of considerable debate in the metropolitan press at this time and accusations of 'street rowdyism' were not only directed at young men, but the behaviour of young women was also criticized.[58]

WOMEN AS CIVILIZERS

As indicated previously, in the years following the formation of the VFA in 1877 and the VFL in 1897, the administration of the game became more formalized and the promotion of Australian Rules became almost evangelistic in its intensity. With this institutionalization of the game came a strong desire to promote the virtues of the indigenous code, and both the Association and the League became concerned with how the on-field behaviour of players was perceived by the public. At the heart of this not altogether altruistic concern was the sometimes violent nature of the game, a topic that increasingly occupied the press at the turn of the century.

According to Geoffrey Blainey, in the early years of the code most footballers displayed goodwill as well as ruggedness in their play. Goodwill was especially needed to support all the unwritten rules of the game, because in the early period there were only a dozen or so written rules.[59] Interpretation of the rules and what was regarded as fair play was therefore largely a tacit agreement between players, umpires and administrators, with the press acting as a barometer for their middle-class readers and supporters of the game. As violence crept more and more into football, it was therefore natural that the press should lead the debate on the changing nature of the game. As in modern-day football, speeding up the code was the usual solution proposed, since it would stop packs forming and assist the flow of the game. But there were also calls for stiffer penalties for players found guilty of deliberate offences, since violent acts were considered to be not only unfair but unmanly. Early in the twentieth century, there were concerns that a number of spectators were turning to other sports and activities that were less violent in nature, and it was with a sense of relief that 'Markwell' of the *Australasian* noted an increase in football crowds for the 1907 season, since 'it indicates that the great body of the public have not permitted their love for the game to be detrimentally influenced by the few rough exhibitions that were presented prior to last Saturday week'. Moreover, he went on to describe recent matches as encounters with 'everything that could be desired, clean, clever and manly'.[60]

Such concerns reflect much broader developments in terms of how men and women viewed and understood their involvement in sport at the turn of the century. In this context, the observations of Michael Messner are especially important, for he claims that the decades from the 1890s through to the 1920s were the first of two great periods of crisis for masculine values in Western society. Industrial capitalism, according to Messner, 'both bolstered and undermined traditional forms of male domination', and changes in work and family relations, along with the growth of urban societies and the closing of the frontier, all contributed to a shift in traditional male roles.[61] Thus, 'Many men compensated with a defensive insecurity that manifested itself in increased preoccupation with physicality and toughness, warfare, and even the creation of new organizations such as the Boy Scouts of America as a separate cultural sphere of life where 'true manliness' could be instilled in boys by men.'[62] In this context, organized sports (such as football) helped to provide men with a psychological and sometimes physical separation from what was widely perceived by the press as the 'feminization of society', while also allowing them to display and observe supposed superior masculine traits such as courage, loyalty and bravery. Sport became, in effect, an anodyne to the social and moral problems created by urbanization.[63]

Other historians have also commented more specifically on the role of football in helping to redefine American masculinity at the turn of the century. For example, Benjamin Rader suggests that football as played in the colleges of North America contributed to a new, more aggressively masculine image among young males.[64] Steven Pope, on the other hand, makes the more expansive claim that 'football touched a deep, vital core within the national soul', for not only was the tradition of staging important football games on national holidays (such as Thanksgiving Day) established, but in his view the game was built around a potent combination of 'aggressiveness, territoriality and a fluid interplay between community and individualism'.[65]

Situated against these broader themes, and given that this was also a period characterized by the push for female suffrage, it is not surprising that the debate about the role of women in society, their relationship with men, and their responses to aggressive on-field behaviour on the sporting field should be debated at length in the press. One of the best case studies to illustrate the discourse over these issues in an Australian context is the international tour of the Canadian lacrosse team. The example is also an especially poignant one, for sports historians have paid little attention to the circumstances and the ramifications of this significant sporting exchange.

Invited to tour in 1907 by the South Australian Cricket Association, and funded by a range of guarantors including a number of state lacrosse associations, this was the first visit of an international lacrosse team to Australia and a hectic schedule of 18 matches across four states in 63 days was organized.[66] Largely a sport for the middle and upper classes and promoted by private schools, the potential of the game to draw crowds was recognized by the administrators of the tour, and it was 'Markwell' who graciously announced that 'In deference to the local Lacrosse Association, leaguers have suspended premiership games for the afternoon, and their doing so is regarded as a sportsmanlike and generous action.'[67] Given that the sport of lacrosse self-importantly saw itself as a potential rival to Australian Rules football for a number of years prior to the tour, the co-operation of the VFL on this matter was surprising.[68] Thus, whatever the motive for suspending a round of matches, the Melbourne Cricket Ground (MCG) was left vacant for the first lacrosse 'Test' match between Canada and Australia. A crowd of between fourteen and sixteen thousand witnessed the game, which, to everyone's surprise, was won by Australia with a scoreline of 5–3.[69] By the time the third 'Test' was to be played, again at the MCG, the Canadians had levelled the series with a win in Adelaide, and interest in the deciding game of the series was high.

What is remarkable, though, is the claim by 'Left Attack', the writer of lacrosse notes for the *Australasian*, that women were giving up their patronage of Australian Rules football in favour of the Canadian game. On the eve of the third 'Test', in comments heavily laden with class overtones, he stated that:

> Twenty years ago ladies were conspicuous at football games; they are still conspicuous, but it is by their absence. Twenty years ago all Melbourne was stirred by a football match; now it is only the crowd that is moved. Then ladies followed football because they knew the players and liked the game; now they shun it on account of the absence of their friends and of the brutality imported into it ... Lacrosse is, as Sir John Madden [Lieutenant-Governor of Victoria], puts it, 'a game for thoroughbreds', and the players are of that type which makes for manly sport.[70]

The implications of such assertions could not go unchallenged by the boosters of football, and 'Markwell' was quick to enter the debate with his comments on the round of football for the following week:

> The attendances were unusually good, and included the customary percentage of ladies, whose presence and bright, attractive costumes added charm and picturesqueness to the proceedings. I mention the presence of the fair sex, not because it is other than every year increasingly common, but in order to counteract any

wrong impression that may have been created by strictures that have recently appeared concerning the game, its players, and its patrons. As a rule, the club reserves at football matches, from week to week, accommodate far more women than men; and this year in the outer portions of the grounds as well the increase in the attendance of the gentler sex is undeniable.[71]

In the light of such debates, then, it may be possible to make a case that the 'battle' over which sports were more attractive for female spectators had important implications for the future of football. After all, if football crowds consisted of such a large percentage of female spectators, the continued attendance of women was quite rightly a matter of concern for the boosters of the game, whether they were press commentators or football administrators. Thus, during the early years of the twentieth century, the push for a less violent code owed at least something to the large presence of women at games. This is clearly evidenced by the middle-class press (exemplified by 'Markwell' of the *Australasian*) which was often at pains to assert that women as spectators had a positive and beneficial effect on the overall tone of the game.

The significant presence and potential influence of women at Australian Rules football games is reflected in a number of photographs and illustrations from the period, and although more research needs to be done on the spatial dynamics of football spectatorship, a number of observations can be made in this regard.[72] Firstly, large groups of women, of various ages, sat together in the stands at both League and Association football games.[73] Moreover, seating around the perimeter of grounds was also usually occupied by women and children.[74] From press commentary of the period, it is clear that because women were seated in such a conspicuous manner, their behaviour was scrutinized to a much greater extent than it would have been if they were dispersed throughout the crowd. 'Phil Garlick', for example, writer of a 'Football Gossip' column for the *Melbourne Punch*, claimed that grandstands were regarded as places to stow the 'parrots', where women could 'talk to their hearts content'. 'The mere male,' he said, 'prefers to be where he can smoke his clay, and emphasize his ideas about the umpire, and generally, to talk in a strain that the gentle Annies wouldn't approve of.'[75]

Stremski's investigation of the Collingwood Football Club also lends support to such attitudes, for he suggests that women at Victoria Park were encouraged to sit together in the stands in order to segregate them from the activities and the domain of male supporters.[76] Grow also claims that such segregation occasionally created animosity between male and female members as the latter group sometimes enjoyed special privileges and more comfortable seating despite their discounted tickets.[77] The relationship between enclosed, or segregated spaces, such as special stands or designated seating areas, and the creation and maintenance of gendered space is clearly a link that has relevance in this context, but there have been no studies of the spatial arrangements or crowd dynamics of football spectators in Australia.[78] It seems clear, however, that there was a belief during this period that the presence of women (and perhaps young children) at most sporting events was conducive to public decorum. Women thus acted as civilizing agents, keeping the vulgarity and asperity of both players and male spectators to socially acceptable levels. It was for this reason, as Michael Smith explains in another sporting context, that 'organizers often permitted women to watch sporting events at a reduced or lower fee'.[79]

Closer to the boundary line and the action on the field, women seated around the perimeter of the oval who were intent on barracking in a partisan manner also exerted another form of influence by their proximity to the game. 'Clio', writer of a regular 'Ladies' Letter' in *Punch*, described a match played in pouring rain where 'the girl-barrackers did not even put up their umbrellas, but stoically let the drizzle sodden their hats and wet their dresses'. Apparently the umpire could not please the Essendon lady members and when he gave a Carlton player a free kick near the Essendon goal, 'one of them leaned over the fence, and in the tense silence said: "You are getting money under false pretences. You don't know the game any more than a baby in arms."' And according to 'Clio', 'the umpire palpably winced'.[80]

While it may be possible to categorize female spectators on the basis of their behaviour and their seating arrangements, it should also be noted that it was certainly acceptable for different social groups of women to be present at football games, with female gossip columnists gleefully describing the antics and dress of both tittering 'shop-girls' and vice-regal patrons.[81] 'Clio', in trying to explain the attractiveness of football for female barrackers, suggested that it had something to do with 'the growth of sportiness in women'. As she said, 'The girl who plays hockey and cricket and a host of other violent games is naturally deeply interested in the violent physical exercises of men.'[82] But 'Clio' was also aware that women were particularly attracted as spectators to matches played by the University football team, first admitted to the VFL in 1908. At pains to point out that all the players were amateurs, 'Clio' believed:

> There is no doubt, as far as the onlookers are concerned, [that] the University team has helped to raise the tone of the game. The very nicest people, who would have scornfully hurled aside the mere suggestion that they would ever look at a football match, are delighted to put on swell costumes and expensive furs and the latest hats, and motor or drive or even tram it to a distant suburb to see University play Richmond or some equally un-aesthetic team.[83]

If press reports and photographic material are any guide, there is clear evidence that the female spectators attending football games, particularly after the formation of the League, exercised an important influence, not only on the behaviour of other sections of the crowd, but also on the development of the game itself. To suggest as Anne Summers does in her feminist history of Australia, that women who watch football are seemingly motivated by less complex notions than male spectators underplays the role that women have had in seemingly masculine sports.[84] While it is acknowledged that newspaper accounts of women's behaviour at the football were mostly written and contextualized by male sports writers, this only makes the commentaries offered by female columnists such as 'Clio' all the more enlightening.

A strong contrast can also be drawn here with the lack of evidence for female involvement in the two rugby codes. Andrew Moore, for instance, specifically comments on 'the absence of female faces in the surviving photographs of club social events' when writing about 'the emergence of the working *man's* code' (emphasis in original) in North Sydney at the turn of the century.[85] Brett Hutchins, although concerned with more contemporary developments in rugby league, refers to the 'hyper-masculinity' of the rugby code and describes how threats to the firmly entrenched gender order of the sport have traditionally been resisted by media institutions dominated by masculine values and ideals.[86] Even though concessions were initially offered to female spectators at both rugby codes, the very low proportion of women attending games, and the lack of commentary by the press on the issue, bears further witness to the unique level of female support for Australian Rules football.

WOMEN AS AUXILIARIES

With the exception of a recent book which seeks to acknowledge the 'vital' role women play in contemporary football settings, it is clear from the above discussion that, by and large, the function and significance of women as spectators at Australian Rules football has been downplayed in almost all of the secondary literature on the game.[87] However, there are other dimensions of the female experience of the game which need to be explored, since women were and are more than 'passive onlookers', 'voyeurs', 'socialites', 'barrackers' or 'civilizers'. Women are manifestly more than just one element of the crowd that goes to watch the Australian code.

Indeed, if sociologists R.W. Connell and T.H. Irving are correct in their claim that women in society act as a form of social cement, binding and holding organizations and sporting institutions together with their informal networks of co-operation, practical support and tacit encouragement of male activities, then the institution of Australian Rules football would appear to be an exemplar of their theory.[88] From the evidence it is clear that a number of cultural assumptions concerning gender roles and the marginalization of women in sport are broken down in the case of the Australian code where the percentage of female spectators is so high, but it is still true that the playing and watching of most male physical activities depends implicitly upon the co-operation of women. Contemporary observations of women's role in football, like those concerned with women as spectators, have often lacked detailed historical context, and therefore it is important that the following discussion of the extent of female involvement as football auxiliaries relies on a close examination of the primary source material.[89]

All of the above discussion serves as essential background to other aspects of women's involvement in Victorian football clubs at the turn of the century. For given the widespread participation of women as spectators, it seems obvious that in an inclusive code such as Australian Rules football, that the involvement of females would be extended to include active participation as club members and auxiliaries. The remainder of this essay examines this contention in the light of selected newspaper accounts and annual reports from two Victorian Football League clubs, notably the Collingwood Football Club and the Fitzroy Football Club. Further research may indicate whether the experiences of women at other clubs were different or similar to these two essentially working class sporting organizations.

Stremski has demonstrated clear links between the Collingwood Football Club and the local community, aspects of which were present in all VFL and VFA clubs and arose from the social and cultural milieux in which the game developed.[90] Nearly all clubs were based upon and identified with a distinct local community, demonstrating what John Bale and others have identified in a more general way as topophilia, literally a 'love of place'. As John Bale explains, 'there are characteristics of sports landscapes which people find attractive, create fond memories, or provide a sense of place', and such sources of topophilia, including visual, aural, olfactory and tactile senses, along with nostalgia and myth, help to foster and sustain communities, and evokes a sense of pride in ownership for members of particular groups.[91] In the case of Collingwood, according to Stremski, the roots of its football fanaticism were, paradoxically, traceable to the low esteem of the municipality. The development of Victoria Park as a sports oval and the creation of the club in 1892 to 'carry the banner of the city in battle against other suburbs' were thus the outcome of a belated, but vigorous, civic pride.[92] As Leon Mann and Philip Pearce postulate in a more general sense, the suburban team functions not only as an institution forming an integral part of the community's social structure, but it can allow local residents to regard their suburb as a legitimate community – 'a place of substance'. Community spirit is thus enhanced by team supporters who develop a kind of 'folk culture', with commercial interests and regional newspapers combining to generate and encourage feelings of pride in the suburb and the individual through sports related news, promotions and advertising.[93]

Understandably, then, although the Collingwood Football Club only had moderate on-field success in its first season in the VFA, the Secretary, Edwin Wilson, was at pains to point out in the first annual report that upgrading of the facilities of Victoria Park for players and spectators was high on the list of priorities. Social functions to offset some of the costs incurred were thus an integral part of the club's activities, and, in the context of this chapter, it is noteworthy that a Mrs Pryde was specifically mentioned as one of nine 'Grand Stand Debenture Holders', and her further donation of several pounds was listed in the 'Statement of Receipts and Expenditures'.[94] Significantly, although both the 1892 and 1893 annual reports were addressed 'To The

Members – Gentlemen – ...', J. Tobin, now the new Secretary of the club, took the trouble to address the 1894 annual report 'To The Members – Ladies and Gentlemen – ...'.[95] The Treasurer, E. Murphy, also astutely recognized the increasing importance of women to the club when, for the first time, a breakdown of membership figures was provided, revealing that 47 tickets for 'ladies' had been sold in 1894. The 'Statement of Receipts and Expenditure' also revealed that a Mrs Russell and a Mrs Coates had joined Mrs Pryde in making financial donations to the club. At a social level, it was also noted that the Mayoress, Mrs Gahan, had formally unveiled the clock which adorned the front of the new grand stand.[96]

The increasingly important role of the club in the community, and the public acceptance of the role of women at the club, was specifically acknowledged in the invitation attached to members in the annual report for 1895. The annual meeting was to be held at the Town Hall and as the invitation records: 'An Excellent Programme under the management of Mr. W. G. Barker will be rendered during the evening. Ladies are specially invited to attend. The Balcony ... will be reserved for Ladies, or Ladies accompanied by Gentlemen till 8 pm.'[97] The evidence thus indicates that women not only supported the club in a social sense, attending club functions with their male counterparts, but as A. Cross, the Chairman of the Committee, indicated in his report, donations had increased substantially and 'Our heartiest thanks are due to these Ladies and Gentlemen for their continued liberality'. Six women, both married and single, were specifically listed as making financial donations to the club, and ladies' ticketholders had more than doubled in number to 116. Vice-regal patronage also reflected the growing success and confidence of the club, and the attendance of John Madden, the Lieutenant-Governor, Lady Madden and their daughter at a fundraising concert was noted as one of the highlights of the 1895 season.[98]

The following year, a successful season for the club, finally saw '"the Magpie" flapping his wings triumphantly on the top of the Premiership Tree', and the 1896 annual report claimed that the club's membership of 797 was 'the largest of any football club in Australia'. Female ticketholders now stood at 187, an increase of more than 33 per cent on the previous season, and five women were again mentioned in the list of donors, with Mrs H. Pryde especially acknowledged for providing 'sumptuous banquets' for the players.[99]

The involvement of females in the club continued in 1897 and the annual report for that season highlights for the first time the work of the Ladies' Committee, which was chaired by the Mayoress, Mrs Cody. Their principal fundraising effort for the year was the 'Fancy Fair', and more than 100 women were engaged in the successful organization of this event. Not only did the fair raise the enormous sum of £415, used to pay off part of the outstanding debt on the grand stand, but the Committee presented to each lady 'a handsome and appropriate card expressive of the deep obligation they felt as well as a Membership Ticket for the season'. In addition to these 115 complimentary tickets, there were also 151 'Ladies' tickets' sold, even though membership figures for the year only showed a slight increase from the previous season.[100]

In 1898 the tradition of 'specially' inviting women to the annual meeting continued, and the annual report also listed six women who had made financial donations to the club.[101] This pattern continued for the next few seasons, with a number of women and 'Lady Members' also listed as donating prizes as awards for players. For instance, Mrs Jackson offered a gold medal to the most consistent player of the season, and a tea and coffee service was presented by the ladies to the captain of the team, Dick Condon, 'in recognition of his brilliant play and success in handling the team'.[102]

Although a similar volume of detailed information is not available from other Victorian football clubs for exactly the same period, it is clear in some anecdotal evidence that the auxiliary support of women was appreciated and acknowledged. At the Fitzroy Football Club, for instance, selected annual reports between 1907 and 1914 routinely address both 'Ladies and Gentlemen', specifically acknowledge by name the financial contributions and donations of female members (Miss McInerney, Miss Rowan, Mrs O'Hagan, Miss Roberts, and so on), and outline details of social functions such as picnics and dances where 'sumptuous' catering was usually provided, with players and 'lady friends' mixing freely. Wives of officials also had the honour of unfurling premiership pennants, and a number of female hoteliers were listed as ticket agents for the club.[103] In this context, it is therefore revealing to note that comparable annual reports from clubs playing the rugby union code in Sydney at this time display an exclusive masculine bias. The 1903 annual report of the Eastern Suburbs District Football Club, for example, makes no reference to any females or even mixed social events, while the report itself is addressed to 'Gentlemen' only, a marked contrast to the inclusive welcome extended to 'Ladies and Gentlemen' who were obviously in attendance at football club meetings in Melbourne.[104]

WOMEN AS PLAYERS

Finally, the role of women as players should be mentioned, for as one contemporary female writer notes in despair, 'Attempts by girls or women to play the game have never been treated seriously. Those who have tried have been ridiculed by other women as well as men.'[105] To illustrate this sense of ongoing ridicule, the reference to 'a football match between teams composed of ladies' in a 1908 edition of the *Ballarat Courier* should be discussed. It listed both teams by surname, their uniform (Blue skirt and white blouse for the 'Single Ladies'; black skirt and white blouse for the 'Married Ladies') and announced that a match would take place that day at the carnival.[106] Since earlier references to games between women are scarce, if non-existent, it could be reasonably assumed that this was, in fact, one of the first female football games in the state of Victoria. However, the match report on the following day reveals that 'the said "ladies" were simply impersonations in the most pronounced back-block styles and colours, the married being represented by the members of Prout's Band and the single by the East Swimming Club'.[107] Moreover, 'their make-up, if not picturesque, was at least humorous, while their general deportment and eccentricities were consistently maintained'.[108] In other words, it was a match between men dressed up as women.

This sense of ridicule, that women would not, and should not, consider playing such a masculine game, of whatever football code, was also apparent in a British cartoon of two female rugby footballers which was published by the *Melbourne Punch* in 1899.[109] As Jennifer Hargreaves observes in a British context:

> Conventional femininity does not incorporate images of physical power and muscularity and female athletes who have such physiques have always stood the risk of being treated in a derogatory way. Women who play traditional male sports, such as cricket, football [soccer] and rugby, face the greatest criticism and exposure to ridicule.[110]

This is not to say that women were never involved in earlier forms of football in Britain, for there is clear evidence that females of various ages participated in Shrovetide and other village football games.[111] But it is clear that those women who played with the British Ladies' Football Club, for example, were not only subjected to heckling, but to censure by the press.[112] Founded in 1890, the club was keen to promote not only the sport of soccer for women, but dress reform as well. Wearing 'blue serge knickers of the divided skirt pattern and cardinal and pale-blue blouses respectively', the Ladies' Football team were often regarded as 'a spectacle for men to gawk at rather than a serious sporting activity'.[113] The Melbourne press also carried reports of their activities and a match in which female soccer players were mobbed and assaulted by spectators at a game in 1896 appeared in the *Herald*.[114] In 1902 soccer's governing body in England, the Football Association, specifically denounced games of soccer involving women and was strongly opposed to males playing against females in so-called exhibition matches.[115]

It was not until the years following the Great War that soccer for women gained a measure of popularity and respectability in England, largely due to new social attitudes and the influence of independent promoters and employers.[116] In 1920, a crowd of more than 50,000 spectators watched a match between two ladies' teams at Goodison Park, Everton, and when the Dick, Kerr's Ladies team (consisting of factory employees) played matches against men on tours of France and North America they were also watched by appreciative audiences. By 1926, however, enthusiasm for the women's game was on the wane and deliberate and continued opposition by the English Football Association prevented widespread involvement by female players.[117]

In Australia, one of the earliest references to females wanting to participate in football games as players is revealed in the school magazine of the Presbyterian Ladies' College. According to Ray Crawford, in 1876, the second year of the college, 'one girl was bold enough to suggest that a "football club be established" at the school because she had observed how much "fun, enjoyment and excitement" boys seem to have in that game'.[118] No record of the formation of such a club exists, but it seems obvious from the lack of evidence that any other similar attempts by women to involve themselves in the game as players were either short-lived or failed to gain the attention of the press. It was not until the 1920s that the involvement of female players in Australian Rules football gained any substantial exposure, although it is evident that even these early games were treated with a certain amount of ridicule and scepticism by male commentators.[119] As Nauright and others explain in different contexts, such negative attitudes by the press toward female athletes simply served to reinforce dominant hegemonic beliefs about the perceived role of women in early twentieth-century society as a whole.[120]

CONCLUSION

From the discussion outlined above, it is clear that the role of women and football in Melbourne must be seen as multi-faceted rather than one dimensional. In support of such a claim, this essay has provided evidence that women were involved in the game in a variety of ways during the late nineteenth and early twentieth centuries. Apart from their obvious presence as spectators, analysed within the framework of a typology, an examination of the role of women as auxiliaries, and possible early evidence for women as players, has also demonstrated the significant gender dimensions of what has traditionally been seen as a male-dominated game.

More particularly, if the case study drawn from press reports and records of the Collingwood Football Club is mirrored at other clubs, then it is manifest that women played an important role in community based football clubs in Melbourne at the turn of the century. Not only were females present in the crowd in large numbers, and sometimes accommodated in specially built facilities, but they were active in various capacities as club members. Far from being token members of the club, acting as adornments at social functions or premiership pennant unfurlings, the evidence indicates that individual women made regular and substantial financial donations to club coffers, joined with other like-minded women to organize large fundraising events, supplied valuable prizes for awards, and offered auxiliary services such as banquets and other forms of catering. Moreover, they were 'specially invited' to annual meetings and their presence at such events was specifically acknowledged by the officials of the club. Although not formally accorded positions of power or status, or rarely bestowed with honours such as life membership, it seems clear that females in VFL and VFA clubs played an integral part in the nexus between community and club during this period.

What strengthens this claim, and therefore makes Australian Rules football unique, is that the role of women in other football codes has been much more exclusivist. On this basis, then, it is possible that aficionados of the indigenous game may, in fact, take the role and presence of women in Australian Rules football for granted, because their involvement has, in the main, been encouraged and valued over a long period of time. Supporters, players and administrators of other codes who have little desire for, and appreciation of, the potential role of women in the game or the club structure, will therefore, at best, be envious, or at worst, have little understanding of one of the most distinguishing features of the Australian code of football.

NOTES

1. R. Pascoe, *The Winter Game: The Complete History of Australian Football* (Melbourne, 1995), pp.55–56.
2. Ibid., pp.56 and 59. See also R. Grow, 'From Gum Trees to Goalposts, 1858–1876', in R. Hess and R. Stewart (eds.), *More Than a Game: An Unauthorised History of Australian Rules Football* (Carlton, 1998), p.28.
3. L. Sandercock and I. Turner, *Up Where, Cazaly? The Great Australian Game* (London, 1981), p.40. See also Grow, 'From Gum Trees', pp.33–4.
4. Gerard Dowling, *The North Story*, Revised Edition (Sydney, 1997), p.31.
5. John Lack *et al.*, *A History of the Footscray Football Club: Unleashed* (Footscray, 1996), pp.11–12. In Great Britain, the *Sportsman*, published in March 1876, claimed to be the world's first daily sporting newspaper, although according to Mason, 'Few working class people could afford a regular daily paper before the first World War.' Tony Mason, '"All the Winners and the Half Times …"', *The Sports Historian*, 13 (May 1993), 4–5.
6. R. Grow, 'Nineteenth Century Football and the Melbourne Press', *Sporting Traditions*, 3, 1 (Nov. 1986), 25.
7. Maggie Indian, 'Formalisation of Urban Leisure: Melbourne 1880–1900', in R. Cashman and M. McKernan (eds.), *Sport: Money, Morality and the Media* (Kensington, 1981), p.277. Footscray and Collingwood were both situated on flat land subject to flooding, making their locations initially suitable only for noxious trades. See G. Davison, *The Rise and Fall of Marvellous Melbourne* (Carlton, 1978), p.146. For more specific detail on the origins of the Footscray Football Club, and the role of civic figures in fostering community involvement, see J. Lack (ed.), *Charlie Lovett's Footscray* (Footscray, 1993).
8. Grow, 'From Gum Trees', pp.23–5.
9. R. Grow, 'The Victorian Football Association in Control', in Hess and Stewart (eds.), *More Than a Game*, p.45. Teams based on occupational groupings, such as Melbourne Police, Hobson's Bay Railway and Port Phillip Stevedores, had limited access to grounds and were usually short-lived. None of these teams entered Association ranks. R. Hess, 'A Sport in Crisis: Melbourne Society and the 1896 Football Conspiracy' (unpublished Honours thesis, Monash University, 1981), 35.
10. *Australasian*, 13 Oct. 1877, cited in Grow, 'The Victorian Football Association', 45–6.
11. Ibid., 46.
12. The literature is somewhat confusing on the early make-up of the VFA. The uncertainty appears to stem from disagreements concerning what constituted 'senior' status. In 1896 the secretary of the VFA, Thomas Marshall, reminiscing on the origins of the game, claimed that there were 11 foundation clubs in the Association, namely Albert Park, Ballarat, Barwon, Castlemaine, Carlton, Geelong, Hotham, Melbourne, St Kilda, Inglewood, and Rochester. *Herald*, 9 May 1896, 3.
13. Grow, 'The Victorian Football Association', 46.
14. Marc Fiddian, *The Blue Boys: A History of the Prahran Football Club* (Armadalel, 1986),

pp.7–8.

15. B. Poynton and J. Hartley, 'Male-Gazing: Australian Rules Football, Gender and Television', in M.E. Brown (ed.), *Television and Women's Culture: The Politics of the Popular* (Sydney, 1990), p.144.

16. W. Broderick in the *Age*, 2 April 1977, cited in Sandercock and Turner, p.248.

17. Sandercock and Turner, ibid., p.248.

18. Women are briefly mentioned in the context of 'cross-generational loyalty' and in terms of players, umpires and board members. Pascoe, *The Winter Game*, pp.60, 246.

19. Ibid., p.xvii.

20. For discussion of hegemonic masculinity as it relates to other football codes, see H. Yeates, 'The League of Men. Masculinity, the Media and Rugby League Football', *Media Information Australia*, 75 (Feb. 1995), 35, and S. Scraton, 'Foreword', in S. Lopez, *Women on the Ball: A Guide to Women's Football* (London, 1997), pp.ix–xiv.

21. See, for example, an earlier version of this essay in R. Hess, 'Women and Australian Rules Football in Colonial Melbourne', *International Journal of the History of Sport*, 13, 3, (Dec. 1996), 356–72, and R. Hess, 'The Victorian Football League Takes Over, 1897–1914', in Hess and Stewart (eds.), *More Than a Game*, pp.99–105.

22. M. Brady, 'Miss and Mrs Football, but no Ms Football', in Sandercock and Turner, *Up Where Cazaly?*, p.249. Brady was the wife of a VFL footballer and mother to six daughters.

23. S. Alomes, 'Tales of a Dreamtime: Australian Football as a Secular Religion', in I. Craven (ed.), *Australian Popular Culture* (Cambridge, 1994), p.57. The estimate of the percentage of female supporters appears to be a personal observation.

24. Anonymous, 'Report from the Politics of Sport Conference, University of London Union, 11 Sept. 1994', *British Society of Sports History Newsletter*, 4 (Spring 1995), 11.

25. A. Guttmann, *Sports Spectators* (New York, 1986), pp.107–9.

26. T. Mason, *Association Football and English Society, 1863–1915* (Brighton, 1980), p.152.

27. Ibid., pp.152–3. See also Lopez, *Women on the Ball*, p.202.

28. D. Birley, *Land of Sport and Glory: Sport and British Society, 1887–1910* (Manchester, 1996), p.232. For further discussion of British female soccer fans in a more contemporary context see Lopez, pp.202–9.

29. Guttmann claims that 45 per cent of fans attending games of the now-defunct North American Soccer League were women. Guttmann, p.110. Murray indicates that a similar percentage of women made up a Danish supporters' association. W.J. Murray, *Football: A History of the World Game* (Hampshire, 1994), pp.196–7.

30. Lindley has expressed the view that women love to look at footballers' 'great legs' as they run, kick, twist, turn and pivot. See T. Chappell, 'Baggy Shorts Risk Loss of Support', *Campus Review*, 22–28 Sept. 1994, 32.

31. Examples of such trivialization by female writers include R. Koval, 'Thighs And Whispers', in R. Fitzgerald and K. Spillman (eds.), *The Greatest Game* (Richmond, 1988), pp.89–94; T. Holmes, *Girls' Guide to Football* (Sydney, 1996), pp.8–13; and C. Perkin, 'The Thighs Have It', *Football Record* (1–3 Sept. 1995), 38.

32. On this point in particular, see J. Hargreaves, *Sporting Females: Critical Issues in the History and Sociology of Women's Sports* (London, 1994), pp.1–2, who specifically warns against dwelling on reductive categories in debates about women's sports.

33. *Herald*, 11 July 1859, cited in J. Ross (ed.), *100 Years of Australian Football, 1897–1996* (Ringwood, 1996), p.21.

34. *Bell's Life*, 15 Sept. 1866, cited in G. Hutchinson (comp.), *Great Australian Football Stories* (Melbourne, 1989), p.17.

35. Grow, 'From Gum Trees', p.20.

36. Ibid., p.21.

37. G. Blainey, *A Game of Our Own: The Origins of Australian Football* (Melbourne, 1990), pp.60–5.

38. Ibid., p.10. Blainey specifically comments on the important role of players, as opposed to officials, during the formative years of the game.

39. S. Zavos, *The Gold and the Black. The Rugby Battles for the Bledisloe Cup.New Zealand Vs Australia, 1903–94* (St Leonards, 1995), p.15. For further details on this point, see T.V.

Hickie, *They Ran with the Ball: How Rugby Football Began in Australia* (Melbourne, 1993), ch.11.

40. T.J.L. Chandler and J. Nauright, 'Introduction: Rugby, Manhood and Identity', in J. Nauright and T.J.L. Chandler (eds.), *Making Men: Rugby and Masculine Identity* (London and Portland, OR, 1996), p.2.

41. M. Phillips, 'Football, Class and War: The Rugby Codes in New South Wales, 1907–1918', in Nauright and Chandler (eds.), *Making Men*, p.163. For a useful analysis of the origins and development of rugby in another Australian colony, see P.A. Horton, 'Rugby Union Football and its Role in the Socio-Cultural Development of Queensland, 1882–91', *International Journal of the History of Sport*, 9, 1 (April 1992), 119–31.

42. *Australasian*, 1873, cited in Hutchinson, p.18.

43. J. Pullman, 'The Gentleman Cricketer: In Search of an Ideal', in Simon Creak *et al.*, *Polemics, Poetics and Play. Essays in Nineteenth and Early Twentieth Century Sporting History* (Melbourne, 1997), p.35.

44. See, for example, a series of full-page photographs of prominent footballers in the *Australasian*, 1907, *passim*.

45. *Argus*, 1909, cited in Marc Fiddian, *The Pioneers* (Melbourne, 1977), p.19.

46. Grow, 'From Gum Trees', pp.40–1.

47. *Australasian Sketcher*, 7 July 1877, 54.

48. *Illustrated Australian News*, 30 Aug. 1879, 137. For a less complimentary report, see the *Australasian Sketcher*, 30 Aug. 1879.

49. M. Oriard, *Reading Football: How the Popular Press Created an American Spectacle* (Chapel Hill, 1993), p.248. See also B.G. Rader, *American Sports: From the Age of Folk Games to the Age of Televised Sports* (Englewood Cliffs, 1996), pp.91–3.

50. Oriard, *Reading Football*, pp.248–9.

51. A. Doyle, '"Causes Won, Not Lost": College Football and the Modernization of the American South', *International Journal of the History of Sport*, 11, 2 (Aug. 1994), 238.

52. *Australasian Sketcher*, 3 July 1880, 157.

53. J. Senyard, '1944 and All That', in Cutten History Committee (eds.), *Fitzroy. Melbourne's First Suburb* (Carlton, 1991), pp.215–16. For a brief explanation of the Australian context for 'barracking', see the entry by John O'Hara in Wray Vamplew *et al.* (eds.), *The Oxford Companion to Australian Sport* (Melbourne, 1994), pp.53–4.

54. R. Stremski, *Kill for Collingwood* (Sydney, 1986), p.52. For an explanation of this ratio, see the comment in the relevant endnote. Ibid., p.296.

55. Stremski also notes that specific ladies tickets were abolished by the VFL in 1922, making further comparisons difficult. Ibid.

56. *Melbourne Punch,* 30 July 1896, 83. and 100.

57. *Argus*, 27 July 1896, cited in R. Cashman *et al.* (eds.), *The Oxford Companion of Australian Sporting Anecdotes* (Melbourne, 1994), p.53.

58. See, for instance, the *Age*, 20 Feb. 1896, 5.

59. Blainey, *A Game of Our Own*, pp.57–8.

60. *Australasian*, 6 July 1907, 23. According to Robin Grow, 'Markwell' was 'the most influential football writer of the day'. Grow, 'The Victorian Football Association', p.75.

61. M.. Messner, 'Sports and Male Domination: The Female Athlete as Contested Ideological Terrain', in W.J. Morgan and K.V. Meier (eds.), *Philosophic Inquiry in Sport*, second edition (Champaign, 1995), p.276.

62. Ibid.

63. Ibid. For a case study that considers how American football became the cultural mainstay for men in a specific city at the end of the nineteenth century, see B. S. Butler, '"Gain Ground and Glory": Metropolitan Athletic Clubs and the Promotion of American Football – the Case of the Louisville Athletic Club', *International Journal of the History of Sport*, 9, 3 (Dec. 1992), 378–96.

64. Rader, *American Sports*, p.90.

65. S.W. Pope, 'God, Games and National Glory: Thanksgiving and the Ritual of Sport in American Culture, 1876–1926', *International Journal of the History of Sport*, 10, 2 (Aug. 1993), 243.

66. For details of the tour, including financial records, see Mat Roberts, 'The Game of Thoroughbreds', Student essay, Department of Physical Education and Recreation, Victoria University of Technology (26 June 1992), 1–11.

67. *Australasian*, 27 July 1907, 218. The VFL had organized a representative game to be played away against the Ballarat Football League and cancelled all Melbourne fixtures. The VFA had a match scheduled against the South Australian League to be played in Adelaide, but also completed a normal round of games in Melbourne. On the middle class, masculine nature of lacrosse in Australia, see Brian Stoddart, *Saturday Afternoon Fever: Sport in the Australian Culture* (North Ryde, 1986), p.138.

68. For an earlier comment on the rivalry between lacrosse and Australian Rules football, see the *Sportsman*, 10 July 1902, 6.

69. The *Australasian*, 3 Aug. 1907, 288, noted that 'Probably nine-tenths of those present were not familiar with the laws of lacrosse, but ... As nearly every point and move that counts for merit in lacrosse would be equally meritorious in the Australian game of football, the onlookers were able to appreciate every bit of skilful play.'

70. *Australasian*, 10 Aug. 1907, 346.

71. Ibid., 17 Aug. 1907, 407.

72. For some brief commentary on this issue, specifically for the colonial period, see Grow, 'The Victorian Football Association, p.73. For a more general discussion of the physical and social boundaries that separate players and spectators in modern sport, see D. Hemphill, 'Revisioning Sport Spectatorism', *Journal of the Philosophy of Sport*, XXII (1995), 50–3.

73. See, for example, photographs from *Melbourne Punch*, 23 July 1907, 120, and 20 Aug. 1908, 268, and the *Australasian*, 22 Aug. 1908, 477. Collingwood was one club that provided a stand specifically for female supporters. A makeshift 'Ladies Pavilion' was opened on 11 May 1900. It was extended to accommodate 300 women just two years later. See Stremski, *Kill for Collingwood*, p.52.

74. See, for instance, photographs from the *Australasian*, 7 Sept. 1907, and *Melbourne Punch*, 30 July 1908, p.164. A photograph (*c.* 1910) of women and children crowded around the perimeter of the Reserve at a game between South Melbourne and Fitzroy is reproduced in Senyard, p.214.

75. *Melbourne Punch*, 24 June 1909, 901.

76. Stremski, p.52.

77. Grow, 'The Victorian Football Association', p.73.

78. The literature on crickets crowds is more extensive. See, for example, Richard Cashman, '*Ave a Go, Yer Mug! Australian Cricket Crowds From Larrikin to Ocker* (Sydney, 1984), and K.A.P. Sandiford, 'English Cricket Crowds During the Victorian Age', *Journal of Sport History*, 9, 3 (Winter 1982), 5–22.

79. M. Smith, '"There's No Penalty When You Hit the Fence": Sporting Activities in Central and Eastern Nova Scotia, 1880s to 1920s', *Sport History Review*, 27, 2 (Nov. 1996), 195.

80. *Melbourne Punch*, 16 July 1908, 96.

81. See, for example, *Melbourne Punch*, 27 Aug. 1896, 173, and 6 May 1909, 28.

82. *Melbourne Punch*, 10 June 1909, 808. Such a view is also previously reflected in the so-called 'Smart Girl's Calendar' for 1904, published by *Melbourne Punch*. According to the poem accompanying the almanac, the 'Smart Girl' participated in a different sporting activity every month, including watching the 'men of mark' during June. *Melbourne Punch* (Special Issue), 8 Dec. 1903, 3.

83. *Punch*, 10 June 1909, p.808. For an earlier comment on the 'little dears' who watched the 'Students', see *Punch*, 13 Aug. 1908, 353.

84. A. Summers, *Damned Whores and God's Police* (Ringwood: Penguin, 1994), p.124.

85. A. Moore, *The Mighty Bears! A Social History of North Sydney Rugby League* (Sydney, 1996), p.21.

86. B. Hutchins, 'Mediated Violence: The Case of Origin Rugby League', *Sporting Traditions*, 13, 2 (May 1997), 30–1.

87. See Kevin Sheedy and Carolyn Brown, *Football's Women: The Forgotten Heroes* (Ringwood, 1998). The book relies almost exclusively on the oral testimony of women who have been involved in the game at different levels in various capacities. There is virtually no discussion

of long term historical trends.

88. R.W. Connell and T.H. Irving, *Class Structure in Australian History* (Melbourne, 1980), p.280. See also Alomes, 'Tales of a Dreamtime', p.56.

89. For academic discussion of the contemporary role of women as auxiliaries in Australian Rules football, see, for example, Senyard, p.225 and Alomes, p.57. For specific detail on the 'behind-the-scenes' activities of women in the survival of one particular AFL club, see Kerrie Gordon and Alan Dalton, *Too Tough to Die: Footscray's Fightback 1989* (Melbourne, 1990). For the active role of women in the 'Fight for Football' organization, see Dave Nadel, 'The League Goes National, 1986–1997', in Hess and Bob Stewart (eds.), *More Than a Game*, pp.237–8.

90. Stremski, pp.1–12.

91. J. Bale, *Landscapes of Modern Sport* (Leicester, 1994), pp.120–1.

92. Stremski, p.1.

93. L. Mann and P. Pearce, 'Social Psychology of the Sports Spectator', in D.J. Glencross (ed.), *Psychology and Sport* (Sydney, 1978), pp.175–6. See also Hess, 'A Sport in Crisis', 31–3.

94. Collingwood Football Club (CFC), *Annual Report, Season 1892*, no pagination.

95. CFC, *Annual Report, Season 1893* and *1894*, no pagination.

96. CFC, *Annual Report, Season 1894*, no pagination. The Mayor, Councillor J. Gahan, was listed as a patron of the club

97. CFC, *Annual Report, Season 1895*, no pagination.

98. Ibid. The 'Club Account' for 1895 reveals that Members' tickets were sold for five shillings, while Ladies' and Boys' tickets sold for two shillings and sixpence.

99. CFC, *Annual Report, Season 1896*, no pagination.

100. CFC, *Annual Report, Season 1897*, no pagination.

101. CFC, *Annual Report, Season 1898*, no pagination.

102. See the CFC, *Annual Report, Season 1899*, no pagination.

103. Fitzroy Football Club, *Annual Reports*, seasons 1907–1918, *passim*. This incomplete series of annual reports is held at the Melbourne Cricket Club library.

104. Eastern Suburbs District Football Club, *Annual Report*, 1903. The author is indebted to Murray Phillips for making this material available. See also Phillips, 'Football, Class and War', pp.159–63.

105. Brady, 'Miss and Mrs Football, but no Ms Football', p.255.

106. *Ballarat Courier*, 11 Sept. 1908, 6.

107. Ibid., 12 Sept. 1908, p.10.

108. Ibid.

109. *Melbourne Punch*, 11 May 1899, p.460. The same cartoon is reproduced in Ross (ed.), *100 Years of Australian Football*, p.43, but the caption erroneously implies that Australian women are depicted.

110. Hargreaves, *Sporting Females*, p.171.

111. Roberta Park, for example, refers to an annual 'standing match at foot-ball' between married and unmarried women in Inverness, Scotland, prior to the nineteenth century. See Roberta Park, 'From "Genteel Diversions" to "Bruising Peg": Active Pastimes, Exercise, and Sports for Females in Late 17th- and 18th-Century Europe', in D.M. Costa and S.R. Guthrie (eds.), *Women and Sport. Interdisciplinary Perspectives* (Champaign, 1994), p.2. J. Goulstone also cites a newspaper report of a match between married gentlemen and bachelors in March 1773 that was decided when the wife of one of the players entered the fray and 'soon determined the victory'. See John Goulstone, 'Shrovetide Football & Related Games', *British Society of Sports History Newsletter*, 5 (Winter 1996), p.10.

112. See K.E. McCrone, *Playing the Game. Sport and the Physical Emancipation of English Women, 1870 – 1914* (Lexington, 1988), p.53.

113. Birley, *Land of Sport and Glory*, p.98. An illustration of the first match of the British Ladies' Football Club on 30 March 1895 is reproduced in Birley, p.161. Lopez claims that this match took place a week earlier. Lopez, p.2.

114. *Herald*, 4 July 1896, 4.

115. See D.J. Williamson, *Belles of the Ball* (Devon, 1991), pp.2–5, and Lopez, *Women on the Ball*, pp.1–10, for more detailed treatment of discrimination against women playing soccer in England at the turn of the century.

116. Williamson, *Belles of the Ball*, p.20.
117. W. J. Murray, *The World's Game. A History of Soccer* (Urbana, 1996), pp.45–6. Lopez also explains how claims of financial mismanagement by the organizers of various charity matches helped to undermine the public acceptance of women's football. Lopez, pp.6–10.
118. Ray Crawford, 'Moral and Manly: Girls and Games in Early Twentieth-Century Melbourne', in J.A. Mangan and R.J. Park (eds.), *From 'Fair Sex' to Feminism. Sport and the Socialization of Women in the Industrial and Post-Industrial Eras* (London and Portland, OR, 1987), p.190.
119. See the photographic collage, 'Should Women Play Football?', in *Table Talk*, 28 July 1921, reproduced in Sandercock and Turner, *Up Where, Cazaly?*, inserted between p.116 and p.117. For recent reflections on the successful development of the Victorian Women's Football League, formed in 1981, see K. Lawrence, 'Making Our Mark: Women Playing Australian Rules Football in Melbourne', *Occasional Papers in Football Studies*, 1, 2 (Aug. 1998), 115–22. From a comparative point of view, it is interesting to note that according to Stell, a 'Ladies Rugby Football League', consisting of five teams, was established in Sydney in 1921. M.K. Stell, *Half the Race: A History of Australian Women in Sport* (North Ryde, 1991), p.57.
120. For perceptive comments on how photographs of female athletes during this period reflected male constructions of female sport, see John Nauright, 'Netball, Media Representation of Women and Crisis of Male Hegemony in New Zealand', in John Nauright (ed.), *Sport, Power and Society in New Zealand: Historical and Contemporary Perspectives* (Sydney, 1995), pp.49–57. For more general reflections on media coverage of sporting females, see Hargreaves, pp.162–73.

7

In Pursuit of Status, Respectability and Idealism: Pioneers of the Olympic Movement in Australasia

IAN JOBLING

LEONARD CUFF

Leonard Albert Cuff was born in Christchurch, New Zealand, on 28 March 1866. He attended Melville House Private School and Cook's College, Cranmer Square before attending Canterbury Agricultural College where he completed a two-year diploma course in 1882. In 1883 he is first recorded as winning the long jump at the Canterbury Amateur Athletics Club and by 1887 he was a founding member of the New Zealand Amateur Athletics Association (NZAAA) and the driving force behind the development of inter-provincial amateur athletics in New Zealand and the creation of inter-colonial championships involving New Zealand and Australia.

Cuff's position as the Honorary Secretary of the NZAAA between 1887 and 1896 allowed him to assist the expansion of that colony's representative athletics. Significantly, in 1890, Cuff organized and managed New Zealand's first international amateur athletics tour, which competed in Sydney at the Australian Championships – being a contest between representative teams from the colonies of New South Wales, Victoria, Queensland and New Zealand. The New Zealand team comprised just eight athletes, including Cuff, who was New Zealand's premier long jumper, yet claimed seven firsts, five seconds and two-thirds in the 12 championship events.

Following this unprecedented success of the NZAAA team, there was strong support for the sending of a NZAAA team to the British championships.[1] On occasion, colonial sporting performances and records were treated with scepticism by the English sporting public; a trip to England was deemed necessary to prove the validity of colonial sporting achievements.[2] The victories of the NZAAA team in Australia were seen as proof that 'there was no finer race under the sun than the New Zealand-born Englishman' and that the colony produced 'men of stamina':[3] 'second generation New Zealanders began to express feelings of self-respect and growing national pride' through these performances.[4]

Cuff was both a competitor and the manager of the New Zealand team[5] which was greeted soon after their arrival to compete in the 1892 English championships with the following welcome from England's *Sporting Life*: 'Who could not but admire their gallantry and pluck in travelling so many thousands of miles in order to test their power against the cream of athletic England.'[6]

The team had not been in England long when Cuff wrote to his NZAAA President, F.A. Wilding, stating that in addition to the three competitions previously scheduled for the NZAAA team in England, 'it is probable that we will compete in Paris on 7 July'.[7] It is likely that Charles Herbert, Secretary of the English Amateur Athletic Association, who had been assisting the team in London only proposed the competition to Cuff after the New Zealanders had arrived in England.[8]

It was at this athletics competition in France that Cuff and Baron Pierre De Coubertin meet for the only time. The New Zealand team, along with clubs from France, Belgium and Great Britain, competed in the athletics carnival,[9] organized by Coubertin in his capacity as General Secretary of the Union des Sociétés Françaises Sports Athlétiques (USFSA) to celebrate the Union's fifth anniversary.[10] Coubertin and Herbert certainly met the New Zealand team at the train station and together Coubertin and Cuff inspected the venue for the next day's competition. However, it is difficult to determine the extent of any interaction between Coubertin and Cuff over those two days in Paris.[11] In Cuff's later letters to Coubertin, dated 24 April and 4 September 1894, his references to the NZAAA's time in Paris paint a very positive picture of the episode, at least from his perspective. He commented that 'my visit to Paris in 1892 will always live in my memory as one of the pleasantest [*sic*] times of my life',[12] and he asked Coubertin to 'remember me kindly to all those who showed me much kindness in Paris in 1892, a kindness "that can never be forgotten"'.[13]

So it was in this way, and through the auspices of Charles Herbert, that Cuff was introduced into the extended network of friends, acquaintances, sporting officials and dignitaries known to Coubertin. It was this network that Coubertin drew on to attend and/or support the International Amateur Athletic Congress at the Sorbonne in Paris in

1894, where he announced the revival of the Olympic Games and nominated the personnel of the International Olympic Committee (IOC). Although he did not attend this Congress, Leonard Cuff, became the member from the Australasian region of the inaugural IOC.

The 1894 International Amateur Athletic Congress (IAAC), held at the Sorbonne, 16–23 June 1894, is worthy of further consideration.[14] The first invitations to the Congress were sent out in January 1894. A preliminary programme indicated that one of the eight topics to be discussed by the Congress members was: 'The possibility of re-establishing the Olympic Games. Under what conditions would it be feasible?'[15]

Most of the associations and clubs throughout the British Empire which received the January letters were those suggested by Charles Herbert in response to a request for names and addresses by Coubertin.[16] Cuff's name was included, along with the comment:

> He will front to all the best clubs in Australia and New Zealand if you ask him. He is the hon. sec. of the NZAAA. You remember him that tall nice looking follower with us in 1892. I have written him to tell him you are sending over [programmes and an invitation]. He will do anything you want in that way. That will cover Australia and New Zealand.[17]

Coubertin's letter of invitation to Cuff requested him to distribute a circular to a number of sporting newspapers and sporting associations throughout Australasia.[18,19] Cuff's reply indicates that he did as requested, presumably sending the circulars to the other major colonial amateur athletics associations in Queensland (QAAA), Victoria (VAAA) and New South Wales (NSWAAA).[20] References to Cuff in the athletics column of *The Referee* of 20 March 1894 shows that this publication was certainly contacted.[21]

Despite being unable to travel to Paris, Cuff was added by Coubertin to the long list of 'Honorary Members' of the IAAC in June 1894. The 79 members who did attend soon divided into two groups: one to discuss the definition, regulation and application of an 'amateur'; the other to discuss the 'revival of the Olympic Games'.[22] Coubertin's adamant advocacy of the Olympics' revival allowed him a free hand in the nomination of the initial IOC.[23] Cuff was one of many 'Honorary Members' of the Congress who was elected unopposed.[24] It is interesting to note that only five of the 14 nominated by Coubertin to the IOC were present at the Congress; they were Coubertin and Callot (France), Lucchesi-Palli (Italy), William Sloane (USA) and Demetrius Vikelas (Greece). Coubertin, as he later admitted, wanted control of the fledgling Olympic Movement:

> Nobody seemed to notice that I had chosen almost exclusively absentee members. As their names figured on the long list of 'Honorary members of the Congress', people were accustomed to seeing their names and readily assumed that they were staunch members always at their tasks. I needed elbow room at the start, for many conflicts were bound to arise.[25]

Clearly, Coubertin had not consulted the 'absentee' members before the Congress about their willingness to join the IOC. All were known to him, either through personal contact or correspondence, and it was through these pre-existing relationships that he imposed upon them to accept their selection retrospectively. They did. Coubertin wrote to Cuff the day after the Congress had concluded, informing him of some of the outcomes with respect to the revival of the Olympic Games and his selection as a member of the IOC. Cuff replied: 'I deem it a very great honour being appointed to represent Australasia, (and) you may depend on my doing everything in my power to assist you.'[26]

Reports in the press in Australasia of the Paris Congress were sparse so there is little evidence of any reaction in the Antipodes to Cuff's selection to the IOC.[27] What is clear is that the Australasian press was more interested in the scheme to stage a 'Pan-Britannic Festival' which had been first been promulgated by the Englishman, J. Astley Cooper.[28] Part of this festival was designed to secure 'a thorough representation of the athletes of the British Empire, as well as of the English speaking race' in Australasia. Clearly, the Pan-Britannic Festival was a symbol of the desire of the British colonies 'to maintain their strong sense of identification with England'.[29]

Although the Pan-Britannic Festival encountered resistance in English athletics (probably because Charles Herbert, Secretary of the English Amateur Athletics Association, was a key supporter of Coubertin's project to revive the Olympic Games and was elected a member of the IOC in 1894), support for the scheme was strong in Australasia, particularly in the colonies of New South Wales and Victoria.[30] Strong evidence for this may be gleaned from the Melbourne-based newspaper, which criticized Cuff's membership to the IOC: 'As the Australasian associations are pledged to Mr. Cooper's scheme, and Victoria and N.S.W. are now trying to frame suitable athletic contests in connection with it, I hope Mr. Cuff will decline the proposed honour until it is shown whether and why this new scheme is intended to supersede that of Mr. Astley Cooper.'[31] As Honorary Secretary of the NZAAA, as well as an IOC member, Cuff's membership was seen as having a detrimental impact on Australasian support for the Pan-Britannic Festival as the NZAAA was the only amateur athletics association in the region officially affiliated with the Amateur Athletics Association in England.[32] However, there are many reasons for the Pan-Britannic Festival not proceeding; Cuff's membership of the IOC did not really play a part in its demise.

Cuff's years of membership of the IOC are worthy of further consideration because of the subsequent representation of the Olympic Movement in Australasia passing to Richard Coombes. Coubertin and Cuff had similar interests, and if Coubertin did indeed select IOC members for their allegiance to 'all sports to all'[33] and not merely one sport, then Cuff's association with athletics, baseball, cricket and rugby in New Zealand positively reflected the Coubertin's attitude to amateur sport which he sought to promote through the Olympic Movement. As mentioned earlier, Cuff's presence in Australasia also provided a useful means through which to promote the Olympic Movement internationally. In later years Coubertin elaborated on his conception of the IOC's membership, describing it as comprising three concentric circles: 'a small nucleus of dedicated and active members; a nursery of willing members capable of being educated along the right lines, and finally, a facade of people of varying degrees of usefulness, whose presence would serve to satisfy national pretensions while lending prestige to the whole'.[34]

Cuff's membership of the IOC, along with members from the USA, Argentina and Russia, has been termed 'geographic propaganda'[35] but helped create an impression of a global organisation. The geographic isolation of Australasia was clearly an obstacle to potential participation in the inaugural Olympic Games in Athens. Nevertheless, Cuff's reputation as a dynamic administrator would have given Coubertin confidence that Cuff's IOC membership would ensure that athletes from the region would compete in 1896. However, as can be seen from the involvement of athletes from Australia and New Zealand in Olympic Games during the period of his membership of the IOC (1894–1905) it would seem Coubertin's confidence was misplaced. No athlete from New Zealand competed in the Olympics during this period, and only six from Australia.[36] The story of Edwin Flack's participation in those inaugural Olympic Games, one of the six from Australia, provides evidence of a fascinating link between the two pioneer IOC members in Australasia, Cuff and Coombes.

EDWIN FLACK

Edwin 'Teddy' Flack, a handsome 22-year-old accountant-businessman, became known as 'the Lion of Athens' at the 1896 Olympic Games when, as the sole Australian competitor, he won both the 800 and 1500 metre track events. Flack's success fostered the development of the Olympic Movement in Australia and began a tradition which has resulted in Australia being represented at every summer Olympic Games. Prior to Flack's success, there was little enthusiasm in Australia for the Olympic Games because, as has already been stated, there was suspicion about Coubertin's Olympic Games and support for the Pan-Britannic athletic festival. Indeed, the *Australasian* of 25 August 1894 reported Cooper's scheme as the 'Pan-Britannic Olympiad' and even as late as May 1895, the *Referee* still seemed to pledge its support to Australia's participation in an empire athletic competition: 'the most striking features of the proposed Olympian Games, no doubt, are borrowed from the "Anglo-Saxon Olympiad" and the "Pan-Britannic" scheme'.[37]

Flack had an opportunity to read about the inaugural Olympic Games to be held in Athens in 1896 because Cuff sent details to Richard Coombes, then president of the New South Wales Amateur Athletic Association and, perhaps of even more significance, the editor and principal athletics writer for the *Referee*. This weekly sports paper published announcements of the proposed programme of events for the 1896 Games[38] and through his 'Pedestrianism – Amateur Athletics' column, and writing under the pseudonyms of 'The Prodigal', Coombes exhorted the sporting associations to become involved.[39]

Without any help from Cuff, but a letter of introduction from Coombes,[40] Edwin Flack not only made the trip to Athens but competed in four events. Although born in London on 5 November 1873, Flack lived in Australia from the age of five after his father, an accountant with Price Waterhouse in London, emigrated in 1878 and established his own accounting firm in Melbourne. Young Edwin attended Melbourne Grammar School, and later became a successful runner. He was the one-mile champion of Australasia in 1892 and 1893, and the two-mile champion of New South Wales and Victoria in 1894 and 1895, respectively.[41] Flack, who had joined his father's accountancy firm, Davey, Flack and Co., in 1892, sailed to England in February 1895 to gain further experience with Price Waterhouse. Soon after his arrival, he joined the London Athletic Club, and both the Thames and the Hampton Court Hare and Hounds. Coombes reported on Flack's activities during the period prior to the Olympic Games but gave no indication that he knew of Flack's intention to compete.[42] Flack later wrote about his intentions: 'Before I left Australia I knew that the Olympic Games were coming off in Athens in 1896 and I decided then that if I could arrange it I would take part in them, or at any rate, go and see them.'[43]

It was not until cabled reports started to filter through to the newspapers that the Australasian public knew about Flack's participation in the Olympics. A letter Flack received from Basil Parkinson, who was a founder of the Victorian Amateur Athletic Association in 1891 and a respondent to solicited comments from Charles Herbert about the proposed Olympic Games, made it clear the Flack family knew of his intentions. Parkinson's letter recounted a conversation Parkinson had with Joseph Flack, who had said he was quite willing for his son to make the trip, provided the cost was not more than 30 pounds.[44] On receiving this news, Flack arranged for extended leave, recounting later that he did not explain to his employer where he was going 'lest Mr Edwin Waterhouse ... might hear of what I was doing, and probably disapproved of a member of the staff careering across Europe to take part in athletic contests'.[45]

Although he had no hard training, and had run only spasmodically with the Thames Hares and Hounds a few weeks prior to his departure to Athens, Flack packed his 'Old Melbourne colours' – the dark blue vest of the Melburnian Hare and Hounds (Harriers) club, left London by train, crossed to Calais, and went by train again via the Swiss Alps to Brindisi, Italy, where he caught a steamer to Patras on the Peloponnese of Greece and then another train to Athens.[46] The journey took six days, during which he kept a detailed diary and wrote most descriptive letters to his father and to Richard Coombes, who reported Flack's travels and athletic feats in some detail in the *Referee*:

I am in a position to give my readers some particulars of the adventures of E H Flack during his visit to Athens which I feel sure, will be read with interest ... The young Melburnian then proceeds to describe the Stadium. It is narrow in width, and, as a consequence, the two turns are very sharp indeed, and difficult to negotiate. The track is of cinders and 'not at all bad,' says EHF, 'although far from perfect.' Thus the slow times are accounted for. When Mr Flack arrived Athens was very full, and everything was bright and gay, the approaching games causing great excitement amongst the Greeks ... Mr Flack speaks warmly of the generous applause of the Greeks when he won.[47]

In addition to winning two track events, Flack also participated in the tennis competition, partnering the sole British athlete in Athens, George Robertson, in the doubles, and almost caused an upset in the Marathon by leading at the 30 kilometre mark. Flack won the 1500 metre race in the final event on the second day of track and field competition, the first occasion on which a non-American had achieved victory. Flack wrote to his father: 'The win was the most popular one to date, so I am told ... I was the first to succeed in lowering their [American] colours.'[48]

Although it is recorded in the official report of the 1896 Olympic Games that the Australian flag was raised after each of Flack's victories, no Australian flag existed at that time, since Australia was a number of separate British colonies until it became a Commonwealth in 1 January 1901. Indeed, no official Australian flag flew anywhere until 1 September 1901. It is probable that, since Flack had been born and lived in London, and had, as he wrote, 'gone across as a member of the London Athletic Club', the British Union Jack was used.[49] Reports in British newspapers regarded him as a Briton and, indeed, the British Olympic Association continued to record him in their official list of medallists for many decades.

The final of the 800 metres was scheduled for the fourth day of the Games. So, on the third day Flack, probably at the behest of his British acquaintance, George Robertson, entered the lawn tennis competition. Flack was beaten in the first round of the singles by the Greek, Akratopoulos. The next morning, even though he was to compete in the 800 metres final in the afternoon, Flack partnered Robertson in the doubles. They were beaten by the Greeks, Dionysios Kasdaglis and Demetrios Petrokokkinos. Later that day Flack won the 800 metres.[50]

Flack's relatively easy victories in all track events, his experience in cross-country races and the euphoria of this international festival probably contributed to his decision to compete in the new event, the inaugural race from Marathon to Athens. In a letter to his father on 9 April he wrote:

> In about six hours time I run off the final of the 800 and then drive straight away to Marathon a few hours journey. The distance is 25 miles. The road is a very bad one and I shall stay the night there and start in the race at 2 o'clock. I am afraid it will prove too far for me. However I intend to have a shot at it as it is the event which is arousing the spectator interest here. And if I can manage to pull it off I shall be quite prepared to retire from the running path.[51]

Flack's aide for the race was V.W. Delves Broughton, personal butler to the British ambassador in Athens. Broughton who, coincidentally, was an ex-student of Melbourne Grammar School, accompanied Flack on a bicycle. Flack had never run a race of more than ten miles and the distance did prove beyond him. But many Greek spectators lining the route and in the stadium in Athens had some anxious moments. As has can be ascertained from Flack's detailed description of the race in a letter written to his father, it was expected that one of the many Greeks in the field of 25 would win: 'The excitement which had been worked up over this event was simply extraordinary and the Greeks were very anxious to win it. They were all in a mortal funk of me and also of the Americans. In the morning I believe a church service was held in the Marathon Church when special prayers were offered up that a Greek might win.'[52] Flack had to retire at about the 30 kilometre mark; the letter continues:

> I got into a carriage and was driven to the stadium which was packed to overflowing with people. All along the roads there were crowds of people ... of course I should have liked to have won very much but everyone said it was better to turn out as it did because the Greeks had so set their minds on winning this event that if a Greek had not pulled it off there was no saying what might not have happened.

Clearly, Edwin Flack's presence and success at those inaugural Olympic Games of the modern era had a remarkable impact on the development of the Olympic Movement in Australia. The *Australasian* of 11 April provided cabled news of Flack's wins under the headline 'An Australian in Greece'. The editor of the *Argus* speculated on that same day that the 'new Olympic Games' may even in due course offer themselves to the delighted gaze of Melbourne'.[53] They did – 60 years later!

But it was the clever use of Flack's letters by Richard Coombes, which reached him several month's later, which had an especially powerful effect on the Olympic Movement in Australasia. In the *Referee* Coombes told Australians the full story of this heroic yet modest young man who had beaten the world. In this way, Edwin Flack, through Coombes, captured the interest and enthusiasm of many Australians who hitherto had little understanding of this auspicious athletic festival. It is now appropriate, therefore, to consider specifically the impact of Richard Coombes as a pioneer of the Olympic Movement in Australia. He not only pursued but epitomized status, respectability and idealism.

RICHARD COOMBES

Richard Coombes was born in 1855 at Hampton Court and attended Hampton Grammar School in an era when a central component of the English public school system was organized sports and games.[54] As H. Perkin has stated, such activities were regarded as the 'cradle of leadership, team spirit, altruistic self reliance and loyalty to comrades – all the qualities needed for the chief goal of upper middle-class education, the public service'.[55] Coombes left school at the age of 15; he showed great interest in such sports as horse-racing, sculling and rowing, cycling, coursing and rifle shooting. His greatest enthusiasm was for athletics and he became renowned in England as a champion walker and cross-country runner.[56]

When Coombes emigrated to Australia in 1886 he brought with him strong beliefs in amateurism and athleticism, and strong imperialistic inclinations[57] Once in Australia, especially after he became a journalist and editor of the Sydney-based sporting newspaper, the *Referee*, Coombes was confronted by an emerging spirit of nationalism in Australia. One example of this may be seen in his response to J. Astley's Cooper's[58] proposed athletic festival, which was designed to 'draw closer the ties between the nations of the Empire'.[59] This appealed to Coombes. He wrote prophetically in August 1892 that 'the signs of the times are that athletics will have a more powerful effect upon the Empire in time to come than has been the case for centuries'.[60]

Coombes responded positively to that part of Cooper's scheme which was designed to elevate the standard and aims of athleticism and to harness the untapped power of imperial sentiment within the colonies of the British Empire. Coombes, as an influential personality in amateur sport in Australia, frequently wrote about the Pan-Britannic Festival in the *Referee*. However, these sentiments did not receive unanimous support. Other local writers, influenced by the rising nationalistic spirit in Australia, were not nearly as positive about them. For example, the British *Australasian* of 5 November 1891 stated, '... the rising generation in Australia is intensely patriotic, but the sentiment is local, and not imperial. In their dear eyes old England does not loom so largely as it does before those as Mr Astley Cooper'. As has been stated, Cooper's plan for a Pan-Britannic Festival did not materialize for both conceptual and organizational reasons.[61] Coombes lamented and questioned the lack of information about this athletic festival, stating in January 1893, 'we are still completely in the dark as to when and where the affair will take place, and the actual conditions under which the various events will be brought off'.[62]

It was then that Coombes began giving support to Coubertin's idea of reviving the Olympic Games. Olympism was based on Victorian ideals of morality, nobility and purity as well as physical endurance and energy. Winning was important but so was the participation and performance to the best of one's ability. This concept of 'sport for sport's sake' concurred with Coombes' own ideals of sport and amateurism.[63] He eventually embraced the Olympic Movement strongly and his support for the concept becomes even greater than his loyalty to the Empire. However, when there was the possibility of encompassing both Olympism and Imperialism, such as the inclusion of a British Empire team in the Olympic Games of 1912 and 1916, he became especially more ardent.[64]

Coombes was also able to pursue nationalism and imperialism, concepts of apparent mutual exclusion, because of his passion for amateur sport which was epitomized through the Olympic Games. Nationalism for Australia was possible for him as long as it did not threaten his loyalty to the British Empire. This loyalty was directed more to the Empire *per se* than to England or Great Britain, a notion consistent with that of Sir John Foster-Fraser who wrote, 'there is loyalty in Australia, but it is loyalty to the Empire, not Great Britain'.[65] Coombes alluded to this in an article in the *Referee* in 1916:

One needs to understand the mind workings of many of the leaders in British sport, and to remember that those in control of some branches still cling to the belief that English Championships are the last word, something considerably more important than the Olympic Games, for example, and in a greater measure so as compared to, say, a Festival of Empire.[66]

The Festival of Empire in England of 1911 was organized to celebrate the coronation of George V but it was also promulgated as a stage to unify the far-diverse and distant countries and colonies of the Empire.[67] The sports committee for this festival, chaired by Lord Desborough, IOC member in Britain, handled the sports arrangements.[68] Only white male athletes from Australasia, Canada and South Africa were invited.[69] Coombes was honorary manager of the Australian team.[70]

Canada won the Lonsdale Cup as victors of the sports carnival, although there appeared to be some discrepancy as to whether the Cup was won on the basis of athletics (track and field) only or for all four sports (athletics, boxing, swimming and wrestling).[71] It was during a concluding celebratory dinner that Coombes and James Merrick, manager of the Canadian team, proposed that athletes from Australasia, Canada, Great Britain and South Africa form a British Empire team to compete at the Olympics in Stockholm in 1912.[72] A month later, Coombes, writing as 'The Prodigal', outlined the proposal:

> The scheme, then, is that the Colonies – Australia, New Zealand, Canada, and South Africa – will select their teams and the whole contingent be brought together in London, say, a fortnight before they are due to leave for Stockholm. The British team will also be concentrated in London as far as is possible, and then the whole army will train together under the care of responsible coaches and trainers, and be got into the best possible condition for the descent on Sweden ... This is surely the very ideal of Empire – the forces of the Mother Country and her children, and Colonies, congregating on the shores of Britain to concentrate the forces of Empire, and then voyaging to the battle-ground of Stockholm to challenge in friendly warfare the best of the world's athletes.[73]

There was initial enthusiasm for the scheme but there was not enough time to organize it for the Olympic Games in Stockholm which began in May 1912. However, for a while there was strong support throughout the British Empire for such a team to participate at the Berlin Olympics in 1916,[74] but then there was disagreement and dissension. A key factor in Australia was a loss of national identity that would result from athletes participating as Australians at the Olympics. The following extract from *The Times* of July 1912 makes an incorrect assumption:

> The glory which accrues to the individual Dominions is but moderate in amount, and the sentimental satisfaction which each derives from its separate representation cannot be great. Certainly the Colonials themselves feel that it would be vastly better to be associated with a powerful Empire team, the flag of which everybody at the Games knows and respects and to help to keep that Empire in its place at the head of the nations.[75]

Although Richard Coombes had supported this notion in a series of articles in the *Referee*, especially when he defended his proposal against criticism from the *Sydney Morning Herald*, it seems increasing political independence and the desire for separate national Olympic representation was gaining momentum.[76] An element of realism, especially when it came to raising funds for an Australian team, was expressed clearly in the *Sydney Morning Herald*:

> At present any competitor sent from Australia competes in the Games as an Australasian, and any victory credited to him is recognized by the hoisting of an Australian flag. Apart from all questions of loyalty to the Empire, there is a narrower local patriotism for Australia, which is certainly gratified by the present system, which is also a tremendous advertisement to this continent. And in this advertisement lies the Australian council's main hope in financing an Olympic team.[77]

From an analysis of Coombes' columns in the *Referee*, it is clear he remained supportive of the British Empire team concept until the British Olympic Association secretary wrote that the question of an Empire Team 'has been settled by the International Olympic Committee and the overseas dominions shall compete separately'.[78] Despite his previous promulgation and support for the British Empire Team, upon its demise he remained active in fund-raising for the preparation and expenses of a prestigious Australian team for Berlin in 1916. The First World War disrupted sport in Australasia and internationally[79] and during this period Coombes focused on school and university athletics and continued to promote amateur athletics in Australasia.[80]

After the war, Coombes continued to write extensively in his newspaper columns about the early selection of Olympic athletes and capable team administrators which was necessary to enhance Australia's chances of victory at future Olympic Games.[81] His power and influence in the Olympic Movement in Australasia remained great: he was the only IOC member in the region; a member of the Australian Olympic Federation (AOF) and president of both the Amateur Athletic Union of Australia and New South Wales Amateur Athletics Association; and perhaps of greatest significance of all, remained editor of the *Referee*, which enabled him to exert influence nationally on a weekly basis. An example of this periodical's steadfast loyalty to the Empire relates to the 1924 Olympics in Paris:

> ... General Kentish (honorary secretary to the BOA) proposes that Great Britain and the dominions within the Empire shall be housed together and parade together with a clear-cut line of demarcation between each unit of the Empire, so that the identity of each shall be well-defined, and with each carrying or flying its own national flag. It is a spirit of Empire, and the proposal appeals to me greatly.
>
> I may point out that, on the alphabetical order basis of parade, the Empire units would be widely scattered ... The British Olympic Association has ascertained that the Empire units will be able to follow one another, provided they are all agreeable to the scheme – and I should say surely would be.[82]

Coombes was delighted that, at the conclusion of the 1920, 1924 and 1928 Olympic Games, athletic contests were held between combined Empire teams and teams from the United States.[83] He felt this was an ideal opportunity for the British (from the Home Country as well as the overseas Dominions) to show their worth, for them to come together and present a united front of 'assembled Britishers', to show the world the merit of the Anglo-Saxon spirit: '... a splendid tribute to the Empire's men ... [and a] ... Real Spirit of Sport'.[84]

In 1928, when it was being proposed that the British Empire Games be held in 1930, Coombes considered them as being the second in the series, the first being put forward by him in 1911: 'Since then I have again and again advocated a revival of the Empire Games, so there is nothing fresh in the suggestion.'[85] The 1930 Empire Games held in

Hamilton, Canada, were so successful[86] that some imperialists openly advocated withdrawal of the British Empire from the Olympic Games to concentrate on the Empire Games.[87] Coombes was not one of those advocates. In 1928 he did acknowledge the importance of the Empire Games for unifying the Empire, but he strongly supported the Olympic Games and noted their dominance in international sport: 'One thing is certain, viz, Empire Games or no Empire Games, the Olympiads will still continue, and Great Britain and the dominions will continue to participate in them.'[88]

CUFF AND COOMBES AND THE IOC

The interaction and exchanges between Leonard Cuff and Richard Coombes in relation to the IOC are fascinating and provide insights to the early decades of the Olympic Movement in Australasia as a whole. Cuff never attended a Congress or meeting of the IOC or an Olympic Games. Cuff wrote just five letters to Coubertin during his ten years as an IOC member, all 'replies'. Two related to his election to the IOC; two regarding his resignation from that body in 1905; and the remaining letter, in 1896, discussed matters pertaining to the Olympic Games, stating that Australasia would not be able to send a team to the 1896 Games, but that he hoped Australasia would participate in the 1900 Games in Paris.[89]

Cuff did not attempt to form a New Zealand Olympic Committee and there is no evidence that he promoted Olympism in Australasia. The New Zealand Olympic Association (NZOA) was not formed until 1911, and there is no record in its early minutes of his contribution towards the development of the Olympic Movement in New Zealand.[90] Indeed, Richard Coombes of Australia is featured more prominently in those early minutes. He is regarded as having 'contributed to the development of the Olympic Movement in New Zealand'.[91]

No New Zealand athlete competed at Olympic Games during Cuff's IOC membership.[92] Athletes from Australia were: Edwin Flack (1896); Fred Lane, Donald Mackintosh, and Stan Rowley (1900); and Corrie Gardiner and Leslie McPherson (1904). Cuff, however, did assist Coubertin by informing associations and clubs in Australasia about the inaugural Olympic Games in Athens. Coubertin reported on Cuff's activities in the *Bulletin du Comité International des Jeux,* although he wrote specifically that Cuff had 'drawn up a list of Australian Clubs likely to participate in the Olympic Games and has communicated to them the general lines of our project'.[93]

Richard Coombes, of course, who at the time was president of the New South Wales Amateur Athletics Association (NSWAAA) and editor of the *Referee*, received this information and copies of the IOC Bulletin of the Olympic Games. This communication from Cuff to Coombes about matters Olympic meant that one the most influential members of Australia's amateur athletics community received regular information directly from the region's IOC member.[94] However, none of this occurred in time for any 'representatives' to be sent from Australasia for the inaugural Olympic Games in Athens in 1896. As early as March, 1895 Coombes prompted a difficulty, stating in the *Referee* that if Australasia is to be represented a team will have 'to be directly selected from the battle at Christchurch', which was to be the venue for the Australasian Amateur Athletics Championships in January 1896.[95] A frustrated Coombes wrote 'it is about time that something in the shape of a pow-wow was decided upon'.[96] No meeting took place. It seems, however, that the list of sports associations compiled by Cuff had some effect. The General Secretary of the Hellenic Olympic Committee, Timoleon J. Philemon, sent a letter of invitation to the New South Wales Amateur Athletic Association to attend the Athens Olympic Games. Although Coombes wrote about this invitation from Athens in his column in October 1895,[97] no specific action was taken. After the Australasian Championships in January, Cuff, Coombes and the other sports officials in Australasia had only three months before the Games commenced in Athens in April, 1896. The result was that no official team from Australasia was despatched to the Athens Olympics. On 28 January 1896 Cuff replied to a letter from Coubertin of November 1895: 'I am sorry to say that I do not think there is any chance of Australasia being represented at the Games in Athens. Probably in 1900 when Paris is the scene of the meeting an effort will be made to send a number of competitors.'[98] As has been stated above, the region was 'represented' at the inaugural Olympic Games by Edwin Flack but his presence in Athens was not the result of specific efforts of athletic clubs or associations within Australia or New Zealand.

There are probably many reasons for Cuff's lack of enthusiasm as an IOC member for the Olympic Movement; one may have been because he saw himself merely as an intermediary for Coubertin.[99] After 1896 he may have felt that Coombes was keeping athletes and administrators in

Australia informed of Olympic matters through the *Referee*. What remains an interesting question is why Cuff did not grasp the opportunity of the Olympic Games to continue to expand New Zealand's international sporting contacts and reputation. Perhaps personal circumstances provide an answer. These changed considerably at about the time of the 1896 Olympics when he moved from Christchurch to Auckland for business reasons. He resigned from the NZAAA and from several other prominent New Zealand sporting organizations based in Christchurch. Then in 1897, after participating in the Amateur Athletic Conference, which resulted in the creation of the Amateur Athletic Union of Australasia (AAUA) of which Coombes became President, Cuff moved to Melbourne and then to Launceston, Tasmania, in 1899, and seems to have withdrawn from the administration of amateur athletics, even though he was to retain his position on the IOC until 1905.

Coombes became the main conduit between the Olympic Movement and Australasia from the time he assumed the presidency of the AAUA. It was he who requested Archie Baird, Honorary Secretary of the NSWAAA, to obtain information about the 1900 Paris Olympics when he travelled to Europe on business in 1898.[100] Much of Baird's correspondence with Coombes appeared in the *Referee*; it was clear that Baird's enquiries about the Paris Olympics were sent to Coombes as President of the NSWAAA and the AAUA rather than to Cuff as Australasia's IOC member. Clearly, Coombes had begun to establish his own links with Coubertin and the IOC and had become frustrated over Cuff's inactivity. He wrote in 1900 that 'all the nations of Europe are represented, but Australia and South Africa appear to be out in the cold'.[101]

Cuff resigned from the IOC in 1905. Interestingly, in his letter of resignation to Coubertin he referred to himself as the IOC representative for 'Australia', not 'Australasia', probably because he had been residing in the Australian state of Tasmania since 1899.[102] Cuff recommended Coombes for his position on the IOC as he was 'in close touch with officials of affiliated Associations, the active members and the likely competitors' for the next 1908 Olympic Games in London.[103] Coombes became the IOC member in 1905 and in this position, and through his presidency of the AAUA, he continued to be the main figure in the development of the Olympic Movement in Australasia until he resigned from the IOC in 1932 citing in his letter of resignation 'advancing years and ill-health'.[104] He died in 1935 at the age of 77.

CONCLUSION

Leonard Cuff, Edwin Flack and Richard Coombes are three significant Australasians who did much to foster the development of sport in the Antipodes and ensured that it became an integral aspect of Australasian culture. Although Flack did not compete internationally again after the 1896 Olympic Games, his success in 1896 stimulated interest and enthusiasm for the Olympics in Australasia. Cuff continued as the IOC member in Australasia until he was succeeded by Coombes in 1906. In short, he was on paper, at least, an Australasian presence at international Olympic deliberations. Coombes was far more active and influential in his several roles in Australia and in his role a successor to Cuff as an Australian IOC member. All three men epitomize the amateurism, nationalism, imperialism and internationalism in Victorian and Edwardian sport in Australasia. They each contributed in their various and different ways to the promotion and promulgation of the Olympic Movement, especially in its fledgling years, not only in Australasia but globally. The philosophy and idealism typical of all three men was summarized by Coombes when writing as 'Argus' in the *Referee* in 1922: 'The good fellowship of sport belongs to no country, no people. It is the possession of the world. To be proficient in some branch is, as a rule, the open sesame to the people of other lands.'[105]

NOTES

1. Newspaper clipping from the *Christchurch Press*, 1890, date unknown. From the collection of Margaret Fraser, Palmerston North, New Zealand. Ms Fraser is a descendant of Derisley and Peter Wood, who were New Zealand athletics champions and team-mates of Cuff's on the NZAAA tour of 1892.
2. The comments of 'Vanderdecken' in the English *Sunday Times* which challenged the validity of Harold Batger's performance which had equalled the English record of 16 seconds for the 120 yards hurdles during a competition in New Zealand, for example, were reproduced in the New Zealand press. Comments such as 'that the particulars of the number and height of the hurdles were not given, and without these comparisons might be more than usually odious' were reflective of the scepticism of colonial records and the attitude to colonial sport as being technically inferior to English sport. The *Christchurch Press*, 1892, date unknown. From the collection of Margaret Fraser.
3. *Christchurch Press*, 1890. Specific date unknown. From the collection of Margaret Fraser.
4. S.A.G.M. Crawford, 'Athletic Images and the Cultural Canvas of New Zealand Sport', *Sporting Heritage*, 1 (1994), 58. For a discussion of the significance of colonial sporting tours to England in the development of national identity in the Antipodes, see also S. Crawford, 'Rugby and the Forging of a National Identity', in J. Nauright (ed.), *Sport, Power and Society in New Zealand: Historical and Contemporary Perspectives*, ASSH Studies in Sport History, 11 (Sydney, 1995), pp.5–20; and J. Nauright, 'Colonial Manhood and Imperial Race Virility: British Responses to Post-Boer War Colonial Rugby Tours', in J. Nauright and T.J.L. Chandler (eds.), *Making Men: Rugby and Masculine Identity* (London, 1996), pp.121–39.

5. The team comprised Harold Batger, Jack Hempton, Peter and Derisley Wood.
6. As quoted in the *Christchurch Press*, 19 July 1892. From the collection of Margaret Fraser.
7. Letter from Cuff to F. Wilding, President of the NZAAA, 13 May 1892. Copies of Cuff's Letter Book from the 1892 NZAAA tour of Europe were provided courtesy of Margaret Fraser.
8. Had Charles Herbert suggested the trip to Paris to Cuff BEFORE the team departed New Zealand, it would probably have been reported in the correspondence at a NZAAA's Committee meetings and in press statements.
9. In addition to managing the team, Cuff also competed in the sprint and hurdles events. On the day of competition, Coubertin and Herbert acted as judges while the New Zealanders performed well, winning three events; Harold Batger set a French record for the 400 metres.
10. Programme de Union des Sociétés Françaises de Sports Athlétiques, 3e Grande Réunion Internationale Paris, 9 July 1892 The event was staged at the Racing Club of Paris.
11. H. Gordon, *Australia at the Olympic Games* (Brisbane, 1994), p.17.
12. Letter from Leonard Cuff to Baron Pierre de Coubertin, 24 April 1894. IOC Archives, Lausanne, Switzerland.
13. Letter from Leonard Cuff to Baron Pierre de Coubertin, 4 Sept. 1894. IOC Archives, Lausanne, Switzerland.
14. See D. Quanz, 'Civic Pacifism and Sports-Based Internationalism: Framework for the Founding of the International Olympic Committee', *Olympika* (1993) 2, 1–23.
15. *Referee*, 31 Jan. 1894, 7.
16. Letters from Charles Herbert to Baron Pierre de Coubertin, 10 Jan. 1894. IOC Archives, Lausanne, Switzerland. David Young refers to some of these clubs, stating that they were contacted despite being too far away to attend the Paris Congress. See D.C. Young, 'The Origins of the Modern Olympics: A New Version', *International Journal of the History of Sport*, 4, 3 (1987), 296, n.46.
17. Letter from Herbert to Coubertin, 10 Jan. 1894.
18. Inference has been made from the reply to Coubertin's letter by Cuff, dated 24 April 1894.
19. *Referee*, 8 May 1895.
20. Letter from Leonard Cuff to Baron Pierre De Coubertin, 24 April 1894. IOC Archives, Lausanne, Switzerland.
21. *Referee*, 20 March 1894, 3.
22. For elaboration, see J. MacAloon, *This Great Symbol: Pierre de Coubertin and the Origins of the Modern Olympic Games* (Chicago, 1981); D. Young, 'The Origins of the Modern Olympics', 271–300.
23. Pierre de Coubertin, 'The Paris Congress and the Revival of the Olympic Games', *Olympic Review* (1981) 101–2, 163.
24. The inaugural IOC comprised: Lord Ampthill (England); Colonel Victor Balck (Sweden); General de Boutowsky (Russia); Leonard Cuff (New Zealand); Jiri Guth-Jarkovsky (Bohemia); Charles Herbert (England); Franz Kemeny (Hungary); Count Lucchosi-Palli (Italy); William Sloane(USA); Demetrius Vikelas (Greece) and Professor Jose Benjamin Zubiaur (Argentina). See D.C. Young, 'Demetrios Vikelas: First President of the IOC', *Stadion*, XIV, 1 (1988), 85–102; and Young, 'The Origins of the Modern Olympic Movement', 271–300. It should be noted that the second Bulletin of the IOC (Oct. 1894) a modified list of members was published: Count Lucchesi-Palli was replaced by Count Andria Carafa, and Count Max de Bousies (Belgium) was added. Norbert Muller, *One Hundred Years of Olympic Congresses, 1894–1994: History—Objectives-Achievements* (Lausanne, 1994), p.36.
25. Coubertin, p.163.
26. Letter from Cuff to Coubertin, 4 Sept. 1894.
27. I. Jobling, 'Australia and the 1896 Olympic Games' (unpublished paper presented at the Fifth International Seminar for Educationalists, International Olympic Academy, Ancient Olympia, Greece, 1982).
28. Cooper was actually born in Adelaide, South Australia, the son of an English clergyman.
29. K. Moore, '"One Voice in the Wilderness": Richard Coombes and the Promotion of the Pan-Britannic Festival Concept in Australia, 1891–1911', *Sporting Traditions*, 5, 2 (1989), 189–90.
30. *Referee*, 12 Jan. 1898, 7. Katharine Moore also writes of this support in the Australian colonies, Moore, '"One Voice in the Wilderness"', 190–2.

31. *Australasian*, 4 Aug. 1894, 194. As quoted in I. Jobling, 'The Crumpled Laurel Wreath: International Sport in Disarray, Australia and the Olympic Movement, 1894–1936', *Sport and the Elite Athlete: Proceedings of the 50th ANZAAS Congress* (Adelaide, 1980), p.121.

32. *Referee*, 26 Jan. 1898, 7.

33. MacAloon, *This Great Symbol*, p.160.

34. Coubertin, p.292. Coubertin's *Olympic Memoirs* were published in 1931 and allowance should be made for comments which occurred nearly three decades earlier.

35. M. Letters and I. Jobling, 'Forgotten Links: Leonard Cuff and Olympic Movement in Australasia, 1894–1905', *Olympika-International Journal of Olympic Studies*, V (1996), 96.

36. Edwin Flack, 1896; Fred Lane and Donald Mackintosh, Stan Rowley, 1900; and Corrie Gardiner and Leslie McPherson, 1904.

37. *Referee*, 8 May 1895.

38. *Referee*, 20 March 1895, for example.

39. Despite earlier efforts, 'Prodigal' wrote in 3 July 1895, 'if Australasia is to be represented at these games it it [sic] about time something in the shape of a pow-wow was decided upon'. As late as Feb. 1896 Coombes wrote in his column under the heading 'Olympic Games at Athens' that 'Australian and New Zealand amateur athletes have been invited, but I don't think any will be able to make the trip'.

40. Coombes provided Flack with 'several letters of introduction to old friends of [his] in London', *Referee*, 20 Feb. 1895.

41. I. Jobling, 'The Making of a Nation through Sport: Australia and the Olympic Games from Athens to Berlin, 1896–1916', *Australian Journal of Politics and History*, 32, 2 (1988), 163–4. A prominent Victorian athlete described Flack as being as 'game as a pebble', but had an action which did not make good use of his arms; like many good-distance runners, he was lightly framed with a free-swinging gait and a sweeping stride. See Gordon, *Australia at the Olympic Games*, p. 2.

42. *Referee*, 20 March, 21 Aug. , 5 Nov., 18 Dec., 1895 and 15 Jan., 1896.

43. *Price Waterhouse and Co. Centenary, 1874–1974* (Melbourne, np., 1978). Flack went with colleagues of the London Athletic Club, not as part of any Australian representation.

44. Gordon, p.3.

45. As cited in Gordon, p.3.

46. Correspondence from Flack to his father, 4 April 1896.

47. *Referee*, 17 June 1896.

48. Correspondence from Flack to his father, 9 April 1896. Flack's letter continues: 'The English visitors are making a great fuss of me and I never seemed to have a minute to myself.'

49. Gordon, p.9.

50. Frenchman Lermusiaux, who regarded Flack as unbeatable over this distance and wanted to save himself for the Marathon, withdrew leaving only a field of three runners. The comment in Flack's diary for the 800 metres heat reads 'won comfortably'; alongside both the 1500 and 800 metres finals are two 'ditto' symbols.

51. Correspondence from Flack to his father, 9 April 1896

52. Correspondence from Flack to his father, 18 April 1896. See also C. Anninos, 'The Marathon Race', in *Olympic Games 776 BC-AD1896*, as cited in A. Bijkerk and D. Young, 'That Memorable First Marathon', *Journal of Olympic History*, 7, 1 (1999), 7: 'Suddenly, unknown how, it is rumoured from mouth to mouth that the Australian Flack is arriving first. The news was brought by the German cyclist Goedrich. A mournful sadness spreads over all the faces and complete silence reigns through the discouragement. But the delusion does not last long. The starter of the Marathon race, covered with dust from the long ride on horseback, is seen to enter the stadium, who going directly to the Royal thrones, announces that Louis is in the lead.'

53. *Argus*, 1896.

54. See J.A. Mangan, *Athleticism in the Victorian and Edwardian Public School* (Cambridge, 1981 and London, 2000). This is regarded as the authoritative study of the games cult (athleticism) of the British public school system. See also J.A. Mangan, *The Games Ethic and Imperialism: Aspects of the Duffusion of an Ideal* (London, 1986 and London, 1998) for details of the diffusion of the games cult into the schools of empire. For specific reference to the influence of the

metropolitan games cult on Australian middle class culture and schools, see J.A. Mangan, 'Noble Specimens of Manhood: Schoolboy Literature and the Creation of a Colonial Chivalric Code', in Jeffrey Richards, *Imperialism and Juvenile Literature* (Manchester, 1989), pp.173–94.

55. H. Perkin, 'Sport and Society: Empire into Commonwealth', in J.A. Mangan and R.B. Small (eds.), *Sport. Culture, Society: Proceedings of the VIII Commonwealth and International Conference on Sport Physical Education. Dance, Recreation and Health* (London, 1986), p.4.

56. P. Serle, *Dictionary of Australian Biography*, 1 (Sydney, 1949), p.193; B. Nairn and G. Serle, *Australian Dictionary of Biography* (Melbourne, 1981), p.105; Colin R. Veitch, 'Play up! Play up and Win the War! The Propaganda of Athleticism in Britain, 1914–1918', in G. Redmond (ed.), *Sport and Politics* (Champaign, 1984), p.1.

57. See G. Henniker and I. Jobling, 'Richard Coombes and the Olympic Movement in Australia: Imperialism and Nationalism in Action, *Sporting Traditions – Journal of Australian Society for Sports History*, 6, 1 (1989), 2–15.

58. J. Blanch and P. Jenes, *Australia's Complete History of the Commonwealth Games* (Sydney, 1982), p.l. These authors refer to J. Astley Cooper incorrectly as 'Reverend'; the Reverend Cooper was J. Astley's father.

59. Cited in Jobling, 'The Making of a Nation through Sport', p.161.

60. *Referee*, 17 Aug. 1892.

61. K. Moore, 'Strange Bedfellows and Cooperative Partners: The Influence of the Olympic Games on the Establishment of the British Empire Games', in Redmond (ed.), *Sport and Politics*, p.119.

62. *Referee*, 25 Jan. 1893. Although a detailed proposal outlining the scheme and possible dates had been published, the 'Amateur Athletics' column written by Coombes in the *Referee* in Sept. 1893, it was clear the idea was dead by 1894. For further details, see Moore, 'Strange Bedfellows', p.9.

63. *Sydney Mail*, 4 Feb. 1899, 292.

64. I. Jobling, 'The Lion, the Eagle and the Kangaroo: Politics and Proposals for a British Empire Team at the 1916 Berlin Olympics', in Redmond (ed.), *Sport and Politics*.

65. J. Foster-Fraser, *Australia: The Making of a Nation* (London, 1910).

66. *Referee*, 8 Nov. 1916.

67. B. Stoddart, 'Sport, Culture and Postcolonial Relations: A Preliminary Analysis of the Commonwealth Games: An Analysis of its Origin and Evolution', in Redmond (ed.), *Sport and Politics*; Moore, 'The Concept of the British Empire Games' (unpublished doctoral dissertation, University of Queensland, 1985), 97.

68. Moore, 'The 1911 Festival of Empire: A Final Fling?', in J.A. Mangan and R. Small (eds.), *Sport, Culture, Society: International, Historical and Sociological Perspectives* (London, 1986), pp.86–7.

69. *Referee*, 5 April 1911; Moore, 'Strange Bedfellows and Cooperative Partners', p.120;

70. *Referee*, 1 March 1911.

71. The report in *The Times* of London on 26 June 1911 implies track and field events only. Moore has cited the Minutes of the Second Annual Meeting of the AAU of Canada held at Toronto on 25 Nov. 1911, pp.49–50 to support that the Lonsdale Cup was awarded on the basis of all sports. Moore, 'The Concept of the British Empire Games', p.96.

72. *Argus*, Melbourne, 2 Aug. 1911; *Referee*, 27 Sept. 1911.

73. *Referee*, 21 Sept. 1911.

74. *Referee*, 17 July 1912. the *Argus* (19 July 1912) considered an Empire team as an alternative at future Olympic Games ' …instead of dissipating their strength by breaking up into units'.

75. *The Times*, 18 July 1912.

76. See *Sydney Morning Herald*, 10 Aug. 1912, 15; 30 Oct. 1912, pall; and Coombes' replies in the *Referee*, Sydney, 14 Aug. 1912, 1, and 6 Nov. 1912, 9.

77. *Sydney Morning Herald*, 30 Oct. 1912.

78. *Argus*, 6 Sept. 1913, 19; *Referee*, 10 Sept. 1913. Jobling has stated that he was unable to confirm from his perusal of minutes and reports of the IOC that this question was ever discussed. Regardless, it is clear that Australian sporting officials and commentators dismissed the idea from this time. Jobling, 'The Lion, the Eagle and the Kangaroo', p.105.

79. *Referee*, Sydney, 17 March 1915; 8 Nov. 1916, 10; 2 May 1917, 10.

80. *Referee*, 18 March 1914, 16; 15 April 1914, p.9; 10 June, 1914, 16; 30 Sept. 1914, 6.
81. *Referee*, 12 May 1920, 20; 19 May 1920, 10; 29 Dec. 1920, 9.
82. *Referee*, 8 Aug. 1923, 9; the columnist was 'Argus'. However, the Empire units did not march as a team; *The Times* of London, 7 July 1924, reported that the teams entered in French alphabetical order, so that South Africa (Afrique du Sud) was followed by Argentina.
83. Moore 'Strange Bedfellows', p.120.
84. *Referee*, 27 Oct. 1920, 9.
85. *Referee*, 5 Aug. 1928, 11.
86. See Jobling, 'Australia and the Commonwealth Games'.
87. *Referee*, 8 Jan. 1930, 15; 5 Feb. 1930, 1; 11 June 1930, 15.
88. *Referee*, 15 Aug. 1928.
89. Letter from Leonard Cuff to Baron Pierre de Coubertin, 24 Jan. 1896. IOC Archives, Lausanne, Switzerland.
90. See New Zealand Olympic Association Minute Book, 1911–1912, 1920, New Zealand Olympic and Commonwealth Games Association Archives, Wellington, New Zealand.
91. New Zealand Olympic Association Minute Book, 1911–1912.
92. Athletes from New Zealand first competed in the London Olympic Games in 1908.
93. However, it does seem likely that Cuff also contacted clubs and associations in New Zealand. The extract in the *Bulletin du Comité International des Jeux*, 2 states:

    A letter from Leonard A. Cuff, secretary of the New Zealand Amateur Athletics Association, member of the International Committee, had just arrived at the general secretariat since the publication of the last number of the Bulletin. The letter gives warm adherence to all the decisions of the Paris Congress and the promise of Australian collaboration which will be as complete as the enormous distance that separates us from the great ocean continent. Mr. Cuff has drawn up a list of Australian Clubs likely to participate in the Olympic Games and has communicated to them the general lines of our project, while waiting to receive the detailed programme that we have announced.

94. This relationship was significant, since the programme of the 1896 Olympics was dominated by athletics events, so the responsibility for sending competitors to the Games lay primarily with the colonial amateur athletics associations of Australia and New Zealand. The expense confronting amateur athletes who were interested in competing in the Olympics reinforced the necessity of the Amateur Athletic Associations as sponsoring agencies. For example, the cost of single passenger births from Sydney to London ranged from 35 to 70 pounds, and 65 to 105 pounds return. *Sydney Morning Herald*, 8 Jan. 1896
95. *Referee*, 20 March 1895, 7. In this edition Coombes also wrote: 'The project (Olympic Games) is becoming daily more popular … Our Associations must not altogether lose sight of this great festival.'
96. *Referee*, 3 July 1895, 7.
97. *Referee*, 16 Oct. 1895, 7.
98. Letter from Cuff to Coubertin, 28 Jan. 1896. IOC Archives, Lausanne, Switzerland.
99. Letters and Jobling, 'Forgotten Links', p.100.
100. *Referee*, 11 May 1898, 7. Cuff did provide Baird with a letter of introduction to Charles Herbert.
101. *Referee*, 19 April 1899, 6.
102. Cuff wrote, 'It has been my intention for sometime back to write and resign my position as a Committeeman on the International Olympic Committee for Australia, owing to having dropped out of Athletics', Letter from Cuff to Coubertin, 18 Jan. 1905. New Zealand Pierre de Coubertin Committee, Report to the IOC, Wellington, New Zealand, 1991.
103. Coubertin replied to Cuff's letter of 18 Jan. asking him to reconsider, but Cuff reaffirmed his decision and reiterated his recommendation that Coombes succeed him. Personal correspondence from Cuff to Coubertin, 17 April 1905, New Zealand Pierre de Coubertin Committee, 1991.
104. Coombes was also regarded as the father of Australian amateur athletics' (see the *Mercury*, 14 Jan. (1924), 8; P. Serle, *Dictionary of Australian Biography*, p.105), as well as the 'father of Empire sport' (*Referee*, 9 Dec. 1931, 21).
105. *Referee*, 6 Sept. 1922, 9.

PART 2

Sport in Later Antipodean Society

8

Surf Lifesaving: The Development of an Australasian 'Sport'

DOUGLAS BOOTH

Many Australians and New Zealanders escape the rigours and stresses of modern life at the beach. There they relax, lounge, picnic, play games, explore and go surfbathing. The latter, a portmanteau term for bathing, swimming and frolicking in open ocean waters and among the waves, is an integral component of contemporary beach culture. In fact, orthodox histories of surfbathing in Australia and New Zealand typically begin with the functionalist assumption that it is a natural activity, synonymous with sunshine, clear and warm water, golden sands, and curling waves. Frank Margan and Ben Finney, for example, claim that 'it was only a matter of time' before Australians 'took the plunge',[1] while Stephen Barnett and Richard Wolfe believe that it was 'inevitable, given [New Zealand's] equable climate and access by the vast majority of its population to a wealth of fine beaches, that ... swimming in the sea would eventually be commonplace'.[2] But there is nothing natural about surfbathing: disinterest is strong in many congenial climates and alluring settings.[3] Furthermore, in the nineteenth century many local governments prohibited surfbathing. In short, culture, and in particular attitudes towards the presentation of the body in public, is the principal determinant of surfbathing.

An examination of the cultural conditions that initially restricted the public display of the bathing body, together with the transformation of those conditions, is therefore necessary to understand the history of surfbathing in Australia and New Zealand. According to the dominant view, initially propagated in the 1930s by officials of the Surf Life Saving Association of Australia (SLSAA), who were delving into the origins of their association, the first surfbathers were young rebels who defied repressive and prudish Victorian laws that prohibited bathing in public.[4] However, surfbathing was never a generational issue. Rather it was a site of tension and debate within the middle classes. Medical practitioners, health faddists and small business interests claimed that surfbathing was a healthy sport that contributed to local economies; moralists condemned it as an indecent pastime.

Middle-class factions organized surfbathing in Australia and New Zealand early this century. They established clubs that became the foundations of surf lifesaving associations. Although initially reluctant to assist surfbathing clubs, local councils quickly reappraised their positions and accepted them as a way to defray the costs of ensuring surfbathers' safety. Yet, despite their identical class composition and similar objectives, the lifesaving movements in Australia and New Zealand adopted distinct philosophies. These reflected critical variations in socio-political circumstances.

LEGALIZING DAYLIGHT SURFBATHING

Medical practitioners in eighteenth-century England alerted the aristocracy to the therapeutic benefits of bathing in cold water. Under aristocratic patronage, the middle classes adopted bathing as a healthy pastime which they pursued as a recreational activity and developed into the sport of swimming. In the nineteenth century, however, moralists voiced concerns about indecently exposed swimmers and bathers. Richard Rutt describes many interventions by English moralists.[5] In New South Wales, governor Lachlan Macquarie banned bathing at the government wharf and dockyard in 1810, describing it as an 'indecent and improper custom'.[6] Two decades later, the New South Wales government prohibited bathing in all waters exposed to public view between 6.00 a.m. and 8.00 p.m.[7] A city by-law in Christchurch, New Zealand, prohibited public bathing in the Avon River.[8]

For most of the nineteenth century bathing and swimming were minority activities. Males and females bathed separately and one could always find an isolated river or beach. Thus, the presentation of the body was not an issue. Judging from the following account of the official opening of Dunedin's St Clair seawater baths in 1884, the state of bathers and swimmers' undress attracted minimal attention:

> Shortly after 4 o'clock Mr Calder [the local mayor] stepped out of the bathing house and approached the brink of the water ... addressing the crowd, he said ... that they now had saltwater baths

wherein they could bathe with security and enjoyment. The speaker then divested himself of his overcoat, and showed himself to be arrayed in nature's garb, with the exception of a pair of bathing trunks, and without more ado took a 'header', followed by about a dozen similarly attired persons. The Industrial School Band was in attendance, and considerably enlivened the proceedings by playing a number of selections.[9]

Nuisance inspectors policed bathing hours in Australia, although they took little action against the unclad. In 1889 the mayor of Manly instructed inspector Leahy to ignore those who bathed naked before 7.00 a.m.[10]

Public presentation of the bathing body became a legal and moral issue in Australia and New Zealand only in the last decade of the nineteenth century. In 1891 Manly Council in New South Wales passed new by-laws requiring bathers to wear costumes at all times.[11] Napier Borough Council and the Dunedin Ocean Beach Domain Board in New Zealand followed in the mid-1890s. Their by-laws demanded that bathers wear 'decent' and 'proper' costumes.[12] Section 10 of the Dunedin by-laws went further and banned bathing 'on any part of the beach under the control of the Board'; the law confined bathers to the St Clair baths.[13]

At issue was the rapidly growing middle classes' obsession with health, and what Christopher Lasch calls the 'therapeutic outlook'.[14] While the established upper classes, who possessed high volumes of both economic and cultural capital, were self-assured and indifferent to the gaze of others and viewed promenading and open bathing as social pleasures, the middle classes, especially those factions which had invested time and effort in acquiring cultural capital, were less secure and less confident in their bodies.[15] In the late nineteenth century these new middle-class factions exposed themselves to endless private and public examination 'for tell tale symptoms of psychic stress, for blemishes and flaws' and 'for reassuring indications that ... life is proceeding according to schedule'.[16] The beach became a favourite site among health faddists, physicians, physical educators, utopians and the like, a place where they could display their therapeutic outlook. By the First World War they would legitimize the revealed body and supplant the reserved, modest, restrained and hidden Victorian body. But initially the therapeutic outlook fuelled an hysteria among conservative middle-class moralists. These 'agents of disgust', as Freud called them,[17] or 'Mrs Grundies' as they were popularly known in Australasia,[18] insisted that bathers lacked restraint and self-control over bodily desires, and that bathing stimulated desire for flesh, aroused erotic thoughts and encouraged sexual crimes. The result was a debate and struggle over daylight bathing.

Australasian surfbathers wanted to bathe in daylight while moralists argued that such activity would corrupt the social order. In 1893 local councillors described as 'disgraceful' the young men who bathed at Devonport (Auckland) in 'full view of passers-by in a perfectly nude condition'.[19] James Wilson complained in 1901 to the New South Wales Legislative Council about 'men in an absolute state of nudity' who appeared at the public baths in the Domain.[20] The Local Authorities Act and the Municipal Authorities Act empowered local councils in New South Wales and New Zealand respectively to pass by-laws governing bathers' behaviour and dress. Within Sydney, Manly and Randwick imposed an 8.00am curfew, although Waverley permitted bathing at Little Coogee (now Clovelly) at all hours provided bathers were 'properly and becomingly clad'. The New South Wales police, however, continued to prosecute bathers under Section 77 of the Police Offenses Act.[21]

Legal jousting and the courts eventually settled the debate. In October 1902 William Gocher, proprietor and editor of the *Manly and North Sydney Daily*, announced through the paper, that he would defy the law and bathe during daylight hours at Manly. Gocher wanted a test case. On three consecutive Sundays he bathed at midday in a neck-to-knee costume. On approaching and leaving the water he wore a mackintosh over his costume. Inspector-general Fosbery declined to prosecute Gocher. Fosbery's discretion becomes clearer in the light of a police report dealing with a similar incident the following month. In November 1902 Waverley Council requested Fosbery to prosecute naked bathers who ran along the beach and who 'appear to take great delight in this somewhat distusing [*sic*] habit, to the annoyance of residents and others'.[22] Two constables proceeded to Bondi Beach where they recorded the names and addresses of 15 bathers, two of whom wore neck-to-knee bathing costumes and the remainder 'small trunks'. In their report the police noted that all the bathers were 'respectable men and residents of the district'. They did not observe any bathers naked or undressing in public view. Further investigation revealed that the complainant was Mr

Farmer, the lessee of Bondi baths. He paid the council £150 per annum and was 'annoyed at seeing so many people enjoying a free bath'.[23] Fosbery thus concluded that:

> so long as bathers wear suitable costume and public decency is not outraged, I am unable to see that a practice permitted for so many years should be stopped. Indeed, I do not suppose that the magistrates would inflict penalties for any breach of the Act ... Unless, therefore, I receive instructions from the government to the contrary, I do not see my way to take action beyond instructing the police that decency is to be observed.[24]

Manly Council initially refused to sanction daytime bathing. Without police support, however, it had little choice but to repeal the by-law in November 1903.[25]

Failed prosecutions paved the way for daylight bathing in New Zealand. When Christchurch police charged a local man with violating bathing by-laws in December 1909, a stipendiary magistrate ridiculed the prosecuting constable and held the by-laws to be *ultra vires* and unreasonable.[26] Similar circumstances occurred in Dunedin several months later. In March 1910 Dunedin police charged Quinton McKinnon and brothers Frank and Albert Gurr with violating local by-laws by bathing after 7.30 a.m.[27] Like the Gocher case in New South Wales, the Dunedin courts never adjudicated the legal arguments for and against daylight bathing. Magistrate J.R. Bartholomew agreed with the bathers' solicitor that the Ocean Beach Domain Board, in requesting an adjournment, had failed to act with promptitude and he dismissed the charges without prejudice.[28]

Cases such as these opened the way for daylight bathing in Australasia. Bathing became an accepted, and popular, practice. But moralists were not silenced: they insisted on new costume regulations that would ensure decency on the beaches.

BATHING COSTUMES AND THE REGULATION OF DECENCY

According to devotees, surfbathing produced youthful, attractive bodies. The *Australian Star* recommended that the public acquaint itself with 'the brown skinned specimens of manhood who spend their weekends at the beach'.[29] J.Q.X., a columnist in *The Dominion* (Wellington, NZ), praised the 'quick, free movements' of youthful 'brown limbs ... on the level sands' at Lyall Bay. 'It is only at such a time,' J.Q.X. added, 'that one sees how truly graceful is the figure of the ordinary healthy youth.'[30] A correspondent to Napier's *Daily Telegraph* poetically described the beauty of the revealed human body: 'trunks (watertight) display every lovely curve and crease as the sportive mermaids rear themselves to the embrace of Father Neptune, or as they race out alongside an Adonis for a flirtation and a sunbath'.[31]

Supporters also portrayed surfbathers as national assets against the inevitability of war. A.W. Relph, a founding member of the Manly Surf Club, claimed that the surfbathing race comprised fine, healthy men, 'quite equal to their brothers who live outback in the bush and open air of the country', and that 'when Australia needs them, as some day no doubt she will, these men, trained athletes, tanned with the sun on the beaches, strong and brawny with the buffeting in the surf, will be well fitted to take up their trust and do duty for their country'.[32] Lastly, surfbathing appeared as a panacea for the ills of urban life. 'We are an open air people', declared Sydney's *Evening News*, and

> in these days when the 'return-to-nature' theory is looked upon with increasing favour, the getting of as much sunshine and fresh air as possible is coming to be looked upon as a moral duty. Sand, surf, sunshine and the free winds of heaven make up the prescription which is confidently recommended as a sort of universal medicine ... This, if not the elixir of life, must surely be part of it, and is certain to tone up the system and lengthen the life. It is plain that he who wishes for a royal road to health and happiness should take the first step to it by getting sunburnt, it is well understood that a well-browned skin is much healthier than a white one. So the sun-worshipper looks with pity upon his pallid brother as one who stupidly neglects a most evident good, and, in fact one who falls short somehow in the standard of true manliness.[33]

J.Q.X. concurred. Surely, the columnist suggested, 'exposure to wind and sunshine, even on Lambton Quay', would 'make for health and vigour'. And,

> would not our natural and proper vanity, deprived of all aid of tailoring, express itself in more shapely and muscular limbs, more erect and graceful carriage? And after a generation or two, would it

not be rare indeed to see a sick body amongst us? Would not ... the light covering of the surfbathers do more for our eugenical future than all our hospitals, military drills and medical inspection?[34]

Moralists agreed that surfbathing was an 'invigorating and healthy pastime'.[35] But they feared that indecent and wanton behaviour would 'retard progress' and undermine 'the common standards of propriety that prevail amongst civilized nations'.[36] Moralists inundated the press, protesting about bathers' costumes, sunbathing and mixed bathing. 'One Disgusted' inveighed against 'vulgar beasts' who lay on the beach at Napier 'absolutely nude with the exception of a towel'.[37] 'A Mother of Girls' said that the 'heaps of sprawling men and lads, naked, but for a nondescript rag around their middle' had forced her to leave Sydney's Balmoral beach.[38]

Moralists frequently compared the behaviour of surfbathers to animals. 'Daily Dipper' said that sunbathers 'put themselves on the same level as dogs'[39] while 'Disgrace' likened surfbathers, 'basking their naked bodies in the sun', to 'alligators watching for their prey'.[40] Moralists labelled surfbathers 'blackguards' and 'larrikins'. 'One Indignant' rebuked 'yahoos' who used the beach for the 'purpose of exhibiting their nakedness under the pretence of bathing',[41] and Sydney's *Daily Telegraph* described 'dirty ignorant louts ... dirty bodily and mentally', who go to the beach 'not to bath, but to indulge unchecked in ... horseplay'.[42]

Moralists' outcries forced local councils to pass by-laws regulating swimwear and sunbathing. A major problem with the then standard Canadian neck-to-knee costume was that it became transparent and revealed too much of the wearer's figure and anatomy when wet. Councils thus ordered male bathers to wear trunks, of dark material, either inside or outside, the costume; females were required to wear a loose-fitting tunic, also of dark material, over their neck-to-knee costumes.

Surfbathers opposed strict costume regulations that they said undermined the benefits of surfbathing. R.D. Meagher, a member of the New South Wales Legislative Council, said if surfbathing was to have a 'salutary effect on skin, nerves, and tissue' then saltwater and sunlight must strike the body. But Meagher also accused moralists of failing to acknowledge the new, independent, Australian:

> Where is Mrs Grundy going to stop? Our Australian girls no longer consider it good to wear pale and uninteresting complexions

like the heroine of the 'Young Ladies' Journal', but are devotees to Old Sol and Neptune – these bronze Venuses, with Ozone in their nostrils, and vitality in their constitutions, are to be the robust mothers of the vigorous race which is to hold white Australia against all comers.[43]

'Baldhead' warned that New Zealand was 'in the claws of Mrs Grundy'. He challenged 'her' morality: 'when a community ceases to be natural, when people see indecency everywhere ... it is a clear sign of mental decay, of moral collapse, incipient degeneracy, and of doom'. There is nothing wrong, he insisted, with 'healthy, jolly girls, full of life, to be gambolling on a beach, or strong, well made athletes to run about with bathing trunks only'.[44]

Two antagonistic moralities – an old morality and a new morality – emerge in this debate. At the centre of the old morality is 'a fear of pleasure and a relation to the body made up of reserve, modesty and restraint'. The new morality combined pleasure with, *inter alia*, the search for self-expression, bodily expression and the cult of personal health.[45] Revealed surfbathing bodies became symbols of the new morality, a morality which, it warrants noting, concerned the public presentation of the European body and did not dampen prevailing racist sentiments. Local councils in Sydney attempted to reconcile the two moralities but their actions prompted protests by surfbathers.

In October 1907 Manly, Randwick and Waverley councils met with the Local Government Branch of the Public Works Department to draft a new set of beach ordinances. According to the proposed by-laws bathing costumes would:

cover the body from the neck to the bend of the knee; and be of such material as not to disclose the colour of the skin [and] ... shall consist of complete combinations, *together with a tunic worn over the combinations*, both covering the body from the neck to the knee, and the tunic shall have sleeves reaching to at least half way from the shoulder to the elbow.

The draft ordinances prohibited males and females mixing on the beaches, undressing and dressing in public view, 'loitering on the beach clad only in bathing costume' and sunbathing outside special enclosures. In addition, the proposed law required bathers in costume to take the most direct route between the dressing pavilions and the water.[46]

Waverley mayor, R.G. Watkins, defended the proposals. 'Some of these surfbathers are nothing but exhibitionists' who go about 'in a worse manner than if they were nude', he said.[47]

Surfbathers interpreted the 'tunics' as 'skirts' and staged demonstrations at Manly, Coogee and Bondi beaches against what they said would undermine Australian manhood. At Bondi, some 250 male bathers donned skirts of various descriptions and marched along the beach. Reporters from the *Evening News* filed an account of the protest:

> The manner in which the spectators, men and women alike, joined in the humour of the thing was evidence of the popularity of the surfbathers, while at the same time the onlookers were afforded an object lesson which plainly indicated the absurdity of the skirt idea as applied to men.
>
> The utmost good humour prevailed on the beach. There were repeated cries of 'Are we downhearted?' and 'Will you wear the skirt?' to all of which came a deafening 'No'. Then someone sang out, 'Well, let us laugh'. But this was unnecessary, for the spectators, as in fact everybody on the beach, processionists included, were already laughing to their hearts content. They had entered earnestly into the humour of the thing, but, at the same time, they were there to heap such ridicule on the skirt ordinance as would successfully kill it for all time.[48]

Laughter is a potent strategy of resistance and the protestors forced local councils to retreat. The new beach ordinances, promulgated seven months later, made no reference to 'tunics'.[49] But surfbathers had learned a valuable lesson; they needed an umbrella association to advocate the benefits of surfbathing, to counter moralists' attacks, and to represent their interests. Sydney surfbathers had begun forming local surf clubs in 1906 and 1907, and at the start of the 1907–8 season officials from these clubs, the New South Wales Head Centre of the Royal Life Saving Society (RLSS),[50] and the New South Wales Swimming Association established the Surf Bathing Association of New South Wales (SBANSW).[51] In New Zealand surfbathers formed the first clubs in 1910 and 1911.[52] In both countries these clubs became the foundations of lifesaving movements.

The lifesaving movements constitute the formal organization of surfbathing in Australia and New Zealand. Before the 1950s the philosophy of these two movements differed as a response to specific local conditions. In New South Wales, the 'skirt' issue acted as a catalyst for the formation of a politically motivated umbrella organization, SBA, which sought to legitimize surfbathing *and* gain control of local beaches: lifesaving was simply the means to those ends. In New Zealand lifesaving developed as a purely humanitarian activity and as an end in itself. As a result, the first surfbathing clubs maintained closer relationships with the RLSS for much longer than those in Australia. But before comparing the nature of organized surfbathing in Australia and New Zealand, it is necessary to analyse the economic history of early lifesaving in both countries. The economic interests of the early leaders and advocates of lifesaving – many of who were land speculators and property developers or owners of food, transport, souvenir and entertainment businesses that depended on beach tourists[53] – is an area largely ignored by historians of surf lifesaving. Standard histories have focused, almost exclusively, on the humanitarian objectives of lifesaving, but economic considerations encouraged local councils to approve the volunteer rescue services organized by surfbathers. This approval encouraged bathers to establish formal lifesaving clubs.

THE ECONOMIC FOUNDATIONS OF ORGANIZED SURFBATHING

Middle-class gentlemen and public figures stood at the helms of the new surf clubs in Australasia. Ironically, however, their economic and social interests meant that they were as conservative as those moralists who opposed surfbathing. At the founding meeting of the Manly Surf Club, inaugural president Frank Donovan recommended that the 'officers and committee be men of some standing'. According to one press report, half of the initial 600 members of Manly were 'leading citizens', including its patron, the state governor.[54] Likewise, 'men of standing' promoted surfbathing in New Zealand. John Brodie, the inaugural president of the Worser Bay Amateur Surf Lifesaving and Swimming Club was mayor of Miramar;[55] D.C. Cameron, who chaired the meeting which launched the Pacific Surf Club, Dunedin's first surfbathing club, was mayor of St Kilda; William Downie Stewart, mayor of Dunedin, advocated the formation of a second surfbathing club in the southern city. Belinda Leckie concludes that 'virtually all' the foundation members of the St Clair Surf Life Saving Club were property owners.[56]

Yet neither the social standing of officials, their appeals and criticisms, nor their references to the health and medical benefits deriving from bathing, persuaded local councils to invest in surfbathing. Dunedin's Ocean Beach Domain Board gave surfbathers permission to build dressing rooms and lockers for storing lifesaving equipment although it refused to contribute financially.[57] Waverley Council debated at length the merits of funding dressing accommodation for surfbathers. Several aldermen objected on the grounds that bathers did not contribute to council coffers.[58] Some local ratepayers echoed these sentiments. C. Anderson opposed council expenditure of ratepayers' money on '50 or 60 bathers'.[59] Waverley Council agreed to erect bathing accommodation subject to contributions from the Lands Department, the Railway Commissioners, and the public.[60]

Councillors could not, however, ignore surfbathing's economic contribution. After the legalization of daylight bathing, beachside suburbs became popular places to live and the beach a favourite site for recreation. Surfbathing officials and their supporters recognized the opportunity. Frank Donovan attributed a 50 per cent growth in Manly's population and huge increases in local property values, housing rents and rates to surfbathing.[61] In 1912 an official New South Wales government inquiry into surfbathing, chaired by John Lord, the president of SBANSW, warned that the lack of suitable dressing accommodation would hinder 'commercial prosperity, and the increase in land and rental values which surfing brings in its train'.[62] The *Otago Daily Times* said that residents would judge the Dunedin Ocean Beach Domain Board harshly if it 'neglect[ed] ... its duties as custodian of the Ocean Beach' and failed to 'provide such facilities as will encourage surfbathing and render St Clair an even more attractive spot'.[63] Columnist 'Pakeha II' advised that surfbathing would 'make the beach a great asset to the city' and urged the 'statutory governing bodies to do their duty' and actively encourage the pastime.[64]

Competition for surfbathers' money persuaded local councils to invest in foreshore development. Before the 1907–8 season, Manly and Randwick councils advertised their respective beaches as Sydney's favourite resorts. Randwick council initiated a programme of improvements at Coogee which included a new dressing shed with a concrete floor and fresh water, lighting for night bathers, a network of footpaths, bandstand, kiosks, and picnic tables and chairs.[65] Quick, cheap transport was an essential prerequisite for development. An electrified tramline (and bathing sheds, band rotunda and waiting shed) transformed Lyall Bay from a 'run for wild pigs and rabbits' to the 'Manly of Wellington'.[66] An extension of the Manly-Brookvale line to Collaroy Beach in 1912 made it 'within easy reach' of day-trippers and picnickers from Sydney and 'guaranteed the area's continued development'.[67]

Economic prosperity did not ameliorate moral concerns. Ironically, those whom historians would later misleadingly call rebels did most to appease the moralists by disciplining fellow clubs members and educating the public about the etiquette of surfbathing. Worser Bay Amateur Surf Lifesaving and Swimming Club appointed a costume steward to ensure that 'competitors were decently clad in such a way as to avoid casting aspersions on the morals of club members'.[68] At its first meeting, the St Clair Branch of the Pacific Surf Bathing Club passed a resolution to 'discourage' members from bathing on Sunday afternoons.[69] A principal aim of SBANSW was to determine rules for the proper conduct of surfbathers.[70] The report of the New South Wales government inquiry into surfbathing recommended that councils appoint members of bathing clubs as beach inspectors: 'by choosing the older and more responsible members [the councils] will secure the aid of men who will use their authority with moderation and discretion for the good of the public, and for the advancement of surfbathing'. The report objected to sunbathing, which it defined as 'loitering on the beach clad only in bathing costume', and to people in bathing costumes mixing with the general public. It also recommended that bathers walk from the dressing pavilions to the water by the most direct route.[71]

Each year large numbers of Australians and New Zealanders drown in the surf and safety has always been a major concern of surfbathers. However, economics generated much of the historical public debate about safety in the surf. Indeed, even William Henry, the founder of the RLSS, told a Dunedin audience during a visit in 1910, that every drowning cost the state £300.[72] It is hardly surprising that economics should play such an important role, given the class and business interests behind organized surfbathing. Foreshore development, increased tourism and higher property values depended upon safe beaches. In Sydney, local realtors at Harbord advertised Freshwater as the 'safest beach in Australia',[73] while the Barrenjoey Land Company, owner of 400 acres on the southern headland of Broken Bay, produced a booklet for potential purchasers which described Palm Beach as 'one of the safest –

if not the safest – surfing beaches in Australia': 'Magnificent breaking rollers, so eagerly sought after by surfers are abundantly in evidence. The beach at one end forms itself into a natural harbour affording an opportunity for the little folks to bathe and romp in perfect safety.'[74]

Similarly, *The Dominion* devoted many column inches to Lyall Bay and ran prominent advertisements for land sales there. It described the Bay as 'well suited to be the playground of children, for it slopes very gently, and there is plenty of room for them to bathe without getting anywhere near dangerous depths … from each point [of the Bay] run lines of rocks that serve to protect the waters still further from rough weather outside'.[75]

In the nineteenth century, local councils assumed authority over local beaches and surfbathers, and they passed by-laws to that effect; they also recognized the economic contributions made by surfbathing. When it came to accepting responsibility for bathers' safety, however, their first reaction was to baulk. Whereas in North America local authorities employed permanent lifeguards, in Australasia most councils believed that their responsibility ended with the provision of rudimentary equipment and notices. For example, Warringah Shire Council, which was responsible for most of Sydney's northern beaches, provided 'life lines' – a neck-to-waist cork belt attached to 50 yards of coir rope and housed in wooden boxes attached to poles.[76] But people were needed to operate this equipment and to patrol beaches, and surfbathing clubs seemed the obvious solution to councils anxious to minimize expenses. Experienced and competent surfbathers had long served as *de facto* lifesavers and the voluntary nature of the clubs enabled the council to defray costs. Manly was one of the first councils to employ a lifesaver – New Zealander, Edward 'Happy' Eyre. He patrolled the beach on weekdays and Saturdays, and the Manly Surf Club took over on Sundays. For their part, most of the early surfbathing clubs affiliated to the RLSS and officials expected members, especially juniors, to learn rescue and resuscitation methods.[77] According to the 1907–8 annual report of the RLSS's New South Wales branch, 33 surf clubs between Tweed Heads in the north to Twofold Bay in the south, were affiliates.[78]

HUMANITARIAN DIRECTIONS (AND DILEMMAS)

Surfbathing clubs in New South Wales severed their links with the RLSS by 1910 and the SBA instituted its own qualification and award systems. 'Independence' refocused attention on the role and legitimacy of the clubs. Local councils and ordinary surfbathers did not automatically welcome the clubs, especially when they demanded public land for clubhouses and seized large sections of the beach for 'private' use. To enhance respectability, SBANSW embellished the RLSS's military-style rescue drills and procedures; surf carnivals were public displays and featured march-pasts, uniforms, insignia, flags and 'strict discipline and concentrated behaviour'.[79] SBANSW also redefined its 'sole aim' as 'the promotion of lifesaving in the surf'[80] and assumed a 'duty of care' for surfbathers. In 1920 the organization reinforced the latter by changing its name to the Surf Life Saving Association, which within three years had became a national body. These strategies proved successful: two years after becoming a *lifesaving* association, the New South Wales government granted it an annual subsidy of £200. Over the next two decades, SLSAA took every opportunity to advertise itself as a volunteer, humanitarian, safety service. For example, it highlighted the number of rescues made each season and the cumulative number of 'lives saved'. The cover of SLSAA's 1925 annual report claimed that a total of 12,000 lives had been saved since the association's foundation in 1907. It was a 'guesstimate' – SLSAA only began to compile accurate statistics in 1923 (647 rescues) and, of course, a rescue does not necessarily translate into a life saved. In 1932, SLSAA adopted the motto 'Vigilance and Service' and in 1940 it boasted, for the first of many times, that no lives had been lost the previous season at beaches patrolled by lifesavers. SLSAA's humanitarian policy certainly led to increased government support. Federal and state governments recognize the cost effectiveness of the voluntary SLSAA. But among ordinary members, SLSAA's humanitarian policy kindled a problem of identity.

SBANSW's initial primary objective was 'to advance the sport and pastime of surfbathing'. As well as the informal, healthy and invigorating act of 'surf shooting' (body surfing and later surfboard riding), the sport of surfbathing increasingly referred to a new genre of formal competitions based on patient rescue. Although the middle-classes regarded sports that encouraged amateur ideals – downgrading victory, self-restraint, masking of enthusiasm in victory and disappointment in defeat, equalization of outcomes, voluntary compliance with the rules and chivalrous attitudes towards opponents – as forms of moral endeavour, the competitive, celebratory and entertainment aspects of sport weakened SBANSW's public credibility.

SLSAA's response was to give greater priority to rescue work; this would supposedly ensure organizational autonomy on, and control over, the beach. From the late 1930s, SLSAA played down the tag of sporting organization. In 1940 it proclaimed:

> We are in a peculiar position of being a body formed primarily and principally with the humanitarian object of rendering safe the healthy and invigorating pastime of surfbathing, and at the same time we are able, by means of competition in our various phases of activity, to introduce into our work a very definite sporting spirit which greatly benefits our Association work and our relations with the general public.[81]

The shift presented a problem for the governing association because the new emphasis conflicted with the desires of ordinary club members. Surfbathing clubs were never bastions of humanitarianism; most people joined the clubs simply to use the facilities or for the camaraderie. The first clubs in New South Wales were popularly called 'dressing shed syndicates',[82] and an early member of Manly recalled the club being 'run by ... old men, who were primarily concerned with having a decent dressing place and showers'.[83] In 1911 the MSC split after the local council refused to set aside an area of beach for a new clubhouse. When the MSC threatened to withdraw its beach patrols unless the council acceded, a small group of club members, who the majority called 'disloyalists' and 'beach scavengers', departed and formed the Manly Life Saving Club.[84] Sean Brawley concluded that 'few if any' people joined the Collaroy or Palm Beach clubs for humanitarian reasons. In the case of the latter, most joined to 'take advantage' of residential facilities and recreational and social activities.[85] Several score of unpublished club histories, usually written by honorary and amateur historians, support Brawley's conclusions. Of course, while alternative lures are not uncommon in the history of voluntary organizations in the twentieth century, including those dealing with sport and leisure, it is an especially pronounced problem for the SLSAA.

By contrast, different circumstances prevailed in New Zealand where surfbathers never confronted a galvanizing political event like the 1907 'skirt' crisis in Sydney and local clubs maintained close links with the RLSS for over two decades. Indeed, Kent Pearson attributes the critical difference between the Australian and New Zealand organizations to their historical relationships with the RLSS. 'In general', he wrote, 'relationships between these two bodies in Australia were characterized by conflict with occasional periods of calm, while in New Zealand the reverse was the case'.[86]

The RLSS had either a direct or indirect involvement in the formation of the original seven clubs in New Zealand. New Brighton, Castlecliff and Sumner were branches of the RLSS. Although Maranui was technically an independent surf lifesaving club, the chairman of the Wellington Head Centre of the RLSS, G.S. Hill, presided over the public meeting that launched the club. He also became a vice-president of the club and helped lobby the Wellington Council for £50 towards a clubhouse.[87] Similarly, the president of the Otago Head Centre of the RLSS, A. Davidson, gave his 'hearty support' when surfbathing enthusiasts launched the Pacific Surf Club (PSC) in Dunedin.[88] Moreover, the St Clair Life Saving Club, formed by members of the PSC's St Clair Branch a month later, 'functioned under the auspices of the RLSS'.[89] Lyall Bay and Worser Bay were initially branches of the New Zealand Amateur Swimming Association (NZASA), which had been founded in Auckland in 1890. NZASA, too, was a RLSS affiliate.

Military symbolism was a feature of both SLSAA and the New Zealand Surf Life Saving Association (NZSLSA). Australian and New Zealand lifesavers both 'inherited the ANZAC tradition'.[90] 'The sloping fields of Waterloo, so often read in our history books, seem to have come to light once again,' wrote Norman Ingram, a former president of NZSLSA, when describing the march-past competition at the 1935 national championships: 'they came over the top of the sloping sand drifts and levelled off again'.[91] New Zealand officers also encouraged club members to compete in sporting events as a way to hone rescue skills and generate interest and keenness. NZSLSA's two most prestigious sporting competitions, the Wigram and Nelson shields, were introduced in 1911 and 1915 respectively.[92] But a sporting ethos did not become ingrained in the New Zealand lifesaving movement until the 1950s. The grand, pulsating surf carnival, a feature of the Sydney beach scene by the First World War, was several decades away in New Zealand. The inaugural competitions for both the Wigram and Nelson shields were held in conjunction with the New Zealand swimming championships and even in the early 1930s RLSS carnivals included only four events. SBANSW championship carnivals featured nine events before the 1920s.[93] In short, the embryonic lifesaving movement in New Zealand remained tied to the RLSS's humanitarian traditions and ethos.

Despite efforts by Canterbury surf lifesavers to form an independent national association immediately after the First World War, the NZSLSA did not emerge until 1932. Ironically, this was a reaction to another attempt by Cantabrians to form a national body. Canterbury was the early home of surf lifesaving in New Zealand. In 1912 Cantabrian lifesavers brought together the RLSS Head Centres in New Zealand which had been established by William Henry during his tour of the Dominion two years earlier.[94] In 1919 and 1920 the Canterbury Surf Lifesaving Association (CSLSA), an affiliate of the RLSSNZ, made 'strenuous' but unsuccessful efforts to 'take control of reel lifesaving away from the RLSS'.[95] In 1931, when the CSLSA again approached clubs to defect from the RLSS, the Society's council 'invited' surf lifesaving officials in Wellington to form a new national association with its headquarters in the capital.[96]

CONCLUSION: THE PHILOSOPHY OF LIFESAVING

Economic and health interests motivated the early generations of surfbathers in Australasia who predominantly came from the middle classes. Yet, different political and social circumstances in Australia and New Zealand led these surfbathers to form two surf lifesaving associations, each with its own philosophy. SLSAA's philosophy celebrates an aggressive, all-conquering, human willpower that, combined with hard labour, strives to overcome, subdue and subordinate the ocean. In *The Lure of the Sea*, Alain Corbin analyses the 'invention' of the beach in early nineteenth-century Western society. He describes a process in which bathers 'harmonise' the beach and set out to 'see, feel, and experience the sea'.[97] But one finds little evidence of 'harmonization' among Australian lifesavers (and surfers). On the contrary, they self-consciously strive to conquer the sea. This philosophy is strikingly evident in the titles of books written about SLSAA: *Heroes of the Surf, Gladiators of the Surf, Surf: Australians Against the Sea* and *Vigilant and Victorious*;[98] it is evident in the aggressive, arrogant manner in which clubs have appropriated tracts of beach and foreshore for their own ends; and it is evident in the array of military and paramilitary groups that appear at SLSAA's annual national championships. By contrast, NZSLSA retained, at least initially, much of the egalitarian and humanitarian traditions of the RLSS. It stressed the rescue and safety component of the movement and played down the sporting aspects of what was viewed as essentially a leisure pastime.

The treatment of women members perhaps best illustrates these two distinct philosophies. Women were an integral, and welcome, part of the early surfbathing and lifesaving movements in New Zealand. They joined clubs as full members, earned proficiency qualifications, performed rescues and competed in carnivals.[99] In Australia, by contrast, official SLSAA policy banned women from rescue work and competition in 1914: conquering the sea was a man's prerogative and women were deemed physically too weak to carry a heavy belt and line or to swim competitively in surf races.[100] Before the Second World War many clubs, especially those outside the Sydney metropolitan region, ignored SLSAA's policy on competition and actively encouraged women to participate in intraclub sport and interclub carnivals. During the Second World War some clubs even allowed women to 'assist' patrols. Such participation makes a mockery of the frailty argument and reveals internal opposition to SLSAA's policy. After the Second World War, however, the SLSAA tightened its policy and effectively excluded women from competitive surf lifesaving until 1980 when it officially reversed the no-women position.[101]

Patricia Grimshaw points out that between 1880 and 1980 'New Zealand women sustained certain advantages over their cross-Tasman sisters' and that 'concepts of sexual egalitarianism received a less hostile response in New Zealand'.[102] This may help explain women's close involvement with the surfbathing and lifesaving movements in New Zealand. But why did women lifesavers in New Zealand face increasing discrimination after the Second World War? Women's lifesaving in New Zealand all but collapsed in the 1960s and 1970s, despite the fact that this period was the beginning of the sexual revolution and radical feminism. While a full explanation awaits further research, there seems little doubt that the demise of women's lifesaving in New Zealand had its origins in SLSAA hegemony; as they attempted to establish the International Surf Life Saving Association in the 1950s, Australian surf lifesavers forged much closer relations with their New Zealand counterparts. From then on, NZSLSA became increasingly caught in SLSAA's sporting orbit.

NOTES

1. F. Margan and B. Finney, *A Pictorial History of Surfing* (Sydney, 1970), p.131.
2. S. Barnett and R. Wolfe, *At the Beach: The Great New Zealand Holiday* (Auckland, 1993), p.8.
3. B. Finney, 'Surfboarding in Oceania', *Wiener Volkerkundliche Mitteilungen*, 2 (1959), 23–36.

4. K. Pearson, *Surfing Subcultures of Australia and New Zealand* (Brisbane, 1979), p.64.

5. R. Rutt, 'The Englishman's Swimwear', *Costume*, 24 (1990), 70–1.

6. V. Raszeja, *A Decent and Proper Exertion* (Sydney, 1992), p.30.

7. Under Act 4 William IV, No.7 of 1833 the government prohibited bathing in Sydney Cove and Darling Harbour between 6.00am and 8.00pm. In 1838 2 Victoria II, No.2 extended the ban on bathing 'near to or within view of any public wharf, quay, bridge, street, road or other place of public resort within the limits of any towns ... between the hours of six o'clock in the morning and eight in the evening'. In 1901, at federation, the bans on bathing in NSW were inscribed in Section 77 of the Police Offenses Act, Act No. 5.

8. 'Early Days of Life Saving in New Zealand', *Royal Life Saving Society, New Zealand Journal*, Eightieth Anniversary Issue (1992), 5.

9. 'The St Clair Baths', *Otago Daily Times* (ODT), 15 Dec. 1884.

10. Manly Pound Keeper's Book, 14 May 1889, Manly Municipal Library.

11. Manly Pound Keeper's Book, 27 April 1891.

12. Barnett and Wolfe, *At the Beach*, p.24.

13. Dunedin Ocean Beach Domain Board, By-law 1, St Clair Public Baths, Section 2 and Section 10, 1 Nov. 1895.

14. C. Lasch, *The Culture of Narcissism* (New York, 1979).

15. M. Featherstone, 'Leisure, Symbolic Power and the Life Course', in J. Horne, D. Jary and A. Tomlinson (eds.), *Sport, Leisure and Social Relations* (London, 1987), p.126.

16. Lasch, *Culture of Narcissism*, p.49.

17. P. Stallybrass and A. White, *The Politics and Poetics of Transgression* (London, 1986), p.188.

18. According to the *Oxford Dictionary*, Mrs Grundy represents the tyranny of social opinion in matters of conventional propriety. The original Mrs Grundy was the neighbour in Thomas Morton's play *Speed the Plough*, 1798. See also Peter Fryer, *Mrs Grundy: Studies in English Prudery* (London, 1963).

19. Barnett and Wolfe, *At the Beach*, p.17.

20. NSW Government, *Legislative Council Debates* (1901), col. 1708.

21. 'Commotion at Little Coogee', *Sydney Morning Herald* (SMH), 2 June 1902.

22. Letter, Borough of Waverley to the Inspector-general of Police, 12 Nov. 1902. Legislative Assembly, Tabled Paper 1902/884, NSW Parliamentary Archives.

23. Police Report, Sub-Inspector J McDonald to Superintendent N. Larkins, 13 Nov. 1902. Tabled Paper 1902/884.

24. Police Report, Inspector-general Fosbery to the Chief Secretary, 14 Nov. 1902. Tabled Paper 1902/884.

25. Mark Doepel, 'The Emergence of Surf Bathing and Surf Life Saving at the Holiday Resort of Manly, 1850–1920' (unpublished MA, University of New South Wales, 1985), 30–1.

26. 'Mixed Bathing', *Evening Post* (EP) (Wellington), 1 March 1910.

27. In 1905, following a petition presented by two surfbathers, the Ocean Beach Domain Board suspended Section 10 of By-Law 1 and allowed people to swim in the sea between 5.00am and 7.30am provided they wore 'proper costume'. Minutes of the Dunedin Ocean Beach Domain Board, 18 Dec. 1905.

28. 'St Clair Bathing Cases. Domain Board Unprepared. Cases Dismissed', *ODT*, 5 April 1910.

29. 'The Sun Bath', *Australian Star* (AS), 14 Oct. 1907.

30. J.Q.X., 'On the Sandhills', *The Dominion* (Wellington), 28 March 1910.

31. Letter to the editor, *Daily Telegraph* (DT) (Napier) 31 Jan. 1911.

32. A.W. Relph, 'Life Saving Methods', *SMH*, 26 Sept. 1908.

33. 'The Value of Sunshine', *Evening News* (EN) (Sydney), 12 Oct. 1907. See also 'Benefits of Sea Bathing', *AS*, 15 Oct. 1907.

34. J.Q.X., 'On the Sandhills'.

35. Archbishop Kelly cited in, F. Crowley, *Modern Australia in Documents, 1901–1939* (Melbourne, 1973), I, p.177.

36. Letter to the editor from 'An Onlooker', *EP*, 31 Jan. 1910; Letter to the editor from 'A Mere Man', *SMH*, 7 Feb. 1907.

37. Letter to the editor, *DT* (Napier), 24 Jan. 1911.

38. Letter to the editor, *SMH*, 12 Feb. 1907.

39. Letter to the editor from 'Daily Dipper', *SMH*, 1 Feb. 1907.
40. *DT* (Napier), 30 Jan. 1911.
41. Letter to the editor, *DT* (Napier), 25 Jan. 1911.
42. Cited in Sean Brawley, *Vigilant and Victorious: A Community History of the Collaroy Surf Life Saving Club* (Collaroy Beach, 1995), p.11.
43. 'The New Bathing Regulations. More Opinions', *EN*, 14 Oct. 1907.
44. Letter to the editor, *The Dominion*, 5 Feb. 1910.
45. Pierre Bourdieu, *Distinction: A Social Critique of the Judgement of Taste* (London, 1984), p.367.
46. Emphasis added in main quote, 'Surf Bathing and Swimming-baths. The Proposed New Regulations', *EN*, 14 Oct. 1907.
47. Cited in, Doepel, 'Surf Bathing in Manly', p.41, and 'Surf Bathing – More Trouble Brewing', *AS*, 17 Oct. 1907.
48. 'Surf Bathers' Revolt. A Demonstration at Bondi', *EN*, 21 Oct. 1907.
49. Local Government Act 1906, Ordinance No. 52, Public Baths and Bathing, NSW Government Gazette, 14 May 1908, para.3.
50. A London based organization founded in 1892 by William Henry and Archibald Sinclair.
51. J.R. Winders, 'Surf Life Saving in Australia', undated manuscript, National Council offices of the Surf Lifesaving Association of Australia, Sydney.
52. New Brighton (Canterbury) was formed in July 1910; Lyall Bay (Wellington) Aug. 1910; Worser Bay (Wellington) Dec. 1910; Pacific Surf Club (Dunedin) Dec. 1910; Castlecliff (Wanganui) Jan. 1911; Sumner (Canterbury) Aug. 1911; and Maranui (Wellington) Oct. 1911. Norman Ingram, *Surf Life Saving in New Zealand* (1952), p.33.
53. Brawley, *Vigilant and Victorious*; S. Brawley, *Beach Beyond: A History of the Palm Beach Surf Club 1921–1996* (Sydney, 1996).
54. 'The Surf Club', *Manly and North Sydney Daily*, 6 Aug. 1907. See also Doepel, 'Surf Bathing at Manly', p.46.
55. T.E. Christie (ed.), *A History of the Worser Bay ASLSC, 1910–1961* (Wellington, 1961), p.3.
56. B. Leckie, 'The St Clair Surf Life-Saving Club, 1911–1925' (research essay, University of Otago, Department of History, 1990), 14–16.
57. Letter, Town clerk to Henry Ward, secretary Pacific Surf Bathing Club, 19 Dec. 1910. See also Minutes of the Ocean Beach Domain Board, 16 Feb. 1911, Dunedin City Council Archives.
58. 'Surf bathing at Bondi', *SMH*, 25 Oct. 1905.
59. Letter to the editor, *SMH*, 10 Jan. 1907.
60. 'Surf Bathing at Bondi'.
61. 'Revolt of the Surfers Against Municipal Laws', *DT* (Sydney), 19 Oct. 1907; 'Manly Council and Surf Bathing', *Manly and North Sydney Daily*, 24 Oct. 1907.
62. Surf Bathing Committee, *Report of the Surf Bathing Committee*, NSW Legislative Assembly, 14 Feb. 1912, paras.138–139 and 141, Mitchell Library, Sydney.
63. 'Surf-Bathing at St Clair', *ODT*, 5 April, 1910.
64. 'Pakeha II', 'Ocean Beach Dunedin. Surf-Bathing and its Requirements', *ODT*, 17 Jan. 1911.
65. 'Manly V. Coogee. A Big Fight On. Good Time Coming for Surf Bathers', *SMH*, 18 July 1907.
66. 'Topics of the Day'; 'Lyall Bay. Wellington's "Latest Discovery"', *The Dominion*, 1 Jan., 1910; 'Lyall Bay. "The Manly of Wellington"', *The Dominion*, 8 Jan. 1910.
67. Brawley, *Vigilant and Victorious*, pp.19–20. Brawley also discusses in detail the importance of transport to the development of Palm Beach. Brawley, *Beach Beyond*, pp.2–7.
68. Christie, *Worser Bay*, p.2.
69. 'Pacific Surf-Bathing Club', *ODT*, 16 Jan. 1911.
70. 'Surf Bathing. An Association Formed. Protest Against Municipal Laws', *AS*, 19 Oct. 1907.
71. SBC, *Report*, paras.148–9, 152 and 154–5.
72. 'Royal Life-Saving Society. Mr Henry's Visit', *ODT*, 24 Nov. 1910.
73. Brawley, *Vigilant and Victorious*, p.15.
74. Brawley, *Beach Beyond*, p.6.
75. 'Lyall Bay. Wellington's Latest "Discovery"'.
76. Brawley, *Vigilant and Victorious*, p.13.
77. RLSS, *Fourteenth Annual Report of the NSW Head Centre, Season 1907* (Sydney 1908), p.12.
78. RLSS, *Fifteenth Annual Report of the NSW Head Centre, Season 1907–08* (Sydney 1909), p.15.

79. Doepel, 'Surf Bathing at Manly', pp.51–2.
80. SBC, *Report*, para.54.
81. SLSAA, *Thirty Third Annual Report 1938–39* (Sydney, 1940).
82. SBC, *Report*, para.22.
83. Edward Reeve, 'The SLSA rules', *Surf in Australia*, 1 March 1937, p.4.
84. Reg Harris, *Heroes of the Surf: Fifty Years' History of Manly Life Saving Club* (Sydney, 1961), pp.6–8. Interestingly, the fate of Dunedin's Pacific Surf Club, like that of the MSC, becomes unclear after bathers, members of the St Clair Branch of the Pacific Surf Club, formed the St Clair Life Saving Club in 1911. Leckie, 'The St Clair Club', pp.5–6.
85. Brawley, *Beach Beyond*, p.103. See also Brawley, *Vigilant and Victorious*.
86. Pearson, *Surfing Subcultures*, p.41.
87. Ingram, *Surf Life Saving in New Zealand*, pp.28–9.
88. 'Surf Bathing. A Club Formed', *ODT*, 9 Dec. 1910.
89. W.F. Kaler, *St Clair Surf Life Saving Club's Souvenir, Fiftieth Anniversary 1911–1961* (Dunedin, 1961), p.13.
90. Leonie Sandercock, 'Sport' in Bill Gammage and Peter Spearritt (eds.), *Australians: A Historical Library, Australians 1938* (Sydney, 1987), pp.376–7.
91. Ingram, *Surf Life Saving in New Zealand*, p.99.
92. Ibid., pp.82–3. Competition for the Wigram Shield originally involved teams of four men swimming 25 yards to a patient and demonstrating four different towing methods. Competition for the Nelson Shield involved a six man rescue and resuscitation drill using lines and reels.
93. Ibid., pp.86–91; Barry Galton, *Gladiators of the Surf* (Sydney, 1984), pp.245–78.
94. '1914–1960: A Stormy Beginning', *Royal Lifesaving Society, New Zealand Journal*, Eightieth Anniversary Issue (1992), 13;
95. L. Tointon, *The History of the Canterbury Surf Life Saving Association* (Christchurch, 1967); Ingram, *Surf Life Saving in New Zealand*, pp.36–9.
96. Ibid., p.39.
97. A. Corbin, *The Lure of the Sea* (Berkeley, 1994), pp.263 and 265.
98. Harris, *Heroes of the Surf*; Galton, *Gladiators of the Surf*; C. Bede Maxwell, *Surf: Australians Against the Sea* (Sydney, 1949); Brawley, *Vigilant and Victorious*.
99. Ingram, *Surf Life Saving in New Zealand*, pp.140–51; Sandra Coney, 'Amazons of the Sea', *Broadsheet*, 128 (1985), 14–19.
100. 'Believes Women "Too Weak" For Surf Events', *SMH*, 11 March 1953.
101. E. Jaggard, 'Forgotten Members: Women in Australian Surf Life Saving, 1906–1980', paper presented at the Annual Conference of the North American Society for Sport History, Springfield, May 1997.
102. P. Grimshaw, 'Tasman Sisters: Lives of the "Second Sex"', in K. Sinclair (ed.), *Tasman Relations* (Auckland, 1987), p.226.

9

Women's Sports and Embodiment in Australia and New Zealand

ANGELA BURROUGHS and JOHN NAURIGHT

Women have had a long history of participation in sporting activities in Australia and New Zealand. At the élite level many women have performed well in international competitions. Despite this, there has always been resistance from the male-dominated public culture to support and promote female physicality as equally as male physicality. Sport is perhaps the most significant site where the gender order is maintained in both societies. In the process of maintaining the gender order, women have been embodied in and through sport and through participation in physical activity more generally. For over a century male (and some female) critics have argued that vigorous physical activity was not appropriate for women. Concerns about female physical activity were centred squarely on the preservation of the female body for its 'natural' function – the reproduction of the race. In the late twentieth century some of these old concerns about the protection of the female body from damage reappeared as women entered physical contact sports, such as the football codes and boxing, previously viewed as off-limits. Many women who participate in these sports have had their sexuality questioned as the kinds of physicality embodied in contact sports are still viewed by many as an inappropriate use of the female body, and ultimately a threat to the gender order in society. In the 1990s in Australia, and to a lesser extent in New Zealand, as a way of both deflecting concerns about sexuality and femininity, many controlling bodies of women's sports or the athletes themselves, began to focus on selling (hetero)sexiness to promote their sports including the releasing of semi-nude and nude calendars.

This essay explores the embodiment of women in sport through an historical examination of the construction of ideal femininity in Australasian sport. Three distinct periods have been evident in this process. First, between the late nineteenth and mid-twentieth centuries women's participation in non-contact sports away from male view was tolerated and at the time promoted for health reasons. In particular, the non-contact sport of netball became the sport thought to best promote female health and ideal feminine physicality.

Second, between the early 1960s and the late 1980s a new focus on the 'heterosexiness' of female players developed through changes in media representation. We use the term 'heterosexy' hegemony in this study to explain the dominant ways in which female athletes have been presented for male consumption in the period since 1960. A heterosexy hegemony has emerged in Australia and New Zealand that has worked to position female athletes in opposition to male athletes and to valorize femininity in women's sport, while in men's sport, violent, hard-hitting muscular action is promoted. Indeed, as Bob Connell relates, 'the body is virtually assaulted in the name of masculinity and achievement. [Male] Ex-athletes often live with damaged bodies and chronic pain, and die early.'[1]

Third, many women have increasingly attempted to move into those sports most readily identified with a violent or strength-based physicality, such as rugby union and other football codes, powerlifting, boxing and many more. During the 1980s and 1990s in particular there was a dramatic influx of women into sports formerly viewed as male-only. Responses to these changes created tensions and led eventually in the mid and late 1990s to the re-incorporation of these sportswomen into a heterosexy hegemony. Those women who failed to conform to such images were marginalized and criticized for being too masculine, had their sexuality called into question and were labelled as not being 'real women'. In particular the promotion of heterosexiness has focused on containing the active female body within accepted male-defined parameters of physical attractiveness so that the gender boundary in sport (and society) is maintained. This heterosexy hegemony has worked so effectively that by the late 1990s many female athletes and organizations voluntarily attempted to market themselves by selling sexual attractiveness to sponsors and consumers.

Until recently, feminist research has largely ignored the female sporting body, 'nor have [feminists] always seen the relevance of physicality or empowerment through physical activity, to feminist politics'.[2] In arguing that the body is at the centre of female oppression, Elizabeth Grosz argues that:

> Instead of granting women an autonomous and active form of corporeal specificity, at best women's bodies are judged in terms of

a 'natural inequality', as if there was a standard or measure for the value of bodies independent of sex. ... By implication. Women's bodies are presumed to be incapable of men's acheivements, being weaker, more prone to irregularities, intrusions, and unpredictability.[3]

In following Ann Hall's call for more work on the body and physicality in women's sport, we discuss the changes that have taken place in both women's sporting participation and in the ways that women have been embodied in and through sport in Australia and New Zealand. Several scholars have examined women's embodiment and sport in the North American context.[4] Helen Lenskyj argues that women were embodied through the medical profession's focus on reproduction in devising attitudes towards physical activity. Further, she states that according to prevailing medical opinion in the late nineteenth century, women's role in reproduction 'disqualified them from vigorous physical activity', indeed sport was thought to waste a woman's vital force, her bodily energy that should be conserved for motherhood and service to the family.[5] Similar views applied to the female body and physical activity in Australasia.

Iris Marion Young suggests that gendered expectations of bodily capabilities have worked historically to create an 'inhibited intentionality' that constrains women's movement in and through space in comparison with that of men.[6] Indeed, in Australasia, the construction of accepted and ideal female physical activities was focused on controlling women's movement through space. This was most especially true in the sport of netball, overwhelmingly the most widely played sport among Australasian women and a sport that was devised in the late 1890s to promote ideal femininity.

THE EMERGENCE OF 'HEALTHY' SPORT AND IDEAL
FEMININITY FOR GIRLS AND YOUNG WOMEN

As women began to participate in sporting activities in the latter decades of the 1800s, most doctors agreed that excessive physical activity would have severe physiological effects on the adult female body, as Lenskyj, P. Vertinsky and others have pointed out.[7] As a result sport for women was widely discouraged. From the late nineteenth century onwards medical 'evidence' was used continually to postulate possible health risks to women playing sport, though similar concerns about male health did not materialize, with the result that science combined with gendered conventions about 'proper' female behaviour severely hampered the development of women's sports in Australasia as elsewhere.

In schools, however, there was some attempt to increase female involvement in sport. As Ray Crawford shows, in 1875 at the first girls' secondary school opened in Australia, the Presbyterian Ladies' College (PLC) in Melbourne, the headmaster, Rugby old boy and Oxford don, Charles Pearson, spoke of the importance of health and physical education.[8] Pearson's view was not universal. When Southland Girls' School in Invercargill, New Zealand, opened in 1879, there were no playing fields and the first full-time sports mistress only appeared in 1912. At Otago Girls' School further north in Dunedin, gymnastics were only made compulsory twice a week by new headmaster Alexander Wilson in 1885.[9] A tennis club was established at PLC in 1879 and tennis became the main sport in the new girls' schools in Melbourne. By 1885 Melbourne schools played tennis matches against each other, though the virtual lack of reporting of results suggests that the male model of competitive, result-focused achievement sport had not yet pervaded female sport.[10] By 1902 six independent Melbourne schools organized a regular sporting competition, and as early as 1907 Gwenneth Morris complained about the 'win at all costs' attitude emerging at Merton Hall school. Female interstate tennis started in Australia in 1910 when Methodist Ladies' College, Adelaide travelled to Melbourne.[11]

Despite steady advances in women's sporting participation and in physical education provision, girls were always under adult scrutiny and 'ladylike' behaviour was always expected and enforced, as C. Smith argues. One of the key ways such behaviour was enforced was through the avoidance of too much physicality and the promotion of sports that did not allow physical contact. By 1910 netball,[12] a modified sport that developed from basketball, became the dominant sport in girls' schools in both Australia and New Zealand.[13] Fears of women becoming too 'mannish' had been expressed as early as the 1880s and 1890s and attacks on girls' sports increased just as young women were taking up sport in much greater numbers. Indeed, their participation challenged the Victorian concept of the ideal woman as the 'angel of the house' and many sports were defined as 'masculine' and unsuitable for women even though some had proved they could play any sport. Restrictions on women playing any type of football and cricket became widely accepted and some attacks were made on the vigorous nature of hockey. Girls' schools had the additional problem of space as most had few playing-fields and had to rely on boys' schools or sports associations controlled by men for access to sports fields.

Although women gained the vote in the late nineteenth century, restrictions on women in public life remained very rigid in Australia and New Zealand. They had to make their own public space and were largely confined to education, health and sports. While middle-class women slowly took control of women's sport, they largely accepted that public society was male dominated and that women should behave in certain ways which were different from men, thus continually reinforcing appropriate 'ladylike' behaviour or ideal femininity, in and through sport. K. McCrone argues that in England 'women's sport was severely circumscribed by the patriarchal nature of social relations and by one's willingness, as in so many other areas, to allow men's perceptions of what was suitable to influence the choice and nature of their activities'.[14] The situation in Australasia was much the same and some feminists, such as Rose Scott who opposed women competing in swimming in public in 1912, even reinforced dominant notions of femininity and use of the female body. Writing in 1913, Mary Richmond, founder of Wellington kindergartens in New Zealand, stated that 'there is a kind of strength which is made perfect in weakness'.[15] Indeed, in the 1890s as the New Woman emerged, efforts were made to contain any crossing of the gender barrier. The *Christchurch Press* argued in 1895 that the New Woman tried 'to obliterate the distinctions of sex, by following the same pursuits, wearing the same kind of clothes, indulging in the same sports as men'.[16] Thus women who were involved in sport faced immediate criticism and most chose to take part in physical activities thought suitable for creating the ideal woman.

These women, therefore, actively encouraged participation in those sports that appeared not to threaten the gender order, particularly hockey, tennis, modified forms of cricket, and most especially netball. Australia and New Zealand have dominated world netball since the beginning of international tournaments in the 1960s and in both countries netball is played by huge numbers of women. Netball in New Zealand receives coverage as one of the nation's four major sports, including the airing of live test matches on prime time television and live coverage of national league games on Saturday and Sunday afternoons.

Regular netball competitions developed in major Australasian cities by the early 1900s. These competitions were important initially in generating images of a school's success and also demonstrated that girls enjoyed sporting competition as much as boys. These sporting opportunities were restricted to the middle and upper classes as equipment was expensive and less than ten per cent of girls went to secondary school by 1900. Netball prospered partly because of restrictions on women in sport. It became the sport for women because it best embodied female attributes and was viewed by doctors, reformers, politicians, the media and middle-class women as the best team sport for women and girls to play. In addition, netball succeeded because women controlled it without male interference. A female sporting culture developed through netball in towns and cities that provided thousands of women and girls with the chance to participate in a cultural activity in spaces dominated by women rather than by men. This separatist pattern was the norm in women's sport in the first several decades of the twentieth century in both Australia and New Zealand and aided the growth of women's sporting organizations.

By 1948 netball had the largest number of players in New Zealand than in any sport except rugby union. In 1991–92 there were more netball clubs than in any other sport, with 10,928 registered teams affiliated to Netball New Zealand (NNZ), the game's governing body.[17] An estimated 155,600 women and school girls played the game in 1988, nearly ten per cent of all females in the country. Only Australia, where up to one million girls and women play social and organized netball, has greater numbers of participants than New Zealand.

The first National Tournament in New Zealand was held in Dunedin in 1926 as part of the Empire Exhibition. Teams travelled from five main centres to compete. Press coverage was minimal at this stage, but the *Otago Daily Times* carried news of the tournament. The paper supported the tournament and netball as a 'game eminently suitable for every girl, especially the business and industrial girl, who gets practically no exercise during the week'. The article also reported that netball was played in every primary school and most secondary schools throughout New Zealand with 2,000 registered senior players.[18] The article shows a shifting attitude towards seeing netball as ideal not only for middle-class girls in schools, but as a sport that could promote health amongst working women.

By the 1920s middle-class reformers felt young working women needed organized activities to keep them healthy and on the high moral path until they fulfilled their ultimate destiny of marriage followed by motherhood. Groups like the YWCA actively promoted team sports for young working women to teach them fitness and co-operation. The YWCA was also active in organizing young women's competitions in Australia in the 1920s.[19] Netball benefited in both countries from the new focus on female health and sport. Many sports were still 'off-limits' to women, but most thought netball the sport most suitable for women. During the 1920s and 1930s subtle shifts in the representation of women began to occur. S. Coney argues that advertisements for menstrual pads played a key role in shifting from notions of female passivity to a more active femininity. Advertisements for menstrual products depicted active women participating in sports and hiking.[20]

During the 1930s and 1940s officials included netball in the girls state school physical education curriculum. The majority of primary schools adopted netball as the winter sport for girls once the medical profession recommended it. In reporting on the establishment of the Wanganui Basketball Association, the local press reported that 'Basketball is regarded by the medical profession as a very suitable game for young women'. In addition, the organizers echoed broader concerns about the health of young women waged-workers: 'The aim ... is to provide a game for young ladies in shops and offices, who at present take part in no winter sport. The game is inexpensive, and at the same time provides very good exercise.'[21]

Although netball expanded in the 1920s and 1930s, few women played at élite levels after marriage. Indeed, in many sports, women who married retired. Former national New Zealand netball coach, Lois Muir, recalls that people expected her to quit playing when she married at 19 in 1954:

> People tended to get married a lot younger then, but very few managed to keep up their sport afterwards. I did and found it difficult; the longer I kept playing, the more certain it was every year that I'd end up at the Nationals. Surprised officials and players would ask what I was doing back there. As soon as you were married they expected you to stay at home, have children, and rock the cradle.[22]

The conservative attitudes of netball officials was not unique. Indeed, social expectations were that even world-class athletes, such as the 1950s Australian Olympic champion Shirley Strickland, also a qualified nuclear physicist, were more identified by their positions as wives, mothers and girlfriends than as sports stars. The linking of female sports stars to males continued to be common even at the end of the twentieth century. In a 1999 article on the World Cup winning New Zealand national women's rugby team, every player except one is identified through their association with males.[23]

By the 1970s, however, the role of women in physical activity began to change. This was presaged by subtle shifts from the focus on internal beauty and character that marked Victorian debates about the female body. During the 1920s and 1930s interest in feminine beauty products developed rapidly in Australia and New Zealand. By the end of the 1940s there was a shift from the concept of inner beauty and morality to that of making the female body attractive to men. By the 1960s the focus shifted further and beauty and (hetero)sexiness became intertwined in society.

WOMEN ENTERING 'MEN'S' SPORTS

After the Second World War, when women proved they could perform jobs vacated by men who went to war, pronouncements against women in sport declined, but still surfaced from time to time particularly regarding the need to protect female bodies from physical damage. Indeed, such 'evidence' was used to limit women's sporting opportunities. Though national athletics championships were held for men in New Zealand as early as 1887, there was no event for women until 1926 when a 100-yard race was included. In 1924, though, the New Zealand Amateur Athletics Association took advice from the New Zealand branch of the British Medical Association which said that athletics were too strenuous for women.[24] The 220 yards was added in 1939 along with field events but the 880 yard race only appeared in 1959 and the mile in 1968. Attitudes, such as those of 1936 Olympic champion Jack Lovelock, who called for the exclusion of women from the Olympics as they were 'foreign to the whole idea of the Games', have maintained barriers to women in sport.[25] Restrictions based on 'medical' evidence continued to haunt women in sport into the late twentieth century. In 1988 the Queensland Life Saving Association banned women from the beach flag events (involving a sprint and dive after a flag placed in the sand). This was done on advice of their medical committee which argued, 'Females contesting flags risk damage to breast tissue and the development of painful lumps which could be a source of worry.'[26]

Conspicuous consumption and the increasing importance placed on the maintenance of the body, however, gave rise to the fitness boom of the 1970s. With more women working out or using exercise as a weight control technique, together with changes in societal attitudes and the introduction of equal opportunity and sex discrimination legislation, women's involvement in physical activity has become more widely accepted. Women have used this critical mass of participation to enter, or in many instances to re-enter, sports that have traditionally been defined as 'men's' activities. Yet, as women have increased their participation in physical activities, there have been attempts define women's sport and physicality as different from that of men.

Women played rugby as early as 1891, for example, though men quickly attacked female participation in the nation's dominant male sport as 'unwomanly'. Maori women played rugby after the Second World War, but it has only been in the 1990s that widespread playing of rugby by women in Australia and New Zealand has emerged. By 1992 there were 87 women's rugby teams in New Zealand along with 8000 more women who played soccer. Soccer teams were organized in Canterbury and Wellington in 1921 and the first inter-provincial match between the two teams drew a crowd of 2000 spectators. New Zealand women first played cricket in 1886, but organized cricket only startedd in 1928 under YWCA sponsorship.[27] These sports did not receive the same amount of open encouragement as netball and rugby and soccer faced outright condemnation causing the sports to largely disappear until the late 1970s and 1980s.

Richard Cashman and Amanda Weaver demonstrate that women who played cricket faced numerous attacks in the media throughout most of the twentieth century.[28] The high point of the media's targeting occurred in 1994 when Denise Annetts, an Australian player since 1984, alleged she was dropped from the Australian one-day team to tour New Zealand because she was heterosexual. All forms of media in Australia and overseas swooped on the allegation and the incident sustained media coverage for over a month. Coverage, however, was devoted to speculation about the extent of lesbianism in women's cricket, possible discriminatory practices and the unfairness of New South Wales legislation that did not protect heterosexuals from unjust treatment based on their sexual orientation.[29] At no time did the coverage analyse Annetts' batting statistics, recent form or past contributions in an attempt to understand the selectors' decision. The media attention fuelled speculation that women who played 'men's' sports were suspect, that not only had cricket been tainted, but other non-traditional women's team sports were implicated. Ironically, the media attention has not deterred women and girls from participating in cricket.

Despite such criticism, women have continued to strive for more and varied sporting opportunities for many decades. In 1921 over 200 women met to establish the Ladies' Rugby Football League in Sydney. Women's rugby league matches continued into the early 1930s with over 2,500 spectators witnessing a charity match in 1930 in aid of Sydney's unemployed women.[30] Rugby league competitions disappeared, however, and rugby league and union competitions only returned in the late 1980s and 1990s. In the 1970s touch football was introduced as a safe alternative to rugby league and immediately became popular with both males and females. The development of touch football was an important precursor to women playing rugby union and rugby league. Rugby union expanded rapidly in the 1990s and in 1994, Australia played New Zealand in the first ever women's rugby union test match between the two countries.

Although soccer for women began in Australia in the late 1960s, its introduction in 1974 to the range of sports available to girls in state high schools led to the rapid explosion in the popularity of soccer among women and girls. By 1978 an estimated 60,000 women were playing.[31] Once the sport gained legitimacy through the school system, women and girls took up the opportunity to play with relish. Soccer proved to be a good winter alternative to netball, and with competitions organized on Sundays (primarily because most fields were used by men on Saturdays), women who played hockey and netball were able to play soccer as well.

Basketball (as opposed to netball) boomed in the 1990s with the strong support of the men's league and the televising of the women's national league by the Australian Broadcasting Corporation. Particularly because of the high profile of star point guard Michele Timms, the Australian national team, the Opals, developed a strong following. The Opals finished fourth at the 1994 World Cup, losing the semi-final against the United States before a capacity crowd at the Sydney

Entertainment Centre. Finishing third at the Atlanta Olympics, the Opals became the first Australian basketball team to win an Olympic medal.

Despite the long history of women's involvement in a range of sports, from the club level to the international scene, little has been written on the subject. Histories of sport invariably focus on men's sports and male sports personalities. What results is a lack of accessible information on women's achievements, performances, records and organization in sport. Instead, it is easier to construct a record of women's sport that is focused on the sexualization of the female athlete.

'FRAMING' HETEROSEXINESS, THE MEDIA AND WOMEN'S SPORT, 1956–2000

In both Australia and New Zealand women have received little press coverage throughout the past century. While the situation improved somewhat during the 1990s, the media still 'frames' public images of women in sport. Women are still frequently categorized as 'girls', displayed in posed, passive shots. Their achievements are compared to those of men and discussed in relation to their marital and family status. A study of Australian newspapers in 1992 found that only 4.5 per cent of sports coverage went to women's sports with a further small percentage to women in mixed sports, making a total of no more than eight per cent of non-horseracing sports coverage given to women.[32] A New Zealand study showed that women there faired slightly better receiving 11.3 per cent of coverage and a portion of the 12.7 per cent coverage of mixed sports.[33] The higher figures in New Zealand can be attributed to the status of netball as one of the four major sports shown on television in New Zealand, while to date, netball has only been shown on the government-owned Australian Broadcasting Corporation and not on commercial stations. This is evidenced by the television figures for both countries. Women's sport comprises only 1.2 per cent of coverage in Australia while it comprises 20.5 per cent of the New Zealand total.[34] Another problem in Australia is that women's sports are often scheduled at the same time as major men's sports, and at times one women's sport competes with male sports on the four other channels.

What little coverage women do receive is more often than not focused on sexualizing, marginalizing or trivializing the athlete. Most commonly sportswomen are treated as 'wives and mothers', 'sex objects' or 'freaks'.

Swimming champion Lisa Curry-Kenny was the 'apotheosis of the sporting "supermum"' of the late 1980s and early 1990s.[35] Then, as an author on women's fitness books who chose to have breast implants because she was unhappy with her body image, Curry-Kenny sent confusing messages to her followers.

Heather Turland, a mother who took up long distance running and at 38 won gold at the 1998 Kuala Lumpur Commonwealth Games, has emerged as the new sports supermum of the late 1990s. In a television advertisement for a sandwich spread she is shown proudly providing for her four children and says, 'my family is my greatest achievement'. Although this portrayal provides an avenue for recognition and sponsorship, it reinforces a view that women's achievement in sport is a secondary consideration and not 'real' work. It suggests that the only advances women have made in the past 30 years is that they can play sport as well as look after the children and husband.

The trivalization of women in sport is most common when the coverage concerns women in traditional 'male' sports as the cricket example of the Annetts case demonstrates. In a 1996 article on women's rugby union, the journalist Roy Masters devoted more attention to allegations of sexual molestation during matches, consumption of beer by players and the players' occupations than commentary on the skill of the players.

Obtaining appropriate, achievement-based recognition is proving almost impossible for women. As J. McKay points out, 'women are being asked to market their sports according to voyeuristic potential rather than other values'.[36] As early as the 1960s this process was starting in New Zealand and Australia when the media began to focus on some female athletes' sex appeal. In New Zealand, the *Evening Post* published a cartoon during the first World Netball Tournament in 1963 that reflected an emerging sexualization of netball. The cartoon showed a man leering at two passing national netball representatives while his wife complained to a friend about her husband's new-found support for the sport.[37] New Zealand national player Joan Harnett received unprecedented media coverage during the 1960s. She was described variously as 'a long legged beauty', 'the male's ideal sportswomen', and 'the essence of femininity'. The media paid much less attention to the fact that Harnett was the outstanding player of the mid- and late 1960s. Thus Harnett became a sex symbol for netball rather than respected primarily for her outstanding playing skill. The power of the sexualization process was such that Harnett eventually internalized the media attention. She stated that she was initially embarrassed, but got used to it as it gave netball publicity.[38] Indeed, Harnett is a classic example of Connell's notion of body-reflexive practice whereby external expectations about the body's appearance or movement are internalized and reproduce bodily performance and draw together social expectations and individual behaviour.[39] By the 1980s little had changed when national star Julie Townsend received substantial media coverage. Journalist Joseph Romanos attributes this to several factors and argues that Townsend received attention because she was 'good looking'. Romanos suggested that coverage based on attractiveness should not be underestimated and sees nothing wrong with the approach.[40] A 1982 book, *New Zealand's Champion Sportswomen*, demonstrated how little had changed over a 20-year period. The chapter on Harnett began with a discussion of her beauty, even listing her measurements.[41] The power of a heterosexy hegemony in presenting women in sport to the wider public is evidenced in the fact that the author of the book is a former national women's cricket representative. By the 1990s the power of sexualized representations of female athletes was such that many women's sports and sportswomen used sexual attractiveness to market themselves in attempts to increase sponsorship and media coverage.

In 1994 a group of female athletes in Australia were photographed in 'sexy' poses for a 'Golden Girls of Athletics' calendar that was organized by athlete and media commentator, Jane Fleming. This calendar sparked tremendous debate in Australia over the ways in which women's sports should market themselves. Photography used in the calendar promotes the heterosexy hegemony in presenting a constructed feminine ideal that represents male constructions of the female as object. The athlete's bodies are presented in a highly sexualized manner in which, in view of some, élite athletes are degraded into sexualized objects.

Despite much controversy, utlizing sex appeal remains one of the few viable sponsorship options available to many women's sports. In 1999 twelve members of the Australian women's soccer team, the Matildas, went beyond sexy poses and posed nude in a calendar for 2000. In defending the calendar one player revealed the extent to which some women's sports are constrained by hegemonic standards of heterosexual/heterosexy attractiveness. Amy Taylor explained that by posing nude she hoped to 'show people that female soccer players are not uncouth and masculine but can be attractive and feminine'.[42] The use of nudity by women in sport to gain attention is in stark contrast to the way men's bodies have been portrayed in sport. Indeed, when an unauthorized nude photograph exposing part of the genitals of the rugby league international, Andrew Ettingshausen, was published in the April 1991 issue of *HQ*, a glossy upscale monthly Australian magazine, he successfully sued the publisher for defamation and was awarded $350,000 in damages (on appeal reduced to $100,000).[43]

In 1994 an Australian study argued that women were important consumers of television and print media and women and men would like to see more women's sports covered.[44] Despite this, women have not been taken seriously enough as a market by television and newspapers. When women in sport are covered it is often as sex objects. The editors of *Inside Sport*, Australia's most popular monthly sporting magazine of the 1990s, openly admit that they use sexual images of women to sell magazines to male readers. *Inside Sport* has a woman, nearly always not a leading sportswoman, usually clad in a bikini on its cover each month with a pictorial section of the woman on the cover in various '(hetero)sexy' poses. The editors also defend the relative lack of coverage of women's sport because there is not much interest. In October 1994 surf-lifesaving stars Karla Gilbert and Samantha O'Brien were presented on the cover in bikinis. In the pictorial spread the accompanying text discusses the introduction of real prize money and a women's series stating 'It's going to be pretty to watch' and 'As you can see, they're well and truly in shape' opposite a full page picture of the two posed in bikinis.[45]

The presentation of female athletes in demeaning or sexualized pictures with captions that reinforce the reader's 'common sense' views of society has contributed to the perception of women's sport as inferior to men's or 'real' sport. In addition the presentation of the female athlete as wife and mother was still extant at the end of the twentieth century. This shifts the focus away from the woman as athlete and onto the woman as domestic, thus negating threats to the gender order posed by females playing sport. All of these 'framings' of female athletes have adversely affected coverage of women's sports and such reporting remained a prominent feature of media coverage of women's sport at the end of 1990s. Women's rapid entry into sports defined as masculine, particularly the tackling football codes, in the 1990s caused even greater difficulties of presentation to the media.

This was particularly true in the coverage of women playing rugby union. Women's rugby has proved difficult to 'frame' in a uniform manner. Coverage in the early 1990s in both Australia and New Zealand, when any appeared at all, tended to 'masculinize' the players. New Zealand national team prop Emma Thomas was described as having 'real strength', 'a touch of intimidating brutality about her on-field behaviour' and as a 'scary granite-hard prop'.[46] The media often presented women's rugby as a novelty event in the 1990s, but two dominant 'framings' emerged. The first followed the example above of portraying forwards in particular as tough, rough and in dirty poses that tried to frame these players as 'ugly' and not 'real' women. On the other hand, some players were shown, especially out of uniform or in non-playing contexts, as attractive. The prime example of this occurred in New Zealand where national team player Melodie Robinson, a former Miss Canterbury, a runner up in the Miss New Zealand competition and a model, helped to de-masculinize the sport and give it a feminine face. An extreme example of the representation of women rugby players occurred in 1995 in a feature article with accompanying pictures in *Inside Sport*. On one page some players were depicted as dirty, unattractive and masculine, while on the opposite page other players were positioned as 'real' women in glamorous and sexualized photographs.

CONSTRAINTS OF ACHIEVEMENT: A NOTE ON THE BODY AND SPONSORSHIP

The positioning of women in over 100 years of involvement in organized sport has moved between two extremes. In its earliest forms, women's physical activity was conducted away from male view. Today the male gaze is actively, perhaps even desperately sought, as individual athletes and women's sporting organisations compete for private sector funding. Despite international successes by Australian and New Zealand women in sport, difficulties in obtaining sponsorship is much greater for women than for men. Increasingly the marketing of many women's sports has become reliant on the promotion of players' sexuality. The body becomes the focal point in this strategy, as the marketing techniques adopted by the Matildas and Golden Girls of Athletics examples most clearly demonstrate. Other sporting organizations have adopted less extreme but similarly insidious marketing strategies that detract attention from athletic achievement and instead position female athletes as objects of male voyeurism. The Women's National Basketball League recently adopted bodysuits as uniforms rather than the usual baggy basketball outfit worn by men and by women in the United States and some netball teams have even gone as far as to wear sponsors' logos on the athletic briefs worn under their skirts. Similar strategies to enhance the (hetero)sexual appeal of sports women have been used by the administrators of hockey, touch football and cricket. Unfortunately there is evidence of the trend to use sex to sell women's sport becoming institutionalized. In 1999 the international organizing body for beach volleyball went as far as regulating the dimensions of the two piece swimming attire to be worn by female participants.

CONCLUSION

Changing attitudes towards female physicality throughout the twentieth century have assisted women in Australia and New Zealand in their pursuit of sporting opportunities. Extraordinary progress is evident, not only in access to an increasing number of sporting opportunities, but in the fact that some women have the chance to develop a career as a professional sportswoman. However, these gains must be set against the still limited avenues available for women to achieve appropriate recognition in sport. In particular, women's sporting progress is limited by the reality that women have not been able to exercise direct control in sport. Unlike early interventions restricting women's participation, control over women in sport and over women's active bodies in the later part of the century and in the new millennium, is no longer direct. Control is the product of the subtle mix of complex ideologies that claim women's physical achievements as inferior to men's, and require women in sport to display other physical qualities in order to receive recognition and acceptance. Consequently, women in sport are pitted against each other as they struggle to promote the most acceptable image. While dramatically increasing the range of expressions of female physicality, the range of forms are still limited by hegemonic notions that confine female expression to images acceptable for male consumption.

NOTES

1. R. Connell, *Masculinities* (Cambridge, 1995), p.58.
2. M.A. Hall, *Feminism and Sporting Bodies: Essays on Theory and Practice* (Champaign, 1996), p.50.
3. E. Grosz, *Volatile Bodies: Towards a Corporeal Feminism* (Sydney, 1994), p.14.
4. For some examples see essays in S. Birrell and C. Cole (eds.), *Women, Sport, and Culture* (Champaign, 1994).
5. H. Lenskyj, *Out of Bounds: Women, Sport and Sexuality* (Toronto, 1986), p.18.
6. I. Young, 'Throwing Like a Girl: A Phemomenology of Feminine Body Comportment, Motility, and Spatiality', *Human Studies*, 3 (1980), 137–56.
7. For examples of doctors' opinions, see H. Lenskyj, *Out of Bounds: Women, Sport and Sexuality* (Toronto, 1986); and P. Vertinsky, *The Eternally Wounded Woman: Women, Doctors and Exercise in the Late Nineteenth Century* (Manchester, 1989).
8. R. Crawford, 'Sport for Young Ladies: The Victorian Independent School 1875–1925', *Sporting Traditions*, 1, 1 (1984), 61.
9. C. Smith, 'Control of the Female body: Physical Training at Three New Zealand Girls' High Schools 1880s-1920s', *Sporting Traditions*, 13, 2 (1997), 61.
10. Crawford, 'Sport for Young Ladies', 66–7.
11. M. Stell, *Half the Race: A History of Australian Women in Sport* (Sydney, 1991), pp. 32–4.
12. Netball was originally called basket ball, shortened to basketball in 1927. It was also referred to as women's basketball or outdoor basketball. The name was officially changed to netball in 1970. To avoid confusion to today's reader, netball is used throughout this paper except in reference to official organisations like the New Zealand Basketball Association.
13. For more detailed histories of netball in Australia and New Zealand, see J. Nauright and J. Broomhall, 'The Development of Netball and a Female Sporting Culture in New Zealand, 1906–70', *International Journal of the History of Sport*, 11, 3 (1994), 387–407.
14. K. McCrone, *Sport and the Physical Emancipation of English Women 1870–1914* (London, 1988), p.13.
15. *Auckland Weekly News*, 22 May 1913; quoted in S. Coney, *Standing in the Sunshine: A History of New Zealand Women Since They Won the Vote* (Auckland, 1993), p.14.
16. Quoted in Coney, *Standing in the Sunshine*, p.15.
17. *Netball New Zealand Annual Report 1991–92* (Auckland, 1992).
18. *Otago Daily Times*, 8 April 1926.
19. I.F. Jobling and P. Barham, 'The Development of Netball and the All-Australia Women's Basketball Association (AAWBBA), 1891–1939', *Sporting Traditions*, 8, 1 (1991), 32.
20. Coney, *Standing in the Sunshine*, pp.96–7.
21. *Wanganui Herald*, 8 May 1929.
22. Stratford, 1988: 160
23. *Sunday Star Times* (Wellington), 6 August 1999. Thanks to Malcolm MacLean for this reference.
24. *Christchurch Press*, 13 May 1924.
25. Quoted in Coney, *Standing in the Sunshine*, p.255.
26. Quoted in Stell, *Half the Race*, p.177.
27. See S. Coney, *Every Girl: A Social History of the YWCA in Auckland 1885–1985* (Auckland, 1986).
28. R. Cashman and A. Weaver, *Wicket Women: Cricket and Women in Australia* (Sydney, 1991).
29. A. Burroughs, L. Seebohm and L. Ashburn, 'A Case Study of Australian Women's Cricket and its Media Experience', *Sporting Traditions*, 12, 1 (1995), 27–46.
30. Stell, *Half the Race*, pp.56–7.
31. Ibid., p.255.
32. Sport and Recreation Minister's Council, *An Analysis of the Media Coverage of Women in Sport* (Canberra, 1994).
33. Ferkins, 1992.
34. SRMC, *An Analysis of Media Coverage*.
35. J. McKay, 'Embodying the "New" Sporting Woman', *Hecate*, 20, 1 (1994).

36. Ibid.
37. Reprinted in J. Romanos and G. Woods (eds.), *The Big Black Netball Book* (Auckland, 1992), p.95.
38. J. Romanos, 'Joan Harnett – A True Kiwi Great', in Romanos and Woods, *The Big Black Netball Book*, pp.46–9.
39. Connell, *Masculinities*, pp.59–64.
40. J. Romanos, 'J. Townsend Calls it Quits', in Romanos and Woods, *The Big Black Netball Book*, pp.73–6.
41. D. Simons, *New Zealand's Champion Sportswomen* (Auckland, 1982), p.138.
42. Waltzing Matildas now the 'Flashing Matildas', www.womensoccer.com.
43. The Ettingshausen case is discussed in T. Miller, 'A Short History of the Penis', *Social Text* (1995),
44. SRMC, *An Analysis of the Media Coverage*.
45. *Inside Sport* (Oct. 1994), 76–7.
46. Quoted in M. MacLean, 'Does Rugby = Man = New Zealand?: Rugby's Challenges to Maculinity in Aotearoa/New Zealand', paper presented at The Real Level Playing Field: Sport, Society and Culture, Stout Centre, Wellington, 16–18 Oct. 1998, 5.

10

Conflict, Tensions and Complexities: Athletic Training in Australia in the 1950s

MURRAY G. PHILLIPS and FRANK HICKS

I

'THE FIFTIES, as a term, has become a cliché', argued John Murphy and Judith Smart in a special edition of Australia's premier historical journal.[1] The 1950s in Australia have commonly been seen as a decade of conformist trends including the dominance of the nuclear family, the return (or re 'conscription') of women to domestic duties and as the period epitomizing ideal forms of suburban life. For conservatives it has been a decade to revere – one in which life was unified and prosperous; for non-conservatives the 1950s were staid, stultifying and monocultural. Historians are starting to question some of the broad generalizations attributed to this decade in order to reveal many of the complexities and contradictions of social life. Tensions centred around the new suburbia, post-war Australian identity, sexual identity and popular culture.[2] In the context of sport, the 1956 Olympic Games illustrated some of the underlying tension that existed as Melbourne and Australia prepared to show themselves to the world. Many of the problems that beset the organizing committee – and resulted in Melbourne almost losing the Games on three occasions – was the conflict between amateur sporting officials and the city's business community. As Graeme Davidson has pointed out: 'Throughout the long tussle to win and keep the Games, two wings of the Melbourne establishment and two visions of national and civic progress contended for mastery.'[3] The Melbourne Games are one example of competing interests that surfaced in the supposed tranquillity of the conformist, conservative decade.

We want to pursue the theme of the underlying tensions in Australian society by looking at an area of sport – coaching – that has not been considered by historians, sociologists or those interested in popular culture. Sport coaching in Australia emerged as modern sports became institutionalized with bureaucracies that administered rules with a fairly extensive degree of codification and standardization. Conditions were provided with sufficient uniformity to meet historically and culturally specific notions of achievement-orientated sporting competition.[4] In order to facilitate performance in sports, coaches provided athletes with not only personal direction, motivation and inspiration but with skill acquisition and training methods to help achieve victory and break records. Coaches assumed an important role in achievement-orientated sport. The value of coaching, however, was not appreciated uniformly and the opportunity to coach as well as the availability of coaches varied considerably across the range of sports. In this sense, coaching like sport more generally, was not a unified or a unifying activity and tended at least to reflect, if not to reinforce, divisions in society along lines of sex, race, ethnicity, socioeconomic status and sporting ideologies.[5] From the 1850s for almost a century, those athletes who did receive coaching, and the coaches themselves, were usually white, Anglo-Saxon males. Women, indigenous peoples, and those of ethnic origins were very rarely coaches, and athletes of such backgrounds very rarely received coaching. Coaching emerged as a by-product of the rationalization of sport, so it was inextricably linked to tensions within modern society that ultimately translated into contradictions within sport. The ideology of amateurism divided coaching further. The expertise offered by professional coaches in Australia by the 1950s was accepted in amateur sports like athletics and swimming, but these coaches were shunned by amateur officialdom, particularly at Olympic and Commonwealth Games.[6] Professional coaches attended many international competitions but were not part of the official Olympic teams until 1968, having to meet their own travel and accommodation expenses and gaining admittance to events by stealth rather than right.[7]

The amateur/professional dichotomy and the contradiction surrounding this ideological divide certainly exposes some of the tensions in sport during the 1950s, but this essay will take another tangent. We examine the different training regimes in coaching because they expose two opposing views of the athletic body, of science in coaching and ultimately the debates about coaching in this period helped to shape many of the features of contemporary sport including the rise of sport science in élite performance, in coach education and in academic institutions.[8] We will detail the views of two of Australia's leading professional athletics coaches in the 1950s: Percy Cerutty and Franz Stampfl. Other prominent coaches like Forbes Carlile, Harry Gallagher, Frank Guthrie and Sam Herford could have been utilized but Cerutty and Stampfl provide a lively case-study because they were contemporaries in the same sport, they devised competing training regimes and they were public adversaries at practical and ideological levels. Cerutty published seven books in Australia and Britain[9] while Stampfl published *Franz Stampfl on Running*[10] that was translated into several languages and sold 600,000 copies in the Soviet Union and Europe.[11] By examining the coaches' publications and their athletes' recollections we interpret their coaching against the backdrop of Australian sporting culture. In particular, we speculate about what framed their approaches to coaching, we link their coaching styles with broader social and cultural issues and we briefly summarize their contributions to contemporary sport.

II

Franz Stampfl was born in Austria in 1913 and was an international skier and javelin thrower. He began his coaching career in 1938 in England. When The Second World War broke out he was interned because of his nationality, was transported to Australia and as he puts it: 'I was one of the last convicts to get out here in the traditional way'.[12] Only after the armistice did he return to the United Kingdom and continue coaching. He coached at Cambridge University (1946), Queen's University, Belfast (1946–51), took control of the Pakistani Olympic team (1952) and concluded his coaching in the Northern Hemisphere at Oxford University (1953–55). At Oxford he was involved with Roger Bannister, the first man to break the four-minute mile barrier in 1954, and several other prominent milers like Chris Chataway, Brian Hewson and Chris Brasher.[13] Stampfl was lured back to Australia in 1955 to run the new Beaurepaire Centre and to coach University of Melbourne students and other promising athletes in Victoria. Stampfl's highest profile Australian protégé was Ralph Doubell, the 1968 Olympic Gold Medallist over 800 metres.[14]

Stampfl's great rival was Percy Cerutty.[15] Much to Cerutty's chagrin Stampfl was imported to coach local athletes at a time when, no doubt, Cerutty thought he could do the job. As Stampfl acknowledged: 'I think Percy couldn't stand anyone else coming to Australia to coach.'[16] Born in

1895 and growing up in the working-class Melbourne suburb of Prahran, Cerutty participated in sport but was not overly athletic and suffered from a number of physical ailments. He was employed in the Postmaster General's Department and was plagued by health problems including migraine headaches when he suffered a physical and mental breakdown at the age of 43. How he recovered from this nadir in his life shaped his views on athletic training. Cerutty rebuilt his health during a six-month leave from work by thrusting himself into athletic exercise, radically altering his diet and developing a philosophy of life. Cerutty worked with many sportspeople at his seaside residence at Portsea where he developed a reputation for alternate forms of training.[17] He coached many national champions in track and field and his most famous athlete was Herb Elliott, the 1960 Olympic Gold Medallist over 1500 metres.[18]

The values and beliefs of both these men, as we shall see, helped to shape their coaching and training regimes. Cerutty and Stampfl used different paradigms of knowledge acquisition to provide the foundation for their training ideas and programmes. Stampfl could be said to have had a 'logic' to his methods – it was a form of applied positive biological reductionism – whereas Cerutty undoubtedly had reasons for his methods, but they were not founded in any formal 'methodology'. Stampfl applied a form of positive empirical science that was committed to theories of measurement and testing of material phenomena (sensations), involving the collection of data that was then subjected to processes of quantitative verification or falsification. It was no accident that Stampfl was literally a child of 1930s Austria with its local philosophical school epitomized by R. Carnap that was committed to philosophical positivism.[19] We should not be surprised that he sought out expertise from scientists whose research had some relevance to athletic principles of training. Cerutty emerged from a rationalist tradition (traceable through Cartesianism) in the sense that like the French *philosophes* he brought reason to bear instead of uncritical acceptance of tradition or 'common sense'. When he was rebuilding his life after his physical and mental breakdown, he consulted a wide range of views to build his approach to sport. Their contrasting approaches to coaching are typified by their sources of inspiration. When Cerutty spoke of his evaluation of Newton, he was referring to Arthur Newton, the world record runner; when Stampfl acknowledged the influence of Newton, he was referring to Isaac Newton, the acclaimed scientist whose name became a metaphor for a physicalist 'clockwork universe'.

Cerutty's faith in the rational tradition of philosophy is evident in his books. His works, in particular *Athletics: How to become a Champion* (1960), are different to other previously published sources on training such as *Athletic Queensland* (1900) and Reginald Baker's *General Physical Culture* (1910).[20] *Athletic Queensland* and Baker's treatise are in the tradition of successful athletes expounding their experiential knowledge about sports they have gained by word of mouth, trial and error and lived experience. These early treatises were similar to those in Britain and North America during the nineteenth and early twentieth centuries that promoted practices including diets of red meat, dry bread and beer and training regimes with regular bouts of purging and sweating.[21] Cerutty's approach, unlike his Australian predecessors, was based on reading a wide range of sources in the areas of anatomy, philosophy, science and sport. Herb Elliott described Cerutty's passion for knowledge after visiting the Portsea residence for the first time in 20 years: 'Feeling as though I was back in time and feeling his presence, I wandered over to his library, mostly untouched since his death. I'd forgotton the wide range of subjects – philosophy, diet, human movement, religion, art, history, the Saints.'[22] The sport specific sources of great influence on Cerutty were Arthur Newton and his ideas on the value of posture and the importance of consistent training, and to a lesser extent George Hackenschmidt and Bob Hoffman and their views on the importance of strength. Cerutty's wide reading was evident in his approach to the very idea of athleticism and, as we shall see, his justification of training regimes, diet and lifestyles for his athletes.[23]

Cerutty's knowledge base centred on his consultation of sport and non-sport literature and around three major tenets which included observation and trials with his own body, and his visualization of movement which in turn was informed by a particular nineteenth-century understanding of anthropology,[24] as it related firstly to the movement patterns of indigenous people (and to a lesser extent young children), and also to undomesticated animals. Cerutty practised movements with his own body using many different styles or patterns. He trialled different stride lengths, varying degrees of knee lift, alternate arm movements, running on the balls of the feet and the toes, and with his head tilted at various angles. This practical self-observation was combined with his study of animal and human movement. Cerutty used forms of visualization to think about the movement patterns of animals: gazelles, apes, panthers, leopards and racehorses. By analysing animal movements, he worked out general principles of motion that he applied to human performance. For instance, he spent considerable time at the racetracks of Melbourne watching horses race and also running against them. He concluded:

> Without some such study (of animal movements), or teachings, no athlete or coach can even hope to aspire, understand, or 'feel' what is perfect human posture and movement (perambulation). The great and finished (perfected) athlete of the future will be seen to have the relaxed power, grace and resiliency of the blood horse both in walking and running – especially the absence of 'haste' in his movements. He will have the 'up'-ness, that 'apparent' faculty of being *over* the ground, that the gazelle suggests in its stance and movement, and the litheness and resolute ferocity that is in the posture and movement of the leopard and panther, whether at rest, walking or moving at full speed.[25]

Whilst it is (and was at that time) possible to dismiss parts of Cerutty's writing as a form of romantic anthropomorphism, and one notable athlete, Ron Clarke, certainly did, it was clearly galvanizing and motivating for Cerutty and his protégés.[26] It is important to point to the passion for human achievement in Cerutty's vision which took precedence over any merely biodynamic account that could ultimately reduce human athletes to some sort of 'mortal engines'.[27]

Complementing his analysis of animal movements was what John MacAloon may have called 'popular ethnography' or 'cross cultural voyeurism' and what we have termed Cerutty's 'athletic anthropology' of indigenous people and their running styles.[28] His approach to studying running movements had many similarities with European scientists during the age of imperialism: the objects of inquiry were essentialized, stereotyped and gendered. Cerutty never premised his athletic anthropology on gender but we assume his gaze was focused on indigenous men because he only referred to athletes in a masculine context and he was very specific, and disparaging, when he referred to female athletes: 'I see no good at all in women competitors'.[29] His understanding must be seen in the context of a popularized nineteenth century ethnology debate that ranked the physical attributes of different 'races'. As a result, Cerutty developed his own categories of racially specific athletic aptitudes and constructed his own idealized athletic type. Cerutty's athletic anthropology was constructed around a variant of the degeneration thesis. Whereas the degeneration thesis of the nineteenth century argued that 'civilization' induced cultural and physical decline, and the Australian version of this thesis spawned questions about the effect of a convict heritage, different climate and modified lifestyle on British stock.[30] Cerutty totally eschewed the Australian immigrant dimension and argued, in more global terms, that wherever 'primitive' cultures had come in contact with civilization, the movement patterns of the inhabitants had been ruined. Therefore those races that had least to do with modern civilization exhibited powerful ways of walking and running; by contrast civilization had destroyed or attenuated powerful movement. 'Indeed, many "whites" were basically less civilized, more primitive, than their coloured brothers, if we judged on naturalistic posture and movements alone.'[31] In line with nineteenth-century Darwinism, human potential was traced back to some primeval essence unobtainable by European people.[32] In this way, the myth of native 'other' was central to Cerutty's understanding of athletic talent.[33]

The two races Cerutty admired were African Americans and Australian Aborigines. He explained his admiration for African Americans within his degeneration thesis. According to Cerutty, the transplantation of Africans to America, had not been of sufficient duration to 'deprive him of his naturalist movements and instinctive relaxation'.[34] These people, however, were not his ideal athletic race. Cerutty revered Australian Aborigines who, because of their separation from Western civilization until 1788, provided 'the key to the art and business of efficient natural perambulation' as they 'had natural capacities without any equal in any other race'.[35] The absence of Western civilization for an existence spanning upwards of 40,000 years, had produced perfect athletes; athletes who walked and ran differently to other races. Lean physiques and running styles which exhibited erect postures, low knee lifts, slightly crooked arms and long effective strides resembled 'the movements of the gazelle in uprightness and the easy grace of a blood-stock horse'.[36] Cerutty's athletic anthropology effectively linked animal and human movement patterns to define the ideal athlete: the Australian Aborigine.

Essentialized, stereotyped, gendered and othered, Australian Aborigines were also flawed. Their capacity for powerful movement was to be analysed and applied, but ultimately they failed for him in athletic performance. The self-same civilization that evinced the idea of athleticism had ruined the ability of Aborigines. Civilization for Cerutty was presumably not the dominance of European over indigenous culture, the exploitation and genocide of Aboriginal tribes, the substandard living, education and health conditions of rural and urban indigenous people, or their lack of political rights in Australia at the time of his coaching.[37] Rather civilization was a nebulous concept devoid of details regarding specific interactions between colonizers and indigenous people. Ultimately for Cerutty, Aboriginal runners lacked 'the drives and incentives that motivate us. Hence racing is purposeless. This is hardly the basis for Gold Medal winning at the Olympic Games'.[38] All of this despite the success of Australian Aborigines in professional running where many sprinters won races from as early as 1883 right through the period of Cerutty's coaching.[39] These contradictions illustrate, as John Bale and Joe Sang have detailed in the context of running in Kenya, the tendency of Europeans to reconstruct, dominate and demonstrate authority in their descriptions of indigenous subjects.[40]

III

By contrast, Stampfl did not place much value on Cerutty's forms of visualization or athletic anthropology in assessing athletic ability or traits. There are no references to evaluations of animal or indigenous peoples' movement patterns in his book nor is there anything to suggest his ideas on running were based on postulations similar to Cerutty. Stampfl deviates most markedly from Cerutty in the value he places on empirical biological science in determining his training ideas and subsequent programmes. The two coaches shared a deep suspicion of dependence on 'traditional ways' of preparing athletes, but their orientations to devise new training techniques contrasted starkly. In *Franz Stampfl on Running*, he makes the point that traditional ideas, like staleness in sport, persist but '... all research must be conducted, and its results accepted, with an open mind if there is to be any progress at all. In other fields, science has shown that many of our cherished beliefs of our grandmothers ... were completely without foundation though at the time they seemed logical and reasonable enough.'[41] In his book Stampfl goes no further in detailing his use of empirical science, it is only in a subsequent interview towards the end of his life that he posed a question that seemed to underpin his beliefs: 'Why could not one standardise the way of doing things which would be more truthful, efficient and have a more scientific background?'[42] The answer to improving athletic performance for Stampfl rested with new training regimes based on empirical science.

While empirical science was paramount to Stampfl's coaching, he was only partially in the mould of Professor Frank Cotton and Forbes Carlile who are commonly acknowledged as the pioneers of sports science in Australia.[43] Cotton and Carlile tested the effects of exercise on athletes' blood pressures, brachial pulse waves, blood haemoglobin levels and heart rates.[44] This experimentation initiated a paradigm shift in the relationship between empirical science and athletes. As John Hoberman has noted in the European context, there was a similar transition in Australian sport in the 1950s from the evaluation of athletes in the name of scientific endeavour to the employment of science to produce high performance athletes.[45] Stampfl used the findings of empirical research in his approach to athletic training, but he neither functioned as nor saw himself as conducting serious, peer-reviewed scientific research; he was an athletics coach. He openly admitted that the information that was gathered about the 'intervals' in his training methodology was not extensive enough, nor sufficiently accurate to support replicable 'proofs'. Nevertheless, he consulted and admired the renowned physiologist Haldane in England, sought in his own way to apply Hans Selye's views on stress adaptation in his revolutionary interval training, and he was oriented by Newtonian principles of motion in his coaching of runners, jumpers and throwers.[46] This emphasis on empirical science was to the exclusion of any acknowledgment of the *social* sciences. Anthropology and sociology could not have been unknown to Stampfl, but certainly his writings show no awareness of how his own thinking could be contextualized culturally by social scientists. There is little sense of any legitimate value in assessing the impact of culture (in any form, at any level) on various understandings of the relationship between science, sport and society, something that Cerutty relished.

The distinction between Cerutty's and Stampfl's appreciation of knowledge is also evident in their views about the body and embodiment. Stampfl's view of the body is one that focuses almost exclusively on the anatomical, psychological and technological factors related to maximal athletic performance. On this basis, his book is written with discrete chapters on athletic fundamentals and training principles for races over 100 and 220 yards, 440 yards, 880 yards, one mile, and three and six miles. It is a book, truly innovative in its era, yet it was a recipe for athletic success that treated the body as a machine.[47] Only on the premise of the body as a machine could Stampfl boast, on his arrival in Melbourne, that he could turn any man in the street into a world champion. While Stampfl acknowledged the need for athletes to have other interests in their lives – friends, hobbies, books and music – these views were not incorporated into the training regimes in *Franz Stampfl on Running*.[48] Stampfl's athletic body was an instrumental one as it was overwhelmingly portrayed as an object to be mechanically conditioned, tuned and managed to improve performance. Stampfl's view of the body is important because when it is linked with Professor Cotton and Forbes Carlile's initiation of sport science, it represents a pivotal moment in Australian sport. This period marked the birth of sport science and the growth of the dominant paradigm of the sporting body as a machine.[49] In contemporary sport: 'the raw material of athletes' bodies becomes *the athletes'* machines, as specific parts of the machine are isolated and transformed into effective components of competitive performance through the application of scientific knowledge'.[50]

In opposition to Stampfl's understanding of the relationship between training and the body, Cerutty retorted that: 'Such concepts as the rigid schedule, the worked-out and laid down day-by-day training routines, find no place in this book, or my ideas as to the fitness of things athletically. Despite the efforts of the industrialist, we are still "humans", not machines.'[51] Cerutty's views were based on an idealized version of Greek sport. In fact, there were many similarities with the values that underpinned sport in Victorian Britain and the Olympic movement. He never referred to the influential books by Thomas Hughes and Charles Kingsley, but these novels and the ideas they fostered in Britain and parts of the Empire permeated Cerutty's notion of the athletic body.[52] Cerutty rejected the naturalist view of the body – a body in which the biological constitution determines human capabilities[53] – and argued that sport added very important moral dimensions to the physical component. Sport provided personal, emotional and spiritual development; it built character: 'the ethics and moralities upon which character is founded – these are the result of education, and experience is a vital part of education'.[54] The Greek ideal of sport was also found in his advocacy of a healthy mind yielding a healthy body. 'Only those who excel in something physical, but yet exercise the mind, can ever hope to be balanced: to live balanced lives …And balance, equilibrium, is the first law of the Universe; without it we have no law, no order, nothing.'[55] While Cerutty steadfastly dismissed amateurism in sport, probably because he was fiercely antagonistic to any sort of authority which might inhibit what he saw as the spontaneous mode of sporting achievement, he had enough in common with its stated values to advocate the adage: 'It is not the "winning" that is important, it is the taking part.'[56] In this sense Cerutty falls on the Socratic side of a divide separating him from the more Aristotelian tradition which helped form the basis for the positive biological reductionism embraced by Stampfl.

With this rationale underpinning sporting participation, it is not surprising that Cerutty's athletes were given a wide range of sporting and non-sporting experiences. At the coastal retreat of Portsea, on weekends initially and then on a full-time basis, athletes were encouraged to read English literature and to listen to classical music. Similarly, Cerutty advocated a number of sporting activities besides athletics for his athletes including basketball, bicycle riding, gymnastics, swimming and table tennis which were 'part of the pattern of living a complete and interesting life'.[57] Variety was also integral to training programmes. The athletes trained on the undulating paths on cliff tops, on the soft sand of the beaches, the dirt roads, the nearby golf courses, the local flat playing field and on some special circuits made up of a composite of surfaces. These are the types of landscapes that, as Bale has argued, may produce topophilia through sensory stimulation.[58] Cerutty combined interesting landscapes with freedom for athletes to choose their training regime: 'I favour that "free expression" and encourage the lads to be self-determining, my role being mostly a supervising and advising one.'[59] Running sessions were augmented with weight-lifting and a fairly rigid dietary approach as Cerutty blended routine with individuality for his charges.

Stampfl's activities included cross country running, gymnastic exercises, 'fartlek' (speed play), repetition and interval training. It is the latter form, interval training, which is synonymous with Stampfl and earned him an international coaching reputation.[60] He started experimenting with interval training in Northern Ireland, refined it when coaching at Oxford University and applied this revolutionary regime during his career in Australia. Stampfl was not the only coach to use interval training, as the Germans were experimenting at the same time, but he acknowledges it as his major contribution to middle-distance running.[61] To understand interval training in a wider context and to reflect on its implications on future sporting practices, we will invoke some aspects of Michel Foucault's work.[62] In contrast to the views that scientific advances were liberating, Foucault contends that science intensified the means of regulation of the body.[63] As we have shown Stampfl's approach to training was based on the empirical science of Haldane, Seyle and Newton, and this body of scientific knowledge provided the basis for a carefully controlled set of training principles where the body was treated as a machine and subordinated to ascetic rules of practice. Stampfl had much in common with Cotton and Carlile who also advocated other forms of external control over the body including heart rate assessments, blood pressure readings and even hypnosis. These were the antecedents of contemporary scientific methods that include maximal oxygen uptake tests, lactate analyses and skin fold monitors.

A Foucauldian approach also helps to point out a contradiction between the training regimes of Stampfl and Cerutty. Foucault addressed the characteristics of certain modern institutions as having practices that fitted his special meanings of 'discipline' and 'surveillance'. Foucault's disciplines were forms of knowledge which were carried in texts and social practises, but which in athletic or sporting terms might be understood as 'enacted embodiments'.[64] In a Foucauldian sense, Cerutty's and Stampfl's coaching regimes were markedly different in their approaches to external control of the body. Where Cerutty argued 'the athlete must never be asked to conform or train according to a set schedule',[65] Stampfl advocated the regimented and repetitive interval training. The public conflict between Cerutty and Stampfl was at this level: unregimented versus highly structured programmes. More subtly, and equally important, the athletes who were trained by the coaches were encouraged to develop some forms of self-administered control or what may be termed a 'sporting conscience'.[66] As much as Cerutty and Stampfl advocated contrasting approaches to training, we contend that the development of sporting consciences in their athletes was remarkably similar.

There are several common features between the disciplinary practices that Foucault found in military institutions, factories, hospitals, schools and prisons, and Stampfl's main coaching programme, interval training. The Marxist critic, Bero Rigauer, summarizes interval training as 'continuous repetition of temporally, spatially, and quantitatively set training tasks, interrupted by controlled pauses for recovery'.[67] The most salient features of the disciplinary practice of interval training were time tabling, the track and the stopwatch. Interval training prescribed timetables for the athletic body in events from 100 metres sprinting through to long distance races over monthly, weekly and daily sessions. The training regime formalized into athletics rhythms and cycles of repetition that were widely found in schools, workshops and hospitals.[68] Time tabling was not a completely new dimension of coaching, but interval training clearly articulated seasonal and temporal dimensions in a number of events to an extent not experienced in athletics. It was this seasonal, temporal and structured model that Australian swimming coaches and subsequently other sports adopted.[69] Beside the timetabling aspect, interval training relied heavily on both the facility of the cinder track and the precision of the stopwatch. Stampfl rated the stopwatch 'as indispensable to every athlete' and it was essential to his training regime.[70] What the stop watch enabled was the refinement of time, the precision necessary to demarcate warm-up from work effort from warm-down, to segregate intense work from recovery and to assess work effort.[71] As Foucault argued: 'Time measured and paid must also be time without impurities or defects; a time of good quality, throughout which the body is constantly applied to its exercise.'[72] The track, like the institutions in Foucault's analysis, was the ideal facility or enclosure for training the body and the preferred medium over other options like bush trails, country roads or the beach.[73] As much as possible the cinder track neutralized the inconveniences of other surfaces. The biggest asset of the cinder track was that it was measured, marked and regulated. It enabled running distances to be prescribed and the athletic bodies' efforts to be acutely assessed by combining geographical markers with the stopwatch.[74] The disciplinary practice of interval training, with its emphasis on timetabling, the ideal enclosure of the track, and the precise measurement of the stopwatch produced what Foucault referred to as 'docile' bodies.[75] The athletic body under Stampfl's interval training had its forces increased in terms of running speed and therefore linear performance, but whose forces were concurrently diminished by obedience to the regime.

It was exactly the dominance of interval training over the athletic body that irritated Cerutty: 'I hold that the athlete must never be asked to conform or train according to a set schedule'.[76] He advocated training in the fields, woods, parklands and the beach on the basis that 'the artificial track is *not* the place to develop our athletics even if it be the place to demonstrate our ability'.[77] Cerutty's degeneration thesis, when linked to his notion of civilization, explains his rejection of modern athletic devices and his adoption of the coastal retreat of Portsea as a residential training venue. Only at a place like Portsea, far from the cinder track, could athletes distance themselves from the harmful effects of civilization. In this idealized environment, Cerutty provided overall guidance in order for himself and the athletes to live out his maxim: 'Always the great athlete creates the schedule – never does the schedule create the great athlete.'[78] Their schedules rarely included the stop watch. This device was occasionally used in time trials, but in the majority of training sessions Cerutty avoided the stop watch. Instead, athletes were encouraged to measure strength, speed and timing on their 'inner time recorders'.[79] This is precisely the self-administered control that Foucault argued was so powerful. Herb Elliott describes the development of his own sporting conscience through Cerutty's methods: 'Pushing yourself ... beyond what you thought were the borders of endurance is of great moral benefit. The purifying quality of the pain that has to be suffered is like that in a confession. You walk away with a clear conscience.'[80]

For Cerutty, control resided within a sense of (athletic) personhood, while in Stampfl's regime the practices were 'imprinted' in the body, but in a context where the shared social assumption was that 'any *body* can do it'. Stampfl's prescribed schedule of training irked Cerutty because 'the human being cannot be reduced to the status of a machine'.[81] He argued that the regimented forms of training worked against developing what might be called the 'humanist' athlete. 'There is some reason to believe that, athletically, the world has had foisted upon it in this age of factory production, regimentation, and unquestioned authority, regimes of training that must prove inimical to all that tends to develop the gifts of personality and athletic ability in the young athlete.'[82] Cerutty, like Rigauer two decades later, made a direct link between Taylorism and Fordist modes of production in the Western world and Stampfl's style of training.[83] Cerutty's rejection of Stampfl's methods were based on a combination of his views on the degeneration thesis of the athletic body via civilization, the explicit rejection of certain uses of technology, and his version of the Greek ideal of sport that rejects the body-as-machine model seemingly epitomized by interval training. There are many senses in which Cerutty's sentiments were precursors of Foucault's critique both of 'the disciplines' and of 'docile bodies'.[84]

IV

The 1950s was an era of change for both performance and coaching in athletics as Cerutty and Stampfl challenged accepted practices in sport. Both coaches argued (and demonstrated) that improved athletic performance could only be achieved through demanding training regimes. Beyond this common denominator and the reality that both men inculcated self-administration and control of their athletes' bodies, Cerutty and Stampfl clashed to provide a sporting example of the complexities that existed in a decade misleadingly noted for its conformist attitudes. These men espoused different ideas about knowledge, understood embodiment in contrasting ways and, accordingly, designed athletic training programmes that bore little resemblance or similarity. Perhaps most important of all, they differed in their sense of the relationship between sport and society. Stampfl made few explicit references, except perhaps on general notions of 'character' and 'manliness', whereas for Cerutty the whole enterprise finally revolved about a conception of sport and society. His athletic practices were strongly linked to a humanist philosophy associated with idealized notions of sport in Ancient Greece and middle-class Victorian Britain. Cerutty gave enormous prominence to the humanist body as an autonomous social (as well as biological) agent in athleticism. Cerutty practised a critical rational form of knowledge acquisition combining his visualization of the athletic body, and his version of the athletic anthropology of human (and animal) movement, with a thesis based on the degenerative effects of civilizing forces.

Stampfl valued the results of a positivist and biological-reductionist empirical science and based his athletic programme of interval training on the practical applications of findings from the world of formal research scientists. Stampfl was not alone, and in fact was only one of several other important people, whose coaching style was based on and stimulated interest in sport science. Stampfl, Cotton and Carlile used scientific research findings in their coaching and inadvertently lent support to the differentiation and emergence of a new branch of sporting intelligentsia in Australia: sports science. This intelligentsia has grown since the 1950s and, at present, has considerable influence at the various institutes of sport throughout the country, where it is viewed as crucial in the production of élite athletes, in coach accreditation programmes where science provides the centre piece of education and in academic programs in Australia.[85] Critics of sports science have questioned the priority of the view of the athletic body that privileges biophysical knowledge over any appreciation of the body in its cultural and social context.[86] As Wendy Seymour argues: 'The perspective of the body as a machine, exemplified in medicine, reaches its zenith in sports science.'[87] For coaches, the increasing influence of sport science has fuelled a contemporary debate about whether their profession is an art or a science.[88] In the academic context, the emphasis on sports science in many curricula has resulted in arguments maintaining that sport, physical education and related academic fields have been 'scientized' to the detriment of competing views of the philosophy of movement education.[89] Stampfl at least, seems to have been unaware, or at least unperturbed by such possibilities: Cerutty was much less sanguine about the future of sport.

NOTES

Our thanks to Bruce James for his comments on a draft of this essay.

1. J. Murphy and J. Smart (eds.), *The Forgotton Fifties: Aspects of Australian Society and Culture in the 1950s* (Melbourne, 1997), p.1.
2. Ibid., pp.1–5.
3. G. Davison, 'Welcoming the World: The 1956 Olympic Games and the Re-presentation of Melbourne', in Murphy and Smart, *The Forgotton Fifties*, p.66.
4. The key authorities on the development of achievement orientated sport are H. Eichberg, *Der Weg des Sports in die industrielle Zivilisation* (Baden Baden, 1973), R. Mandell, 'The Invention of the Record', *Stadion* (1976), 250–64 and what has been termed the 'Eichberg/Guttmann/Mandell hypothesis' is debated in J. Carter and A. Krüger (eds.), *Ritual and Record: Sports Records and Quantification in Pre-Modern Societies* (Westport, 1990). My access to Eichberg's work has been through *Ritual and Record* and S. Brownell, 'Thinking Dangerously: The Person and His Ideas', in J. Bale and C. Philo (eds.), *Body Cultures: Essays on Sport, Space and Identity: Henning Eichberg* (London, 1998). Where these debates are important for this study is that they provide an understanding of the conditions in which coaching emerged as a worthwhile and, eventually, a crucial activity in achievement-orientated sport.
5. D. Adair and W. Vamplew, *Sport in Australian History* (Melbourne, 1997); R. Cashman, *Paradise of Sport: The Rise of Organised Sport in Australia* (South Melbourne, 1995); B. Stoddart, *Saturday Afternoon Fever: Sport in Australian Culture* (North Ryde, Sydney, 1986).
6. M.G. Phillips, *From the Sidelines to Centrefield: A History of Sports Coaching in Australia* (Sydney, forthcoming).
7. H. Gordon, *Australia and the Olympic Games* (St. Lucia, Brisbane, 1994).
8. J.A. Daly, *Quest for Excellence: The Australian Institute of Sport* (Canberra, 1991); D. Kirk, 'Science as Myth in Physical Education', paper presented at the American Educational Research Association, San Francisco, April 1992; D. Booth, 'Sport History: What Can Be Done?,' *Sport, Education and Society*, 2 (1998), 191–204; J. McKay, J. Gore and D. Kirk, 'Beyond the Limits of Technocratic Physical Education', *Quest*, 41 (1990), 52–76; J. Maguire, 'Human Sciences, Sport Sciences, and the Need to Study People "In the Round"', *Quest*, 43 (1991), 190–206; R. Tinning, 'Physical Education and the Sciences of Physical Activity and Sport: Symbiotic or Adversarial Knowledge Fields', paper presented at the Congreso Mundial de Ciencias de la Actividad Fisica y el Desporte, Granada, Espana, November 1993; D.

Whitson and D. MacIntosh, 'The Scientization of Physical Education: Discourses of Performance', *Quest*, 42 (1990), 40–51.

9. P.W. Cerutty, *Running with Cerutty* (Los Altos, 1959). We have frequently referred to P.W. Cerutty, *Athletics: How to become a Champion: a Discursive Textbook* (London, 1960) because Cerutty is expansive on a whole range of issues in this book.

10. F. Stampfl, *On Running: Sprint, Middle Distance and Distance Events* (London, 1955).

11. B. Lenton, *Through the Tape* (Australian Capital Territory, 1983), p.111.

12. Lenton, *Through the Tape*, p.107.

13. Ibid., pp.107–8.

14. R.K. Stewart, 'Franz Stampfl' in W. Vamplew, K. Moore, J. O'Hara, R. Cashman and I. Jobling (eds.), *The Oxford Companion to Australian Sport*, second edition (Melbourne, 1994), pp.401–2.

15. Nearly every source written about these coaches stress the rivalry between Cerutty and Stampfl. See R. Clarke and N. Harris, *The Lonely Breed* (London, 1967), pp.23–4, 166–9; G. Kelly, *Mr Controversial: The Story of Percy Wells Cerutty* (London, 1964), pp.71–8; H. Elliott and A. Trengove, *The Golden Mile* (London, 1961), pp.68–73.

16. Lenton, *Through the Tape*, p.111.

17. R.K. Stewart, 'Percy Wills Cerutty: "Genius Coach" or "Good-Ordinary" Trainer' (unpublished paper, Victorian University of Technology, 1994), pp.1–20.

18. R.K. Stewart, 'Percy Cerutty' in Vamplew *et al.*, *The Oxford Companion to Australian Sport*, p.94.

19. R. Carnap, *The Unity of Science* (London, 1934). See A.F. Chalmers, *What is This Thing Called Science?* (St Lucia, Brisbane, 1982) for a more contemporary view of positivism.

20. W.B. Carmichael and H.C. Perry, *Athletic Queensland: A History of Amateur Rowing, Boxing and Physical Development, Pedestrianism and Cycling in Queensland* (Brisbane, 1900) and R. Baker, *General Physical Culture* (Melbourne, 1910).

21. See R.J. Park, 'Athletes and Their Training in Britain and America, 1800–1914', in J.W. Berryman and R.J. Park (eds.), *Sport and Exercise Science: Essays in the History of Sports Medicine* (Urbana, 1992) for an excellent discussion of the acquisition of knowledge by trainers, coaches and athletes. Diets and training regimes are comprehensively detailed in P.G. Mewett, '"Nothing is Better for Dinner Than a Pint of Good Dry Champagne": The "Gentleman", Amateur and Sports Training in the Second Half of the Nineteenth Century', paper presented at the ANZALS Conference, Wellington, 1995.

22. H. Elliott, 'Foreword' in Phillips, *From the Sidelines to Centrefield*.

23. See in particular Cerutty, *Athletics*.

24. M. Banks and H. Morphy (eds.), *Rethinking Visual Anthropology* (New Haven, 1997).

25. Cerutty, *Athletics*, p.59.

26. R. Clarke and A. Trengove, *The Unforgiving Minute* (London, 1966), p.43.

27. J.M. Hoberman, *Mortal Engines: The Science of Performance and the Dehumanization of Sport* (New York, 1992).

28. J.J. MacAloon, *This Great Symbol: Pierre de Coubertin and the Origins of the Modern Olympic Games* (Chicago, 1981), p.262.

29. Cerutty, *Athletics*, p.83.

30. R. White, *Inventing Australia: Images and Identity 1688–1980* (North Sydney, 1981), pp.63–84.

31. Cerutty, *Athletics*, p.61.

32. Hoberman, *Mortal Engines*, p.56.

33. J. Bale and J. Sang, *Kenyan Running: Movement Culture, Geography and Global Change* (London, 1996), p.188.

34. Cerutty, *Athletics*, p.61.

35. Ibid., p.62.

36. Ibid.

37. Many of these issues are covered in H. Reynolds, *Why Weren't We Told? A Personal Search for the Truth about Our History* (Ringwood, Victoria, 1999).

38. Cerutty, *Athletics*, p.63.

39. C. Tatz, *Obstacle Race* (Sydney, 1995), pp.87–106.

40. Bale and Sang, *Kenyan Running*, pp.50–5.

41. Stampfl, *On Running*, p.40.

42. Lenton, *Through the Tape*, p.107.
43. F.S Pyke 'Sport Science', in Vamplew *et al.*, pp.397–9.
44. For a summary of this work see F. Carlile, *Training for All Sports* (Sydney, 1953) and F. Carlile, *Forbes Carlile On Swimming* (London, 1963).
45. Hoberman, *Mortal Engines*, pp.11, 91, 98.
46. Lenton, *Through the Tape*, p.107.
47. C. Shilling, *The Body and Social Theory* (London, 1993), p.37.
48. Stampfl, *On Running*, p.49.
49. J. McKay, *No Pain, No Gain?: Sport and Australian Culture* (New York, 1991), p.141.
50. W. Seymour, *Remaking the Body: Rehabilitation and Change* (St Leonards, NSW, 1998), p.6.
51. Cerutty, *Athletics*, p.16.
52. For some major sources see R. Holt, *Sport and the British: A Modern History*, (Oxford, 1989); W.J. Baker and J.A. Mangan (eds.), *Sport in Africa: Essays in Social History* (New York, 1987); J.A. Mangan, *Athleticism in the Victorian and Edwardian Public School: The Emergence and Consolidation of an Educational Ideology* (New York, 1981); J.A. Mangan, *The Games Ethic and Imperialism* (Harmondsworth, 1985); J.A. Mangan, *Pleasure, Profit, Proselytism: British Culture and Sport at Home and Abroad, 1700–1914* (London and Portland, OR: Frank Cass, 1988); J.A. Mangan, *The Cultural Bond: Sport, Empire, Society* (London and Portland, OR, 1992); J.A. Mangan, *Tribal Identities: Nationalism, Europe, Sport* (London and Portland, OR, 1996).
53. Shilling, *The Body and Social Theory*, p.79.
54. Cerutty, *Athletics*, p.90.
55. Ibid., p.105.
56. Ibid., Introduction.
57. Ibid., p.152.
58. J. Bale, *Landscapes of Modern Sport* (Leicester, 1994), pp.139–45.
59. Cerutty, *Athletics*, p.22.
60. E. Cashmore, *Making Sense of Sports*, second edition (London, 1996), p.19.
61. Lenton, pp.107–8.
62. For a sample of Foucauldian analyses in sport see J. Hargreaves, 'The Body, Sport and Power Relations', in J. Horne, D. Jary, and A. Tomlinson (eds.), *Sport, Leisure and Social Relations* (London, 1987), pp.139–59; D.L. Andrews, 'Desperately Seeking Michael: Foucault's Genealogy, the Body, and Critical Sports Sociology', *Sociology of Sport Journal*, 10 (1993), 148–67; J. Heikkala, 'Discipline and Excel: Techniques of the Self and Body and the Logic of Competing', *Sociology of Sport Journal*, 10 (1993), 397–412; J. Heikkala, 'An Introduction to a (Non)fascist Sporting Life', in L. Laine (ed.), *On the Fringes of Sport* (Sankt Augustin, 1993), pp.78–83; R. Gruneau, 'The Critique of Sport in Modernity: Theorising Power, Culture, and the Politics of the Body', in E.G. Dunning, J.A. Maguire and R.E. Pearton (eds.), *The Sports Process: A Comparative and Developmental Approach*, (Champaign, 1993), pp.85–109.
63. Of particular use for our analysis has been M. Foucault, *Discipline and Punish: The Birth of the Prison* (London, 1977). The issue of scientific advances and control of the body pervade Foucault's work and for a brief summary see B.S. Turner, 'The Discourse of Diet', in M. Featherstone, M. Hepworth and B.S. Turner (eds.), *The Body: Social Process and Cultural Theory* (London, 1995), pp.157–60.
64. Foucault, *Discipline and Punish*.
65. Cerutty, *Athletics*, p.72.
66. The concept of a 'sporting conscience' is drawn from W.B. James, 'Watching the Footy on Telly: Making Meaning of the AFL' (unpublished Honours Thesis, University of South Australia, 1995); W.B. James, 'The Construction of a (Post)Modern Footy Fan', paper presented at the third biennial conference – 'Postmodernism in Practice', Adelaide, 1998; W.B. James, 'A History of the Sporting Present: Genealogy and the Cultural Practices that have Made Me What I Am', paper presented at Sporting Traditions XII, Queenstown, February 1999; W.B. James, 'The Practice of Sport Spectatorship: Desire, Pleasure, Meaning, Motility and Memory', paper presented at the Australian and New Zealand Association for Leisure Studies Conference, Hamilton, January 1999.
67. B. Rigauer, *Sport and Work* (New York, 1981), p.33.
68. Foucault, *Discipline and Punish*, p.149.

69. Interview, Forbes Carlile, Sydney, 15 February 1997. For two examples of the application of interval training to swimming see Carlile, *Forbes Carlile On Swimming* and H. Gallagher, *Harry Gallagher on Swimming* (London, 1970).

70. Stampfl, *On Running*, pp.35–6.

71. For an historical analysis of the stop watch in sport see H. Eichberg, 'Stopwatch, Horizontal Bar, Gymnasium: The Technologizing of Sports in the 18th and Early 19th Centuries', *Journal of the Philosophy of Sport*, 9 (1982), 43–59. Eichberg argues that the development of the stopwatch was 'social' and was driven by the achievement orientation of modern sport.

72. Foucault, *Discipline and Punish*, p.151.

73. The athletic track provides a sporting example of the need of enclosures for disciplinary practices (Foucault, *Discipline and Punish*, pp.141–3). For a thorough geographical analysis of the enclosure in track and field see Bale, *Landscapes of Modern Sport*, pp.100–19.

74. John Bale contends that the replacement of cinder tracks with synthetic tracks was not in order to make training easier, but to prevent interruptions to training regimes. (J. Bale, *Sports Geography* (London, 1989), p.178). In effect, a more efficient enclosure has been created.

75. Foucault, *Discipline and Punish*, p.138.

76. Cerutty, *Athletics*, p.72.

77. Ibid., p.16.

78. Ibid., p.77.

79. Ibid., p.130.

80. Elliott cited in H. Gallagher, *Memories of a Fox* (Adelaide, 1998), p.184. Our thanks to Bruce James for this citation.

81. Cerutty, *Athletics*, p.23.

82. Ibid., pp.44–5.

83. Rigauer, pp.32–40.

84. Foucault, *Discipline and Punish*.

85. See Daly, *Quest for Excellence* for science in élite sport; Phillips, *From the Sidelines to Centerfield* for science in coach education; and B. Abernethy, V. Kippers, L.T. Mackinnon, R.J. Neal and S. Hanrahan, *The Biophysical Foundations of Human Movement* (South Melbourne, 1996) for science in tertiary sport education.

86. McKay, *No pain, no gain?*, pp.139–48.

87. Seymour, *Remaking the Body*, p.6.

88. F.S. Pyke, *Towards Better Coaching: The Art and Science of Sports Coaching*, (Canberra, 1984); L. Woodman, 'Coaching: A Science, an Art, an Emerging Profession', *Sports Science Review*, 2 (1993), 1–13.

89. See for example, Kirk, 'Science as Myth in Physical Education'; Booth, 'Sport History: What Can Be Done?'; McKay, Gore, and Kirk, 'Beyond the Limits of Technocratic Physical Education'; Maguire, 'Human Sciences, Sport Sciences, and the Need to Study People'; Tinning, 'Physical Education and the Sciences of Physical Activity and Sport'; Whitson and MacIntosh, 'The Scientization of Physical Education'.

11

From a Club to a Corporate Game: The Changing Face of Australian Football, 1960–1999

IAN ANDREWS

> ... crisis consists precisely in the fact that the old is dying and the new cannot be born; in this interregnum a great variety of morbid symptoms appear.
>
> Antonio Gramsci, *Selections from the Prison Notebooks*

In 1896 the Victorian Football League (VFL) was formed as a breakaway competition from the Victorian Football Association (VFA).[1] From its inaugural season the following year, the VFL became an integral component of the cultural fabric of Melbourne, due in part to the broad social reach of the code,[2] and in part to the passionate commitments that the clubs engendered in players and supporters alike. Indeed, this combination was sufficient to see the VFL quickly emerge as the nation's premier sports competition, a status it maintained into the second half of the twentieth century.[3]

Despite its sustained pre-eminence, however, from the end of the Second World War the VFL's traditional cultural role was progressively subordinated to, and problematized by, an economically driven process of restructuring. Ultimately, this process transformed the competition from a 12–team, semi-professional, metropolitan concern, into a 16-team, fully professional, and thoroughly commercialized national league. In 1989, these developments were reflected in the renaming of the competition as the Australian Football League (AFL).

The purpose of this essay is to make sense of this post-war transformation of the VFL/AFL.[4] The argument is divided into four sections, corresponding to four chronological periods. Each is taken to mark a distinct, qualitative shift in the way the League has been organized (its *structural* aspects), as well as experienced (its *cultural* aspects). In order to differentiate these periods analytically, the historical analysis is interwoven with, and guided by, a social-scientific conception of 'crisis'.

Although the word 'crisis' is typically used haphazardly in everyday discussion, in the social sciences it has been productively employed to refer to a quite specific state of affairs. Drawing on J. Habermas[5] and J. Keane,[6] we can identify three aspects to a satisfactory social-scientific conception of the term. Firstly, a true 'crisis' constitutes an *objective* 'fateful phase' or 'turning point' in the development of a social system, which severely tests that system's capacity for reproduction in its existing form. In this sense, 'crisis' tendencies constitute 'ruptures' or 'moments of discontinuity'.[7] Secondly, a *bona fide* 'crisis' represents a process of *transformation*, whereby the destruction of the old is intimately bound up with the creation of the new. Thus, we are not dealing with an absolute endpoint, or a total collapse, but with an unfolding process of *transition*. Here, a qualitative shift must be evident, and not merely quantitative or incremental changes within the existing structure. Finally, for a 'crisis' to be genuine, it needs to be *experienced* as such. That is, a fully-fledged 'crisis' is not only an objective transformative process, impacting upon the structure of a social system; it also possesses a *subjective* dimension, experienced and expressed through the medium of culture.[8]

Where a genuine 'crisis' is occurring, a sequence of 'crisis phases' is typically evident. For present purposes, we can designate four such phases – those of 'origin'; 'manifestation'; 'high-point'; and 'resolution'. When assessing a 'crisis' retrospectively, it should be possible to identify each of these discrete phases in turn.

On the basis of these conceptual reflections, the argument below explains the post-war history of the VFL/AFL as an unfolding 'crisis process'. Specifically, this history is discussed in terms of four chronological periods, which correspond to the four 'crisis phases' identified above. During the first period, covering 1946 to 1963, the societal context in which the VFL operated was transformed, and this comprised the *origins* of the post-war 'crisis' in the competition. In the second period, spanning 1964 to 1974, an intensifying process of commercialization gripped the VFL, producing the formative *manifestations* of the 'crisis'. The third period, from 1975 to 1984, constituted the *high-point* of the 'crisis', during which time escalating television rights and corporate sponsorship underpinned a chaotic financial restructuring of the competition. The final period, dealing with the years since 1984, has witnessed the (partial) *resolution* of the 'crisis'. Here, it is argued that although the policies of an independent Commission have stabilized and strengthened the finances of the League, this 'success' has been tempered by ongoing tensions associated with the cultural dimensions of the game.

The 'crisis' framework employed in this article highlights a key theme in the post-war history of the VFL/AFL, that being the tension between its *economic restructuring* on the one hand, and its *cultural reproduction* on the other. In short, it shows that structural changes have seriously disrupted and threatened the social fabric of the competition, necessitating an intricate renegotiation of its economic and cultural facets. In turn, this reflects the complex nature of the League as a social institution, one that simultaneously serves a dual function – economic and cultural. Many of the controversies in its post-war history stem from tensions and contradictions between these roles, and the period can only be fully understood when the changing balance between the two is carefully assessed. This complicated question is taken up in the conclusion.

1946–63

In Australia, the society which developed after the Second World War was strikingly distinct from that which had existed before it. This contrast centred on the 'Long Boom', an unprecedented period of economic prosperity, stretching from the late 1940s through to 1974. Leaving behind the hardship that had blighted most of the years since 1890, the post-war boom witnessed a pronounced fall in unemployment, coupled with a continual rise in real wages and living standards. Progressively, a new consumerism emerged, embodied in the 'Great Australian Dream' of home ownership.[9]

A key component of Australia's post-war boom was an expansion of the manufacturing sector, fuelled by a mass immigration programme. The latter saw more than 2 million migrants arrive between 1947 and the mid-1960s. Along with the post-war 'baby boom', this led to an increase in population from 7.6 million to over 11 million.[10] Immigration also impacted upon the demographic composition of the population, as large numbers of non-English speaking background migrants – especially Yugoslavs, Greeks, and Italians – entered the country. As a result, the proportion of the population born outside of Australia and the British

Isles climbed from 3 per cent in 1947, to 10 per cent by the mid-1960s.[11] The majority of migrants settled in the major metropolitan centres, thereby intensifying longstanding trends towards urban sprawl and suburbanization. These trends were facilitated by a rapid growth in car ownership, which reduced the importance of locality-bound communities, and broadened people's work and leisure options.

This societal transformation was felt strongly in Melbourne, and it harboured major implications for the VFL. Thus, during the 1950s, Melbourne's population grew by almost 40 per cent; its metropolitan boundaries were repeatedly extended; and its ethnic diversity increased markedly.[12] These developments irreversibly altered the context in which the VFL operated, and ultimately this would necessitate changes in the League's organization and culture. However, such changes were neither immediately, nor conspicuously, evident in the competition. Indeed, the period 1946 to 1963 was generally characterized by a 'business as usual' approach to the administration of the game.[13] In short, there was to be a pronounced time-lag between the transformation of society, and the transformation of the VFL.

This lag was partly due to a continuity of personnel at the top of the game. Until 1956 the President of the League remained Dr W.C. McClelland, who had held this position since the mid-1920s. His continuing tenure reflected a quest to recreate the perceived 'golden era' of the mid-1930s. During the Depression VFL football had cemented its place in the lives of many Melburnians, and these years were marked by growing crowds, 'star' players, and an intensification of 'tribal allegiances'. There was now a strong desire to revive these features, and to leave behind the disruptions associated with the war years.[14]

With the exception of a short-lived attempt in 1952 to make Australian Rules *the* football code across the nation,[15] McClelland's administration of the game was marked by a conservative approach. Upon his retirement in 1956 he was replaced by Kenneth Luke, who held the presidency for the next 15 years. Unlike his predecessor, Luke advocated a wide range of reforms, including changes to labour market controls, higher player payments and the professionalization of the game's administration.[16] However, during his first decade in charge, most of these plans went unfulfilled, and it was largely in the area of ground reforms that his presence and vision were strongly felt.

Football grievances with cricket clubs and local councils were a longstanding issue in the VFL. Stretching back to the nineteenth century, cricket administrators and local councillors had controlled the grounds that were used by football clubs. From the start, the latter had felt the arrangements unfair, arguing that football was being forced to pay excessive sums of money for grounds with sub-standard facilities. Luke now resolved to increase the game's autonomy, by building an independent 'home' for football. After promoting the idea in the late 1950s, in 1962 he oversaw the purchase of a site in Waverley – a south-eastern suburb of Melbourne. In time, the commitment to the Waverley project would have major repercussions, however construction on the new venue did not commence until the mid-1960s.[17]

Notwithstanding Luke's goal to professionalize the administration of the VFL, during this period, the game continued to be largely under the control of amateurs. Specifically, the central organizing body remained the traditional Board of Directors, comprised of delegates from each of the clubs. Although this body was marred by divided loyalties, it sufficed to oversee what was essentially a stable competition. Throughout this period, the same 12 clubs vied for honours, and all had been in the VFL since at least 1925.[18]

The theme of continuity carried through to the finances of the competition, as reflected in the regulation of players' labour, and the limiting of their match payments. These occurred respectively through a system of metropolitan zoning, dating back to 1915, and the Coulter law of 1930. The former bound Melbourne-based players to a single club in perpetuity, thereby restricting their bargaining power. For its part, the Coulter law set a maximum match payment that could be paid to players. Although these measures led to an abortive attempt to set up a players' union in 1955,[19] together they helped to contain player payments. Indeed, over this period payments actually *fell* both in real terms, and as a proportion of average weekly earnings.[20]

This limited financial return to players was difficult to justify, given the game was coasting on the post-war tide of prosperity. Not only were crowds strong, culminating in record aggregate attendances and receipt figures in 1963,[21] but a new source of revenue appeared from 1956 – that of television broadcasting rights. This source began modestly, with the League receiving just £50 per game in 1957, but it climbed rapidly thereafter. Indeed, the figure tripled the very next year, with each of the 12 clubs receiving £500 from television rights, in addition to a sum of £90 for radio rights.[22]

Although broadcasting revenue was welcomed, until the 1970s it remained marginal to the finances of the VFL, representing less than 5 per cent of the total income of the clubs.[23] Throughout this period then, primary sources of revenue – namely admission fees and membership subscriptions – were sufficient to fund the competition, thus securing its financial independence from television. Indeed, in the late 1950s and early 1960s the central administration was highly suspicious of the new medium, severely restricting the form of television broadcasts. The fear was that live coverage of matches would reduce attendances, thereby starving the game of its lifeblood. Consequently, live telecasts were limited to the last quarter of matches from 1957, and banned altogether from 1961.[24]

In retrospect, this fear was misplaced, as television – along with the press and radio – proved an ideal means of promoting the competition. This role was crucial in the post-war period for two main reasons. Firstly, the traditions of the VFL needed to be sustained for the growing number of supporters who were relocating to Melbourne's outer suburbs, away from the inner-city heartland of the competition. Secondly, along with the education system, the media served to socialize many newly arrived migrants into the rules and culture of the 'indigenous' game. Thus, in the face of sweeping demographic changes, the media helped to create, and to sustain, relationships between clubs and their supporters.[25]

In promoting the VFL, the media orchestrated an enormous quantity of football 'talk'. By the 1960s television coverage was extensive, with multiple channels screening programs from Thursdays to Sundays.[26] In general, the *style* of media coverage was acritical, stimulating interest over scrutiny and making 'stars' out of the best players. This resulted in the game becoming more popular while, for the most part, VFL administrators escaped public scrutiny. At this time then, the League enjoyed a positive public image, and 'could do little wrong as far as supporters were concerned'.[27]

Overall, following the uncertainties of the war, the years 1946 to 1963 were prosperous ones for the VFL, during which it regained its central place in the cultural life of Melbourne. What is more, due in no small part to the media coverage it received, the League actually improved its position relative to rival sports and football competitions, including the VFA. During this period, where changes were evident in the VFL, they tended to occur *within*, rather than *to*, the basic structures of the competition. That is, they were largely incremental and quantitative in nature, and did *not* constitute pronounced organizational and operational shifts. Nevertheless, behind this facade of stability and continuity, the societal foundations of the VFL had been transformed, and the competition was soon to experience the 'morbid symptoms' of 'crisis'.

1964–74

Although the 'origins' of the post-war 'crisis' in the League did not give way to its 'manifestations' in a single instant, a useful marker for the transition is the 'Barassi affair', which erupted at the completion of the 1964 season. At that time, after a long association with the Melbourne Football Club, Ron Barassi was lured to its rival at Carlton, taking up a position as captain-coach. Whilst many star players had shifted their allegiances in the past, this case was distinct in several respects.[28] Firstly, Barassi's biography ensured that hitherto he had been regarded as an integral member of the Melbourne 'family' and the quintessential embodiment of the club's 'spirit'.[29] Secondly, these impressions were strengthened by the fact that during the 1950s and early 1960s, he had formed the linchpin in the most successful team in the club's history. Thirdly, Barassi was the first VFL captain to move directly to another club and therefore the first to be seen to disrespect this prestigious office. Finally, for the time, the move to Carlton was extremely lucrative, involving a sum of £20,000 over three years.[30]

Given this potent combination of factors, it is hardly noteworthy that many Melbourne supporters regarded Barassi's departure as an act of betrayal. However, such sentiments were not restricted to this group; rather, they were echoed across the competition and exacerbated by numerous sensationalist media reports.[31] In this context, the episode served as a flashpoint for escalating concerns over the *general* direction in which the game appeared to be heading.

These concerns were not misplaced. Indeed, from the mid-1960s there were numerous signs that the VFL was entering a period of 'dislocation and uncertainty'.[32] Following in the wake of sustained stability and prosperity, these 'new times' caught some in the football community off-guard, and were therefore treated as entirely novel. In truth, however, they were the cumulative outcome of the various post-war trends outlined above. Together, these trends increasingly came to threaten the traditional structure and culture of the competition.

An immediate issue confronting the VFL was the perpetual problem of grounds. In addition to the longstanding gripes outlined above, the post-war movement of Melbourne's population to the outer suburbs resulted in a growing imbalance between the location of the clubs, and the distribution of their supporters.[33] Notwithstanding the capacity of the media to offset the impact of this change partially, the view strengthened that these festering ground issues needed to be tackled as a matter of urgency.

In response to these problems, in 1965, three clubs – Richmond, Saint Kilda, and North Melbourne – relocated to new home grounds, with varying motives and outcomes.[34] Further relocations followed in 1967 and 1970, when Fitzroy moved firstly to Carlton's Princes Park, and then to Saint Kilda's old base at the Junction Oval. The final relocation of this period occurred in 1974, when Hawthorn shifted from its traditional home at Glenferrie, to Princes Park.[35]

Beyond these responses at club level, the League as a whole sought a wider solution to the problem of grounds, in the form of the Waverley project. Building on the stadium began in 1966, and the result – christened 'VFL Park' – staged its first match in 1970. In theory, this venue would ease ground problems, by substantially reducing football's dependency on local councils, cricket clubs in general, and the Melbourne Cricket Club (MCC) in particular.[36] In practice, however, VFL Park posed problems of its own. These included its outer suburban location, which made it difficult to access, especially given the area was prone to traffic jams, and poorly served by public transport.[37] A further problem stemmed from the flawed stadium design, which curtailed the sense of intimacy and atmosphere that could be generated.[38]

These shortcomings ensured that VFL Park failed to solve all of the League's ground problems. What is more, the cost of the project – amounting to some $12 million – was a drain on the game's finances. This had two major repercussions: firstly, it reduced the funds available for upgrading the remaining venues; and secondly, by raising the financial stakes, it intensified the search for outside revenue, in the form of broadcasting rights, sponsorship, and marketing income.[39] In retrospect, this contribution to the turn to external revenue sources was the major consequence of the Waverley project.

Linked to ground problems was another issue facing the VFL – declining crowds. The League's annual reports show that the aggregate attendance figure in 1969 was 2.4 million, down from 2.7 million in

1963. Whilst this did not represent a dramatic fall, it concerned administrators who, in the post-war period, had grown accustomed to continual growth in this area. The view emerged that unevenness in the competition was a contributing factor to the decline. Between 1946 and 1965 a mere four clubs (from 12) accounted for 16 (from 20) premierships.

In this context, the League instigated a series of reforms, including two rule changes designed to limit congestion and to speed up play.[40] These revealed a growing preoccupation with the broad 'entertainment value' of football, which in turn reflected the goal of attracting new supporters, particularly television viewers. Other reforms were geared to evening-up the competition. For instance, in 1967 a Victorian country zoning system was added to the existing metropolitan scheme. The following year, a series of revenue sharing measures, designed to see the rich clubs subsidize the poor, furthered the administration's equalization objectives.[41] These reforms were based upon research which suggested that spectator sports were characterized by a 'peculiar economics', whereby unevenness and predictability might well undermine the interest in, and demand for, a sports competition.[42]

The most pressing problem confronting the League during this period was growing player disenchantment over wages and conditions.[43] In the wake of the 'Barassi affair', a trend towards professionalism emerged across the competition. Matters came to a head in 1970, with two key disputes at the Collingwood and Essendon clubs. Here, after threatening to withdraw their services a number of established players secured substantially higher wages. One of these, Geoff Pryor of Essendon, went on to become the first president of the VFL Players' Association, formed in 1973.[44] Around this time, player payments climbed rapidly, such that by 1974 they were twice that of 1972.[45] However, this increase had little to do with the power of the Players' Association, which was slow to gain legitimacy in the eyes of the League, and which faced several structural problems common to player unions in team sports.[46] Instead, the upward spiral was driven primarily by an intense competition between clubs for quality players.

The growth in player payments was made possible by the increasing availability of, and turn towards, external sources of revenue. For instance, during this period television rights increased steadily, and by 1973 they stood at $200,000 per year.[47] In 1968 the League's first major sponsorship deal was secured, with the tobacco company W.D. & H.O.

Wills, and this source grew in importance from that point on.[48] More generally, at both the League and club levels increasing efforts were made to court business, with corporate boxes being introduced at a number of grounds, including VFL Park.[49] Collectively, these developments signalled a growing trend towards the commercialization of the VFL.

The essence of this period was most clearly expressed at the North Melbourne Football Club. Following the election of Allen Aylett as President in 1971, North embarked upon a wholesale restructuring programme. The reform agenda comprised two central planks, the first of which centred on the corporatization and professionalization of the club's administration. Most importantly, a full-time fundraiser was employed to maximize the revenue derived from 'non-traditional' sources – that is, from sources other than membership subscriptions and gate receipts. This led to an expansion of the social club's operations; to a range of travel and insurance services being offered to members and supporters; and to corporate sponsorship being actively sought. The result was a massive increase in club turnover, such that by 1974 it stood at $247,000, approximately four times the figure for 1968.[50]

The second plank in Aylett's strategy was to use this additional revenue to fund a player recruitment program. A 'chequebook approach' was adopted, whereby player talent was immediately bought, rather than painstakingly developed. This strategy dovetailed with the players' push for higher wages, and was facilitated by the VFL's introduction of the 'ten-year rule' in 1973. This allowed those who had played in the competition for ten years (or more) to switch clubs without the customary imposition of a hefty transfer fee.[51] Although the rule was only in place for a year, this was sufficient to enable North to purchase the playing services of several VFL 'stars' and these were supplemented by a series of high-profile interstate recruits. Subsequently, the club's on-field performances improved markedly, and having come no higher than seventh for more than a decade, in 1974 North finished second on the ladder.[52]

Taken as a whole, the years 1964 to 1974 witnessed a new phase in the development of the VFL, characterized by the linked processes of commercialization and professionalization. Commencing with the 'Barassi affair', this period culminated with the rise of North in the early 1970s. In turn, the latter's 'corporate approach' served as an indication of what was to come. No longer, it seemed, was the running of football to be left largely to amateurs, all be they knowledgeable about the game. Instead, administration was now the business of professionals, and should be unashamedly carried out in accordance with the logic and practices of the broader marketplace. This management style, which began as a controversy at North, was soon to become a commonplace throughout the League. The result would be a period of great structural change, and accompanying cultural trauma: the 'high-point' of the post-war 'crisis' in the game.

1975–84

In 1975 two events combined to intensify the rate of change in the VFL. Firstly, North secured its first ever premiership, a testimony to its new way of 'doing business'. The club followed this with three consecutive grand final appearances, including a second premiership in 1977, a record that accelerated the adoption of its off-field strategies throughout the league. The second event was the introduction of colour television, an innovation that rapidly began to transform the financial underpinnings of the competition.

Coming in the wake of these events, the 1976 election for League President represented a watershed in the history of the VFL.[53] The two contenders – Phil Ryan and Allen Aylett – represented competing sets of forces acting upon the game. On the one hand, Ryan was more aligned with the weight of tradition, symbolising continuity and stability; on the other, Aylett stood defiantly at the cutting edge of the corporate and commercial revolution, as his years at North had ably demonstrated.

With the ballot of the club delegates ending in a deadlock, the vote of the incumbent President – Sir Maurice Nathan – was required to determine the outcome.[54] Ultimately, it was Aylett who triumphed, making him the youngest President in the history of the League. The closeness of the result reflected the volatility of the period: at that time, the VFL stood at a crossroads. In retrospect, Aylett's victory marked a shift in the relative importance of the cultural forces of tradition, versus the economic imperatives driving 'modernization'. Clearly, Aylett personified the latter, his election confirming the course for the future.[55]

In February 1977 Aylett commenced his term as President, forming a partnership with Jack Hamilton, who the previous month had been appointed General Manager. Until the end of 1984 this partnership – dubbed the 'dynamic duo' by the press[56] – oversaw the most tumultuous period in the history of the VFL. The tone of their 'vision' was reflected at an 'Administration Seminar' in 1978, where a range of issues were discussed, including a corporate plan, sponsorship, legal matters, and recruitment policies.[57] The following year, a full-time corporate planner was appointed, to investigate and advise on such controversial issues as ground rationalization and the prospect of interstate expansion.[58] In this highly corporatized context, the VFL emerged as the fastest-growing sports competition in the country, and it increasingly left behind its troubled interstate rival – the New South Wales Rugby League (NSWRL).[59]

Throughout the Aylett–Hamilton reign, the trajectory of the VFL was closely bound up with the money and interests of commercial television. The inception of colour transmission in 1975 had increased the attractiveness of televised sport and this set in train an intensified bidding process for the rights to broadcast the VFL, historically the most watched sports competition in Australia. In the late 1970s this trend was given further impetus by research which confirmed that VFL telecasts drew an attractive demographic, comprised of a high proportion of affluent men.[60] This made for a lucrative 'audience commodity', with a strong appeal to advertisers, one that had traditionally proved difficult to attract through other forms of programming. The result was a rapid increase in broadcasting rights, with the figure rising more than tenfold between the mid-1970s and the mid-1980s, to a total of approximately $2.5 million per year.[61]

The financial benefits accruing to the VFL from television were not limited to the sale of broadcasting rights. Instead, by broadening the following and raising the profile of the competition, television fuelled another source of secondary funding – corporate sponsorship. Although it had been evident from the late 1960s, sponsorship grew rapidly over this period, both at the League and club levels. Indeed, whilst in the mid-1970s none of the clubs had drawn revenue from this source, over the ensuing decade *all* managed to secure six-figure sponsorship deals.[62]

The increased revenue from secondary sources contributed to major changes in the administration of the game. These included pronounced trends towards corporatization and bureaucratization, as well as evidence of an expanding entrepreneurial logic in the League's operations. These were reflected in the establishment of the Properties Division, which in 1976 began licensing and marketing the 'VFL' logo. Within a year this operation had become the third biggest source of revenue – behind gate receipts and television rights – contributing some $300,000 to League coffers. The following year, the figure climbed to $500,000, and then to more than $1 million by 1979.[63]

Similar trends were evident at the club level, where restructuring was rife. Mirroring the changes pioneered at North, a growing proportion of staff came to be employed in areas not directly related to football. The archetypal example was at Carlton where, between 1977 and 1979 the club embarked on an ambitious project of diversification. This included a range of ventures that had nothing whatever to do with football, including a medical centre, travel and insurance services, and a female dance troupe called the 'Carlton Bluebirds'.[64] The latter met with the ire of supporters, from Carlton and beyond, as it was seen to undermine the traditions of the VFL, and to reflect a crass 'Americanization' of the game.[65]

All of these trends combined to create a new structural reality in the VFL, with the shift to secondary revenue sources undermining the game's self-sufficiency. Thus, during the 1970s, although gate receipts and membership subscriptions remained the major sources of income, they ceased to be sufficient to fund the competition fully.[66] Many supporters and journalists regarded this loss of autonomy as a disturbing trend, given that it meant football literally could not afford to ignore the interests of outside, commercial concerns. It was feared that the latter were not committed to the game itself, and that their involvement was as conditional, not to mention as precarious, as any other business investment.

Heightening this unease were the intensifying connections between the VFL and conspicuous figures in the broader business community. During this period numerous status-seeking entrepreneurs entered the game as club presidents, including Bob Ansett at North Melbourne, Lyndsay Fox at Saint Kilda and John Elliott at Carlton.[67] Although such figures typically had little first-hand knowledge of the game they increasingly met (privately) to discuss matters pertaining to the running and future of the VFL.[68]

The League justified the turn to secondary revenue sources, and the growing presence of corporate identities, by pushing arguments on two fronts. Firstly, the income derived from television and sponsorship was presented as a means of keeping down admission prices, by alleviating the 'common' supporter from the burden of underwriting the costs of the game.[69] Secondly, coupled with the perceived managerial flair of the corporate celebrities, this revenue was put forward as a solution to any existing financial problems faced by the clubs and as the key to a prosperous future for the competition.

These arguments, however, were confounded by the facts. For instance, from the mid-1970s to the mid-1980s, the cost of admission to VFL matches doubled in real terms, despite rapid increases in corporate funding.[70] Furthermore, whilst this funding *did* greatly increase club revenue, it merely elevated the level of financial problems, rather than eliminating them altogether. That is, because there was no systematic framework for regulating or containing the cost structures of the clubs, these new funds were simply absorbed into those structures, fuelling inflationary pressures in the process.[71]

The two main factors driving this inflation were player payments and transfer fees.[72] With the greater availability of secondary revenue, costs in these areas spiralled due to the intense competition for quality players; the increasing presence of player agents; and the failure of the League to establish an effective regulatory framework. Consequently, from the mid-1970s to the mid-1980s player payments rose by 1800 per cent, and transfer fees more than doubled in real terms.[73] As a result of such hyper-inflation, over this period, the annual cost of fielding a team soared from $300,000 to around $3 million.[74]

This escalation in costs exerted great financial pressure on the more vulnerable VFL clubs, particularly those languishing near the foot of the table. These clubs were faced with an acute dilemma. On the one hand, their precarious financial status made the purchase of expensive talent seem an extravagance. On the other, the only way out of trouble was through an enhanced on-field performance, which – in the short term at least – required the purchase of new players. Put simply, these clubs found themselves in a double-bind, whereby they could neither afford to buy players, nor could they afford not to. The result was an entrenched unevenness in the VFL, such that between 1975 and 1984, just half of the clubs appeared in a grand final, and only five out of twelve managed to secure a premiership.

Despite the periodic forebodings of Aylett, little was done to alleviate these internal problems.[75] Instead, the *primary* focus of the central administration was outwards, with an emphasis being placed on maximizing television and sponsorship revenue, and cementing the VFL's position as the nation's pre-eminent football competition. These preoccupations were reflected in the League's plan to increase its market share, via the development of Sunday football. Traditionally, the VFL had been prevented from staging Sunday matches by the State Government, and since 1960, this day had been the exclusive preserve of the VFA. Along with television coverage on Channel 0 (later 10) from 1967, this sole use of Sundays had enabled the VFA to carve out a stable market niche for itself.[76]

In 1978 the VFL began an intensive lobbying campaign to have the Government lift its restrictive Sunday legislation. However, when this strategy stalled, the League sought to bypass it by scheduling matches beyond the state borders of Victoria. From 1979 an increasing number of fixtures were played in Sydney and beamed back live to a receptive Victorian television audience. The result was more money for the VFL, in the form of broadcasting rights and sponsorship, and the progressive crippling of the viability of the VFA. In 1982 Channel 10 dropped its coverage of the latter's home-and-away rounds, and despite more than a century of tradition, from this point on, the VFA was 'in decline and beyond protection'.[77]

With the assistance of television, it seemed the VFL had secured its dual aim regarding Sunday football: that is, to increase secondary revenue and to destabilize one of its direct rivals. However, the League was not content with scheduling fixtures outside Victoria, and in 1982 it embarked upon the more ambitious goal of relocating the South Melbourne Swans to Sydney on a permanent basis. This initiative rekindled the dream of making Australian Rules *the* national football code and proved to be one of the most controversial episodes in the game's history. The move divided the club, as it was approved of by most players and club officials, but vehemently opposed by many supporters.[78] This opposition led to the formation of a pressure group – Keep South at South (KSAS) – which engaged in a three-and-a-half month court battle to prevent the relocation from proceeding. These efforts, however, were unsuccessful, and from 1983, the 'old' South Melbourne played as the 'new' Sydney Swans.

The Swans relocation saga highlighted the growing social distance between VFL clubs and their traditional support bases. More specifically, it was indicative of a wider trend towards 'appropriation', whereby commercial interests were wresting control over the clubs from their traditional supporters. This process required that the latter be transformed from *active producers* of their clubs, into more or less *passive consumers* of a sports commodity.[79] As KSAS had shown, however, this 'required transformation' was unlikely to proceed smoothly, and it could be expected that economically driven restructuring would meet with cultural resistance. Indeed, this pattern was to become a familiar one in the years ahead.

A further repercussion of the Swans relocation flowed from the *Foschini Case* of 1982–83. Citing work and family reasons, Silvio Foschini – a Swans player – refused to relocate to Sydney. Backed by Saint Kilda, who were eager to secure his services, Foschini challenged the League's labour market regulations in the courts. In the final ruling, Mr Justice Crockett deemed them an 'unreasonable restraint of trade'. Along with previous judgements, which had compared the rules governing the movement of football players to feudal bondage, the *Foschini Case* left the League's labour market regulations in tatters.[80]

The Foschini debacle forced the League into a major strategic and policy re-think. This exercise was informed by a 1983 reconnaissance trip to the United States, where VFL officials met administrators from the National Basketball Association (NBA), and the National Football League (NFL). At these meetings, a range of issues were canvassed, including the merits of a player draft system and salary cap. In addition to these discussions, the VFL commissioned a Task Force, charged with investigating the overarching framework of the game.[81]

In the meantime, the depth of the 'crisis' confronting the League became clear. At the financial level, in 1984, a confidential internal document was leaked to the media. Known as the Tilley Report, it revealed that in 1983 the VFL had incurred a loss of almost $2 million, and at this time half of its clubs had been technically bankrupt.[82] This dire financial situation was exacerbated by the fact that crowds had been falling since the early 1980s, suggesting both a waning enthusiasm for the game, and growing competition from other sporting and entertainment rivals.[83]

The League's problems did not stop there. Instead, the 'financial crisis' was coupled with a pronounced 'cultural crisis' in the game. This extended beyond declining crowds, to include explicit attacks on the public image of the VFL and its chief administrators. Both were increasingly portrayed by the press as greedy and power hungry, and they were repeatedly criticized for being out of touch with the 'common supporter'.[84] Lest it regard these reports as unrepresentative of the football public, the League was directly confronted with the latter's hostility on Grand Final day in 1983, when Aylett and Hamilton were roundly booed by the crowd.[85]

In March 1984 this burgeoning 'crisis' culminated in an attempt to form a breakaway league. Orchestrated by John Elliott, the President of the Carlton Football Club, the plan was to create a national competition, in which every participant club would fully pay its way. The Elliott 'vision' was put forward at a clandestine meeting, involving representatives from nine out of the 12 VFL clubs.[86] Although the proposal failed to garner the required support, this had more to do with a general mistrust of the motives of Elliott and Carlton, than with a firm belief in the capacity of the central administration to cope with the challenges facing the present competition. Regardless, the breakaway attempt served as a warning of what was likely to happen if the VFL failed to quickly take charge of the situation.

In the wake of the breakaway threat, in August 1984 the League received the first of three Task Force reports, which recommended an overhaul of the game's administration. Specifically, it called for the traditional Board of Directors to be replaced by a streamlined, independent commission. This, it argued, was the surest means of securing a united central body, capable of transcending the conflicts between clubs and of advancing the overarching interests of the competition. After much discussion and debate, the clubs finally relinquished some of their powers, by voting in favour of this recommendation.[87] The decision signalled a recognition of the depth of the 'crisis' confronting the game, and it acknowledged that major reforms were required to resolve it.

In October 1984 a five-person Commission was appointed. At the same time, the role of President was scrapped, and Hamilton – as the inaugural Chief Commissioner – replaced Aylett as the VFL's top administrator. In hindsight, the establishment of the Commission represented a key juncture in the development of the League, as the administrative framework was now in place to embark upon the next phase of restructuring. Put simply, the 'high-point' of the post-war 'crisis' had been negotiated, although the move towards its 'resolution' was to prove a lengthy and traumatic process.

1985–99

When the Commission was appointed at the end of 1984, the League's future appeared bleak. The following year, the new administration released a detailed strategy to redress this situation, entitled

'Establishing the Basis for Future Success'. The blueprint outlined in this document became the prime shaper of the competition, its sweeping recommendations clustering around four central axes: 1) a programme of national expansion; 2) a policy of ground rationalization; 3) an integrated system of labour market regulation; and 4) a broad-ranging equalization scheme. This four-pronged strategy was to be secured by means of a licensing agreement, struck in 1985, which legally bound the clubs to the Commission's directives.[88]

In addition to pursuing this new strategy, the Commission was faced with the existing problem of the Sydney Swans. Since their relocation, the Swans had struggled to carve out a niche for themselves in the heartland of rugby league. In 1985, in an ill-fated attempt to remedy this situation, the Commission sold the Swans to Dr Geoffrey Edelsten – a medical entrepreneur – for $2.9 million.[89] This experiment with private ownership soon ran into trouble, and a complex series of events ensued, which included a second sale of the licence to a private consortium in 1988.[90] After further difficulties, in 1993 the Commission devised a rescue package, which saw the club return to a traditional membership structure. Flirtations with private ownership also occurred at two other clubs – the Brisbane Bears and the West Coast Eagles[91] – but with similarly unsuccessful results. Consequently, the private ownership of clubs was removed from the Commission's policy platform.

Despite these problems in establishing interstate clubs, the Commission has never wavered from its goal of national expansion. Building on the Swans relocation to Sydney, this process commenced in earnest in 1987, with the acceptance of teams from Queensland (the Brisbane Bears) and Western Australia (the West Coast Eagles). In 1991 further expansion occurred with the belated inclusion of a team from South Australia (the Adelaide Crows);[92] and in 1995 a second Western Australian team was accepted (the Fremantle Dockers). Finally, following the demise of Fitzroy in 1996 (see below), a second team from South Australia (Port Power) was admitted.[93] Currently then, the Commission oversees a total of 16 franchises – ten in Victoria; two each in Western Australia and South Australia; and one each in New South Wales and Queensland.[94]

Underpinning this national expansion has been the aim to secure a wider market for the League's 'product', which in turn attracts greater revenue from broadcasting rights, corporate sponsorship, and marketing activities. The Commission has sold the policy to the Victorian-based clubs on these grounds, and successfully so given the pronounced financial difficulties many of them faced by the mid-1980s. Indeed, in the short-term the $666,666 windfall (per club) from the combined West Coast and Brisbane licence fees was crucial to the survival of several Melbourne clubs. Thereafter, direct cash injections from further licence fees, coupled with indirect funds flowing from increases in secondary revenue, have become pivotal to the finances of *all*. In this context, the old VFL clubs mostly came to accept that their financial viability hinged upon national expansion, even if they remained uninspired by the concept.[95]

From a financial standpoint, there is no doubt that national expansion has proved a major success. Indeed, the League's annual reports reveal that total revenue has climbed from $20.6 million in 1986 – the year before the entry of teams from Perth and Brisbane – to $92.4 million in 1998. Much of this improvement is attributable to increases in broadcasting rights and corporate sponsorship. Regarding the former, in 1999 the League received $40 million from Channel 7, covering free-to-air and pay television rights. In 1997 it was even able to charge the network a fee of $20 million for the right to bid last when the current contract expires in 2001. In addition to these direct injections, by capitalizing on media exposure, the League has also increased its sponsorship and merchandising revenue, both of which stood at record levels in 1998.[96]

Although national expansion has greatly increased the volume of money in the League, the experiences of the 1970s and early 1980s warned against seeing this as a panacea. Indeed, these years confirmed that additional revenue might only result in elevating existing financial problems. Thus, from the outset, the Commission has recognized the need for measures to contain the cost structures of the clubs. This recognition has underpinned the remaining three planks in its strategy – ground rationalization; labour market regulation; and equalization.

Ground rationalization has been a priority of the League since the late 1970s. The aim has been twofold: firstly, for clubs to cut costs, via the sharing of facilities; and secondly, to maximize attendances by fully utilising the biggest venues. Under the Commission, the pace of rationalization has been intensified, to the point where the ten Melbourne clubs currently share just five venues. This number is set to fall further still, with the closure of Victoria Park in 1999; the pending sale of Waverley; and the uncertain prospects for Optus Oval. Into the future, the likelihood is that *all* of the Melbourne-based clubs will play at just two venues – the MCG, and the new Docklands stadium.[97] Whilst the League may deem this situation (economically) 'rational', many supporters have opposed the changes, as they are seen to undermine the traditional links between the clubs and their 'communities'.[98]

In a further effort to curb the cost structures of the clubs, the League has developed an integrated system of labour market regulation. This has involved the introduction of a range of measures, including a salary cap (1985); the virtual abolition of transfer fees (1988); the progressive limiting of senior player lists; and a national player draft (1991).[99] Collectively, these measures have eliminated the anarchic hyper-inflation associated with the market for players during the Aylett–Hamilton years. Indeed, over the last decade, whilst players' wages have increased substantially in absolute terms, they have declined as a proportion of the total revenue generated across the League.[100]

The Commission's labour market regulations have formed part of a broader objective of 'equalization'. That is, in an attempt to even-up the competition, so as to attract and hold the interest of supporters, the Commission has sought to have the rich clubs subsidize the poorer clubs. This has been realized by means of a complex system of revenue-pooling, whereby broadcasting rights, merchandising revenue, and a proportion of the gate are distributed evenly among the clubs. In 1997 this scheme saw more than $8 million flow from the wealthier to the poorer franchises.[101] On the field, since 1994, equalization has been pursued through a selective approach to allocating fixtures, such that clubs which have performed poorly in a given year are (theoretically) given an easier draw for the following season. The result has been an increasingly even and unpredictable competition.[102]

In comparison with the situation in the mid-1980s this combination of policies has not only produced a more financially stable competition; in numerical terms at least, it has also strengthened the League's following. This is evident in aggregate attendance figures, which in 1998 were at an all-time high, and more than twice their pre-Commission level. Crucially, attendances per game were also higher than at any other point in the competition's history. The trends are similar with club memberships, which are often regarded as a barometer for hardcore support. Thus, in 1998 memberships increased for the twelfth consecutive year, both in aggregate and per-club terms. Finally, interest in the competition is also reflected in television statistics, which reveal that in 1998, over 90 per cent of Australian households tuned into AFL television broadcasts at some point.[103]

Predictably, the Commission has drawn upon such statistics to vindicate its policies. However, taken in isolation, they mask the fact that this 'success' has come at the expense of other football interests, both external and internal to the League. With regard to the former, the Commission's expansion has threatened the viability of other football competitions. For instance, its increasing presence in the Sunday football market progressively undermined the viability of the VFA. Indeed, after a lengthy period of decline, the latter was subsumed by the AFL in the mid-1990s, effectively being reduced to the status of a feeder competition.[104]

Beyond Victoria, a similar dynamic impacted upon both the West Australian Football League (WAFL), and the South Australian National Football League (SANFL). Here, after the establishment of the West Coast Eagles and the Adelaide Crows, the WAFL and SANFL respectively found it impossible to compete directly with the VFL/AFL. Thus, attendances and marketing revenue declined by over 50 per cent and, like the VFA, these leagues became little more than nurseries for potential AFL players.[105] These examples highlight that much of the VFL/AFL's expansion has been attained through direct competition with other fractions of 'Australian Rules' capital, and thus can more accurately be coined 'market concentration'.

In terms of internal threats, the Commission's agenda has endangered the existence of some of its own clubs. With time, the Commission came to renege on its earlier assurances that a national league would not involve the eradication of existing franchises.[106] Instead, it became increasingly clear that its plans *did* require a reduction in the number of Melbourne teams.[107] To this end, from 1989 the Commission offered financial incentives to encourage clubs to merge, and these incentives peaked at $6 million in 1996. This shifting stance suggested that the Commission's real goal was not to ensure the welfare of the incumbent clubs; rather, it was to build a lucrative national league. Ultimately, this goal was more closely aligned with the profit-driven interests of commercial television and corporate sponsors, than with the interests of a number of its own clubs.

The push towards mergers has been resisted by groups of supporters keen to preserve the autonomy of 'their' clubs. To this end, a number of fundraising campaigns have been run. For example, to save their club from a forced merger with Fitzroy in 1989, Footscray Bulldog supporters waged a 'fightback' crusade which managed to raise over $1.4 million in less than a month.[108] Similarly, in the early 1990s supporters of the Fitzroy Lions and the Richmond Tigers amassed million dollar sums to save their clubs from 'extinction'. More recently still, in 1996, Melbourne and Hawthorn supporters successfully resisted the pressure to merge. These examples confirm that the efforts of supporters have, in the short term at least, successfully obstructed the economic forces that were threatening vulnerable clubs.

The lengths to which supporters are prepared to go in order to rescue 'their' clubs clearly indicates that these institutions continue to serve a significant cultural function. However, the recent history of the League reveals that this function is progressively being subordinated to the demands of commercial rationalism. Here, the subsequent histories of Footscray and Fitzroy are instructive. In the case of the former, despite the 1989 'fightback' victory, soon after officials still felt the need to change the name of the club from the 'Footscray' Bulldogs, to the 'Western' Bulldogs. This was done in an attempt to broaden the demographic base of the club and it signified a realization that the local pool of support was no longer sufficient for economic survival. Presently, the club is considering playing a number of its 'home' games in Sydney, for similar reasons.

In the case of Fitzroy, in 1996, the efforts of supporters to maintain an independent existence for their club came to nought. At that time, it was forcibly merged with Brisbane, and a foundation member of the League was no longer. Whilst long-standing supporters may have struggled to make sense of this development, it appeared that the Commission had no such problems. In an official publication, the *Football Record*, the Commission editorialized as follows:

> During any change there are those who suffer. When workplaces are reconstructed good people lose their places; when governments bring down budgets, good causes are slashed ... when sporting institutions spread their wings from a narrow market to a national one, old brands disappear, even those with 113 years behind them: the weak, unfortunately, are lost.[109]

This passage clearly demonstrates how football has come to be conceptualized at the Commission: it is a commodity in the broader mass entertainment market, understandable within an explicit entrepreneurial discourse. In these terms, Fitzroy was an uncompetitive 'brand' in a highly competitive 'market', and its demise was therefore inevitable.

The destinies of Footscray and Fitzroy attest to the fact that the cultural resistance to economic restructuring is best understood as a 'residual' social force in the AFL. Drawing on Raymond Williams, this means that the social base of this resistance is grounded in the past, although it continues to exert an influence upon the present.[110] Crucially, however, this influence has been progressively lost to once 'emergent', now 'dominant', economic forces. In this context, the cultural traditions of the game have become increasingly *reactive* in nature, responding to an agenda for development that is being set elsewhere, in the capitalist economy.

CONCLUSION

In the early 1980s two seminal works in the emergence of a critical, scholarly literature on the history of the VFL appeared – Sandercock and Turner's *Up Where, Cazaly? The Great Australian Game* (1981), and Bob Stewart's *The Australian Football Business* (1983). Published at the 'high-point' of the post-war 'crisis' in the League, both (rightly) understood the contemporary VFL to be in a state of flux – that is, to be betwixt and between 'the old' and 'the new'. Thus, Sandercock and Turner argued: 'Aussie Rules has been wandering between two worlds for two decades now. One is lost – destroyed by the forces of technological and economic change that brought television and big money into the game. The other world is yet to be found.'[110] In a similar vein, Stewart stated that the problems plaguing the League could most accurately be seen as 'symptoms of a rather lengthy transition from the world of parochial amateurism to a broad-based, professional competition'.[111]

Notwithstanding the likelihood of further refinements to the organization of the AFL, it is now evident that the fundamental structural transformation alluded to by these authors *has* been negotiated. Reflecting upon the nature of social change, Gramsci reminds us that an 'appropriate political initiative is always necessary to liberate the economic thrust from the dead weight of traditional policies'.[112] In the post-war history of the League, there were two moments which signified such 'initiatives', each clearing the way for the next phase in the restructuring of the competition. The first moment was the formation of the Aylett–Hamilton partnership in 1977; the second, the decision taken by the VFL clubs in 1984 to relinquish some of their powers to create a streamlined, independent Commission.

Under the reforming zeal of the Aylett–Hamilton partnership, and subsequently the 'economically rationalist' strategies of the Commission, the VFL/AFL has been transformed from a semi-professional, metropolitan concern, into a fully professional and thoroughly commercialized national league. This transformation has been driven largely by economic forces, emanating both from within and beyond the competition itself. Taken together, these have resulted in more than incremental changes *within* the traditional structure of the League; rather, they have marked a qualitative transformation *of* that very structure. At the aggregate level, this restructuring has proved a striking financial success, as all of the League's key 'performance indicators' attest.

Of course, the League has never been merely a unidimensional, *economic* institution; rather, it has always possessed a dual character, in that it simultaneously serves an additional *cultural* function, which includes the construction of individual and collective forms of identity. Over the post-war period, and especially since the mid-1970s, this dual character has been the source of a major tension or contradiction in the League. Put simply, the continuing process of *economic restructuring* has run up against, and has threatened, the competition's traditional forms of *cultural reproduction*. In other words, a conflict has arisen between that which has been deemed *economically necessary* by League officials, and that which had become *culturally ingrained* over generations. Crucially, there is no guarantee that what is perceived as economically rational will immediately, or necessarily, be experienced as culturally salient.

This pivotal tension has been expressed through a series of post-war disputes over the League's development, centring on such issues as professionalism and commercialization; the Waverley project; ground rationalization; the League's relationship with rival competitions; the decision to expand interstate; and the volatile questions of club relocations and mergers. These issues have periodically pitted key stakeholder groups – including supporters, sections of the media, and some VFL/AFL clubs – against the thrust of the central administration's reform agenda. Collectively, these disputes have underscored the fact that the economically driven restructuring of the

League has been bound up with highly problematic processes of cultural adjustment and resistance.

As shown in such examples as the 1989 'Footscray fightback', and the successful 1996 campaign to stave off a merger between Hawthorn and Melbourne, supporter resistance *has* had structuring effects on the competition. However, such resistance has fallen well short of being the dominant force directing the League's development, and ultimately it has not significantly altered the *general* trajectory of the game's development. In other words, supporter resistance seems only to stand as a temporary hindrance to the economically driven restructuring agenda. Once more, Gramsci's insights into the process of social change are instructive: 'mass ideological factors always lag behind mass economic phenomena, and therefore, at certain moments, the automatic thrust due to the economic factor is slowed down, obstructed or even momentarily broken by traditional ideological elements'.[113] This recognizes that traditional cultural and ideological elements exert an influence in the short term, but that they are typically rendered impotent in the face of relentless economic forces.

This essay has attempted to clarify the duality – economic and cultural – of the post-war transformation of the VFL/AFL. This has been attempted through the application of a social-scientific conception of 'crisis'. It has been argued that this framework enables us to see that, over the course of the post-war period, the League has passed through a series of distinct 'crisis phases'. These have involved an economically driven restructuring of the competition, coupled with a traumatic adjustment in the culture of the game. Whilst the former has been successfully negotiated, the latter is still fraught with conflicts and tensions. In other words, although the restructuring process is complete, issues remain, and resistance persists, in terms of the cultural reproduction of the game.

Finally, the complex relationship between the League's economic restructuring on the one hand, and its cultural reproduction on the other, should not blind us to the fact that the *balance* between these two roles has shifted irreversibly over the post-war period. In short, the League has moved from an institution that is *primarily* bound up with culture, including the construction of identity, to one that is *primarily* driven by the economic imperative to produce exchange value, often for external television and sponsorship interests. It must be recognized that these represent competing modes of institutional integration, and that they produce different paths for development. Ultimately, it is this switch of developmental paths that will stand as the central legacy of the post-war 'crisis' in the VFL/AFL.

NOTES

1. The VFA was established in 1877, making it the oldest Australian Rules football competition. The 1896 split revolved around the vexed issue of professionalism – the VFA retaining an official commitment to amateurism; the VFL openly accepting player payments. The acrimonious nature of the breakaway heralded the start of a long and bitter relationship between the two leagues, which only ended with the demise of the VFA as an independent entity in the 1990s (see below).
2. One of the distinctive historical features of Australian Rules, as compared to other football codes, is the extent to which the former has tended to stretch across class and gender boundaries. See R. Hess and B. Stewart (eds.), *More Than A Game: An Unauthorised History of Australian Rules Football* (hereafter *More Than A Game*) (Melbourne, 1998).
3. This claim to 'premier' status can be justified according to numerous criteria, including attendance figures, membership levels, media profile, sponsorship, and turnover. In all of these areas, the VFL significantly out-performed its domestic sporting rivals.
4. Due to word constraints, this essay will not discuss the distinctive features of the Australian Rules code of football, and it will overlook changes in the style of play during the post-war period. These issues are dealt with at length in a number of publications, including R. Pascoe, *The Winter Game: The Complete History of Australian Football* (Melbourne, 1995).
5. J. Habermas, *Legitimation Crisis* (Cambridge, 1988), pp.1–31.
6. J. Keane, *Public Life and Late Capitalism* (London, 1984), pp.10–13.
7. Ibid., pp.11–12.
8. 'Culture' is one of the most complicated words in the English language, and it is defined and used in numerous ways by different writers. Here it is being employed to refer to the socially produced symbols, values, ideas and beliefs that are shared by the members of a social group. 'Culture' helps to bestow on human existence a sense of 'meaning' and 'purpose', and it is integral to the process of constructing individual and collective identities.
9. Elsewhere I have outlined the post-war transformation of Australian society, and its impact on the League, in greater detail. See I. Andrews, 'Redrawing "Community" Boundaries in the Post-War AFL', *Football Studies*, 2, 1 (1999), 106–24.
10. A. Jamrozik, C. Boland and R. Urquhart, *Social Change and Cultural Transformation in Australia* (Cambridge, 1995), p.44.
11. Ibid., p.46.
12. M. Lewis, *Melbourne: The City's History and Development*, 2nd edition (Melbourne, 1995), p.129.
13. B. Stewart, 'Boom-time Football, 1946–1975', in Hess and Stewart (eds.), *More Than A Game*, p.167.
14. For a succinct summary of the VFL during the Depression, and the Second World War, see R. Holmesby, 'In a New League, 1925–1945', in Hess and Stewart (eds.), *More Than A Game*, pp.139–64.
15. In 1952, the League ran a 'National Aussie Rules Day', with fixtures being played in three other states (see Stewart, 'Boom-time Football, 1946–1975', p.175). Although attendance figures were solid, the experiment was not repeated until the 1970s, and the 'national vision' was not pursued in earnest until the 1980s (see below).
16. L. Sandercock and I. Turner, *Up Where, Cazaly? The Great Australian Game* (London, 1981), p.141.
17. L. Frost, *The Old Dark Navy Blues: A History of the Carlton Football Club* (Sydney, 1998), pp.103–4.
18. In 1925 North Melbourne, Hawthorn, and Footscray were accepted into the VFL. From this

point through until the 1980s, the competition was comprised of the same 12 clubs.

19. Stewart, 'Boom-time Football, 1946–1975', pp.179–80.
20. Ibid., pp.179–81.
21. With the exception of a brief decline in the late 1950s, crowds throughout this period increased, and aggregate attendances were over 2 million in all but one year. In 1963 a record attendance figure of 2.74 million was set. *AFL Annual Report 1995*, pp.49–50.
22. Stewart, 'Boom-time Football, 1946–1975', p.174.
23. B. Stewart, *The Australian Football Business: A Spectator's Guide to the VFL* (Kenthurst, 1983), pp.116–17.
24. Stewart, 'Boom-time Football, 1946–1975', pp.173–5.
25. Andrews, 'Redrawing "Community" Boundaries in the Post-War AFL', p.113.
26. Pascoe, *The Winter Game*, p. 159; Sandercock and Turner, *Up Where, Cazaly?*, pp.157–8.
27. Stewart, 'Boom-time Football, 1946–1975', p.181.
28. The most notable examples occurred after 1937, when the VFA revoked a longstanding permit agreement with the VFL, which had prevented players from switching between the two leagues. This led to numerous VFL 'stars' being lured over to VFA clubs. See Holmesby, 'In a New League, 1925–1945', p.155.
29. In 1941 Barassi's father – a Melbourne player himself – was killed in the Second World War. After Ron's mother remarried and moved to Tasmania in 1952, Norm Smith – the legendary Melbourne coach at the time – took the 16-year-old Barassi into his home, to enable him to pursue a career in the VFL.
30. See Frost, *The Old Dark Navy Blues*, pp.117–19; Pascoe, *The Winter Game*, pp.140–2, 162–3.
31. There were, however, those who supported Barassi's right to pursue his own interests, including the Melbourne Football Club, and Norm Smith himself. See Frost, *The Old Dark Navy Blues*, pp.118–19.
32. Stewart, 'Boom-time Football, 1946–1975', p.188.
33. Ibid., pp.184–5.
34. For Richmond and Saint Kilda, the moves proved highly successful, with both clubs strengthening their support bases and on-field success in subsequent years. In the case of North, however, the move was a fiasco, and within a year the club had returned to its original home at Arden Street. See ibid., pp.185–6.
35. Stewart, *The Australian Football Business*, pp.97–8.
36. The MCC was based at the Melbourne Cricket Ground (MCG), which was the biggest venue used for football matches, and the traditional home of the VFL Grand Final. For decades, the League felt that the MCG had creamed profits from football, and that the latter was thereby subsidising cricket. See G. Linnell, *Football Ltd: The Inside Story of the AFL* (Sydney, 1995), pp.263–4.
37. In turn, this lack of public transport provision was indicative of both the poor relationship that prevailed between the VFL and the State Government, and the lobbying power of the MCC. By ensuring that VFL Park was difficult to access, the Government helped to maintain the League's dependency on the MCG.
38. Stewart, 'Boom-time Football, 1946–1975', pp.194–5.
39. Sandercock and Turner, *Up Where, Cazaly?*, pp.167–9.
40. Stewart, *The Australian Football Business*, pp.118–19.
41. Pascoe, *The Winter Game*, pp.183–4.
42. Stewart, 'Boom-time Football, 1946–1975', pp.186–7.
43. This process was indicative of a broader trend towards industrial militancy. In 1969 more than a million workers struck against the gaoling of Tramway union leader, Clarrie O'Shea, and in 1974 the number of working days lost to strike action hit a record 6.2 million. S. Deery and D. Plowman, *Australian Industrial Relations*, 3rd edition (Sydney, 1991), p.53.
44. Linnell, *Football Ltd*, pp.206–7.
45. Stewart, *The Australian Football Business*, p.87.
46. See B. Dabscheck, 'Playing the Team Game: Unions in Australian Professional Team Sports', *The Journal of Industrial Relations*, 38, 4 (1996), 608–15, and Linnell, *Football Ltd*, pp.199–200.
47. Stewart, *The Australian Football Business*, p.65.

48. Stewart, 'Boom-time Football, 1946–1975', p.191.
49. Ibid., p.195.
50. Ibid., p.197.
51. Pascoe, *The Winter Game*, p.187.
52. Stewart, 'Boom-time Football, 1946–1975', pp.197–8.
53. D. Nadel, 'Colour, Corporations and Commissioners, 1976–1985', in Hess and Stewart (eds.), *More Than A Game*, pp.200–1.
54. Linnell, *Football Ltd*, pp.12–13.
55. This is *not* to say that an entirely different trajectory would have transpired had Aylett been unsuccessful. Indeed, the structural constraints and pressures acting upon the League at this time were profound, and it is difficult to resist the conclusion that the *general* direction of change was inevitable. Nevertheless, Aylett's victory was of great symbolic significance, and it ensured that the forces of 'modernization' would operate unfettered, and in fact would be actively encouraged, by the philosophy of the game's chief administrator.
56. Linnell, *Football Ltd*, p.41.
57. Nadel, 'Colour, Corporations and Commissioners, 1976–1985', p.207.
58. Ibid., p.207.
59. See Linnell, *Football Ltd*, pp.49–50.
60. *The Australian Financial Review*, 13 Sept. 1979.
61. R.K. Stewart, 'The Economic Development of the Victorian Football League 1960–1984', *Sporting Traditions*, 1, 2 (1985), 4.
62. B. Stewart, 'Sport as Big Business', in G. Lawrence and D. Rowe (eds.), *Power Play: The Commercialisation of Australian Sport* (Sydney, 1986), p.68.
63. Linnell, *Football Ltd*, pp.46–9.
64. See Frost, *The Old Dark Navy Blues*, pp.152–3.
65. Around this time, there were growing concerns about the impact of 'American cultural imperialism' on Australian society. These concerns were particularly pronounced on the organised Left. See, for example, the analysis of the mass media provided by Humphrey McQueen – an erstwhile Maoist – in his *Australia's Media Monopolies* (Melbourne, 1977), pp.144–82.
66. Frost, *The Old Dark Navy Blues*, p.163.
67. Linnell, *Football Ltd*, pp.59–70.
68. The most cited example of such meetings was the lunchtime gathering in Toorak of the so-called 'Gang of Four' – Carlton's Ian Rice, Melbourne's Wayne Reid, North Melbourne's Bob Ansett, and Saint Kilda's Lyndsay Fox – in April 1980. At this meeting, the discussion centred on how the VFL was to be opened up to a free enterprise culture, consistent with the ethos underpinning the wider economic sphere. Sandercock and Turner, *Up Where, Cazaly?*, pp.239–40.
69. This line held that corporate penetration of the VFL resulted in a form of 'football socialism', whereby the rich (corporate interests) subsidised the poor (supporters). See *Inside Football*, 7 (June 1984).
70. F. Reynolds, 'Fiasco', *Sports World Australia*, 1, 5 (1984), 30.
71. B. Stoddart, *Saturday Afternoon Fever: Sport in the Australian Culture* (Sydney, 1986), p.113.
72. During this period, when one club wished to sign a player currently contracted to another, the former was liable to pay the latter a transfer fee, as a form of compensation.
73. *The Age*, 10 Sept. 1986; Nadel, 'Colour, Corporations and Commissioners, 1976–1985', 210.
74. A. Attwood, 'Big Men Fly National: Australian Rules and Rugby League Reach Across the Nation for Survival', *Time Australia*, 1, 8 (1986), 27.
75. See, for example, Aylett's 'President's Message' in the 1980 *VFL Annual Report*, p.3.
76. Stewart, 'Boom-time Football, 1946–1975', pp.181–2.
77. Nadel, 'Colour, Corporations and Commissioners, 1976–1985', pp.205–6.
78. Those officials who supported the relocation deemed it a financial necessity. For their part, the players saw the move as the only means of guaranteeing the considerable back-pay that they were owed from the club. See ibid., pp.214–16.
79. B. Wilson, 'Pumping Up the Footy: The Commercial Expansion of Professional Football in Australia', in D. Rowe and G. Lawrence (eds.), *Sport and Leisure: Trends in Australian Popular*

Culture (Sydney, 1990), p.36.

80. B. Dabscheck, 'Abolishing Transfer Fees: The Victorian Football League's New Employment Rules', *Sporting Traditions*, 6, 1 (1989), 65–7; Linnell, *Football Ltd*, pp.73–6.
81. Linnell, *Football Ltd*, pp.201–5.
82. Nadel, 'Colour, Corporations and Commissioners, 1976–1985', pp.220–1.
83. Although critics suggested the fall in attendances was a consequence of declining loyalties and traditions in the game, in truth the causes were more complex, and they formed part of a national and international trend. The reasons included a broadening of people's entertainment options, and growing competition from other team sports. See C. Morley and K.G. Wilson, 'Fluctuating VFL Attendances: Some Insights From an Economic Analysis', *Sporting Traditions*, 3, 1 (1986), 69–81.
84. See, for example, the following: B. Birnbauer and M. Coward, 'VFL Needs Watchdog', *The Age*, 11 Aug. 1983; G. Hobbs, 'VFL: The Last Straw!', *The Sporting Globe*, 4 Jan. 1983; G. Hutchinson, 'Football, Finis?', *The National Times*, 21–27 Sept. 1984.
85. Linnell, *Football Ltd*, p.263.
86. Ibid., pp.26–31.
87. The Commission's powers were increased substantially with the acceptance of the major recommendations of the 1992 *Crawford Report*. See Andrews, 'Redrawing "Community" Boundaries in the Post-War AFL', p.115.
88. Linnell, *Football Ltd*, pp.136–9.
89. This final figure was less than half the $6.3 million bandied about in the press at the time. J. Goldlust, *Playing for Keeps: Sport, the Media and Society* (Melbourne, 1987), p.178.
90. For details, see Linnell, *Football Ltd*, pp.91–117, 331–44; D. Nadel, 'The League Goes National, 1986–1997', in Hess and Stewart (eds.), *More Than A Game*, pp.225–7.
91. The Bears private ownership fiasco was just as complicated as the Swans, and was intertwined with the collapse of Christopher Skase's Quintex Corporation in the late 1980s. See Linnell, *Football Ltd*, pp.243–59, 321–30; Nadel, 'The League Goes National, 1986–1997', pp.228–30. In the case of the West Coast Eagles, events unfolded quite differently, due in part to the fact that the Eagles were based in a traditional Australian Rules state. See Linnell, *Football Ltd*, pp.243–59; Nadel, 'The League Goes National, 1986–1997', p.230.
92. This delay reflected the long and bitter history between the VFL and its South Australian equivalent – the South Australian National Football League (SANFL). Ultimately, it took a rebel bid by the Port Adelaide club to force the hand of the SANFL, and the latter finally entered the national competition in the shape of the Adelaide Crows. For Port, the failure of their bid resulted in their exclusion from the AFL until 1997. See Linnell, *Football Ltd*, pp.345–61.
93. It is worth noting that with the two most recent additions to the competition – the Dockers and Port Power – the AFL has accepted teams that have a more secure basis for entry. Both are located in Australian Rules football states, and in communities with strong, working class traditions and football clubs.
94. In 1999 the Commission embarked upon a gradual process of increasing the competition's presence in New South Wales, by scheduling five of the Kangaroos 'home' games in Sydney. Prior to 1998 the Kangaroos had been known as North Melbourne, and had been based in Victoria. The club's decision to rename itself, and to play a proportion of its 'home' games interstate, was based upon the belief that this would help secure its long-term future, in the face of the threats to Melbourne clubs outlined below.
95. Nadel, 'The League Goes National, 1986–1997', p.228.
96. *AFL Annual Report 1998*, pp.16–18.
97. Ibid., pp.19–20.
98. Andrews, 'Redrawing "Community" Boundaries in the Post-War AFL', p.115.
99. Dabscheck, 'Playing the Team Game: Unions in Australian Professional Team Sports', *Journal of Industrial Relations*, 38, 4, 600–28.
100. Ibid., p.607.
101. *AFL Annual Report 1998*, p.58.
102. Pascoe, *The Winter Game*, p.18.
103. *AFL Annual Report 1998*, p.40.

104. Nadel, 'The League Goes National, 1986–1997', pp.246–7.
105. AFL, *Background on Development of the National Competition* (Melbourne, 1991).
106. Even as late as 1991, the Commission was persisting with this line. See ibid.
107. 'The Gamekeepers', *Four Corners*, ABC Television, 22 May 1995.
108. K. Gordon and A. Dalton, *Too Tough To Die: Footscray's Fightback* 1989 (Melbourne, 1990).
109. Cited in J. Small, 'My Club Survive? I'd Like To See That!', *Socialist Alternative*, 11 (1996), 15.
110. R. Williams, *Marxism and Literature* (Oxford, 1977). Elsewhere I have applied Williams' framework of dominant, emergent, and residual social forces to an analysis of the changing nature of 'community' in the VFL/AFL. See I. Andrews, 'Towards a Conceptual Framework for Community', *Football Studies*, 1, 2 (1998), 103–14; Andrews, 'Redrawing "Community" Boundaries in the Post-War AFL', pp.106–24.
111. Sandercock and Turner, *Up Where, Cazaly?*, p.236.
112. Stewart, *The Australian Football Business*, p.136.
113. A. Gramsci, *Selections From the Prison Notebooks* (London, 1971), p.168.
114. Ibid., p.168.

12

Football as Social Critique:
Protest Movements, Rugby and History in Aotearoa, New Zealand

MALCOLM MACLEAN

Ten years on I can't be sure about who won the tour war or even quite what was at stake ... That final violence seemed an unavoidable, sought, even just conclusion for both protesters and police. The 1981 demonstrations became a major blowout of idealistic concern, after which liberals were passé and the Kiwi and South African worlds so changed that all the pain and passion were rendered largely irrelevant.[1]

The scale and intensity of the discontented winter's campaign against the 1981 Springbok tour, the extent of respectable New Zealand's involvement in mass direct political action, and their confrontation with state power in a material and personal sense has overshadowed the politics of the 1970s and early 1980s to become seen as unique – even if, like Tony Reid, there no is longer any certainty about the reasons for and effects of that confrontation. It is almost as if, in popular memory, the tour has become a singular event through which New Zealand, as a nation, had to go to reach maturity, or is an unrealized promise of a new world. This summer of maturity, in which the sun of York is an amnesic popular memory, has buried the tensions of the era and the resulting widespread social protest in the ocean-deep bosom of nostalgia. These nostalgias, one a liberal-Left nostalgia yearning for a more just world, the other a conservative nostalgia seeing the attainment of national maturity, operate by denying the political context of the anti-tour campaign and the significance of the historical frame of the 1950s and the post-1984 era.

This sense of quantum leap associated with the trials and tribulations of the campaign against apartheid exposes the amnesia of popular memory that forgets, or is encouraged to forget, each generation's action to constrain state power – be it on the waterfront in 1890, the mines, railways and wharves in 1912 and 1913, the dole queue in 1932, or the waterfront again in 1951. It also ignores the tensions of the 1970s and 1980s, and the widespread social protest they provoked. The New Right ravages of the Fourth Labour Government have overshadowed all but the near civil war of 1981. A key element of this 'overshadowing' is that the power of the consensus around the New Right drive begun under the Fourth Labour Government and continued through more recent National Party and Coalition governments has embedded the notion that there is no alternative – opposition to the framework seems either futile or utopian, or both. The intensity and relentlessness of the New Right drive and the associated sense of powerlessness is accompanied by a sense of betrayal by Labour held by many in the oppositional movements who believed they shared a vision of liberal egalitarianism or social democracy with the Labour Party.[2] Embodied in this imaginary shared vision was a reliance on the state to act as an agent of the transformation sought by dissident politics.[3] There is a nostalgia on the liberal Left about the period before 1984 when it is held that there was a vision of something different, when oppositional forces had not been incorporated into state structures, or crushed by the less fettered power of the consensus of the powerful.

Only the campaign against apartheid sport has risen above the blandness of pre-1984 politics to stand out. The anti-apartheid activity of 1981 was the pinnacle of a 60-year era of discontent at sporting contact between New Zealand and South Africa. The discontent between 1921 and the mid 1960s was largely expressed as a sense that the New Zealand Rugby Football Union was effectively importing apartheid by agreeing not to select Maori players for tours to South Africa. In 1960 the anti-tour movement's central slogan was 'No Maoris [*sic*] No Tour'. Starting in 1949 voices began to be raised against the practice of apartheid in South Africa. By the time the All Blacks toured South Africa in 1970 with three Maori and one Samoan in the team the campaign was organized around the demand for the total sporting isolation of apartheid. Despite these 60 years of opposition, little had prepared New Zealand for the intensity and extent of protest in 1981. The tour had came to represent all that was wrong with the country: the arrogance of the political leadership, the pattern and effects of colonial dispossession, the maintenance of patriarchal power. Most of all, opponents saw the tour as representing an elite that seemed to be endorsing apartheid as legitimate.

The opposition campaign was potent because of rugby's metonymical role in Aotearoa/New Zealand. Critical analyses of New

Zealand rugby have held it to embody the nation as a Pakeha masculine entity.[4] These analyses have focused on rugby as a site of national celebration and valorization, the continuation of a masculinist frontier ethos, or the outcome of a particular pattern of colonization. Regimes of cultural power in Aotearoa/New Zealand are fully imbricated with rugby union. Rugby is seen as significant, if not instrumental, in building the nation. The character and ability claimed as the arbiters of national membership are tested only in competition with other nations: usually in sport or in war. In a popularly held dominant view of New Zealand history the young colony proved its mettle against the home countries during the 1905 All Black tour of Britain and reached maturity on the battlefield at Gallipoli in 1915. In this view, sport is a worthy substitute for war and a precursor for the national worthiness the war proves, whilst also preparing young men for combat. In both New Zealand and South Africa, rugby union was the game of the dominant group and was seen to encapsulate the characteristics and traits of nationhood. Before 1987 and the launching of the Rugby World Cup, an international series between New Zealand and South Africa was held by many to be the world championship of rugby. Supporters of the 1981 tour were expecting to see this unofficial world championship played out before them, and expecting a New Zealand victory. This desire came into conflict with competing views of nation, rugby, masculinity and the politics of apartheid sport.

The liberal-left romanticization for the pre-1984 era connects with another yearning for the pre-1984 conditions to build a more specific nostalgia that sees the events of the tour as necessary. It is this sense of the necessary that is linked to the tour-as-maturation analysis. This sense that the tour was necessary for national maturation was clearly revealed during the 1994 Springbok tour. In 1981 the Springboks had a special relationship with the Waikato provincial rugby team. Having lost the first game to Waikato in 1956, the South Africans saw the game in 1981 as the chance for revenge. It was as if the Springbok victory over Waikato in 1965 had been forgotten. That desire remained unfulfilled as an occupation of the rugby field by protesters lead to the game being cancelled. The first big match of the tour had been prevented and the resulting turmoil exposed a schism in attitudes to rugby and nation. Writing in 1994 of the 1981 cancellation, a week before the Springboks were due to play Waikato for the first time in 29 years, Gilbert Wong noted that 'Godzone was redefined that day'.[5] Wong's sense of fundamental change is explicitly linked to the maturation argument by suggesting that this event created the conditions for what Hamilton City Councillor Margaret Evans called 'a tremendous growing up with the dawning recognition of the renaissance of the tangata whenua [people of the land, Maori] and the acceptance that we have many issues of our own to talk through'.[6] Other commentators and participants are not so specific about the cancellation of the Waikato game as Wong and Evans preferring to see a wider and more complex series of changes running through and resulting from the events of the tour. For some, the effects of the tour are conservative. Former police officer and National Party Member of Parliament Ross Meurant argues that the tour 'was probably a force for good. The turmoil was the price we had to pay at the time for the preservation of democracy as New Zealand knows it.'[7] Journalist Tony Reid suggested this complexity when he argued that 'the sheer scale of the Springbok tour disruption permanently altered psychological and tactical relationships between the state, the rugby world, the wider citizenry and the police'.[8] The key and problematic word in this assessment is 'permanently' in that Reid undermines the amnesia of the popular by immediately stating that the 1981 tour was, in this sense, similar to the effects of the 1951 Waterfront Lockout. The widespread view is that these changes were caused by or resulted from the tour. A more historically informed assessment of the era would show the tour to be concentration of the conditions that promoted this series of changes, but would not and could not use the tour as the explanation of them.

Although the quest for origins is not in itself nostalgic, there is a sense of glorying attached to the events of the winter of 1981. Meurant, considering his time as senior member of the Red Group, a special unit travelling with the Springbok party, has described the tour as 'halcyon days' pointing to the sense of 'togetherness' and 'team spirit' within the unit.[9] It is worth noting, however, that not all share this glorying and some are contemptuous of it. From the other side of the gap between police and protester, Wellington Marshalls' Committee convenor Alick Shaw resisted the tendency to reminisce noting that 'the nostalgia of the returned protester is even more tedious than that of the returned soldier, and with rather less justification'.[10] Shaw reflected more openly a tendency running through comments by many in the protest leadership during this ten years after recap. There is a sense that the scale and intensity was something that developed unwillingly, that the times were difficult and that there were so many other things that could have been done during that time. Central to this is a rejection of the sense that these were the good old days, the 'wasn't it great' element of the nostalgia of the returned protester Shaw implies.

Although every 20 to 30 years Pakeha New Zealand has taken action against excessively exercised state or class power, the events of 1981 are a break from earlier patterns of political struggle and resistance. There are four distinguishing characteristics:

- the events follow a longer period of activism than had previously been the case;

- the campaign was not run by trade unions focusing explicitly on working people's concerns;

- women were actively involved in organizing and leading anti-tour action, not in the 'ladies auxiliary', while raising and gaining support for feminist concerns in a broader political movement; and

- the campaign saw the active involvement of Maori at all levels and a growing focus on colonial relations in Aotearoa/New Zealand.

Interpretation of the nostalgic view and perception of maturity is aided by a consideration of Europe in 1989. Events during this year saw a growing debate and awareness about the meaning and significance of history.

Building on these European events, in 1992 Francis Fukuyama published his celebration of capitalism, *The End of History and the Last Man*.[11] Fukuyama argues that collapse of the Soviet Union represented the defeat of socialism and the victory of capitalist power. It was the end of a 200-year struggle and an absolute victory for capitalism. As the 'defeat of communism' allowed liberal capitalism to be constructed as the only viable model for social and economic organization, History ended. Fukuyama recently has argued that the collapse of communism proves the fundamental error of the Left – the assumption that equality is both a desirable objective and proof of historical progress. His argument now is that inequality is the motor of progress because it both drives the capitalist economy and is 'right'.[12] Fukuyama's declaration of the End of History now seems as premature as the often proclaimed End of Ideology. The continuing crisis of finance capital and effects of the falling rate of profit, beginning with the collapse of Asian economies in

1997, is the most recent of many events suggesting that capitalism has not been as victorious as Fukuyama and his ilk would hope. History is still alive.[13]

It is not just the present crisis of capitalism and the continuation of a class struggle that undermines Fukuyama's position. The past itself suggests that he is merely one of many to argue that we have entered a post-historical era. L. Neithammer's review of declarations of post-history shows that there is a more widespread disenchantment with nineteenth-century, or even post-Enlightenment, philosophies of history that lie behind assertions of the end of history by writers as diverse as Junger, Heidegger and Baudrillard (the English translation of the original 1989 book was published the same year as Fukuyama's).[14] At the heart of this recurrent proclamation lies not the end of history, but the apparent collapse of a particular historical project. He calls for an engagement with the 'legacy of bourgeois individualism [that dispenses] with its ideal of greatness and power' to find a space for action within and against its structures.[15] In the wake of the campaign against the 1981 Springbok tour, this space was squeezed to near disappearance by the inability of increasingly demobilized social and political campaign groups to resist the ethos of 'bourgeois (sovereign) individualism' at the core of the New Right political project.

At the same time as Fukuyama's book appeared, a new understanding of the events of Eastern Europe was developing. In this framework, the reassertion of the independence of nations in the former Soviet bloc was being understood as the 'Rebirth of History' as each of the states that (re)emerged 'rediscovered' its national past.[16] The period from 1945 to 1989 was seen as a period without history, 1989 therefore represented the rebirth of history. This development had a number of disturbing corollaries as anything to do with the Soviet era was rejected as nationality and nationalism were reasserted, including the rampant national-chauvinism seen most horrifically in the former Yugoslavia, and significant setbacks for women's social and citizenship advances of the Soviet era.[17] In Aotearoa/New Zealand, the nostalgic view of the events of 1981 that Shaw regrets, when considered in the context of the 1970s and early 1980s, suggests an unfulfilled Rebirth of History in the yearning for a reinvention and recreation of struggle. The complexity of this view of 1981 lies in its interface with the maturation argument that suggests that there will no longer be a need for struggle: there is, in this sense, a concurrent rebirth and end of history.

After a long period of apparent economic growth and social inclusion, in the late 1960s Aotearoa/New Zealand became aware of diversity and difference as women began to demand recognition of and further inclusion in non-reproductive life, and as Pakeha New Zealand came to confront a Maori presence that was real and was now. It seemed as if nothing had happened since the Second World War except the 1951 Waterfront Lockout, the 1954 Royal Tour and three South African rugby tours. The strength of the consensus around this perception meant that even many of those at the heart of the dissident lives of the 1950s see it as a bleak and grey time, as a changeless and ahistorical time.[18] This perception and the reality were quite different. The period was characterized by continuing population shifts from South to North and from country to city, the later especially so for Maori. At the same time, there was an ongoing peace movement, moral panics associated with the invention of the teenager, a vigorous equal pay campaign and growing opposition to sporting contact with South Africa.[19]

Tensions and dissent began to manifest themselves more openly late in the 1960s, following a pattern similar to that seen in much of the rest of the capitalist world – opposition to the war in Vietnam and a broad anti-imperialism. As with much of the rest of the international experience, this dissent was remarkably non-reflexive failing to recognize the specificity of local colonial conditions and the politics of class and gender.[20] The dissident campaigns of the long 1970s began with anti-war protest in the late 1960s (which itself built on the peace movement and anti-apartheid campaigns of the 1950s and 1960s) and was maintained until the campaign in support of homosexual law reform in 1984–85. Manifest in this period was a fundamental shift from affinity to identity politics. These tensions and dynamics began to be played out during the 1970s, but the gap in relation to colonialism remained significant as seen in the responses to D. Awatere's essays on Maori sovereignty in 1982 and 1983.[21] The campaign against apartheid sport brought these concerns to the fore.

This anti-apartheid movement, the most intense of those dissident campaigns, reached its zenith in 1981 when countless people took to the streets to oppose sporting contact with South Africa. As expected, protest activity took place in the major centres – but the stories abound of the dozen or so people who marched in Eltham on 3 July, or the ten in Kaikohe on 1 May. Before the tour began, the anti-tour movement tapped the 51 per cent opposition to the tour, according to an early July

Heylen public opinion poll.[22] There was enormous confidence and genuine belief within the anti-tour movement that the tour would be stopped if the movement remained disciplined and focused on the objective. Hamilton anti-apartheid activist Mike Law spoke for many at the May 1981 Halt All Racist Tours (HART), the New Zealand Anti-Apartheid Movement, National Council meeting: 'I'm convinced we're going to win this one, provided we don't drop the ball in next few months.'[23] This confidence lasted until the police attack on protesters in Wellington's Molesworth Street on 29 July. This brought the realization that the tour would not be stopped, but it could be disrupted, police resources would be stretched to breaking point and no tour would ever happen again. Molesworth Street was a sign of changing police tactics. By 1 August in the provincial centre of Palmerston North, the army had joined the police in ensuring no rugby grounds were invaded again.

There was a widespread feeling that the campaign against the tour was part of something bigger. There had been a series of major anti-government campaigns over the previous five years; Muldoon's National Party government was increasingly unpopular and looked certain to loose the 1981 election – despite the year long electoral campaign involving a royal tour and the visit of the Springboks. Even staunch and long-term National Party supporters were turning against Muldoon and his 'style', which many found objectionable in contrast to the recollected image of former Party leaders Keith Holyoake and John ('Gentleman' Jack) Marshall. Significantly, the breadth of opposition gave rise to a widespread feeling that change was possible: campaigns against apartheid and for improved reproductive rights for women, increasing awareness of Maori colonial dispossession and demands for improved social services were all premised on a notion of improved equality and precisely and explicitly reject the argument that inequality is the key to progress.

Despite this sense of progress through a quest for egalitarianism, deficiencies remained in the broader progressive movement. Alongside the colonial and gender based gaps within the various dissident trends of the 1970s was increasing isolation from the trade union movement. This isolation from trade unions can be seen as part explanation for the longevity of this period of political struggle. Distinction between these socio-political struggles and the trade union movement meant that the various campaigns, during the period the Labour was in opposition, generally avoided the constraints of 'Labourism' and electoralism. At the same time, though, there was a general failure to develop a class analysis of events and to involve working-class organizations or people. This was to prove fatal to these campaigns once Labour came to power.

By 1981, although the leadership of the trade union movement called for opposition to the tour, workers' support for this position remained weak. The exception was in Wellington where a strong activist union membership had been active in broader social movements for several years. During 1981 a number of factory committees against the tour were formed, mainly in Wellington's Hutt Valley. A number of those involved in these committees went on to become leading anti-tour activists.[24] The other key exception, although less obvious than Wellington, was in Auckland where an organized leftist union leadership was able to build some working-class support of the anti-tour campaign, and the Trade Union Centre was the headquarters for the anti-tour coalition. A more general trade union response was seen in late February 1981 when the National Union of Railwaymen had announced its opposition to the tour and stated that its members would not provide any support for the touring party. Within three weeks NUR branches in Tauranga, Gisborne, Ashburton, Stratford, Lower Hutt, Hawera, New Plymouth, Timaru and Christchurch had either dissociated themselves from the national position or opposed it.[25] The NUR was not alone in its isolation from the anti-tour movement: the 9,000 members of the Canterbury Branch of the Engineers Union, the largest affiliate of the Federation of Labour, opposed any moves to 'interfere' with the tour.[26] They were joined in this position by the Auckland branch of the Allied Liquor Trade Workers' Union, which rejected the Federation of Labour stance.[27] While the Engineers' Union was one of the most conservative unions, the NUR had a tradition of strong action on a broad range of issues, as did the Drivers' Union. Yet even within this more militant group there was considerable support for the tour. After a strong anti-tour vote in 1980, a similar resolution in 1981 saw considerable debate within the Wellington Branch and a much closer vote. Branch Secretary Jackson Smith described the supporters of the tour as 'quite a hefty number' although the resolution attracted a clear majority.[28]

This division exposed two tendencies within the trade union movement. The first was the trade union abandonment of mass action and the politics of class struggle. In the second, the resulting concentration on legislatively constrained industrial instruments meant that there was a basic failure to confront broader cultural issues or cultural politics. As a result, other than in Wellington and to a lesser degree Auckland, anti-tour debates within the trade union movement were played out in terms largely defined by a wider polity and encapsulated a non class-specific position on the tour. The outcome was a trade union movement isolated from the anti-apartheid movement and a weakened anti-tour campaign.

The role of women in the tour campaign was less ambivalent, however. The women's movement in New Zealand followed a trajectory very similar to those in other first world countries. Early work centred on identifying the nature of women's liberation as opposed to women's rights with major campaigning around the question of equal pay.[29] As the 1970s saw a rapid emergence of new groups, there was also a clear diversification within the movement with interest groups forming, Maori and lesbians organizing separately and significant differences developing. The predominant themes running through the women's movement's activities by the late 1970s were sexuality, reproductive rights and violence against women.

Maori women and lesbians criticized elements of the movement in ways heard in other first world nations. Women's liberation was seen to be colour blind assuming that Maori and Pakeha women shared common interests that were more significant than the differences between them. Discontent among Maori and Pacific Island women's groups grew and in 1979 they attacked the United Women's Convention as the 'White Women's Convention' before moving to organize the National Black Women's Hui in 1980.[30] In addition, there was a clearly identifiable lesbian community within the movement by around 1980.[31] By the beginning of the 1980s these differences were becoming too difficult for the movement to manage. The 1979 United Women's Convention proved to be a test for unity that the movement failed: no one offered to organize another.

Other differences were beginning to become clear at this time. While the liberationist tendency split over the question of censorship in anti-pornography politics, the reformist tendency with its women's rights orientation divided over its tactical options.[32] A femocratic tendency had been, at first appearance, highly successful with women in senior positions in government and the bureaucracy, and a range of other consequences. It is this element of the women's movement that strikes so many visitors, along with a discourse where official New Zealand English seems to have lost much of the gender-specific terminology prevalent elsewhere.

A significant factor in this seeming naturalization of liberal/ reformist feminism was the willingness of many New Zealanders during the 1980s to consider and accept elements of the critique of hegemonic nationality and masculinity to emerge during and as a result of the scrutiny of rugby in 1981.[33] As a result, there has been a significant shift in national imagining and a resulting acceptance or tolerance of non-hegemonic forms. The assertion of feminist anti-rugby politics during 1981 raised issues outside the question of apartheid that anti-tour organizers had not considered in any great detail.[34] While the extent of support in 1981 for and the impact of groups such as Women Against Rugby (WAR) is hard to assess, by the time of the proposed 1985 All Black rugby tour to South Africa, WAR had organized in Wellington.[35] Whether a significant number of women actually withdrew their domestic support for rugby is much harder to assess, however there is anecdotal evidence from provincial and rural areas of a clear gender split in attitudes to both rugby and sporting contact with South Africa. WAR was seen by many active in the anti-apartheid movement as a significant move towards more explicit sectoral organization within the movement and as a means to broaden its appeal.[36] The nostalgic re-imagining of nation and masculinity of the 1990s, however, suggested that this acceptance of diversity manifest during the mid to late 1980s was being reconsidered as was the manufacture of a new, hegemonic, biculturalism.[37]

Maori have played a crucial role in the depiction of New Zealand identity. New Zealand was held to have the best race relations in the world and among Pakeha the notion of one nation held strong. The reality is more that Pakeha and Maori lived apart with a clear rural/ urban divide where contact between Maori and Pakeha communities was almost non-existent. The answer to Sinclair's 1971 question about why New Zealand's race relations were 'better than' elsewhere is simply that they appeared so good because Maori and Pakeha stayed apart.[38] The move by Maori to the cities during the 1950s and 1960s changed the situation as contact between Maori and Pakeha increased, and as Maori became more isolated from their quotidian association with hapü and other traditional structures.[39] Maori politics changed, becoming less polite than had been the case in the previous decades.

The Maori Organisation on Human Rights, formed in 1969, and Ngä Tamatoa,[40] formed in 1970 were the first of a series of groupings dissatisfied with the traditional approaches of lobbying, requesting, petitioning and, as they saw it, failure. Campaigns began around land rights, Pakeha appropriation of Maori cultural icons and artefacts, language protection, civil rights and institutional racism. The tactical approach relied on direct action and mass protest, and the strategic objective was fundamental social change rather than limited or short-term reform. This was a clear shift in Maori politics, and the emergence of a new civil society politics.

This emerging, vocal Maori polity presented problems for many Pakeha: the common belief was that the answer to Sinclair's question was a combination of superior colonists and superior natives. New Zealand's claimed exemplary race relations was a key element of the national image, yet here was a broad based series of Maori opinions clearly stating that the one-people approach had not worked. Public (Pakeha) attention was focused on the new spirit in Maori politics during a series of events between 1975 and 1979. The Maori Land March of 1975 directed attention to the past, the history of land theft and the inability of any systems to deal with the problems this caused. The Third Labour Government (1972-75) had introduced the Treaty of Waitangi Act 1975 instituting a mechanism to deal with breaches of the provisions of the Treaty of Waitangi after 1975.[41] Many Maori pointed out that most of the land had already been appropriated so the injustices of the past could not be dealt with. The National Party victory in the 1975 general election, however, reasserted a political force firmly wedded to the one-people notion. The 1977/8 occupation of Takaparawhā (Bastion Point) in central Auckland by members and supporters of Ngāti Whātua, the traditional owners of the land, directed attention to the issue of land rights. The forced removal of protesters 507 days later by police with army support focused critical vision on the power of the state and its intransigence.[42] A nearly concurrent occupation of a golf course in Raglan made it clear that the issue of land theft was widespread and in need of urgent attention. Finally, the attack by He Taua[43] on a mock haka party staged by engineering students at Auckland University in May 1979 revealed that the issue was about more than just land rights.

The occupation of Takaparawhā exposed the diversity of Maori approaches to political action. A number of Ngāti Whātua kaumātua[44] publicly called on those occupying the land to withdraw and continue negotiations with the Crown and developers planning luxury apartments on the site. This public dissension was later seen in other campaigns.

The most significant of these was the ongoing action around the annual Waitangi Day celebrations, a commemoration of the signing of the Treaty of Waitangi in 1840. For Maori leaders from Tai Tokerau, hosting these events was an honour. For many others, a century and a half of breaches of the Treaty provisions by the Crown and settlers made the rallying cry for protest 'The Treaty is a Fraud'. Emerging from this political debate, Awatere's Maori sovereignty articles prioritized colonization over class, and challenged the liberal Left to reconsider its history and its past.

During the early 1980s a change in attitude to the Treaty of Waitangi began to emerge. The call for Maori sovereignty coincided with a reassessment of the Treaty, and its promise of *te tino rangatiratanga*.[45] A new argument emerged that the Treaty should not be considered fraudulent, but had not been honoured by the Crown or by Pakeha. Justice could be achieved by honouring this agreement which guarantied Maori sovereignty, and gave the Crown rights to govern. The step from this to the vision of a bicultural polity is philosophically small, but politically and emotionally enormous. The Treaty of Waitangi Amendment Act 1985 allowed consideration of Treaty breaches back to 1840. This contributed to a fundamental shift in Maori–state relations and, by the early 1990s, a higher degree of Maori incorporation into state networks.

Maori politics merged closely with the campaign against the 1981 Springbok tour. For some Maori, the anti-tour campaign presented an opportunity to have Pakeha 'turn their eyes from overseas racism to *te take* Maori'.[46] Awatere contends that it was the most significant event in Maori history since the Second World War and allowed many Pakeha to realize that New Zealand's racism was 'different in degree but not in kind from what was happening in South Africa'.[47] The intense focus on issues of race and racism and the passions these generated through involvement with rugby union, created an environment conducive to a more comprehensive assessment of New Zealand's colonial experience, and the position of Maori in contemporary society. It also coincided with a shift in political focus from issues abroad to those at home. Increasingly high rates of unemployment and an ongoing economic crisis, growing concern about nuclear testing and the presence of US nuclear vessels in New Zealand waters and other existential concerns combined to make the campaign against the 1981 tour the last mass movement dealing primarily with issues outside New Zealand. A dynamic focus on colonial relations brought political struggle home in a way that had not been seen before 1981.

As the crisis of the final years of the Muldoon government intensified there was a change in perspective among key elements of the Pakeha protest movement leadership. Writers associated with the magazine *The Republican* attempted a theoretical and practical meshing of ideas of Maori sovereignty with Western Marxism.[48] The formerly Maoist Workers' Communist League, the second largest Marxist grouping in the country and influential in a number of social movements, abandoned the Leninist notion that a single party could lead the revolutionary struggle in favour of a coalition of forces united around a programme addressing contradictions based in capitalism, colonialism and patriarchal dominance.[49] Events surrounding the tour challenged the hegemonic identities New Zealand had adopted and, at least during the final Muldoon years, prepared fertile ground for intensified protest actions.

Despite these shifts on the left, the key factor in the changing dynamic and impact of the dissident networks was increasing support from the Labour Party, which lost the 1981 election by one seat, and could smell victory. Labour gave support to a number of movements, especially those around reformist feminism and anti-nuclear politics. Labour's 1984 election victory provided the impetus for a resurgence of 'Labourist' politics in the dissident groups where the 'don't rock the boat' attitude demobilized dissent and undermined resistance to Labour's New Right agenda. J. Kelsey has convincingly argued that it was only the political imperative to resolve the historical claims against breaches of the Treaty of Waitangi that undermined that political-economic drive.[50] Despite this, the focus on historical claims itself has effectively demobilized Maori anti-colonial politics.

For the purposes of considering events in regard to the Springbok tour, protest movements in some other areas are significant. Rising discontent around environmental issues, especially the campaign around the National Party's 1981 election strategy – Think Big, contributed to the sense of struggle against growing state power and totalitarianism. This sense was fed by campaigns against significant other National Party legislation that increased the power of the state. Legislation in 1976 and 1978 weakened the ability of trade unions to protect workers, in 1977 strengthened the Security Intelligence Service, and in 1980 the National Development Act gave the government the power to over-ride public consultation requirements for planning permission. These moves came on top of dawn raids on Pacific Islanders' homes in the quest for immigration permit overstayers, and built on a widespread sense that dissent was no longer tolerated.[51] The era saw increasing trade union campaigns and mass public protest around cuts to social programmes, especially education funding, that fed into a sense of national crisis. The economy was seen to be troubled with rising unemployment, stagflation and declining living standards with an ineffectual policy response. Crucially for many, even its traditional supporters, the government was seen to have no way out of the crisis choosing instead to mount a series of populist campaigns, around gangs, welfare 'cheats', 'subversives' and others, instead of effective policy initiatives.

The anti-apartheid movement built on this growing sense of discontent and struggle. The profile and significance of rugby union is crucial to an effective understanding of the high profile of this component of dissident politics. Rugby union is an integral part of New Zealand's national identity situated at the nexus of strands involving the maintenance of colonial power, a sustained hegemonic masculinity operating through both patriarchal and fratriarchal sites, common-sense capitalist rationality and generational dominion.

The social relations of rugby continue to assert this hegemonic role in such a way as to make both rugby and the nation sacred. Despite its ambiguous relationship with other identities of both modernity and post-modernity, the nation exercises considerable moral and emotional sway over self-imagining. The identification of the All Blacks as nationally representative in all ways when combined with rugby watching as a scopophilic activity serves to fetishize both the nation and the characteristics with which rugby is imbued. The All Blacks are thus both totemic and fetishistic. These processes conflate to grant rugby in general and the All Blacks in particular a sacrosanct position in the iconography of New Zealand.

Rugby's significant role in New Zealand's received hegemonic national identity and the traditional importance placed on competition with South Africa combine to make attendance at All Black–Springbok matches akin to visiting the temple. This secular sacredness meant that these contests needed to be isolated from the profane world of politics and the sacrilege of those who would challenge those identities. By the end of the 1970s the doubters of these identities had been granted voice and were being listened to. Against this cultural assault, the defence of

rugby contact with South Africa protected the highest manifestation of
national, totemic identity assertion, and restated the value of the
received version of national imagining against those agnostics and
heretics who would challenge its veracity. It was the strength of the
conviction of those who would defend the traditions that made the 1981
tour protests so intense. Tour opponents had made the tactical decision
that the tour could be stopped so set out to do just that, while tour
defenders saw it as the last stand against blasphemy. It was the polyvalent
nature of that tradition, and the deeply ingrained place of rugby within
the national and masculine imagining, that allowed that political struggle
to stand in for a much wider set of social and political changes.

In seeking to stop the tour the anti-apartheid movement was striking
a blow at New Zealand's hegemonic identities. It has become a veritable
truism that the capitalist world saw the rise of an intensely politicized
popular protest movement during the 1970s. It is a myth (in the
Barthesian sense) premised on the centrality of 1968 as a turning point
in modern world history. It is associated with the invention of youth as a
political and social rather than life-cycle entity and perpetuates a notion
of prosperity and economic well-being. This myth invests a student
rising in Paris and a party convention in Detroit with an impressive array
of consequences around the world. There is a sense that New Zealand
History as written and understood inflates the significance of the long
1970s, which coincides with the young adulthood of that new group of
historians emerging from the expansion of university access from the
late 1960s, at the expense of the previous two post-war decades.[52] This is
not to imply that the 1950s and early 1960s were not characterized by a
lower level or form of political action than either the late 1940s or the
long 1970s, but to argue that the drama and significance of this era of
political action presumes and intensifies a perception of dullness about
the earlier decades, and is in part premised on a need to find an origin in
some sort of 'big bang'.

New Zealand has not escaped this fable. The question of continuing
sporting contact with South Africa gave rise to the biggest mass political
movement of the 1970s and 1980s in New Zealand. This anti-apartheid
movement, however, has a sensibility extending back for decades, and, as
a post-1960 activist network, built on the peace and anti-nuclear
movement of the post-war years. Accompanying anti-apartheid protests
were other issue-based protest movements.[53] Only the campaign around
the Homosexual Law Reform Bill in 1984 and 1985, a threat to

hegemonic masculinity rivalling the protests against the rugby tour, provoked a sense of social division comparable to the question of sporting contact with South Africa. This, in itself, is telling: masculinity's wagons were secure in their circle.

The anti-apartheid movement took many years to develop, shifting focus from its pre-1960 identity centred on a 'No Maoris [*sic*] No Tour' campaign to a position completely opposed to any contact with apartheid by the mid-1970s.[54] These shifts mirrored changes in the international campaign, and in New Zealand represented a change from the position that saw apartheid as threatening good domestic race relations to one that saw ongoing domestic colonial oppression as well as the need to support the southern African liberation movements by isolating apartheid. A planned Springbok rugby tour of New Zealand in 1973 had been cancelled by Norman Kirk's Labour Government, and 'sporting freedom' had become key part of National's successful populist election campaign in 1975.[55] Their electoral success meant that there was a resurgence in action against apartheid sport. The World Softball Championships in January 1976 was followed by an All Black tour of South Africa in June and July which saw the re-emergence of an increasingly widely supported anti-tour feeling. The South African tour could not have come at a worse time: in coinciding with the Soweto rising and massacre it was a public relations disaster for the NZRFU and Government. Although the Montreal Olympic organizers managed to avoid a boycott over the presence of Taiwan, the vast majority of African states stayed away because New Zealand did not.[56] By 1981, when it was clear that the increasingly unpopular Muldoon government was using the tour as an election tool, it seems that wide ranging frustration had laid the basis for a well-supported protest movement.

During the 1970s opposition to sporting contact remained limited in New Zealand. The common-sense ideology that sport and politics were separate had wide support and the cultural significance of rugby made these tours a crucial event for many New Zealand men. New Zealand's self-satisfied complacency that it was still the world's social laboratory, that it had the best race relations in the world and that women had little about which to complain had been questioned, but little else had happened to shake those beliefs. Throughout the later 1970s, however, the questioning grew louder and in some specific areas, particularly regarding colonial and patriarchal relations, actions defied those certainties. The anti-apartheid movement still had a small core of activists, primarily in the main centres, but there was an increasingly sympathetic constituency for its message. The factors M.N. Pearson identifies as preventing action against the 1956 tour – the dominance of rugby in the national self-image, latent racism that made apartheid tolerable, and lack of appreciation for anti-colonial and black nationalist feeling – had been weakened.[57] Rugby certainly remained a crucial element in the hegemonic national identity, but increasingly public discussion of racism in New Zealand and several years of high profile activity around anti-colonial issues had severely undermined the hold the other two factors had over political opinion.

These circumstances, and the growing international isolation of South Africa, served to make apartheid a crucial issue. Along with the increase in Maori politics, other concerns arose during the 1970s to sharpen the issue of 'race'. Rising unemployment and increasingly restrictive immigration controls had led to a concerns about Pacific Island 'overstayers' resulting in deportations, dawn raids on Pacific Island households by police and immigration officials, and Pacific Islanders being questioned in the street.[58] Yet in 1978 Immigration Minister Frank Gill defended policies that allowed migration by white Rhodesians and South Africans. This reinforced the image of increasingly racist state policies derived from government opposition to boycotts of South Africa and from the growing awareness provoked by Maori protest. In conjunction with a growing women's movement this was fertile ground for the anti-apartheid movement to grow.

By the end of the 1970s the campaign against contact with apartheid combined a number of elements facilitating broad support. It retained a strong focus on an international issue while also prioritizing 'race' as the basic contradiction. Furthermore, the most high profile target of the campaign was rugby union. In combining these dynamics, the anti-apartheid movement could draw support from those concerned about matters of international concern, women critical of patriarchal and fratriarchal cultural mores and Maori seeking to focus on issues of domestic racism as well as build support for black struggles. In addition, the growing international isolation of apartheid and the increasingly strong boycott movement increased the number of sportspeople opposing contact, albeit often from self-interest. Others were concerned that New Zealand was increasingly out of step with world opinion and risked becoming a pariah, especially in a world where market diversity was crucial for an exporting nation. Finally, the tour was to held in an election year: an election it was widely expected National would lose. In a climate where even traditional supporters were turning away from National in favour of third parties, the irony of this political use of sport was apparent to many. Simply, 1981 was a period of intense social tension with the Springbok tour focusing widespread discontent on a single event.[59]

This singular focus is crucial to understanding the consequences of the anti-tour movement. The debates within and around the movement during late 1981 and 1982 centred on two broad issues, both of which came to a head at a particularly fractious HART Annual General Meeting in November 1982. The first was the question of support for the liberation movements: HART had consistently taken a position of non-sectarian support for the South African liberation groups, unlike other national groupings in both Australia and the United Kingdom that supported positions advanced by the African National Congress. The upshot of the November meeting was weakened non-sectarianism and a weakened movement. The second, and in the long term more difficult, debate was the issue of 'domestic racism'. Maori and other supporters of the anti-tour campaign became increasingly frustrated at a perceived failure by the anti-apartheid movement to confront issues arising from a national colonial past. Looking back after ten years, Alick Shaw noted this problem when he noted the movement's singularity: 'It was set up as a single issue organization, not a political movement. You couldn't just take these thousands of people and turn their attention to domestic racism or whatever.'[60] Shaw's observations direct attention to the problems of campaigns to come. Although the anti-tour campaign was important in raising issues about New Zealand's race relations and colonial history, it was neither solely responsible nor was it sufficient to promote or provoke a political movement. In some ways it was easier to consider the question of apartheid: there was less involved in terms of a (re)examination of identity that would result from a reassessment of national history required by a political movement addressing issues of domestic racism.[61]

Subsequent political struggles ranged across a number of issues with the most consistently high profile being the question of colonial relations. The symbol and focus of this struggle, the Treaty of Waitangi, became equated with the totality of the issue, and the high profile of historical grievances has directed focus to those concerns. However, the vibrancy of political debate and struggle in the immediate post-tour period promised far more in terms of changing colonial relations. In effect and in popular memory, the anti-tour campaign was, as has been said of May 1968, 'a turning point in history where history refused to turn: as a beacon of the future it revealed nothing so vividly as the past'.[62] Memory of that past, of that promise and of its potential for change has been expunged as the demobilization of politics allowed and caused by the New Right's Borg-like ravages where resistance seems futile has further sapped the potential of campaigns of struggle and the quest for equality. As the vision Fukuyama represents retains its social and political power and as Neithammer's call to historical action is squeezed as a political option, the dual nostalgias that view the campaign in 1981 as containing either the potential for the rebirth or the actual end of Aotearoa/New Zealand history are exposed as a denial of both the historicity of the 1950s and the nature of post-1984 politics and history.

NOTES

An earlier version of this essay was presented to 'The End of Sports History?', the 1999 Conference of the Australian Society for Sport History, Queenstown, New Zealand, 1–5 February, 1999.

1. T. Reid, 'The Days of Rage: Ten Years After', *Listener and TV Times*, 22 July 1991, 29.
2. The literature suggesting this is extensive. See, for example, C. James, *New Territory: The Transformation of New Zealand 1984–1992* (Wellington, 1992); B. Jesson, *Fragments of Labour: The Story Behind the Labour Government* (Auckland, 1989); J. Kelsey, *Rolling Back the State: Privatisation of Power in Aotearoa/New Zealand* (Wellington, 1993).
3. For a clear statement of this vision, see R. Campbell and A. Kirk, *After the Freeze: New Zealand Unions in the Economy* (Wellington, 1983).
4. Pakeha are New Zealanders of European descent. On the role of rugby as a masculinizing pastime see J.O.C. Phillips, *A Man's Country? The Image of The Pakeha Male: A History*, second edition (Auckland, 1996).
5. G. Wong 'Boots, Batons, Fists' *New Zealand Herald*, 9 July 1994, Sec 3, 2.
6. Wong, 'Boots, Batons, Fists'.
7. A. Morrison, 'The Moment Meurant Regrets', *The Dominion*, 18 July 1991, 11.
8. Reid, 'The Days of Rage', 28.
9. Morrison, 'The Moment Meurant Regrets'.
10. K. Coughlan, B. Hawkins, B. Edwards and P. Elsino, 'Battle of the Boks', *The Evening Post*, 10 July 1991, 5.
11. F. Fukuyama, *The End of History and The Last Man* (London, 1992).
12. G. Bosetti interview with Francis Fukuyama, *L'Unita*, 4 Dec. 1997, cited in N. Bobbio 'At the Beginning of History', *New Left Review* 231 (Sept 1998), 85.
13. For a comprehensive recent treatment of these issues, see R. Brenner, 'Uneven Development and the Long Downturn: The Advanced Capitalist Economies from Boom to Stagnation, 1950–1998', *New Left Review*, 229 (May 1998), special issue.
14. L. Neithammer *Posthistoire: Has History Come to an End?* (London, 1992).
15. Ibid., p. 149.
16. See M. Glenny, *The Rebirth of History: Eastern Europe in the Age of Democracy* (London, 1993).
17. There are many treatments of the worst of the nationalist excesses in Yugoslavia. See M. Glenny, *The Third Balkan War* (London, 1993); B. Magas *The Destruction Yugoslavia: The Break-up of Yugoslavia* (London, 1993). On the setbacks of the post-Soviet era see B. Einhorn,

Cinderella Goes to Market: Citizenship, Gender and Women's Movements in East Central Europe (London, 1993); and N. Funk and M. Meuller (eds.), *Gender Politics and Post-Communism: Reflections from Eastern Europe and the former Soviet Union* (London, 1993).

18. See, for example, A. Hoffman *Tales of Hoffman – Part One* (Wellington, 1998).

19. E. Locke, *Peace People* (Christchurch, 1992); R.Yska, *All Shook Up: The Flash Bodgie and the Rise of the New Zealand Teenager in the Fifties* (Auckland, 1993); R. Shuker and R. Openshaw with J. Soler, *Youth, Media and Moral Panic in New Zealand (From Hooligans to Video Nasties)* (Delta Research Monograph No. 11, Massey University, Palmerston North, 1990); M. Corner, *No Easy Victory: Towards Equal Pay for Women in the Government Service 1890–1960* (Wellington, 1988); and R. Thompson, *Retreat From Apartheid: New Zealand's Sporting Contacts with South Africa* (Wellington, 1975).

20. There is a considerable body of literature on these matters. Drawing from US material alone, reference should be made to S. Sayers, A. Stephanson, S. Aronowitz and F. Jameson (eds.), *The 60s Without Apologies* (Minneapolis, 1984); and M. Wallace, *Black Macho and the Myth of Superwoman* (London, 1990). In the Aotearoa/New Zealand context, as a contemporary text T. Shadbolt's *Bullshit and Jellybeans* (Wellington, 1971) can be read to show the gaps in the dissident movements of the early period while work by C. Dann, *Up From Under: Women and Liberation in New Zealand, 1970–1985* (Wellington, 1985); and R. Walker, *Ka Whawhai Tonu Mātou/Struggle Without End* (Auckland, 1990) show the gaps between women and Maori aspirations and the campaigns of the 1970s.

21. D. Awatere, 'On Māori Sovereignty', *Broadsheet* (June 1982), 36–42; 'Māori Sovereignty, Part 2' *Broadsheet* (Oct. 1982), 24–9; 'Te Mana Māori Motuhake: Beyond the Noble Savage', *Broadsheet* (Jan./Feb. 1983), 12–19. Also published as D. Awatere, *Māori Sovereignty* (Auckland, 1984).

22. G. Chapple, *1981: The Tour* (Auckland, 1984), pp.42, 43, 50–1.

23. Ibid., p.43.

24. *Unity*, 4,10, 18 June 1981, 8; *Unity*, 8, 5, 7 May 1985, 7.

25. *Sunday Times*, 22 Feb. 1981; *New Zealand Herald*, 28 Feb. 1981, 3 March 1981; *Auckland Star*, 4 and 5 March 1981; *New Zealand Truth*, 24 March 1981.

26. *Auckland Star*, 24 Feb. 1981.

27. *New Zealand Truth*, 14 April 1981.

28. *Auckland Star*, 14 April 1981.

29. Dann, *Up From Under*, pp.3–27.

30. Ibid., pp. 23, 33–9. A hui is a meeting, gathering or assembly.

31. Ibid., *Up From Under*, pp.31–3.

32. See A. Ryan, 'Policing Pornography: A Repressive Strategy', in Macdonald, (ed.), *The Vote*, pp.231–5; J. Bean, A. Corich, P. Hall-Jones and S. Jackson, 'Pornography: What, Why, What To Do?', *Race Gender Class*, 3 (1986), 6–14; C. Cheyne and A. Ryan, 'Anti-Pornography: How Should We Proceed?', *Race Gender Class*, 4 (1986), 10–14.

33. Phillips, *A Man's Country?*, pp.270–89.

34. S. Thompson. 'Challenging the Hegemony: New Zealand Women's Opposition to Rugby', *International Review for the Sociology of Sport*, 23, 3 (1988), 205–12.

35. *Unity*, 8, 5, 7 May 1985, 1.

36. Ibid., 7.

37. On nostalgia see J. Nauright, 'Reclaiming Old and Forgotten Heroes: Nostalgia, Rugby and Identity in New Zealand', *Sporting Traditions*, 10, 2, (1994), 131–40. On biculturalism, see M. MacLean, 'The Silent Centre: Where Are Pākehā in Biculturalism?', *Continuum*, 10, 1 (1996), 108–20; and P. Spoonley, 'Constructing Ourselves: The Post-Colonial Politics of Pākehā', in M. Wilson and A. Yeatman (eds.), *Justice and Identity: Antipodean Perspectives* (Wellington, 1995); Augie Fleras and Paul Spoonley, *Recalling Aotearoa: Indigenous Politics and Ethnic Relations in New Zealand* (Auckland, 1999).

38. See Walker, *Ka Whawhai*, pp.215–19; I.H. Kawharu, *Land as Turangawaewae: Ngāti Whātua's Destiny at Bastion Point* (Wellington, 1979).

39. Hapü is usually translated as 'extended family'. It is the primary political and organization element of Maori society.

40. The Young Warriors.

41. The Treaty of Waitangi, signed between Maori and the Crown in 1840, legitimated

colonization, gave guarantees of certain Maori rights and placed certain obligations on the Crown to protect Maori. Its provisions have been hotly contested and its validity intensely debated since the day it was signed. It has only in the last fifteen years acquired any constitutional or jurisprudential authority on Aotearoa/New Zealand.

42. See Joe Hawke *et al.*, *Takaparawhā Bastion Point: 506 Days on Ancestral Māori Land* (Auckland, 1978); Walker, *Ka Whawhai*, pp.215–19, I.H. Kawharu, *Land as Turangawaewae*.

43. The war party. See K. Hazelhurst, *Racial Conflict and Resolution in New Zealand: The Haka Party Incident and it's [sic] Aftermath, 1979–1980* (Canberra, 1988).

44. Male elders.

45. All the characteristics of chieftainship or sovereignty.

46. Māori demands or issues. Ripeka Evans '*From* The Māori Strategy', in Witi Ihimaera, *Te Ao Marama 2. Regaining Aotearoa: Māori Writers Speak Out. He Whataatanga o Te Ao: The Reality* (Auckland, 1993), p.91, originally published in *Broadsheet* (Oct. 1982).

47. Donna Awatere Huata, *My Journey* (New Zealand, 1996), p.64.

48. *The Republican* carried a significant number of articles around these issues between 1982 and 1984. See B. Jesson, 'Conflict in the Anti-Racist Movement', *The Republican*, 40 (1982), 4–5; Black Unity, 'A Statement on the Attempt by White Leftists to Divide Pacific Peoples', *The Republican*, 41 (1982), 4–7; B. Jesson, 'Māori Radicals and the Pākehā Left: How Much in Common', *The Republican*, 41 (1982), 13–16; M. Mita, 'Correspondence', *The Republican*, 42 (1982), 11–13; L. Gale, 'Correspondence', *The Republican*, 42 (1982), 13–15; P. Lee, 'Donna Awatere and Māori Sovereignty: A Marxist View', *The Republican*, 43 (1982), 7–16; S. Webster, 'A Pākehā Answer to Awatere', *The Republican*, 46 (1983), 17–19; B. Jesson, 'Reviewing the Māori Sovereignty Debate', *The Republican*, 48 (1983), 3–4, 19–20; C. Guy and G. Simpkin, 'Correspondence', *The Republican*, 49 (1984), 11–12.

49. D. Steele, 'Where to the Socialist Left Now? the Implications of Eastern Europe and Other Questions', *The Republican*, 69 (1990), 16. Details of the policy shift can be seen in Workers' Communist League, *Socialism and Liberation: Workers' Communist League – A Policy Summary* (Wellington, WCL, 1984) and 'The WCL Takes a New Direction', *Unity*, 8, 12, 10 Oct. 1985, 1, 6–7.

50. J. Kelsey, *A Question of Honour? Labour and the Treaty 1984–1989* (Wellington, 1990).

51. The issue of overstaying and the crisis of the late 1970s is still a delicate question in many Pacific Island communities. See Tamara Ross, 'New Zealand Overstaying Islander: A Construction of the Ideology of Race and Immigration' (unpublished MA thesis, Victoria University of Wellington, 1994).

52. There is little written in New Zealand that deals with the cultural and intellectual impact of this expansion of tertiary education. A useful parallel might be the mid-1980s debate in the US concerning the embourgeoisement of the US working-class and the creation/emergence of the 'Professional-Managerial Class'. See especially B. Ehrenreich and J. Ehrenreich, 'The Professional-Managerial Class', in P. Walker (ed.), *Between Labour and Capital* (Boston, 1979), pp.5–45; and F. Pfeil, 'Makin' Flippy Floppy: Postmodernism and the Baby-Boom PMC', in M. Davis, F. Pfeil and M. Sprinker (eds.) *The Year Left: An American Socialist Yearbook Volume 1* (London, 1985), pp.268–95. The significance of these arguments lies in the proportion of this generation within the PMC. The different economic and class structure in New Zealand means that the parallels should be cautiously assumed, but the structural and class cultural implications of the argument suggest provocative questions for our historical analysis and understanding of the post-war era.

53. These campaigns, referred to above, included protests against New Zealand involvement in the Vietnam War, around environmental causes, and for a nuclear-free New Zealand. By the later 1970s campaigns and struggles had developed around issues of colonization and as a result of the women's movement. Significant protest movements developed around unemployment and a raft of other social policy concerns while increasing state power attracted broad-based public opposition movements.

54. There are several useful accounts of the development of the anti-apartheid movement. For the most recent see M. Templeton, *Human Rights and Sporting Contacts: New Zealand Attitudes to Race Relations in South Africa 1921–94* (Auckland, 1998); and T. Richards, *Dancing On Our Bones: Rugby, New Zealand and South Africa* (Auckland, 1999).

55. W. David MacIntyre, 'From Dual Dependency to Nuclear , in Geoffrey Rice (ed.), *The Oxford History of New Zealand*, second edition (Auckland, 1992), pp.520–38.

56. B. Houlihan, *Sport and International Politics* (Hemel Hempstead, 1994), pp.132–51; and D. Macintosh and M. Hawes (with contributions from D. Greenhorn and D. Black), *Sport and Canadian Diplomacy* (Montreal and Kingston, 1994), pp.37–58.

57. M.N. Pearson, 'Heads in the Sand: the 1956 Springbok Tour to New Zealand in Perspective', in R. Cashman and M. McKernan (eds.), *Sport in History: The Making of Modern Sporting History* (St Lucia, 1979), pp.272–92.

58. Ross, 'New Zealand Overstaying Islander'.

59. See, for example, Chapple, *1981*; R. Shears and I. Gidley, *Storm Out of Africa: The 1981 Springbok Tour of New Zealand* (Auckland, 1981); T. Newnham, *By Batons and Barbed Wire: A Response to the 1981 Springbok Tour of New Zealand* (Auckland, 1981).

60. Coughlan *et al.*, 'Battle of the Boks'.

61. The extensive literature and intensity of cultural and political debate concerning the effects of moves to address historical grievances under the Treaty of Waitangi is testament to the difficulties of reassessing a national history and the orthodoxy of identity it has produced. These same difficulties were exposed by the outrage expressed by many in letters to the editor columns and elsewhere after the Television New Zealand broadcast of the revisionist history of the *New Zealand Wars* during June and July 1998. This series was presented by James Belich and based on his 1986 book *The New Zealand Wars and the Victorian Interpretation of Racial Conflict* (Auckland).

62. G. Marcus, *Lipstick Traces: A Secret History of the Twentieth Century* (Cambridge, MA, 1989), p.431.

13

Australian Sport in a Postmodern Age

BOB STEWART and AARON SMITH

The impact of postmodernism on the arts, architecture, literary criticism and organizational life has been comprehensively examined, but little research has been undertaken into sport to determine the extent to which it, too, may have been affected. This essay examines the impact of postmodernism on Australian sport. We aim to show that sport has been transformed by the process of postmodernism, which commenced in the middle of the 1960s when it threw away many of its moralistic pretensions and repressive formality, and locked itself into the corporate world. By the 1990s a number of professional sport leagues had emerged as amateurism lost its snobbish appeal and sport went about building its commercial value. Corporate signage saturated the major venues, and players were marketed as celebrities. Excitement, speed, the 'quick grab' and sensory bombardment became the defining features of the spectator experience. Spectacular and dramatic contests became just as important as skill and aesthetic display. Fans increasingly narrowed their attention span, but were no longer bound by a parochial tribalism. They took on multiple identities that could shift from an élite European soccer team one week, to a suburban Brisbane rugby team the next. At the same time, branding and image making were used tó attract fans and corporate supporters. Moreover, the television programmer became the final arbiter on how the game should be scheduled and played.

CHANGING TIMES

Peter Drucker, the eminent American writer on corporate affairs, concluded that sometime between 1965 and 1973 Western society 'passed over' a cultural and economic divide, 'entered the next century' and in doing so moved from a modern to a postmodern state.[1] David Harvey, an English social critic, posited a similar turning point that produced 'a full blown, though still incoherent (postmodern) movement'.[2] The shift was gradual, but of sufficient strength to suggest that:

> What appears on one level as the latest fad, advertising pitch and hollow spectacle is part of a slowly emerging cultural transformation in Western societies, a change in sensibility for which the term 'post-modern' is actually, at least for now, wholly adequate. The nature and depth of that transformation are debatable, but transformation it is.[3]

While there was (and still is) a raging debate as to what exactly this transformation entailed, a number of core cultural and commercial changes were identified. Many artists, architects, designers and intellectuals challenged the taken-for-granted hierarchies in literature, the arts and even the fashion industry. They understood that society had become a complex mix of values and cultures where ambiguity and contradiction had undermined the search for universal truths. Moreover, business organizations not only 'loosened up' their management philosophies and work methods, but 'customers' also changed their patterns of buying and consumption.[4] Bureaucracy and mass production gave way to more fluid and organic ways of managing,[5] and more customized delivery of products and services. At the same time, the commercialization of activities like the arts and sport blurred the traditional distinction between culture and commerce.[6] These changes created a new way of viewing the world as Western capitalism entered a post-industrial stage of 'flexible accumulation'.[7]

There was also a significant change in the structure and practice of sport in Australia around this time. According to some critics, our most popular pastimes had been either seduced or fractured by the forces of commercialism and television.[8] For example, in 1968 the divide between amateur and professional tennis was eliminated with the establishment of 'open' tournaments. For the first time, professionals could play in the Australian Open, or any of the other three premier international or 'grand slam' events. In the following year the Australian Cricket Board created a one-day, limited over competition involving all the Australian states and New Zealand, and sponsored by the Vehicle and General Insurance Company.[9] This constituted a radical break with traditional forms of unsponsored first-class cricket that occupied a minimum of four days' play. During the 1960s a surfing culture emerged that challenged the rigid authority and conformist traditions of the surf life saving movement.[10] The concurrent emergence of postmodernity and new forms of sport, and their common ambivalence about tradition, hierarchy, and conformity, immediately suggests a possible connection between the two. There is the tantalizing possibility that the cultural and economic changes that occurred in post-war Australian society directly explain the changes that occurred in the structure and practice of Australian sport over the last 40 years.

MODERNISM

Postmodernism is a slippery term, and can take on a variety of meanings, depending on whether you are talking to an artist, social theorist, literary critic, architect, or business commentator. However, no matter what perspective postmodernism is viewed from, it can only be understood by reference to its modern antecedents.[11]

The modernization process[12] arose out of the Age of Discovery in fifteenth-century Europe, reaching its intellectual zenith during the eighteenth century's Age of Enlightenment. During this period science and technology combined with capitalism to overturn the traditional belief systems and practices associated with Feudalism and Christianity.[13] As a result of this process, Western society underwent a rapid process of industralization and urbanization, culminating in the twentieth-century feature of corporate bureaucracy. As well as generating economic growth through the application of science and technology to commerce and industry, modernization created two contradictory qualities in twentieth-century Western capitalism. On one hand it induced increasing levels of differentiation and specialization which was encapsulated in the mechanistic management principles of Frederick Taylor and Henry Ford.[14] On the other hand this obsessive emphasis on co-ordination and organization produced homogenized commodities, conformist patterns of consumption and a plethora of regulatory institutions. Modern industrial societies therefore embraced the welfare state, government enterprises, centralized control of fiscal and monetary policy, high tariff barriers and fixed exchange rates. Suburban cars and houses were mass-produced, and people's lives were increasingly steered by a corporate planning system.[15]

The modernist emphasis on control and organization was also revealed in its changing belief systems. Whereas reactionary feudalistic structures, superstition and dogmatic religious practices moulded pre-modern values, modern values centred on a utopian belief in rational enquiry and material progress.[16] Modernists understood that that while capitalism was fundamentally chaotic, the application of reason and knowledge would create stability and prosperity and temper its tendency to creative destruction.[17] According to the modernist world-view, capitalism also had universalizing tendencies, which could be discovered and understood through the formation of a grand narrative or meta-theory.[18] While Marxists focused on monopoly capital as the basis of all exploitative social relations, Liberals insisted that markets were the prime example of universal modes of human conduct.[19]

Modern society was therefore framed by a desire for rationality and order, where uniformity and standardized designs characterized most organizations, buildings, artefacts, symbols and services.[20] The institutions of modern life 'were faithfully replicated by modern mentality', and bound by an ideology that centred on universality, hierarchy, regulation and homogeneity.[21] Modern Australian sport fits this description in nearly every respect.

MODERN SPORT

Modern sport arose out of a variety of games and ceremonies that featured in European rural life in the seventeenth and eighteenth centuries. During this pre-industrial period sport was essentially unorganized and local in nature. Rules of games were fluid and varied from one region to another. High levels of violence were tolerated and emotional spontaneity was encouraged. Sport was closely connected to the customs, rituals and ceremonies of the wider social life, and reflected the religious practices and seasonal rhythms of society. No controlling organizations or governing bodies existed. The village was the focal point for what historians have subsequently called 'folk games'.[22] Modern industrial capitalism transformed sport. A traditional, customary way of life was replaced by a modern society that emphasized reason, individualism and order. Allen Guttmann concluded that sport in the modern world exemplified the triumph of Weberian rationality as it became secularized, democratic, specialized, rationalized, bureaucratized, quantified and record oriented.[23] Modern sport was therefore a specific cultural expression of regulated and rule-bound urban society. As a result: 'violent, disorderly and disorganised sports gave way to more carefully regulated ones adapted to the constraints of time and space imposed by the industrial city, embodying the Victorian spirit of self control and energetic competition as well as taking advantage of the development of the railway and the mass press'.[24]

Wray Vamplew's analysis of sport in late Victorian and Edwardian Britain, added support to Guttmann's argument. Sport became a mass consumption industry as it changed its focus from recreational to commercial. He identified the growing professionalism in sport, the establishment of formal administrative structures, the control over sport exerted by the middle classes, and the emergence of sporting monopolies. Vamplew's primary thesis was that the development of mass spectator sport during this period was only possible because of rapid economic growth in the wider society. He identified four economic variables: the structure of the economy, including technology; the volume of non-working time; income levels; and the supply of energy. Vamplew concluded that the productivity-raising innovations associated with urbanization and industrialization led to an increase in both incomes and leisure time, and that this led, in turn, to a demand for commercialized, spectator sport.[25]

Jean-Marie Brohm, Berno Rigauer and George Sage extended the conclusions of Guttmann and Vamplew by asserting that not only was modern sport a product of capitalist development, but that it also exactly mirrored its workplace practices. Sport was a 'mechanism of the body', 'treated as an automation' and 'governed by the principle of maximising output',[26] in which 'incentives and rewards were instituted to motivate athletes to perform better'. Athletes learned the 'dominant–subordinate relationships' that characterized the hierarchical structures of complex organizations.[27] In particular, top-level sports 'copied this model of ordered status and role' and were therefore managed in the same way as any business organization.[28]

The proliferation of sporting organizations in Australia during the nineteenth and early twentieth centuries coincided with the process of modernization. During its early industrialization Australia pioneered the formal organization of sport. Between 1820 and 1850 sporting clubs were established in horse-racing, boxing, cricket, rowing, sailing, billiards, golf and lawn bowls.[29] The colonies hosted a touring party of English cricketers in 1861, standardized rules were established for Australian football in 1866, while an inter-colonial cricket competition, the Sheffield Shield, began in 1892. National and state governing bodies for football, cricket and tennis had all been established by the beginning of the twentieth century, and throughout the first half of the twentieth century this trend to greater codification and formalization continued.[30]

In addition, the work-place need for a compliant labour force was replicated in the paternalistic ethos of obedience and discipline that characterized twentieth-century sport. Australian players and athletes were poorly represented on decision-making boards and committees,[31] and for the most part meekly submitted to official authority. Insubordinate behaviour, like speaking out on team selection, was punished, and strict dress codes were enforced. For example, in Australian cricket during the 1940s and 1950s all test players were required to sign a contract that required them 'not to write for the press, or to make any broadcasts during the currency of the tour'.[32] Neither could they have their wives accompany them on an overseas tour or 'commit any act which rendered them unfit to play'.[33] The rules also stipulated that the Australian Board of Control for International Cricket (the game's governing body) would not approve the selection of any cricketer who 'during the season in which such a team is selected, publicly comments upon play and selection'.[34] Tennis officials had the same rigid views on how sport should be organized. Coaches put curfews on their players. They would speak only when spoken to and the all-white dress code was ruthlessly enforced.[35] Sport officials demanded homogenized dress and 'gentlemanly' behaviour. Individuality was sacrificed to the 'good' of the game, team, and club.

Moreover, the language of sport reflected the technocratic values and structures of the modern business world. Golfers and car racing drivers had a 'hard day at the office', while cricketers 'accumulated runs' and 'worked hard to achieve a win'. The most telling use of a techno-bureaucratic metaphor to describe modern sport came from the English cricket writer, R.C. Robertson-Glasgow, in an assessment he made of Australia's most famous cricketer, Donald Bradman, in 1947:

> But, above all Bradman was a business–cricketer. About his batting there was to be no style for style's sake. If there was to be any charm, that was for the spectator to find or miss. His aim was the making of runs. He seemed to have eliminated error, to have perfected the mechanism of stroke. No other batsman, surely, has ever been able to score so fast while at the same time avoiding risk. He was, as near as a man batting may be, the flawless engine.[36]

To summarize, modern Australian sport up to the 1960s was structured, regulated and conformist. Participants were constrained by rules and codes of conduct that not only set limits to their on-ground practices, but also regulated their public behaviour. There was a clear demarcation between officials and players, which gave the officials most of the privileges, perks and power. The amateur ethos was used to not only keep players in their place, but also to maintain those traditions that sustained these paternalistic relations. Traditional values were used to connect with the past and also to prevent changes to current practices. Most sports activities had few direct business and commercial connections, and in the case of the main spectator sports, the core income came from fans. For example, in the Victorian Football League, the premier Australian football competition at this time, clubs secured more than 90 per cent of its income from memberships and gate receipts.[37] However, the values and structures that underpinned modern sport were the same values and structures that supported modern industrial capitalism. Order, paternalistic authority, and coercive discipline were some common themes.

THE RISE OF POSTMODERNISM

According to Stephen Crook, David Harvey and Fredric Jameson, the origins of postmodernism can be traced to the economic crises that coincided with the social permissiveness of the 1960s, the growth of an influential counter culture and new left movement, and the end of the 'long economic boom'.[38] During the 1960s and early 1970s the Taylorist, Fordist and Keynesian supports of capitalism were undermined by a combination of political protest, student activism, union militancy, declining productivity, and falling profits. The oil crisis of 1973,[39] and the consequent drop in international demand, led to a period of chronic unemployment and escalating prices and wages.[40] The rise of postmodernism has its commercial base in the rejection of the welfare state and regulated markets in favour of competition, free trade and globalization.[41] Its cultural manifestation was based in an 'antagonism to the oppressive qualities of … technical-bureaucratic rationality',[42] and neatly illustrated by the practices of architects and designers who reacted against 'monolithic modernist structures' and standardized forms in favour of anarchy, artifice, fragmentation, and randomness.[43] This reaction against monolithic modernist structures was also found in

Australian sport at this time. It was succinctly revealed in the growth of the surfing movement and the expanding popularity of Percy Cerutty's anti-modern naturalistic athletics training philosophy.

During the 1950s surfing was a marginal sport that existed on the periphery of surf lifesaving, but by the 1960s had become a popular recreational activity. In 1964 the world surfing championships were held in Sydney, at Manly Beach, and attracted about 65,000 spectators. By 1965 an estimated 50,000 surfers had become members of the Australian Surfriders Association.[44] Surfing also became a symbol of a growing counter culture that challenged the ways in modern sport was organized, and its underlying values. Surfing was unorganized, geared around the natural rhythms of the sea. Surf lifesaving, on the other hand, centred on traditional practices like line and reel rescues and resuscitation and beach 'march pasts'. They were all tightly regulated and task oriented, and emphasized routine and disciplined training. The rescue and resuscitation was particularly stylized and mechanistic, but was justified on the grounds that a 'well-drilled precision team' would be rewarded both in competition and a 'real' rescue. Surfing was a therefore a threat to the lifesaving clubs' regimented atmosphere. Whereas surf lifesavers or 'clubbies' were conformist and conventional, surfers or 'surfies' saw themselves as non-conformist and adventure seeking.[45]

Modern sport's emphasis on structure, routine and discipline was also rejected by Percy Cerutty, Australia's most famous athletics coach of the 1960s. Cerutty eschewed the interval training of well-known coaches like Franz Stampfl in favour of a more naturalistic approach. Interval training epitomized the foundation values of modern society. It aimed to regulate, systematize and 'routinize' athletic training, in order not just to improve athletic performance, but also to use scarce training time more efficiently. It centred on the track, the stopwatch, repetition training and rigidly balancing work rates against recovery rates. Cerutty saw little value in interval training. He called it a 'pseudo science' which gave the athlete no autonomy, and reduced training to a system of fixed schedules.[46] Cerutty preferred a more naturalistic system of training that used bush tracks, sand hills and the beach to condition athletes. Cerutty saw little value in reducing athletic training to an exercise in routine and stifling discipline. He said:

> Civilisation and the daily routine of school and work, discipline him, conditions him, and mostly reduces him to an automation, a

robot. How futile to add such a regime to his athleticism. How much better to use his training, conditioning and racing as a means, as it should be, to at least temporarily remove him from this artificial, and harmful, civilising medium … Why add his exercise, his athleticism, to the list of compulsions. Athletics should be, and with me, is, the prime means to escape from these imprisoning conditions.[47]

The growth of surfing and the success of Cerutty's training methods were two core antecedents of the transformation of Australia's sporting landscape. Like the counter culture, their anti-modern response to current ways of doing things undermined the values of modernism, and laid the foundation for sport's subsequent postmodernizaton.

POSTMODERN PRODUCTION

From the commercial and cultural space created by the reaction against modern structures and systems arose a series of radical experiments in business practice and organization design. This resulted in a shift to flexible specialization,[48] or as it was alternatively called, 'post-Fordism'.[49] It involved intensified rates of commercial, technological and organizational innovation, and entailed a new round of space–time compression.[50] The time horizons of both public and private corporations shrunk as microcomputers, satellite communications and faster aircraft accelerated the dissemination of information and visual images. Post-Fordism produced a multi-skilled and flexible work force comprising contract employment, casuals, temporaries and subsidized trainees. As a result much looser organizational structures were designed.[51] Decisions could be made quickly without the cumbersome approval of 'Boards' and committees, and authority was delegated to those people directly producing the goods or providing the services.[52] The modern or Fordist focus on mass production was offset by the post-Fordist concentration on producing a variety of goods in small batches, and the custom-built product.[53] Markets were segmented on the basis of specific customer needs and lifestyle profiles, and product lines were continually updated. For example, the competition between Adidas and Nike at this time not only centred on improving the overall quality of their sports footwear, but also on making sure each of the élite athletes, competitive amateur, recreational jogger, and casual user segments, were catered for.[54] Attention shifted from the product to the customer, as marketeers replaced engineers and accountants as the 'navigators' of corporate success.

POSTMODERN MARKETING

The forces of postmodernism shifted the marketing focus away from the consumption of goods and into the consumption of services; not only personal, business, educational, welfare and health services,[55] but also festivals, entertainment spectacles and sporting events. The 'lifetime' of such services, whether visiting a museum, going to the cinema, 'working out' in a fitness centre, or attending a sporting event, was far shorter than that of an automobile or washing machine. Since there were limits to the accumulation and turnover of physical goods, then it made good commercial sense to turn to the provision of ephemeral services.[56]

The volatility and ephemerality that surrounded personal services and leisure experiences were compounded by the dynamics of a 'throwaway' and disposable society, which became evident during the 1960s. This meant not only throwing away produced goods, but also throwing away values, lifestyles, personal relationships and attachments to things, buildings, places and people. Individuals were forced to deal with disposability, novelty and the prospects for instant obsolescence. Sport was caught in this web of disposability, since it was so intangible. Also, because it often produced strongly felt experiences, it seduced players and fans alike into experimenting with a variety of new activities, which in part explains the growing popularity of extreme sports.

Advertisers also used images rather than information to manipulate desires and taste. Brand name recognition became an important marketing outcome as the emphasis went from the product's tangible features to more intangible things like symbolic representation, prestige and novelty.[57] As a result customers remained loyal to brands only in so far as they maintained a 'fresh and up to date image'.[58] For example, Nike quickly understood it was in the business of branding and 'crafting images', not 'selling shoes'.[59] The concern for image over form and substance created a depthlessness that allowed people to enjoy the moment without needing to fully understand the experience. In sport this was revealed in the growth of the so-called theatre-goer, who valued the sport experience for its immediate fun and pleasure, rather than any strong and prolonged feeling of tribal identity.[60]

Postmodernization therefore represented a further extension of the market system over a whole range of cultural practices, including the arts, sport and leisure.[61] In a postmodern world, then, everything from sex and religion, to art and sport has commercial value, and a market price.[62] The term 'hyper-commercialization' was coined to describe these changes.[63]

POSTMODERN CONSUMPTION

The postmodern emphasis on fragmentation, disposability, and image making was associated with three significant developments in consumer behaviour. First, whereas modernism emphasized a standardization and unification of consumption, postmodernism produced an enormous pluralization of tastes and pleasures,[64] and gave way to a 'vast smorgasbord'[65] of possible lifestyles and identities.[66] Increasingly, identities were chosen 'through the shop window of the pluralised social world'. In other words what we consume largely determines who we are.[67] In sport, traditional identities based on local and suburban loyalties were undermined by the use of club brands, team images and player personalties to form a fluid but often superficial and shifting sense of self.

Second, the increasing preference for ephemeral experiences was accompanied by a gradual dismantling of the barriers between high and low culture. The concept of a superior cultural form was undermined by a postmodern denial of universal truths. The idea that all art and culture could be ranked according to some objective criteria was also rejected. Not all classical was superior to popular music and soccer was not intrinsically superior to American football. The embrace of cultural relativism meant that there was no longer any consensus about what was good or bad, or what was tasteful or tasteless. Synchronized swimming was therefore no less valid an Olympic sport than gymnastics. The modernist search for a hierarchy of excellence was abandoned in favour of the exploration of a variety of equally significant experiences.

The third trend involved the creation of a hyper-reality that combined fantasy and technology to produce an eclectic conglomeration of sensory experiences.[68] These experiences were often modelled on some historical artefact, story or incident and reproduced in an exaggerated form. Theme parks were designed according to these principles and exemplified by Disney's entertainment parks. Disney copied historical events and places with no great concern for authenticity, but showed great concern about the need to manufacture a worked out vision on a grand scale, followed by a massive promotion campaign.[69] This 're-constructed' experience subsequently over whelmed its historical antecedent. According to Jean Baudrillard, who became a postmodern guru, the 'simulation' of reality could become more real and relevant than reality itself.[70]

POSTMODERN CULTURE

Postmodernism consequently provided a radically different way of viewing the world. The search for grand narratives, or all-embracing theories of social behaviour, gave way to the search for indeterminacy, ambiguity and paradox in art, architecture and literature. Difference and contradiction replaced conformity and certainty as dominant cultural themes.[71] The modernist concern for standardized forms was rejected in favour of mixing opposite structures and different historical styles. To be postmodernist was to emphasize the fragmentary, ephemeral and constantly changing face of capitalism, in which novel and superficial images were juxtaposed against coherent and traditional forms.

The practice of pastiche[72] in particular signified a profound break from modernism. Pastiche involves taking symbols, icons and forms from the past and different cultural settings, and fusing them with the present into a clashing constellation of ideas, parodies, pictures and stories. For example, television commercials may sell cat food and a career in the army to the accompaniment of Mozart or Beethoven; while a major sport event may be marketed by using images usually associated with pop music, contemporary art, or 'art house' cinema. The division between traditional and contemporary, popular and élite, and highbrow and lowbrow became blurred. For a number of critics like Fredric Jameson, this emphasis on fragmentation, image and pastiche was a disturbing trend, since it created superficial lifestyles and limited the capacity of people to sustain long-term attachments to anything. On the other hand it also created highly imaginative advertisements of sporting events and sport products. Adidas and Nike created a number of audacious and surreal promotions for their footwear in order to grab the attention of increasingly flighty customers. The fascination with pastiche also explains the enormous popularity of the Australian Football League's 1998 promotional campaign that juxtaposed athletic and sexual imagery against the ageing American comedian, George Burns.

POSTMODERN MEDIA

Postmodernism also embraced technology and television. This connection was first signalled by Marshall McLuhan's idea of the 'Global Village'. McLuhan's views exemplified the postmodern concern for the contradictions inherent in change and progress,[73] as well as demonstrating the impact of satellite technology on international communications and the 'globalization' of television audiences. The era of globalized mass television was characterized by an 'attachment to surface rather than roots, to collage rather than in depth work' and the dominance of superimposed, decentred images over narrative flow and worked surfaces.[74] Its primary concern was the strong image and quick grab, which meant that collision sports, adventurous recreation and dramatic 'news' became increasingly popular 'products'. Television was a vehicle for stimulating wants and mobilizing desire and fantasy. Above all, television, particularly when in colour, had an enormous capacity to mobilize sensory involvement from its audience. Unlike newspapers, which could only provide limited visual stimulation, television possessed diverse qualities like image, colour, movement and sound. Drama and spectacle were to become the dominant themes of television, and any sports event that wanted a 'regular spot' on television had to be dramatic and spectacular.[75] It also had to be abbreviated to accommodate the television viewer preference for time-compressed and high impact experiences. This was all part of the 'cultural logic of late capitalism'.[76]

Postmodern media also provides for a diversity of delivery formats. The free-to-air television broadcasts of major international sport like tennis, soccer and motor racing, and local sports like Australian football and cricket are increasingly complemented by pay television, the Internet, and video games. It has in turn greatly enhanced the revenue base of sport organizations. Whereas gate receipts and memberships for clubs, and government grants for state and national associations traditionally provided the lion's share of revenue, options such as the Internet and pay television represent tantalizing possibilities for financial independence. The Australian 'Review 2000' report, which examined government involvement in sport and recreation, considered the feasibility of Internet-based gaming, national football tipping competitions and pay television for generating revenue to support sport.[77]

A list of the economic and cultural distinctions between modernism and postmodernism is given in Table 1.

TABLE 1
MODERNISM AND POSTMODERNISM:
ECONOMIC AND CULTURAL DISTINCTIONS

Modernism	Postmodernism
Economic Distinctions	
Specialization	Multi-skilling
Mass production and consumption	Variety and segmentation
Rigidity and central control	Flexibility and delegation
Durability	Planned obsolescence
Cultural Distinctions	
Culture protected from market	Culture seduced by market
Common universal values	Multiple values
Leisure as cultural experience	Leisure as a commodity
Real and the permanent	The hyper-real and the disposable
Sacred traditions	Superficial nostalgia
Single identity	Multiple identities
Form, depth and substance	Image, surface and style
Unity and order	Fragmentation and uncertainty
Hierarchy of taste and quality	Cultural relativism
Aesthetics, skilled performance	Spectacular entertainment

In summary, whereas modernization commodified material relations, postmodernization commodified social and cultural relations.[78] Not only were standard household goods embraced by the market, but so too was information and knowledge, community services, the arts and sport. Australian sport always had cultural and social value, but its commercial value was rarely realized in its modern form. Postmodern sport is mainly about re-working its cultural and social traditions to produce a desirable consumer experience, and therefore add to its commercial value.

Postmodernism also involved a shift away from centralized mass production to a decentralized, fragmented structure to attract the market 'niche' and the idiosyncratic customer. A large part of Australian sport has re-invented itself in this respect. New experiences like limited-over cricket, indoor cricket, aerobics, mixed gender softball and netball, and snowboarding were invented to meet the special needs of the sport customer. Diversity is a fundamental part of the postmodern world.

A fundamental difference between modernism and postmodernism centres on how each movement has approached the discontinuity and contradictions of capitalist society. Modernists aimed to counteract it, and hence the obsession with rationality, control, order and conformity. On the other hand, postmodernists preferred to 'wallow' in the 'chaotic currents of change'.[79] In this respect sport is now quintessentially postmodern, since it too underwent dramatic change. Rules were changed, formal dress codes were overturned, tournaments and competitions were re-named, games were converted to spectacles, and players claimed a stake in the future of their sports.

Postmodernism also has a fascination with pastiche, ambivalence and contradiction. Different ideas, incidents, icons and symbols are brought together to create a novel and frequently surreal experience.[80] Sport also moved in this direction as it experimented with new rules, new venues, different playing schedules and mixing old traditions with new technology.

A 'hyper-reality' was also constructed in which the commodities were dominated by fantasy and nostalgia.[81] The popularity of the multi-media sport museum, the growing fascination with sporting memorabilia, and growing interest in watching ageing sports legends going through the motions, demonstrated a need to recreate a spectacular but not necessarily authentic past, and locate it in a technocratic present.

POSTMODERN SPORT

A few scholars and researchers have explored the changing face of sport using postmodern themes. Allen Guttmann touched upon the connection between the growth of naturalistic and transcendental sports, like surfing and mountaineering, and postmodernism.[82] John Loy, David Andrews and Robert Rinehart used a postmodern framework when discussing the current 'obsession' by the consumerist society with the production of images and the way in which the body image is connected to television images.[83] John Bale linked the growing popularity of road running at the expense of the track, as an indicator of a disenchantment with modern sport's focus on formalized systems of organization. Bale also saw the construction of multi-functional, 'playful' aquatic centres in preference to mono-functional swimming pools, as examples of the shift to a post-Fordist, postmodern cultural practice.[84] Jim McKay, Geoffrey Lawrence, Toby Miller and David Rowe have seized upon global markets and globalized sports as another example of the postmodern experience,[85] while Ian Harriss described one day cricket as the triumph of postmodern cultural practice because of its obsession with surface, spectacle and excess.[86] With the exception of Harriss, none of these writers have tackled the relationship between postmodernization and changing sporting practices in much detail, or provided a convincing connection. However, as Harriss hints, there is strong support for the view that changes that took place in Australian cricket from the middle of the 1960s can be explained by this shift in economic structures and cultural practices.[87]

In fact, many spectator sports were radically restructured during the 1970s. For example, at the international level, tennis was organized as an amateur sport until the late 1960s, at which time it became fully professional. Soccer was bureaucratized around the same time as FIFA, the game's international governing body, extended its influence over the world game. Soccer's global and commercial expansion during the 1970s was comprehensively examined by Bill Murray.[88] Locally, Australian football, cricket and rugby league extended their sponsorship arrangements, sold off of exclusive telecast rights and massively increased player payments.[89] Australian rules footballers were paid up to $3,000 per game for a season of winter play, while cricket, players could earn more than $2,000 from a single test match, which was well above average weekly earnings. In contrast, match payments for the leading competition, Victorian Football League (VFL), players during the 1950s rarely exceeded $50, and for test match players averaged at around $100. Spectators and viewers were increasingly attracted to time compressed and colourful sporting contests, while management became entangled in a complex web of commercial arrangements, legal constraints, and marketing 'deals'.[90] By the late 1970s Australian spectator sport transformed its commercial foundations. Sponsorship and media rights rivalled gate receipts as the dominant funding source, and television created an audience which was sometimes a hundred times larger than 'at ground' attendance. There were factors pushing sport in a new direction.

Australian cricket provides a stark picture of how sport was transformed during the 1970s and beyond. Customized stadium seating in the form of private boxes and suites, and the deployment of venues by business as a vehicle for entertaining clients were in place by the middle of the 1970s.[91] By 1975 the Victorian state cricket association had, with the co-operation of the Melbourne Cricket and Football Clubs, introduced a number of private boxes for lease by business firms. An eight-seat box attracted a rental of $1,200 per season. In 1977 the introduction of Kerry Packer's World Series Cricket produced many changes. Instant television replays on giant video screens were introduced, games were played under floodlights and marketing plans were designed to improve cricket's public profile.[92] Heroic and sexual images were used to promote the game, and players like Dennis Lillee and Jeff Thompson became celebrities. The radically different one-day, limited-over international matches played with modified rules and in coloured uniforms, took fans away from the slow moving traditional five-day test matches.[93] The sporting public was fed a 'fast food' diet of time-efficient and time compressed contests that changed the face of first class cricket.

Television also had a significant role to play in transforming sport during the 1970s and beyond. By the 1980s it had became not only the dominant cultural icon and transmitter of cultural values, but also the medium by which most people experienced big time sport in Australia. Its hyper-real emphasis on excitement, speed, the intimate close up, a variety of slow motion re-plays, 'quick grab' and the 'short attention span', conditioned viewers to demand constant entertainment, sensory stimulation, compressed dramatic tension and its quick resolution.[94] As a result, the customary emphasis on the subtle if slow build-up of tension and the fundamental skills were relegated to a secondary position. Improvements in satellite technology during the early 1970s also enabled global markets to emerge, and expanded the sports audience beyond the wildest dreams of administrators who managed the game a decade earlier. A nationwide audience for live sport telecasts in Australia was created in 1971 and sport's growing nexus with television was consolidated in 1975 with the introduction of colour television. Two years later the video replay was enhanced and international sporting telecasts via satellite were introduced.[95] When Kerry Packer's Channel 9 television station mounted a full-scale telecast of the 1977 test series in England, it signalled the globalization of sport for Australian sport fans, and the internationalization of its commercial arrangements.

The paternalistic relationship between players and officials was eroded throughout the 1980s. A number of legal judgments undermined restrictive transfer and recruitment rules, and player conditions improved. Strong player unions emerged, and collective bargaining agreements were struck in Australian football, basketball, rugby league, rugby union and soccer.[96]

By the 1990s sport's postmodern transformation was nearly complete. The Olympic Games threw away its amateur pretensions and aristocratic patronage. In its place emerged a hybrid sporting competition where amateur players mixed with highly paid professionals and where crusty 'Eurocentric' officials bound by tradition and hierarchy deferred to globalized, corporate giants like NBC, Coca Cola, McDonald's and Reebok. Whereas the modern Olympics were underwritten by aristocratic privilege, the postmodern Olympics are sustained by its corporate and commercial connections.[97] Television is now the pivotal revenue source. In 1956 the Melbourne Olympics Organising Committee received a few thousand dollars for newsreel rights, while the television rights for the 2000 Sydney Games will generate about $900 million for the Organising Committee. The Olympic ideals of friendly competition and the joy of participation have been subjugated to the spectacular event and the big performance.

According to Michael Real, the Olympics have become a 'pastiche of cultural artefacts' where titillation, superlatives and historical allusion are used to bombard the viewer's senses.[98] Real sees the Games as an exemplar of the ways in which pastiche is used to overlay the athletic competition with 'promotions, commercial interruption, sponsor logos, abrupt transitions and entertainment packaging'.[99] As a result, the 'classical, coherent single-author focused artistic experience' has been replaced by a fast paced presentation of multiple-events with on-screen graphics and (multi) announcer commentary.[100] Indeed, the proliferation of Olympic logos, sponsorships, memorabilia, merchandising and marketing has meant that the Olympic's commodification is now virtually accepted as part of the Olympic creed.[101]

By the mid-1990s Australian rugby union also decided that its amateur traditions could no longer be sustained in the face of growing commercial interest in the game. At the international level commercialization overwhelmed the game when Rupert Murdoch's global television network entered into a multi-million dollar agreement with the major national governing bodies of Australia, New Zealand and South Africa.[102] In late 1995 the International Rugby Federation, the governing body for world rugby met in Paris and Tokyo where it was agreed that the amateur principles on which the game had been founded, would be repealed.[103] From 1996 players became fully professional and subsequently earned massive salaries, while marketers re-positioned the game as a spectacular experience that combined brute force with finesse and athleticism. As a result, rugby administrators had to reconcile the game's traditional middle class exclusiveness with a commercial requirement for a broad supporter base.

At the same time, no sport could be secure in the knowledge that its fans would retain their singular loyalty. Many fans now had multiple identities and loyalties and seamlessly shifted their allegiances between sports and teams. One week it would be Manchester United, and another week it would be the Chicago Bulls. At the local level, it would be the Sydney Kings basketball team one week, and the Canberra Raiders rugby league team the next. Moreover, their identification and loyalty would be often based on nothing more than a television image.[104] Suburban tribal loyalties based around a place or location were slowly superseded by identities based on a club's profile or corporate personality, star players, team colours or theme songs. In other words, club and team attachments were frequently the result of strong brand identification rather than neighbourhood and family pressures.

This coincided with the segmentation of sports markets based on the values and lifestyles of fans.[105] While it was still appropriate to put sport watchers under the single umbrella of fan, there were now a variety of fan types each type taking their own angle on the game and making its own interpretation of the sports experience. One study divided fans on the basis of their emotional involvement and frequency of attendance. Those fans committed to a single team were labelled 'passionate partisans', those with a preference for strategy and aesthetics were labelled 'aficionados', while those with a more general interest in the event and the match experience, were labelled 'theatregoers'.[106] Moreover, fans could shift between categories. For one game they may be fanatical partisans supporting their local team, but for the next game they may be theatregoers seeking an entertaining experience.

A mass, or homogeneous sports market, in which fans, members and clubs are single entities with common and relatively enduring needs and aspirations, has been replaced by a proliferation of segmented markets, each with their own special requirements. In the new generation stadiums, seating and viewing arrangements are differentiated according to their proximity to the play, the availability of hospitality services, access to closed circuit television, protection from the weather and the potential for business client contact.[107] Both the Docklands 'Colonial' stadium in Melbourne and Sydney's Olympic Games stadium in Homebush have been designed with these features in mind.[108] Colonial

Stadium, which was designed primarily for Australian football, is also an exemplar of how the postmodern stadium takes multi-functionalism to a new level. Not only does it have a retractable roof, but it can also re-configured to alter the playing space. As a result, games can be insulated from poor weather, portable cricket wickets can be installed as appropriate and extra seating can be installed for rugby and soccer matches.

The importance of catering to a diversity of needs is also mirrored in the growth of designer and niche market sports. These new sport products include indoor cricket, beach volleyball (both indoor and outdoor), mixed netball and softball and competitions for special groups such as the disabled, primary school students, adolescents, teachers, professional employees, public servants, police officers and firefighters, gays and lesbians and veterans. In order to meet these challenges, sports managers have developed a range of strategic marketing skills, delivered timely and varied packages of services to increasingly discerning customers and continually monitored the changing needs of players, members and fans.

The preparedness of sports managers and marketers to modify the sports product and intervene in its delivery has also created new ways of 'massaging' some of the troublesome characteristics of sport, such as its inconsistent quality. In doing so, they have further blurred the boundaries between sport and entertainment. Professional wrestling, for example, once a parochial American pseudo-sport now commands a formidable international television audience, including an increasing number of Australians. Professional wrestling contains all the ingredients of sport theatre, neatly packaged it into a dramatic contest between a heroic protagonist and a despicable opponent. The formulaic match includes carefully scheduled action peaks and troughs, culminating in a desperate struggle and a triumphant hero. While professional wrestling scarcely qualified as a sport in the modern world, it encapsulates the postmodern attraction to the spectacular, the fantastic, and the ephemeral. Fans willingly suspend their disbelief just as readily as if they were attending live theatre or watching a film. In a postmodern sports world, fans are prepared to be manipulated and teased provided they can vicariously enjoy a consistently dramatic and tension packed spectacle. It satisfies the apparently contradictory need for 'predictable unpredictability' in their leisure experiences.

The postmodern sporting experiences that emerged in the 1980s, and which were expanded in the 1990s, therefore constituted a dramatic change from the modern, standardized, early post-war experiences. The order, paternalistic authority, coercive discipline and collectivist regimentation that characterized modern sports were replaced by a more diverse, eclectic, and in many ways, chaotic sporting landscape. The postmodern landscape was dominated by its corporate alliances, but also gave its participants an enormous variety of experiences that ranged from mixed gender netball to snowboarding. It gave fans and spectators spectacular events in which the complementary entertainment often overshadowed the game itself. Sports were frequently modified to suit the television audience at the expense of players and spectator. At the same time players were no longer constrained by rigid codes of discipline and dress codes, and for the first time were consulted on the organization and management of their sporting activities. Table 2 summarizes the differences between modern and postmodern sport.

A NEW WORLD OF SPORT

Australia, like other advanced Western countries, has been enveloped by a postmodern, consumerized and customized culture which values fashion, image and surface as much as tradition, substance and depth. In turn, sport has been integrated into the leisure and entertainment industries. Australian sport can now be more aptly described as 'Sportsbiz', a term used by Stephen Aris to identify the fusion of sport's cultural and commercial dimensions.[109] Ritual, myth and tribalism have been conflated into an interdependent cultural and commercial system dominated by the hyper-real and mediated television experience. Not even the Olympic Games, élite rugby union, or first class cricket, with their rich traditions and reactionary cultures, could escape the clutches of the marauding postmodern marketers, promoters and entrepreneurs. In their search for new and novel sports products and markets, they left no sporting stone unturned. Sports administrators now not only view their pastimes as a form of business, but also use professional staff trained in marketing, finance, management and the law. It no longer makes much commercial sense to maintain traditional sporting practices for their own sake, or even as a means of understanding the past. In a postmodern sporting world, history and tradition are valuable only in so far as they can be used to 're-capture an atmosphere', re-invent an experience, or exploit a niche in a competitive and constantly shifting recreation market.[110]

TABLE 2
AUSTRALIAN SPORT: MODERN AND POSTMODERN DISTINCTIONS

	Modern Sport	Postmodern Sport
Game Structure	Emphasis on conventional game plans and cautious innovation; matches end when result achieved; rules are sacred	Experimentation encouraged, traditional practices challenged; rules modified to provide better spectacle
Team Leadership	Conservative leadership Preference for proper technique & risk avoidance	Adventurous leadership Preference for tactical innovation and the 'surprise move'.
Values and Customs	Amateurism and fair play, Conformity; acceptance of custom and tradition Deference to, and respect for, authority figures Sport as character building	Professionalism, Questioning of traditional practices Undermining of authority figures Sport as a personal challenge
Organization and Management	Central control Player subservience Part-time support staff	Diffusion of authority Consultation with players Full-time specialist staff
Financial Structure	Commercial viability dependent on gate receipts; small contribution from radio Arms length relation ship with 'business'	Commercial dependence on sponsorship, television rights, endorsements, merchandise and & gate receipts Sport 'is' a business
Venues and Facilities	Stadiums provide standardized seating, standing room and basic catering Viewing complemented by transistor radio	Customized seating with reserved sections, private boxes with customer service and full hospitality Video screens used to replay critical incidents
Promotion	No active promotion of league or teams, dependent upon publicity from radio & newspaper reports; the game and its traditions will sell itself	Direct promotion to target markets; television the dominant promotional medium. Games tailored to suit needs of specific customer/spectator groups
Viewing of Game	Live match attendance	TV audience dominates
Spectator Preferences	Display of traditional craft, skill & ritual; emphasis on the contest and tribal rivalry	Eclectic blend of entertainment, amusement, on the spectacular image and the big experience
Fan Loyalties	Singular and parochial loyalty to teams and players	Multiple loyalties, shift between sports, and from local to global
The Sports Market	Fans and members comprise a common undifferentiated mass; they see sport in the same way; need to provide only-one experiences	Fragmented and niche markets; 'boutique' sports; fans have multiple ways of viewing and participating; need to provide a variety of experiences
Coaching and Training	Rigid adherence to formularized interval training and repetitive practice	Blend of science support and naturalistic training that involves a variety of training modes

Postmodernism has consequently removed the traditional metaphysical, mythical and social barriers that were thought to have divided commerce from sport. As a result, athletic contests are just another disposable product for sale in a global market place. Sport's traditional practices are no longer unchanging and sacred. The postmodern imperatives of flexibility and customized innovation means that game rules and playing schedules can be changed to suit the ephemeral needs of customers, and in particular the television viewer. Blandness, uniformity and monotony are the curse of postmodern sport, unless of course enough fans want it that way, and the sport entrepreneur can make it a profitable event. Spectacular, entertaining, novel[111] and time compressed contests are the defining characteristics of postmodern sport. Postmodern sport has fans, who are also customers. It is a cultural experience, but also has varying degrees of commercial value. It can be experienced at the venue or through television, with each experience having its own special qualities. One is no longer privileged over the other. Fans have both global and local perspectives and rules can be bent to ensure an entertaining contest. Sport is both business and recreation. Indeed, postmodern sport is whatever we want it to be and is only limited by our imagination and our preparedness to pay for the experience.[112]

NOTES

1. P. Drucker, *The New Realities* (New York, 1989), pp.3–4.
2. D. Harvey, *The Condition of Postmodernity* (Oxford, 1989), p.38.
3. A. Huysens, 'Mapping the Postmodern', *New German Critique*, 3 (1984), 5.
4. A.F. Firat, N. Dholakia and A. Vinkatesh, 'Marketing in a Postmodern World', *European Journal of Marketing*, 2, 5 (1995), 40–56.
5. W. Bergquist, *The Postmodern Organization: Mastering the Art of Irreversible Change* (San Francisco, 1993), pp.43–5.
6. Art galleries are now businesses as much as they are repositories for cultural artifacts.
7. See for example D. Bell, *The Cultural Contradictions of Capitalism* (New York, 1978); S. Crook, J. Pakulski and M. Waters, *Postmodernisation: Change in Advanced Society* (London, 1992); F. Jameson, *Postmodernism: The Cultural Logic of Late Capitalism* (London, 1991); and D. Harvey, *The Condition of Postmodernity* (Oxford, 1989)
8. See, for example, A. McGilvray, *The Game Is Not The Same* (Sydney, 1985), p.10; R. Cashman, 'Crisis in Contemporary Cricket', in R. Cashman and M. McKernan (eds.), *Sport Media and the Morality* (Sydney, 1980), pp.304–12; J. McKay, *No Pain, No Gain? Sport and Australian Culture* (Sydney, 1991). C. Tatz, 'Bought Sport', *The Age* (Melbourne), 22–24 Nov. 1986; B. Wilson, 'Pumping Up the Footy', in D. Rowe and G. Lawrence (eds.), *Sport and Leisure: Trends in Australian Popular Culture* (Melbourne, 1990), pp.27–38.
9. Australian Cricket Board.
10. D. Booth, 'Surfin' Australia 60s', unpublished paper presented at the Sporting Traditions IX Conference, Launceston, 1993; K. Pearson, *Surfing Subcultures* (Brisbane, 1983).
11. See Brown, *Postmodern Marketing* (London, 1995), p.64.

12. The distinction between modernism (a way of viewing the world), modernity (a state or condition) and modernization (the process by which societies move from a state of modernity to postmodernity) is described in *Theory Culture and Society: Special Issue* (June 1988), 195–208. A similar distinction is made in D. Lyon, *Postmodernity* (Milton Keynes, 1994), pp.6–7, and D.F. Ruccio, 'Postmodernism and Economics', *Journal of Post Keynesian Economics* (Summer, 1991), 499–500.

13. L. Spencer, 'Postmodernism, Modernity and the Tradition of Dissent', in S. Sim (ed.), *Postmodern Thought* (Cambridge, 1998), pp.158–9.

14. The theories and practices of Taylor and Ford have in recent times been reduced to the terms 'Taylorism' (after Taylor's pioneering work on time and motion study), and 'Fordism' (after Ford's use of assembly lines to mass produce motor cars). For an examination of Taylorism and Fordism see F. Webster and K. Robins, *Information Technology: A Luddite Analysis* (New Jersey, 1986).

15. One of the most succinct analyses of this practice was provided in J.K. Galbraith, *The New Industrial State* (London, 1969). According to Galbraith, one of the major functions of the planners, or 'technostructure', was to manage demand.

16. I.H. Grant, 'Postmodernism and Politics', in S. Sim (ed.), *Postmodern Thought*, p.29.

17. A term invented by the Austrian economist, Joseph Shumpeter.

18. See for example J.F. Lyotard, *The Postmodern Condition: A Report on Knowledge* (Manchester, 1990). Lyotard defined modernism as any science that legitimates itself to a meta-discourse and makes explicit appeal to some grand narrative (p.xiii).

19. K. Mannheim, *Ideology and Utopia* (New York, 1936).

20. D. Brown, 'Institutionalism and the Postmodern Politics of Social Change', *Journal of Economic Issues*, 26, 2 (1992), 547–59.

21. Z. Bauman, 'A Social Theory of Postmodernity', in P. Beilharz, G. Robinson and J. Rundell, *Totalitarianism and Modernity* (Cambridge, MA, 1992), p.149.

22. J. Bale, *Sports Geography* (London, 1989), pp.38–40.

23. A. Guttmann, *From Ritual to Record: The Nature of Modern Sport* (New York, 1978). See also A. Guttmann, *A Whole New Ball Game: An Interpretation of American Sports* (University of North Carolina Press, 1988), pp.5–6.

24. R. Holt, *Sport and the British: A Modern History* (Oxford, 1989), p.3.

25. W. Vamplew, *Pay Up and Play the Game: Professional Sport in Britain, 1875–1914* (Cambridge, 1988); also see J.R. Betts, 'The Technological Revolution and the Rise of Sports', *Mississippi Valley Historical Review*, 40 (1953), 231–56. Betts, in reviewing the development of sport in the USA between 1850 and 1900, concluded that industrialization and urbanization were more fundamentally responsible for the changes in sport than any other cause.

26. J. Brohm, *Sport: A Prison of Measured Time* (London, 1978), p.55.

27. G.H. Sage, *Power and Ideology in American Sport* (Human Kinetics, 1990).

28. B. Rigauer, *Sport and Work* (New York, 1981), pp.48–9.

29. R. Cashman, *Paradise of Sport: The Rise of Organised Sport in Australia* (Melbourne, 1995), pp.25–33.

30. See W. Vamplew *et al.*, *The Oxford Companion to Australian Sport* (Melbourne, 1992), pp.36–7 (football), pp.212–13 (tennis) and pp.100–1 (cricket).

31. This was particularly the case in cricket. Between 1907 and 1950 only four ex test match players were represented on the Australian Board of Control for International Cricket, the governing body of Australian cricket.

32. Player contracts 'forbade the presence of wives on tour' from 1921. Cited in R. Robinson, *On Top Down Under: Australia's Cricket Captains* (Sydney, 1975), p.188.

33. Australian Board of Control for International Cricket (Board of Control), *Ordinary General Meeting (OGM) Minutes*, March 1946, pp.17–18.

34. Board of Control, *Annual General Meeting (AGM) Minutes* (Sept. 1947), p.10.

35. Harry Hopman, the tennis coach and Davis Cup captain was notoriously autocratic in this regard.

36. R.C. Robertson-Glasgow, 'Bradman', in B. Green (ed.), *The Wisden Papers: 1947–68* (London, 1988), pp.26–7.

37. B. Stewart, *The Australian Football Business* (Kenthurst, 1984), pp.62–75.

38. Crook, *Postmodernisation*; Harvey, *Postmodernity*, and Jameson, *Postmodernism*.

39. During 1973 the international price of crude oil quadrupled, and in doing so, 'transformed a general, but gradual rise in prices into a price revolution, the kind of which the world had never before experienced over so short a period'. P. Johnson, *A History of the Modern World: From 1917 to the 1980s* (London, 1983), p.669.

40. Between 1960 and 1969 unemployment rates in Australia rarely exceeded 2% of the workforce. Between 1972 and 1975 the unemployment rate increased from 3% to 5%. Price levels throughout the 1960s were also stable. However, in 1972 the inflation rate was 6%, and by 1975 had reached an annual rate of 16%. A concise summary of Australia's economic development between 1950 and 1985 is contained in D. McDonald, 'A Description of Recent Developments in the Australian Economy in an Historical Context', *Australian Economic Review* (1st Quarter, 1988), 42–54.

41. T. Friedman, *The Lexus and the Olive Tree* (New York, 1999).

42. Harvey, *The Condition of Modernity*, p.38.

43. M. Ryan, 'Postmodern Politics', *Theory Culture and Society*, 5 (1988), 559.

44. Booth, 'Surfin' 60s', 6

45. K. Pearson, *Surfing Subcultures*, p.114.

46. P. Cerutty, *Success in Sport and Life* (London, 1964), pp.33, 114. Also see the contribution by Phillips and Hicks in this volume.

47. P. Cerutty, *Athletics: How to become a Champion* (London, 1959), p.17.

48. This phenomenon is examined in M.J. Piore and C.F. Sobel, *The Second Industrial Divide* (New York, 1984). The pioneering regions of flexible specialization were identified as northern Italy, central Austria and parts of Germany.

49. In the minds of some writers, flexible specialization is not the same as post-Fordism; rather it is a variant or subset of post-Fordism. See, for example, P. Hirst and J. Zeitlan, 'Flexible Specialisation versus post-Fordism', *Economy and Society*, 20, 1 (1991), 1–45.

50. Harvey, *Postmodernity*, pp.201–39.

51. K. Weik, 'Organisational Redesign as Improvisation', in G. Huber, and W. Glick (eds.), *Organisational Change and Redesign* (New York, 1993), pp. 346–79.

52. See M.I. Reed, 'The End of Organised Society', in P.T. Blyton, and J.A. Morris (eds.), *Flexible Future: Prospects for Employment and Organisation* (New York, 1991), pp.23–39; and M. Rustin, 'The Politics of Post-Fordism: or The Trouble with New Times', *New Left Review* (May–June, 1989), 56–8.

53. Brown, 'Institutionalism', 550–1.

54. Ibid.

55. Rustin, 'The Politics of Post-Fordism', 59.

56. This, according to Ernest Mandell, becomes the defining characteristic of late capitalism. See E. Mandell, *Late Capitalism* (London, 1975).

57. Harvey, *Postmodernity*, pp.287–9.

58. Firat, 'Marketing in a Postmodern World', p.194.

59. Ibid., p.46.

60. C. Rojek, *Decentring Leisure* (London, 1995), p.152.

61. F. Jameson, *Postmodernism*, p.56. Jameson concludes that as a result, postmodern culture is judged in term of what gives pleasure and makes money.

62. Refer to Brown, *Postmodern Marketing*, p.80.

63. See for example, Crook *et al.*, *Postmodernisation*.

64. F. Feher and A. Heller, *The Postmodern Political Condition* (New York, 1988), p.142.

65. Metaphors abound when the essential characteristics of postmodernity are discussed. In keeping with its complicated, intertwined and changing nature, it has also been compared to a labyrinth, a whirlpool, a kaleidoscope and even a carnival. See for example, Harvey, *Postmodernity*, p.5; Bauman, 'Postmodernity', p.150; and T. Peters, *Liberation Management* (New York, 1992), pp.15–17.

66. Brown, 'An Institutionalist Look', 1092.

67. D. Slater, *Consumer Culture and Modernity* (London, 1997), p.85.

68. J. Hannigan, *Fantasy City* (London, 1998) p.69.

69. Firat, 'Marketing in a Postmodern World', p.47.

70. See C. Lemert, *Postmodernism is Not What You Think* (Oxford, 1997), p.33.
71. R. Cooper, and B. Gibson, 'Modernism, Postmodernism and Organisational Analysis, An Introduction', *Organisation Studies*, 9, 1 (1989), 94–9.
72. Jean Baudrillard, the French social theorist, uses the word 'implosion' to describe much the same thing; that is, where all binary opposites like high and low culture, and real and simulated, are 'conflated' and fused into the one category or experience.
73. The 'Global Village' paradox states that the enlargement of the world through modern communication techniques actually makes it smaller. The postmodern slogan that connects with the earlier views of McLuhan is the phrase 'think global, act local'.
74. See Harvey, *Postmodernity*, p.61; and D. Kellner, 'Popular Culture and the Construction of Postmodern Identities', in S. Lash and J. Friedman (eds.), *Modernity and Identity* (Oxford, 1992), p.146.
75. S. Barnett, *Games and Sets: The Changing Face of Sport on Television* (London, 1990), pp.123–8.
76. The term was coined by Fredric Jameson in *Postmodernism*.
77. Sport 2000 Task Force, *Shaping Up: A Review of Commonwealth Involvement in Sport and Recreation in Australia* (Canberra, 1999).
78. See D. Kellner, 'Postmodernism as Social Theory', *Theory, Culture and Society*, 5 (1988), 258–9.
79. Harvey, *Postmodernity*, p.44; see also Jameson, *Postmodernism*, pp.5–10, where he proposes that the postmodern condition confines people to a perpetual present and perpetual change which obliterates tradition.
80. Bauman, 'Postmodernity', pp.149–51.
81. According to Stephen Frosh, it is the image 'which constitutes the most vibrant metaphor for modern reality'. He concluded that the television image in particular has no substance behind it, and is created, played and gone, 'all in an instant'. S. Frosh, *Identity Crisis: Modernity, Psychiatry and Self* (London, 1991), p.31. See also Peters, *Liberation Management*, pp.3–8
82. Guttmann, *A Whole New Ball Game*, p.179.
83. J. Loy, D. Andrews, and R. Rinehart, 'The Body in Culture and Sport', *Sports Science Review*, 2, 1 (1993), 82.
84. J. Bale, 'Racing toward Modernity: A One-Way Street?', *International Journal of the History of Sport*, 10, 2 (1993), 215–32; and J. Bale, *Landscapes of Modern Sport* (London, 1994).
85. J. McKay, G. Lawrence, T. Miller and D. Rowe, 'Globalisation and Australian Sport', *Sports Science Review*, 2, 3 (1993), 10–28.
86. I. Harriss, 'Packer, Cricket and Post Modernism', in Rowe and Lawrence (eds.), *Sport and Leisure*, pp.109–21. Harriss commented thus: 'whereas cricket under modernism was characterized by rationalism, depth, order and constraint, cricket under the influence of post modernism had become geared to surface, spectacle and excess. Cricket was no longer approached as a highly elaborate range of possible risk averse strategies, but was instead an explosive, decentred, glossy spectacle, packaged ready for immediate consumption by both the 'at ground' spectator and television viewer'.
87. Harriss, 'Packer, Cricket and Post Modernism', pp. 102, 104.
88. W.J. Murray, *Football: A History of the World Game* (Aldershot, 1994), pp.200–1.
89. Australian football's commercial development during the 1970s is detailed in B. Stewart, *The Australian Football Business*.
90. Changes in the commercial structure of Australian sport during the 1970s, including cricket, are documented in G. Lawrence, and D. Rowe (eds.), *Powerplay: The Commercialisation of Australian Sport* (Sydney, 1986).
91. See Victorian Cricket Association, *Annual Report* (1975), p.20.
92. A detailed analysis of the origins of the Packer sponsored WSC quickly followed its introduction. See E. Beecher, *The Cricket Revolution* (Melbourne, 1978); H. Blofeld, *The Packer Affair* (London, 1977), A. Caro, *With a Straight Bat* (Hong Kong, 1979); C. Forsyth, *The Great Cricket Hijack* (Melbourne, 1978), and P. McFarline, *A Game Divided* (Melbourne, 1977). A number of 'serious' books written on Australian cricket history since 1980 have also included a section on WSC and its aftermath. Some of the more interesting accounts are by Cashman, *'Ave a Go*, pp.153–69; G. Haigh, *The Cricket War: The Inside Story of Kerry*

Packer's World Series Cricket (Melbourne, 1993); C. Martin-Jenkins, *Cricket Contest: 1979–80: The Post Packer Tests* (London, 1980), pp.1–14, 54–74, 130–7; C. Martin-Jenkins, *Cricket: A Way of Life* (London, 1984), pp.174–9; and S. Quick, 'World Series Cricket, Television and Australian Culture' (unpublished Ph.D. thesis, Ohio State University, 1990).

93. Between 1980 and 1984 the average daily crowds for test matches fell from 16,000 to 12,000. By contrast, average daily crowds for one day international matches increased from 20,000 to 30,000.

94. According to Kenneth Thompson, television was able to create a sense of 'collective effervescence', particularly when it covered sporting events. Thompson, 'Social Pluralism', p.251.

95. Although satellite pictures of cricket from overseas had been used since 1972, it was not until 1975 that a full match from overseas was telecast back to Australia. The inaugural World (one day) Cup was played in England in July, and Australia met the West Indies in the final. The match was telecast by the ABC over a nine-hour period and in colour, starting at 8 p.m. It was a 'dramatic contest'. The ABC reported 'unprecedented interest', and overseas cricket matches subsequently became an attractive 'product' for both the ABC and the commercial stations.

96. For a detailed account of recent developments in player unionism see B. Dabscheck, 'Early Attempts at Forming Soccer Playing Unions in Australia', *Sporting Traditions*, 10, 2 (1994), 25–40; and B. Dabscheck, 'The Professional Cricketers Association of Australia', *Sporting Traditions*, 8, 1 (1991), 2–26.

97. M. Real, 'MediaSport: Technology and the Commodification of Postmodern Sport', in L. Wenner (ed.), *MediaSport* (London, 1998), p.18.

98. M. Real, 'The Postmodern Olympics: Technology and the Commodification of the Olympic Movement', *Quest*, 48 (1996), 9–24.

99. Real, 'MediaSport', p.22.

100. Ibid., p.23.

101. Ibid., p.21.

102. J. Skinner, 'Environmental Turbulence and its Impact on Organisational Change: The Case of Queensland Rugby Union' (unpublished paper presented at second conference of the Football Studies Group, Melbourne, Victoria University, June 1998), 8.

103. Skinner, 'Queensland Rugby Union', p.9.

104. G. Rail, 'The Dissolution of Polarities as a Megatrend in Postmodern Sport', in *Sport: The Third Millennium* (Ste. Foy, 1991), pp.745–51.

105. B. Mullin, S. Hardy and W. Sutton, *Sport Marketing* (Champaign, 1993), pp.123–32.

106. A. Smith and B. Stewart, *Sports Management: A Guide to Professional Practice* (Sydney, 1999), pp.170–3.

107. J. Hall, R. Stewart and M. Shaw, 'The Value of the Venue', *Australian Leisure Management* (June/July 1998), 51–2.

108. G. John, and R. Sheard, *Stadia: A Design and Development Guide*, second edition (Oxford), pp.131–6.

109. S. Aris, *Sportsbiz: Inside the Sports Business* (London, 1990).

110. Thompson, 'Social Pluralism and Postmodernity', p.233.

111. According to Tibor Scitovsky, novelty and stimulation had become major sources of 'consumer' satisfaction by the middle of the 1970s. T. Scitovsky, *The Joyless Economy: An Inquiry into Human Satisfaction* (Oxford, 1976), pp.31–57.

112. According to some commentators we have now entered an era where the core source of economic value is the experience. The stronger the expected experience, the greater its value. This is an extension of the Scitovsky argument cited above. See, for example, J. Pine and J. Gilmore, *The Experience Economy* (Boston, 1999).

14

The Reinvention of Australia for the Sydney 2000 Olympic Games

TARA MAGDALINSKI

Following the announcement of Sydney's candidacy for the 2000 Olympic Games in 1991, the city was cast as an ideal host in several ways. Australian historian Frank Farrell suggests that there is a particular 'Australian reverence' for the Olympics that makes it a plausible host. In addition, he argues 'Australia has been regarded as a safe haven for the Olympics because the Games are taken seriously, no effort is spared to make them a success, and there is an absence of any organised opposition'.[1] Furthermore, the reliance on Sydney's natural beauty, on the friendliness of the population and on the city's commitment to an environmentally friendly games culminated in an image of Sydney as a successful and worthy host. Since then, civic boosters continued to generate internal and external interest in the Games and to present Australians as unified behind this sporting event. Nationally, attempts were made by not only the Sydney Organising Committee for the Olympic Games (SOCOG) but a plethora of other corporations, taskforces, educational institutions and media concerns to create and sustain a frenzy of interest and the unqualified support of the Australian public.

The mechanisms used to generate such interest have been wide-ranging. Games organizers teamed with state and federal education departments to create Olympic education packages designed to teach Australia's children to 'Share the Spirit', advertising campaigns were devised with Olympic themes for products as diverse as soy milk and insurance, and Olympic memorabilia and souvenirs have been hawked on the internet and in The Olympic Stores to provide Australians and tourists alike with the chance to 'experience' the Olympics. Despite the variety of these campaigns, they have been unified by a common theme. Each relied on a knowledge and appreciation of the nation's sporting past, as well as Australia's current position in the global sports fraternity, to provoke public interest. At the same time, Australia as a progressive nation, described as hosting the first Games of a new millennium, has been positioned as a 'clean' nation, one that is interested more in the 'pure performance' of the amateur ideal than in overly and overtly professionalized sport. Such sentiments are embodied in the environmental rhetoric of the bid, the hardline stance on performance enhancing drugs and the promotion of past and present 'wholesome' Aussie sporting heroes.

The presentation of Australia as clean and green symbolizes more than simply a return to the 'ideals' of Olympism. It is part of (white middle-class Anglo-Celtic) Australia's quest to 'return' to itself, to a mythical Australia, an idealistic nation caught in the imagined monocultural paradise of 1950s suburbia. It is, as Roger Bromley suggests, the projection of a utopia into the past.[2] Part of this utopia is the memory of the Melbourne 1956 Olympic Games, staged during the 'glory years of Australian sport'.[3] It is remembered variously as 'Australia's greatest contribution to world sport',[4] 'one of Australia's proudest sporting moments'[5] and 'the last of the innocent Games'.[6] Success in international sport was regarded as evidence of the 'successful development of Australian society', whilst the 'gradual slide' in Olympic performance between Melbourne and the 1980 Moscow Games revealed a stagnation in this progress.[7] The reorganization of Australian sport that catapulted it into the scientized and technological realm, beginning with the opening of the Australian Institute of Sport (AIS) in 1981, heralded the return to international sporting prestige that remained within living memory of many Australians. The culmination of the restoration to sporting renown is the reappearance of the Olympic games on Australian soil.

Despite the fact that Australia's sporting past is a prevalent theme throughout preparations for the Olympic celebration,. the role of sports history is generally underestimated when dealing with the production of national identities and histories. Whilst many have agreed that a sense of shared history and an understanding of a common path is crucial in asserting identification with a particular national territory, few have identified the processes whereby sports history is incorporated into initiatives to create collective identities. The case of the Sydney 2000 Olympics provides a useful insight into the ways that sport, and more specifically sports history, can be included in national activities designed to inculcate an appreciation of a common past and shared destiny amongst its citizens. Specifically, as they are consolidated in commemorative events and national celebrations, sport and sports history become part of an overall process of producing an image of national unity.

It is this link between future and past sporting glories and its implications for Australian identity as well as the process of producing an idealized national sporting history that is explored in this essay. The focus is initially on the process of history in identity construction. In contemporary societies it is impossible to discuss the making of histories in popular imagination without some discussion of the media, which, in Australia, is highly centralized. The focus then turns to two main themes that have emerged in reinventing Australia and the sporting past for the 2000 Olympics: the history of Australian Olympic performance and Australia's role in the modern Olympics; followed by the massive scientization of Australian sport since 1980. Australia has been a leader in the development of scientific approaches to sport and élite sports training spending hundreds of millions of dollars in the pursuit of greater international sporting glory. Yet, at the same time, there have been moves to downplay this reliance on technologies to enhance bodily performance by positioning Australia as a clean sporting nation, one that supports the level playing field and 'fair play', and as a crusader against the use of illegal performance enhancing substances.

WINNING THE GAMES

The 2000 Olympic Games were awarded to Sydney in 1993 after the International Olympic Committee's (IOC) lengthy electoral procedure, during which delegates initially favoured Beijing. Sydney's success was explained by reference to its 'clean, green' approach, and by default because of Beijing's appalling human rights record.[8] Despite an expensive campaign to procure votes for Sydney, success for the Australian city was only assured in the final round of voting with Sydney winning by 45 votes to 43 after trailing Beijing in the first three rounds of voting.[9] Yet the millions spent to guarantee Sydney's success pale into insignificance when compared with the hundreds of millions spent on infrastructure to stage the Games. To pay for the Olympics, public resources have been diverted from other sectors such as education and health. On the day that the Sydney victory was announced, the New

South Wales State Government closed three hospitals at the loss of 225 beds and 800 jobs.[10] Despite the expense of hosting the Games, the Sydney Olympics was expected to generate a large return primarily through increased tourism. Australian academic and media critic Mackenzie Wark stated in 1994:

> Sydney, I can tell you, is in it for the money. It's part of the local poker-machine mentality about economic development: gambling 29 million Australian dollars on winning the Olympics is the developmental equivalent of putting your wages into one of those one-armed bandit poker machines in any licensed club in Sydney, hoping to hit the jackpot.[11]

The Sydney Olympic Bid Committee ensured their chances would exceed normal casino odds. Yet, from late 1998, there have been public revelations about the Sydney bid team's use of 'inducements' to various IOC delegates. As the scandals intensified throughout 1999, officials from SOCOG as well as other public leaders involved in both the bid process and the subsequent organization of the Games argued that the strategies employed to secure IOC votes were not dissimilar to those employed by rival bidding cities.[12] Given the potential economic returns that could be generated from a successful Olympics, the prize was regarded as far too great to leave to chance and every plausible opportunity to procure pledges of support from IOC delegates was pursued, including pairing New South Wales schools with individual IOC members to assist in the lobbying process.[13]

Since then, Games organizers have been beset with a number of controversies, including the investigation of Australian IOC members Phil Coles and Kevan Gosper, ticketing fiascos and fears of a budget shortfall, each of which have been discussed regularly in the popular press despite a largely compliant and highly-centralized domestic media. Notwithstanding these setbacks, Olympic officials, state and federal governments and the media in general have colluded to promote Australia as most 'sporty' and as a nation that embodies the true spirit of Olympism. Even academics have entered into this discourse, reiterating, without supporting evidence, that 'the Olympics are probably taken more seriously, and watched more avidly, in Australia than in any other country'.[14]

The 2000 Olympic Games, the onset of a new millennium and the centenary of Australian federation in 2001 have provided potent opportunities for the exploration of Australian identity and nostalgic remembering in a climate of economic restructuring and social turmoil. In a growing era of political disquiet, where right-wing fundamentalism is increasing, where indigenous and migrant issues are threatening the homogeneity of Australia's political and social landscape and where the Asian economic crisis threatened national economic security, the Olympic Games provided a useful cultural focal point around which images of the Australian nation could be generated. In particular, Australia's sporting past assumed a primary position in the process of provoking a cohesive national identity. Before an analysis of the nexus between the Olympic Games and Australian identity can occur, we must consider the processes by which 'histories' are produced and elements of past cultural identities are selected in order to gloss over social and political change. Of significance in this process is the construction or 'invention' of national traditions that link the present and the future with a chosen past. While Eric Hobsbawm has pointed out the significance of sport to the emergence of mass national traditions in late nineteenth-century Europe, this has been intensified many times over in the mass mediated televisual cultures of the late twentieth century.[15]

HISTORY AND IDENTITY

Stuart Hall explains that 'national cultures construct identities by producing meanings about "the nation" with which we can *identify*'.[16] 'Meanings' about the nation are easily drawn from a national history that posits the new state as the legitimate outcome of a linear development through the display of myths of a common heritage. Anthony Smith suggests that the reliance on the past for legitimacy is not uncommon and that in such cases of rapid social upheaval there is an overriding need to 'mask the radicalism of social change with a veil of tradition and continuity with an assumed past, usually a national one'.[17] He further argues that a return to the past is essential for the formation of identity as 'there can be no collective cultural identity without shared memories or a sense of continuity'.[18] According to Hall, national histories belong to the 'narrative of the nation' that provide 'a set of stories, images, landscapes, scenarios, historical events, national symbols and rituals which stand for or *represent*, the shared experiences, sorrows, and triumphs and disasters which give meaning to the nation'.[19] In many ways, ceremony and symbolism are responsible for the success and durability of national identity as 'it is the area in which individual identity is most closely bound up with collective identity'.[20]

People locate their historical consciousness or identity within traditions, defined by Hobsbawm and Terence Ranger as 'a set of practices, normally governed by overtly or tacitly accepted rule and of a ritual or symbolic nature, which seek to inculcate certain values and norms of behaviour by repetition, which automatically implies continuity with the past'.[21] For a nation, traditions provide a sense of continuity by linking the present and future with aspects of a nation's past deemed positive and appropriate, for as Paul Gottfried states, traditions 'look for a correlation between various contrived pasts and the political and social changes of the modern era'.[22] Yet, whilst we regard ourselves and our society as the culmination of all that has gone before, traditions remain crucial as they supply individuals with an historical comfort that provides tangible evidence of their relationship to former times and places. As a result, the (idealized) past provides the present not only with an ancestral basis but also with historical legitimation. But it is not as simple as relying on past events or a narrative to provide a sense of order, progress and rationality to what are largely random events. There is a proclivity to 'project utopias into the past, rather than the future',[23] which demonstrates that remembering and nostalgia are more about what we wish we were than about 'the way we never were'.[24]

Drawing upon Stephanie Coontz's work on American families and the 'nostalgia trap', I argue that the Australian nation is: 'Like most visions of a "golden age", ... an ahistorical amalgam of structures, values, and behaviors that never coexisted in the same time and place'.[25] The Australia of the public's imagination is, upon closer examination, revealed to be just such 'an ahistorical amalgam'. Yet such images allow citizens to retreat into nostalgic recollections of a happier past when their world appeared to be more stable and when they had more individual or collective, real or imagined power, even if they personally did not experience the era. As F. Da J. Silva and Faught argue, 'Nostalgia requires a collective emotional reaction toward, if not an identification with, a symbolization of the past.'[26] But as Bromley suggests, 'nostalgia is never simply a passive reflection of the "good old days". In fact, it is an active process of styling and "making" the past.'[27] It is this active process of making the past that is of interest in this essay. The cultural narratives that surround sport are part of a larger project to ensure the continued support for public expenditure on events of corporate interest disguised as being beneficial for everyone. Given that most Australians, indeed most of the several billion people globally who will 'participate' in the Olympic Games, will do so in the comfort of their own living room via a bricolage of images, soundbites and commentaries, it is important to identify some of the processes by which the nation is actively constructed through sporting events whilst drawing upon historical images that are promoted as representative of 'ordinary', 'Mums and Dads' of Australia.

National celebrations become increasingly significant during times of rapid social change, as societies or states 'project themselves into the future', while at the same time 'grappling' with the 'legacy of the past'.[28] On a national scale, public recollection demands an encompassing revival and analysis of history, as the 'reassuring presence of the past allows the society to move into the future with confidence'.[29] Australian sports history, however, does not reveal a continuous golden era, thus the myths of a cohesive and triumphant sporting past must be carefully orchestrated. James von Geldern suggests that 'to avoid ensnaring the new culture in the old, the past had to be remembered selectively'. Positive and appropriate elements of the past are designated as events to be celebrated and the past is transformed into a 'myth of destiny'.[30]

Connecting the present to the past through a recovery of sports history has proven useful in the evocation of an Australian identity at the end of the twentieth century, particularly as major sports events are imbued with significant cultural power. Included in a recovery of this past is the search for sporting figures, both past and present, who embody those ideals considered representative of Australians, such as the bushman, or the 'Aussie battler'. The values and ideals of 'Australianness' can be communicated effectively through this cultural medium to the citizenry. Indeed, the political 'neutrality' that pervades hegemonic Western concepts of sport allows it to become a powerful site of socialization. Sports history and the ideals of Australianness are packaged for public consumption through the construction of sporting traditions. Sporting traditions are fashioned and perpetuated making use of the broadcast media, newspapers and popular magazines, books for the popular market written by journalists or sport historians, the work of academic sport historians as well as public celebrations such as the Olympics, which rely on a combination of emotion and history to construct potent meanings about the state.

SPORT, THE MEDIA AND THE STATE IN LATE
TWENTIETH-CENTURY AUSTRALIA

The media have been the primary site where hegemonic opinions and images of the Australian nation have been disseminated to the populace. Whereas once national communities relied almost exclusively on a sense of a shared past, a common future and perhaps a shared genetic heritage to 'imagine' the nation, the nation is now consumed by the citizenry as a pastiche of images and texts that augur 'a sense of connectedness and solidarity' to other members of the 'televised' community by providing 'information … about the past and present that helps to create a common culture and system of values, traditions and ways of looking at the world'.[31] Stuart Cunningham and Elizabeth Jacka argue that communication technologies, in this sense, have the ability to 'respatialize' the world, 'to create new cultural geographies, that is, to link already existing communities or even to create new ones'.[32] The Olympics and other major sporting events operate within this system in a similar manner. Not only is the Australian nation 'brought together' as the Olympics is experienced, both prior to and during the Games, as a televisual narrative, but new imagined (national and global) communities can be invented for and just as easily dismantled after this event. In a sense, it is a mediated 'Olympic truce', where social, economic and political differences are obscured in favour of a 'unifying' experience that encourages viewers to 'share the spirit'. What is significant in terms of sport's and in this case study, the Olympics', ability to generate preferred understandings of the national community, is that 'sport does not antagonize political authorities. It provides drama and excitement while remaining politically uncontroversial and trivial'.[33] Thus political agendas are more easily communicated through the guise of an allegedly apolitical activity. This process is augmented by the fact that in the 1990s three media groups controlled virtually all of Australia's commercial media, News Corporation, Consolidated Press Holdings and John Fairfax, with Rupert Murdoch's News Limited controlling seventy per cent of the Australian print media.[34]

   The pervasiveness of television in particular has prompted conservative and liberal politicians alike to regard sport as a mechanism to 'reach' the people, to present themselves as accessible, as 'everyday' and as traditional Australian 'blokes'. Jim McKay and David Rowe argue that sport supplied the requisite mechanism by which Prime Minister

Bob Hawke could advance his government's policies throughout the 1980s.[35] Hawke used numerous sporting events to promote national healing and a 'can-do' attitude. Beginning with the victory of Australia II over the United States in the 1983 America's Cup, successive Australian governments, prime ministers and corporations have increasingly sought popular legitimation or market exposure by linking themselves with sporting successes. Yet, the use of sport by politicians in particular is by no means a recent phenomenon. Prime Minister Robert Menzies, during his long tenure in office from the late 1940s through to the mid-1960s, often linked himself to the largely successful Australian cricket team in his speeches and references to Australia's all-time greatest cricketer, Sir Donald Bradman.[36] Recent advertisements encouraging Australians to prepare for and celebrate the centenary of federation draw upon Australia's first Prime Minister Edmund Barton's interest in cricket. The ad further questions what kind of nation would have a cricket team before a federation, further propagating an image of a 'sporty' Australia.

INVENTING AUSTRALIA'S OLYMPIC HISTORY

It is often reported that Australians have a 'passionate attachment' to sport that surpasses any other nation.[37] Such notions developed out of late nineteenth-century conceptions of Australia as having a healthy climate where people spent more time in active outdoor pursuits than their English counterparts. By the early 1900s there was a belief that Australia and other settler colonies produced healthier manly specimens. These thoughts were confirmed for many post-Boer War reports of numerous commissions called to investigate reasons for the poor physical condition of British recruits. Reports, such as the 1904 *Report of the Interdepartmental Committee on Physical Deterioration*,[38] established that young men from Australia, Canada and New Zealand were healthier and made better troops in the war.[39] On many indicators, however, Australians have not been particularly more 'sporty' than people from many other nations, though the per capita rate of success in some international sports has been relatively high.[40] Although academics have begun to partially deconstruct assertions about sporting success, the national (and international) perception that Australians are an outdoor, rugged, athletic breed, encompassed in the 'bronzed Aussie', the Ironman or surf-lifesaver, is perpetuated by the media, particularly leading up to international sporting events.[41] Such representations draw upon a long line of international observers such as Mark Twain, Anthony Trollope and D.H. Lawrence, who each commented on the robust nature of Australians and their interest in sporting activities.[42] This myth of physical prowess has also been reinforced by Australia's long history of successes in several international sports such as rugby union, rugby league, cricket and netball. Winning the right to host the Olympics, however, put Australia squarely on the world sports stage, or, as former Prime Minister Paul Keating asserted, in the 'swim with the big boys'.[43]

Part of the myth of the national passion for sport has relied on the construction of close ties between Australia and the modern Olympic Games. This relationship has been dated back to the first modern Games in 1896 and was extended forward to the staging of the Sydney 2000 Games, capping off over a century of 'uninterrupted' involvement in this international multi-sport festival. Some academic historians have enthused that, as a result, 'Australia has had a long love affair with the Olympics'.[44] Australian athletes attending the Olympics have been described as 'among the most dedicated participants'.[45] Farrell further suggests a direct link between Olympism and the 'Australian character', which is enhanced by what he terms the 'special historical connections between Australia and modern Greece'.[46] The media are also complicit in this process. Channel Seven's *The Olympic Show* provides those who surf their website with a potted history entitled 'The Olympics – An Australian Tradition' outlining the significant moments of Australia's Olympic history, categorized neatly into three distinct timeframes: 'Sporting Australia Pre-World War II', 'The Golden Days (1956–1972) and 'Return to Glory' (1992–).[47] This periodization demonstrates the misremembering of Olympic history and the way in which this invented tradition is used to position Australia as central to the modern Olympics and the modern Olympics as central to the construction of Australian identity.

Olympic historians in Australia are proud to announce that Australia is one of two countries in the world to have participated in every modern Olympic Games since their inception in 1896.[48] The claim is rather dubious given that firstly, Australia was not a nation in 1896 when its 'sole representative' Edwin Flack won the 800 and 1500 metres. Secondly, Flack was born in England and was studying there when he decided to go to Athens as a representative of the London Athletic

Club.[49] Australian Olympic historian Harry Gordon points out that Flack's 1896 victories were attributed to Great Britain as late as 1936 and that reports at the time referred to him as an Englishman.[50] Despite these British ties and his English birth, Gordon discusses Flack's 'real origin' as being Australian, thus joining those who have eagerly claimed Australia's one link to 1896. So pervasive is the myth of Flack's heritage that Ian Jobling's entry on the Olympic Games in the second edition of the *Oxford Companion to Australian Sport* does not mention Flack's British connections, proposing instead that 'the success of a sole Melbourne athlete, Edwin Flack … established the history and tradition of Australian and the Olympic movement'.[51]

Even after the IOC only recognized nations, not individual competitors, in 1908 and 1912, Australia and New Zealand competed together as Australasia with the flag bearers on both occasions being New Zealanders (H. St. A. Murray and Malcolm Champion). Furthermore, Champion won a gold medal as a member of the 4 x 200m swimming relay team in 1912 along with three Australians.[52] There has been much trans-Tasman interaction and migration, particularly during the early twentieth century. Australasia's first IOC member, Leonard Cuff, was a New Zealander at the time of his appointment, though he moved to Tasmania later in his career.[53] This shared Australasian history has been obscured to the extent that in many accounts the Australian Olympic history that celebrates the nation's international dedication to sport has become fact and is subsequently replicated without question or rigorous historical analysis. In addition, Australia's imperial connections are overshadowed amongst these attempts to cast Australia as near unique in Olympic history. As Katharine Moore has demonstrated, this era was also the pinnacle of moves to create a Pan-Britannic Festival of sports, and debates about the fielding of a British Empire Olympic team abounded.[54] Indeed, 'Australian' victories in 1896 and 1900 occurred under the British flag with Australasian symbols used in 1908 and 1912. Thus Australian Olympic symbols consistently appear only from 1920 onwards.

The next historical moment that has been used to confirm Australia's 'glorious' sporting history is the Melbourne Olympic Games, which were held at the height of the 'golden days' of Australian sport. The 1956 Olympics frequently reminds, or is used to remind, Australians of their young country emerging on the world stage, of a happier Australia, of a time when young Australians could dream of reaching the Olympics with a few hours training each week; it was a simpler time for the country and for sport. As a result, 1956 has held a powerful place in the Australian Olympic imagination representing not only a yearning for 'our' Olympic yesteryear, in a time when Australia was 'united', but a time when sport was amateur and when Australians staged the best Games in the world. Most potently, the 1956 Olympics is remembered as 'the last of the innocent Games',[55] in other words, the last of the amateur Olympics, without corruption and without scandals. This 'innocence' is reclaimed through the advertising of the Sydney Games and is framed by athletic bodies and the 'environmentally friendliness' of the Olympic site, culminating in the conviction that Australia will return not only the Games but the nation to a state of innocence.

'Innocence' is embodied, for example, in the athletes who represented Australia during the 1950s and who are regularly paraded as evidence of the triumphs of the past, as well as current representatives who are deemed to be 'clean' and healthy, free from the scourge of performance enhancing drugs. According to Smith, a nation must be able to 'unfold a glorious past, a golden age of saints and heroes' who are venerated as role models. Australian sports history is replete with designated heroic events and people, effectively supplying a plethora of apolitical, sanitized heroes.[56] Australian sporting greats, such as Dawn Fraser and Herb Elliott, are exhibited at national and international sporting events to substantiate the nation's 'golden age of saints and heroes'.[57] These heroes have been further packaged by Channel Seven, the local host broadcaster, as the network's 'Olympic legends'.[58] Six of the seven 'legends' participated during this golden era, with four of them winning medals at the 1956 Games. Despite this memorializing, the 1956 Olympic organizers were confronted with a range of problems, including the threat of losing the Games, boycotts, post-colonial struggles and Cold War politics. The 'war on the water' between Soviet and Hungarian water polo players, the Egyptian boycott and other more 'unsavoury' elements have been all but erased from the popular Australian remembering and reconstruction of 1956.

'RETURN TO GLORY'[59]

Between 1956 and the 1976 Montreal Olympics, there was a steady decline in Australia's overall medal count at the summer Games, as the nation dropped to 32nd in the world, suggesting that Australia was out of step with the top performing nations in élite sport. As Brian Stoddart has suggested, however, 'it was not so much that Australian sports fortunes had slumped since 1956, it was just that the rest of the world had drawn away'.[60] Indeed, as Cashman argues, Australia's dismal performance in Montreal was more a demonstration of the problem of relying on philanthropic financial backing, whilst other national teams received generous public funding.[61] Despite a public belief in the virtues of amateurism and the support of mass sport, changes in élite sports funding were quickly mooted, supported by a 1975 report that strongly recommended the establishment of the AIS.[62] Sport had become part of the Commonwealth's agenda from 1972 and by the end of the 1970s there was increasing bipartisan support for the governmental funding, though by the 1980s, the federal commitment to sport lay primarily in the area of élite sport, which, it was suggested, would encourage greater grass-roots participation.[63]

The foundation of the AIS was perhaps the first major step in the construction of a 'gold medal factory' that would ensure Australia's 'return to glory'. The growing financial backing of élite sport, the foundation of the AIS and the increasingly centralized organisation of sport throughout the 1980s were tied to the recognition that Australian sport could not match the successes of communist nations without adopting the organizational strategies and the more professional and scientific approach to 'producing' athletes that had underscored the success of Eastern Bloc athletes. Thus, the popular image of a 'monster' eastern European sports network, intent on seeking and selecting future star athletes, no longer had currency as Australia increasingly and whole-heartedly adopted so-called 'communist' training and managerial techniques. This is not to say, however, that the Australian sporting fraternity abandoned the principles of amateurism, including the notions of natural talent and hard work, in favour of scientized professionalism. The amateur rhetoric remained in force throughout the 1980s and into the 1990s, even as Australian sport's 'new order' was launched into the international arena, a 'new order' that came at a tremendous cost.

In the financial year 1973–74 Australian government expenditure on sport was A$5.7 million dollars rising only to A$8.2 million in 1980–81 before the opening of the AIS. By 1984–85 A$31.2 million was spent on promoting both élite and mass sport.[64] The Confederation of Australian Sport, which formed in 1976, urged the government to formulate a national sporting policy and to increase its support of élite athletes. A *Master Plan for Sport* was released in 1980 and by 1983 a *National Sports Plan* appeared. Two government reports in 1988 and 1990, *Going for Gold* and *Can Sports Be Bought?* solidified consensus around a national sports strategy. By 1994–95, 25 per cent of Australian schools were involved in talent identification programmes whereby children between the ages of 12 and 17 are tested for a range of sporting skills and subjected to a series of tests and measurements devised to predict sporting success. About two per cent of those children are invited to a second phase of sport-specific testing programs run by state and regional academies and institutes of sport.[65]

In 1994, after Sydney had won the bid for the 2000 Olympics, the Australian Sports Commission, which distributes government funding for sport, began a six-year élite development programme aimed at winning 60 medals in Sydney including 20 gold. The Olympic Athlete Program (OAP), which has a stated objective of 'medal success', received a total of over A$400 million through a combination of state and federal government funding including A$72 million from the Australian Olympic Committee.[66] This programme operates on the assumption that increased funding of élite sport will return a larger number of medals, and as a result, the funding profile was increased considerably after a performance review of summer Olympic sports conducted following the Atlanta Games.[67] In 1995 the OAP director argued that they 'have charts that have mapped funding increases from 1976 through to 1994 for all sports against their international results and they do correlate. We're as confident as we can be that if you provide more money, you can get better performances.'[68] By the late 1990s around 90 per cent of government funding of sport and physical activity, which surpassed $100 million in the 1999–2000 federal budget, went to support élite sporting programmes. While other sectors such as education and health care have been cut in recent years, funding for athletes and Olympic projects has increased dramatically.[69]

The new commitment to élite sport delivered sought-after results, and as early as 1982–84 the increased investment seemed to be making returns. Stoddart pointed out in 1986 that in the euphoria of 1983–84 most people did not recognize the changing circumstances surrounding renewed Australian international sporting success: 'these victories were made possible by sporting conditions quite different from those of earlier generations ... A careful reading of the 1983–84 experience delves into the realms of finance, professionalism, technology, the media, the commercialisation of sport and it advancing connections with the world of work.'[70] The Australian public, on one hand, continued to regard sporting successes as a result of simple dedication and hard work rather than 'serious' training methods. The end result of the new finance and commercialism was fully revealed in successful performances at subsequent summer Olympic Games with Australia's tally rising to seven gold and 27 overall medals at the 1992 Barcelona Games and culminating in a record haul of 41 medals for Australia at the 1996 Atlanta Olympics. It was Australia's 'return to glory' that was supplied by a 'new order of Australian sport'.[71] Expectations for 2000 were thus raised considerably.

Despite formative changes in the philosophy of élite sport in Australia, the dramatic ideological shifts have been contextualized in a more palatable manner. John Daly's history of the AIS initially foregrounds the athletic successes of the 1950s and 1960s, but then argues that the situation changed by the 1970s when 'other nations had realised the value of sporting success in developing national pride, in encouraging a healthy emulative lifestyle and perhaps even as an extension of foreign policy ... Australians found themselves amateurs in a world of professionals – possessing a sporting past but not a future unless they were prepared to buy success'.[72] Such an analysis concurs with more popularist depictions of this era. *The Olympic Show* website reveals that: 'A dearth of gold in Montreal in 1976 coincided with a cut in government spending on sport and, as would later be revealed, an increase in drug-induced performances, particularly from Eastern Bloc countries.'[73] Presenting Australia as a lost amateur soul adrift in a sea of professional scientists 'frames' the changes in Australian sport from the late 1970s as an inevitability. Rather than acknowledging that Australian politicians recognized the potential prestige to be gained from the Olympics and in fact drove this transformation, the implication is that if Australia wanted to remain competitive then it simply had to give in and adopt these new training regimes.

CONCLUSION

In order to legitimate the diversion of massive national resources to sport, there has been a renewed emphasis on promoting a successful Australian sporting past, which has relied on establishing and promoting links between the Sydney 2000 Olympic Games, Melbourne's Games in 1956 and the origins of the modern Olympic movement. The reconstruction of the historical record to legitimate an Australian claim to have been at all the summer Olympics immediately demonstrates the manipulation of history to confirm Australia's reputation as a 'sporty' nation, and as a deserving recipient of the Sydney Olympics. In the process, an Australian Olympic tradition is constructed which is largely mythical. From 'our' first gold medallist, Edwin Flack, in 1896, to the 'glory days' of the Melbourne Olympics, through the desolate years of the 1970s, to finally a return to the international centre stage, Australians are raised on a steady diet of sporting nationalism that positions the nation as a important world sporting power, confirmed by a largely undisputed athletic heritage.

The 1956 Games in particular have become a focal point for the promotion of the Sydney Olympics, which has relied heavily on nostalgic representations of Australia in this more innocent era. This 'golden era' of Australian sport has been celebrated as the truest and perhaps the last expression of the philosophies of Olympism, whilst promulgating the middle-class ideology that valorizes suburbia and conservative politics. As a result, the emergence of a 'new order' that 'returned Australia to glory' on the back of science and technology has been couched in the familiar discourses of family and nostalgia, reminding the Australian public of the values of a not forgotten era. These images collude to present an Australian Olympic tradition that has more to do with the projection of a utopia back onto Australia's post-Second World War past, than with any effort to accurately capture and portray Australia's sporting traditions. These processes effectively construct a homogeneous Australian identity that relies as much on a bush mythology of colonial Australia as it does on the 'bronzed' Aussie athlete. Australia has moved into the twenty-first century with commemorative markers – the 2000 Olympics, the 2001 centenary of the Federation and a host of other major events – scheduled by politicians and media for the opening years of the nation's second century together with the 'reconstruction' of an imagined national history based on the projection of selected memories and the obliteration of rejected memories, the purpose of which is to define what it means to be Australian and to marginalize alternative interpretations of Australian identity and the Australian past.

NOTES

1. F. Farrell, 'Australian Identity', in Richard Cashman and Anthony Hughes (eds.), *Staging the Olympics: The Event and its Impact* (Sydney, 1999), p.59.
2. R. Bromley, *Lost Narratives: Popular Fictions, Politics and Recent History* (London, 1988), p.5.
3. D. Booth and C. Tatz, *One-eyed: A View of Australian Sport* (Sydney, 2000), p.136.
4. Farrell, 'Australian Identity', p.63.
5. B. Stoddart, *Saturday Afternoon Fever: Sport in the Australian Culture* (Sydney, 1986), p.27.
6. H. Gordon, *Australia at the Olympic Games* (Brisbane, 1994), p.203.
7. Stoddart, *Saturday Afternoon Fever*, p.25.
8. D. Prasad, 'Environment', in Cashman and Hughes, *Staging the Olympics*.
9. D. Booth and C. Tatz, 'Swimming with the Big Boys?: The Politics of Sydney's 2000 Olympic Bid', *Sporting Traditions*, 11, 1 (1994), 20; A. Burroughs, 'Winning the Bid', in Cashman and Hughes, *Staging the Olympics*, p.43.
10. Booth and Tatz, 'Swimming with the Big Boys?', 16.
11. M. Wark, *Virtual Geography: Living with Global Media Events* (Bloomington, 1994), p.147.
12. R. McGeoch, *The Bid: How Australia won the 2000 Games* (Melbourne, 1994), pp.78–96; Burroughs, 'Winning the Bid'; D. Booth, 'Gifts of Corruption? Ambiguities of Obligation in the Olympic Movement', *Olympika*, 8 (1999), 43–68.
13. McGeoch, *The Bid*, p.142.
14. Farrell, p.59. In this chapter Farrell makes a number of unsubstantiated sweeping assertions about Australian identity; for a critique see J. Nauright, '"The End of Sports History?": From Sports History to Sports Studies', *Sporting Traditions*, 16, 1 (1999), particularly pp.9–10.
15. See E. Hobsbawm, 'Mass-Producing Traditions: Europe 1870–1914', in E. Hobsbawm and T. Ranger (eds.), *The Invention of Tradition* (Cambridge, 1983), pp.288–91, 299–306.
16. S. Hall, 'The Question of Cultural Identity', in S. Hall, D. Held and T. McGrew (eds.), *Modernity and its Futures* (Cambridge, 1992), p.293.
17. A. Smith, 'The Nation: Invented, Imagined, Reconstructed?', *Millennium: Journal of International Studies*, 20, 3 (1991), 356.
18. A. Smith, 'National Identity and the Idea of European Unity', *International Affairs*, 68, 1 (1992), 58.
19. Hall, 'The Question of Cultural Identity', p.293.
20. A. Smith, *National Identity* (London, 1991), p.162.
21. Hobsbawm and Ranger, *The Invention of Tradition*, p.1.
22. P. Gottfried, 'Second Thoughts on Traditions', *Telos*, 94 (1993), 71.
23. Bromley, *Lost Narratives*, p.5.
24. S. Coontz, *The Way We Never Were: American Families and the Nostalgia Trap* (New York, 1992).
25. Coontz, *The Way We Never Were*, p.9.
26. F. Da Silva and J. Faught, 'Nostalgia: A Sphere and Process of Contemporary Ideology', *Qualitative Sociology*, 5 (1982), 49.
27. Bromley, *Lost Narratives*, p.4.
28. P. Connerton, *How Societies Remember* (Cambridge, 1989), p.5.
29. J. von Geldern, *Bolshevik Festivals 1917–1920* (Berkeley, 1993), p.140.
30. Ibid., p.12.
31. E. Herman and R. McChesney, *The Global Media: The New Missionaries of Global Capitalism* (London, 1997), pp.2–3.
32. S. Cunningham and E. Jacka, *Australian Television and International Mediascapes* (Cambridge, 1996), p.8.
33. Herman and McChesney, *The Global Media*, p.76.
34. Wark, *Virtual Geography*, p.8.
35. J. McKay and D. Rowe, 'Ideology, the Media, and Australian Sport', *Sociology of Sport Journal*, 4 (1987), 265.
36. R. Cashman, *Paradise of Sport. The Rise of Organised Sport in Australia* (Melbourne, 1995), p.120.
37. For a recent example, see F. Farrell, 'Australian Identity', p.68.

38. Cd 2175, *Report of the Interdepartmental Committee on Physical Deterioration* (London, 1904).
39. For a fuller discussion of this issue, see J. Nauright, 'Colonial Manhood and Imperial Race Virility: British Responses to Post-Boer War Colonial Rugby Tours', in J. Nauright and T.J.L. Chandler (eds.), *Making Men: Rugby and Masculine Identity* (London, 1996), pp.121–39.
40. J. McKay, *No Pain, No Gain. Sport and Australian Culture* (Sydney, 1991); W. Vamplew and B. Stoddart, *Sport in Australia: A Social History* (Melbourne, 1994); Senate Standing Committee on Environment, Recreation and the Arts, *Report on Physical and Sport Education* (Canberra, 1992).
41. See Cashman, *Paradise of Sport*; and McKay, *No Pain, No Gain*.
42. Stoddart, *Saturday Afternoon Fever*, p.15.
43. Booth and Tatz, 'Swimming with the Big Boys?', 4.
44. Farrell, 'Australian Identity', p.59.
45. Ibid., p.59.
46. Ibid., pp.60, 67.
47. 'The Olympics – An Australian Tradition', *The Olympic Show* website, http://www.the olympicshow.seven.com.au/text/history.asp, date of access, 23 March 2000.
48. Ibid.; Farrell, 'Australian Identity', p.59.
49. Gordon, *Australia at the Olympic Games*, p.2.
50. Ibid., pp.8–9.
51. I. Jobling, 'Olympic Games', in W. Vamplew, K. Moore, J. O'Hara, R. Cashman and I. Jobling (eds.), *The Oxford Companion to Australian Sport*, 2nd edition (Melbourne, 1994), p.316.
52. Gordon, *Australia and the Olympic Games*, p.51.
53. For a discussion of Cuff's role in Australasia's early international sporting links and the porous nature of Australasian sporting identity in this period, see M. Letters, 'Leonard Cuff and the Australasian Olympic Movement' (BA Honours thesis, The University of Queensland, 1994).
54. K. Moore, 'One Voice in the Wilderness: Richard Coombes and the Promotion of the Pan-Britannic Festival Concept in Australia 1891–1911', *Sporting Traditions*, 5, 2 (1989), 188–203.
55. Gordon, *Australia at the Olympic Games*, p.203.
56. Smith, *National Identity*, p.161.
57. T. Magdalinski, 'Drugs, Sport and National Identity in Australia', in W. Wilson (ed.), *Doping in Sport* (Champaign: Human Kinetics, 2000).
58. These 'legends' include Dawn Fraser, Murray Rose, Herb Elliott, Shane Gould, Shirley Strickland, Majorie Jackson and Ron Clarke. 'Meet Seven's Olympic Legends', *The Olympic Show* website, http://theolympicshow.seven.com.au/list/legends.asp, date of access 23 March 2000.
59. 'Return to Glory (1992–)', *The Olympic Show* website.
60. Stoddart, *Saturday Afternoon Fever*, p.186.
61. Cashman, *Paradise of Sport*, p.120.
62. D. Booth and C. Tatz, *One-eyed*, pp.174–5.
63. Cashman, *Paradise of Sport*, pp.123–4.
64. D. Semotiuk, 'Commonwealth Government Initiatives in Amateur sport in Australia, 1972–1985', *Sporting Traditions*, 3, 2 (May 1987), 154.
65. J. Nauright, 'Money, Methods and Medals: The Australian Elite Sports System in the 1990s', in K. Hardman (ed.), *Sport for all: Issues and Perspectives in International Context* (Manchester, 1996).
66. Australian Sports Commission, Olympic Athlete Program, , date of access, 23 March 2000.
67. 'ASC sharpens its focus on best Olympic chances', Australian Sports Commission Media Release, 25 Nov. 1998, http://www.ausport.gov.au/ascpress/19981125.html, date of access, 24 March 2000.
68. S. Baker-Finch, *Sports Report* (Canberra, 1995), p.14.
69. (Industry, Science and Resources Portfolio – Agency Budget Statements, Australian Sports Commission, ASC annual reports 95/96; 96/97; 97/98).
70. Stoddart, *Saturday Afternoon Fever*, p.184.
71. 'Return to Glory', *The Olympic Show* website.
72. Daly, *Quest For Excellence*, p.2.
73. 'The Golden Days', *The Olympic Show* website.

Sport and Future Australasian Cult

JOCK PHILLIPS

In May 2000 the sports columns of New Zealand's newspapers, letters to the editor and even editorials were given over to two incidents in the sporting world. The first concerned two rugby players, Tana Umaga and Gordon Slater, who decided to stay at home with their partners and see their daughters born rather than fly to South Africa to play rugby for their Super 12 team, the Hurricanes. The Hurricanes were in contention for the semi-finals of the competition, so many fans were outraged that family responsibility had come before team loyalty. Accusations flew that tough rugby players had become 'snags' (sensitive new age guys). They were 'soft', effeminate, self-centred and regarded the playing of rugby not as an honour but purely as a job. Others pointed out that as professional rugby players, Umaga and Slater were indeed paid to play rugby and that in taking paternal leave, they were acting as would any other paid worker. But to those who saw rugby as a noble endeavour, above the workaday world, to put the family above rugby was sacrilege. The second incident concerned the decision of Russell Coutts and some of his team-mates to desert Team New Zealand and sail for a Swiss syndicate in the next America's Cup. Some six weeks before, the team had paraded through the streets of the country in triumph. People had comforted themselves with the fact that although Australia, not New Zealand, had won the Rugby World Cup the previous year, yet Team New Zealand had demonstrated old-fashioned Kiwi sporting virtues – team-work, modesty, hard work, physical strength, love of country. The yachting triumph reaffirmed sport's moral virtues. Now all this was seen to be empty. Russell Coutts and his men were accused of sacrificing patriotic loyalty for the lure of the dollar. Of course, any objective observer might have noted that dollars had always played a major part in the America's Cup. It was big business, and like any other professional

Coutts was simply responding to a better job offer. But to many in New Zealand his decision was seen as the act of a traitor, by a man who valued love of money above love of country.

The anger which lay behind these two incidents expressed a conflict between two very different understandings of the relationship between sport and society. The two models are explored in various ways in nearly all of the essays in this volume, and it is important to understand them if we are to gain some sense of future trends in Australasian sport and make sense of the anger which we have just described. The first model which was dominant in New Zealand and in most of Australian sport up to about 1960 emphasized the importance of sport in character formation in a modern capitalist world. It saw sport as having a moral imperative. The second model which has become increasing powerful in the last 30 years regards sport as part of the mass media entertainment world in a post-industrial society. Its motivation is money. It is sport as economics, not sport as morality, which is the dominant force. If we want to have an understanding of future trends, it is worth analysing these two models rather more closely.

As British historians have demonstrated, organized sport emerged out of political, cultural and educational change. In order to create order out of disorder, sport required rules and therefore structures and institutions to lay down and enforce those rules. In the nineteenth century British society experienced a change in economic activities, political imperatives and cultural life, sport became a natural ally in the effort to impose new patterns of behaviour and new moral codes on people.[1] In the colonial societies of Australia and New Zealand the value of organized sport in promoting new codes of behaviour was eagerly grasped. Sport was encouraged by the state and especially by schools where the training of young people was centred. In this volume Martin Crotty, J.A. Mangan and Colm Hickey, and David Kirk devote their essays to the important role of sport in the educational system. They emphasize the efforts made predominantly in the past to encourage widespread participation in sport because through playing the game, rather than watching it, important moral training would occur. Sport was then an integral part of socialization.

What was this training meant to accomplish? It was partly designed simply to encourage obedience to rules, to be part of Elias's 'civilizing process'.[2] This was particularly important in late nineteenth-century Australia and New Zealand for two reasons. First, colonial societies have always been anxious about giving in to the frontier mentality and losing civilized standards of behaviour. Organized games became a way of controlling possible frontier anarchy and violence. In New Zealand the enthusiasm with which sports, especially rugby, were encouraged among the Maori reflected an extension of this process to the indigenous people or 'savages'. Both societies were, despite their colonial origins, highly urbanized places. Sport communicated the message that obedience to rules was required in city life. However, one of the fears in both societies as they became even more urbanized and sensed they were losing their 'bush past', was that this urban life might make men 'soft' and 'effeminate'. Sport, as Mangan and Hickey and Crotty lucidly argue, so the argument went, kept men manly and muscular. This was especially important because as the century drew to a close it became clear that the British Empire was faced with likely major military encounters – the war in South Africa was but a prelude for the world conflagration of 1914.[3] In this situation there was no doubt that participation in sport became a training in the discipline and character required for war.[4] And as Douglas Booth shows in his fascinating essay, martial values even penetrated the world of surf lifesaving. Sport as training for war made male sport and associated concepts associated concepts of manliness especially important to the wider culture.

What other moral lessons were thought to have been taught by sport? Some people at the time believed, and some historians subsequently have suggested, that sport also conditioned participants for industrial society. As Australia and New Zealand provided employment for people in factories and bureaucracies, rather than as self-employed rural workers, so team games, it was thought, inculcated values of hard work (through training), delayed gratification and the gains to be made through team-work and cooperative endeavour. Competitive group performance was clearly one model of economic activity in the industrial world. While people did undoubtedly make this connection with sport, there was also an equally strong tendency to view sport as inhabiting a quite separate world from that of business, commerce and money matters. To a considerable degree, of course, this tendency had a class and ethnic dimension. The sports which had been introduced from the British middle and upper classes – cricket, rugby union, tennis – held strongly to the amateur tradition of games as 'above the world of money', while rugby league and Australian football came to accept a semi-professional status. But even in those games, from a 'spectator' perspective, Saturday afternoon was regarded as relief from the everyday grind and a moment for heroic actions. What kept alive such views was partly, of course, the sense of sport as training for war, for in sport as in war men were expected to put themselves on the line for more than just commercial gain and demonstrate the higher male virtues of courage, strength and aggression.

These higher virtues for which sportsmen sacrificed themselves included love of locality and love of country. In colonial societies where there was a high level of geographical mobility, sport was seen as a way of cementing loyalty to place and region – to the inner city communities of Melbourne through the Victorian Football League, to the suburbs of Sydney through their rugby league teams, or to the provinces of New Zealand through the Ranfurly Shield. In test matches love of country was demonstrated and strengthened. Interestingly, before the Great War sport also became a vehicle of 'colonial' identity. New Zealanders tended to back Australia in tests with the MCC because they saw in Australian success a manifestation of the 'colonial' spirit, a reassurance that the colonies could 'foot' it with the 'mother country'. Because sport became a visible outlet for patriotism it inevitably attracted political involvement – for sporting patriotism helped to define the nation, while fighting for one's country on the sports field was a preparation and an inspiration for patriotic death on the battlefield. By the turn of the century diplomacy, politics and sports were enmeshed. In New Zealand after the highly successful 1905 All Blacks Tour, the Prime Minister Richard Seddon became popularly dubbed the 'Minister of Football' and showered the state's largesse on the team;[5] in Australia in 1932–33 the bodyline series led to diplomatic cables at the highest level.

In summary, in the period up to 1960 the perceived value of sport in inculcating moral virtue, 'character' and patriotism was the driving force in the development of sport in Australia and New Zealand. This helps explain its official support and its institutional structure, even if it fails to explain fully why individuals participated in it. Moral virtue embraced hard work, self-discipline and team-work which were of great value in a new, disordered capitalist, urbanized world. It also included physical strength, bravery, endurance and love of country. These qualities were seen as assets in the military struggles of Empire. What followed from this was an emphasis on participation rather than spectatorship, on male sport (for men were the future soldiers) and a view of sport as essentially separate from, and above, the world of money.

What of the last 40 years? Sport as morality is no longer the impetus. Sport as televised entertainment shapes sporting experience. People still play and watch sport for the sheer excitement and thrill of the game; but the context in which this occurs has changed dramatically. The least radical changes, of course, have occurred in the professional games, rugby league and Australian football, but even there, as Ian Andrews shows in this volume, a revolution has occurred. Semi-professional teams of local players who were paid relatively low wages to perform in front of their local communities, have been replaced by highly professional teams whose players earn very high incomes predominantly from sponsorship, advertising and the dues from international television broadcasts of their games. The greatest changes, however, have occurred in the 'English gentlemen's' games of rugby union and cricket. In both cases, the revolution has been brought about primarily through the influence of international television interests. Kerry Packer's 'circus' introduced professionalism and the one-day game to cricket; and Rupert Murdoch's News Corp Ltd was responsible for professional rugby union and the Super 12 and tri-nations' competitions which have become the game's standard-bearers in Australia and New Zealand.[6] Television interests have also been primarily responsible for the traumatic changes to both rugby league and VFL competitions. In 1995–96 there was a ferocious battle for control of Australasian rugby league between Rupert Murdoch's Superleague and Packer's Australian rugby league. The destiny of the sport was determined in the boardrooms of the media moguls.[7] Of course, previous media innovations, especially radio, had a substantial influence upon games – the construction of large rugby grandstands in New Zealand in the inter-war period was partly a consequence of radio producing increased spectator interest – and as Frazer Andrewes points out in this volume, radio played a key role in developing spectator interest in cricket in Australia in the 1930s. But radio never determined the game to the extent that television interests have done.

Television is now part and parcel of the structure and operation of sport in Australia and New Zealand. Spectators at major events now expect to see replays on a big television screen at the ground while the adjudicators – the referees or umpires in all the codes – have now become dependent upon television for determining close calls. On the pitch and around the ground, advertisements are placed there so they can be beamed to the living room audience. The stadiums are no longer designed to ensure the maximum attendance of packed banks of standing males. Television ensures that the codes are not dependent for their revenue upon a large audience at the game itself. So the stadiums focus instead upon providing corporate boxes for the sponsors and comfortable seating for those wanting family entertainment. That entertainment package includes cheer-leaders, performance artists before games, canned music during games and of course, television replays, so that the spectators experience a multimedia television-style experience. Whereas in the 1930s the radio announcers in Australia tried to recreate the sounds and atmosphere of the action at the ground, now television determines the action at the grounds. The timing of the games fits television schedules – Saturday afternoon, when audiences are out shopping or perhaps even playing their own games and when people do not want to be inside watching television – is no longer a favourite time. Instead evenings and Sundays have become popular. People have become so used to watching the game on the screen, that 'virtual games' on the computer have become a significant form of entertainment.

As for the games themselves, they too have been adapted to enhance their entertainment value: test cricket has virtually been replaced as the dominant form of the game by one-day cricket; in rugby the rules have been changed to encourage a more fluid and flowing game. In both codes brand names – the 'Waratahs', the 'Hurricanes' and so on, – build on the media hype and new highly coloured, 'designer' uniforms have made their appearance. The determinative impact of television may be seen sharply in two antipodean examples. One is the extraordinary increase in interest in basketball which followed the increased exposure of the game on television. By 1998 basketball was the second most preferred sport among all New Zealand adolescents.[8] Michael Jordan had a huge following. The second example was the sustained television promotion of Australian rugby league on New Zealand television in the late 1980s and early 1990s. Sydney league teams and players quickly became household names and the seeds were sown for the establishment of the Auckland Warriors.

Several other significant changes follow from the thrusting impact of professional, commercial and media interests. When sport was a form of character and military training, a degree of violence, so long as it was not out of control, and a reasonable number of injuries were acceptable. But television brings violence in slow motion and in replay into the living rooms of the nation, and this arguably is not helpful if you wish to broaden the audience to include women. Further, when players are worth million of dollars in salary and promotion, they are valuable items

– to be kept as far as possible from being hurt. In cricket helmets have been introduced and limits placed on the number of bouncers, while in contact sports such as League and Union increased penalties and judicial procedures have been introduced for rough play.

If sport is no longer a training for war, but part of the entertainment industry, then it need no longer be available primarily to men, nor is there any need to give priority to male sport. Efforts have been made, with some success, to attract women spectators to rugby games. Television New Zealand claimed that 54 per cent of female viewers over the age of five watched the Super 12 semi-final between the Blues and the Highlanders in 1998 which was only 7 per cent less than the figure for male viewers. A quarter of the Canterbury Rugby Supporters Club in that year was female.[9] Attraction is not simply a matter of increased spectatorship; it embraces increased participation. In a year notable for the failure of the All Blacks, the success of the Black Ferns in winning the women's rugby World Cup brought some satisfaction and consolation to the nation. There has also been increasing promotion of exclusively women's sport. The most obvious example is netball where in New Zealand, at least, a sustained exposure on prime time television has significantly broadened male interest in the game. Participation has another aspect to it. Interestingly the most spectacular recent growth in team sports in the country has been in touch rugby – perhaps because of its less violent character, or perhaps even more because the code has set out to encourage participation by women as well as men.

A further consequence of the dominance of television interests over moral training in determining the shape of sport has been the declining importance of local or even national loyalties. In the old order, players were expected to serve their local club, their province, their state and eventually their country loyally throughout their careers. Sport helped promote local and patriotic cohesion and even for the semi-professional codes local loyalty was essential to fill the grounds which brought in the revenue. But television has a national and international audience. Frequently a high proportion of the watchers are not local to one of the teams, in the jargon of the trade they are pure 'theatre-goers' looking for entertainment, and their passions and interests must be aroused. So the 'brand' – the 'Brumbies' or the 'Broncos' – becomes the defining name as if their ACT and Brisbane origins are largely irrelevant. Players follow the money. Rugby, teams are cobbled together from other places; the 'Brumbies', for example, are largely composed of players from

Queensland and New South Wales. Even love of country becomes subordinate to love of fee. New Zealand rugby players now ply their skills in France and Japan, and they have been a significant influence in the teams of the British home unions. A South African Super 12 team has accepted a New Zealand coach. Fiji, Argentina and Ireland have also been coached by New Zealanders. As we have already noted, in yachting, a sport which has been revolutionized in both its funding and public appeal by the invention of computer graphics for display on television, skippers, crew and designers now sell their talents to the highest bidder. Cricket has been rocked by allegations that players have accepted bribes to throw games. Money has even penetrated deep into the world of spectatorship, where Australian bookies and the New Zealand TAB (Totalisator Agency Board) now offer odds on rugby and cricket matches.

Love of country is now superseded by love of the dollar for high-performing sportsmen and women. This has become a source of some concern to the state – not because the state views sport as a preparation for war, but because the state is synonymous with the nation and wishes to encourage feelings of national pride, and because a successful sports team brings international attention and its success aids the economy. Australia's success in attracting the Olympics to Sydney and New Zealand's ability to retain the Americas Cup for Auckland will make a significant difference to the economies of the two countries. So the political response has been to pour money into high-performance sport to create national icons to counter the growing power influence of the mass media dollar. The Australian government's heavy investment in the Australian Institute of Sport and the New Zealand government's $5 million grant to retain America's Cup sailors are good examples.

Political investment has increasingly been directed at the high performers, rather than at mass participators. This is a logical consequence of new imperatives. If sport is no longer about moral training, then mass participation in sports activity is no longer hugely significant. But if sport is about television audiences then attracting spectators through the performances of the élite few is a necessity. There is no longer any need to institutionalize universal participation in team games by means of the school system. Rather energy goes into promoting the élite competitions and attracting the largest audience. To these ends, all the tricks of the entertainment industry are brought to bear – including fast-paced advertisements and the promotion of stars. Of course, even the old order had stars, but they were presented in terms of the moral values they were supposed to embody – physical toughness, loyalty to mates and team, decent and modest behaviour, the image of the well-behaved, heroic soldier in making of Empire. Now the heroes are presented differently: their bodies are used in pin-up calendars; their extrovert often cosmopolitan lifestyles are publicized; their romantic entanglements are scrutinized. Private life was off-limits to the old culture, but in the new it is part and parcel of the means by which audiences are attracted to sport as entertainment.

Since spectatorship, not mass participation, is the goal, it is hardly surprising that the number of active sportsmen and women is not keeping pace with the growing population, for example, in the major codes such as cricket or rugby. In New Zealand in 1974–75, 36 per cent of men under the age of 25 were involved in rugby; by 1991 only 15 per cent aged 19 to 24 were playing the game.[10] Schools and clubs report increasing difficulty in keeping up their numbers. Because traditional team games are now presented as enjoyable entertainment, rather than moral inculcators, they find themselves competing with other sports entertainments. Individualistic pursuits, rather than organized team sports, are now attracting participants, especially those activities which have a spice of thrill and danger such as surfing, mountain-biking and diving. Such pursuits are neither school-based nor team games, nor generally spectator sports. Moral health is no longer the motivation. Individuals do them at their own volition, when they choose to do so. Furthermore, such pursuits importantly are generally more gender-balanced and integrated than traditional team games. Significantly, the team games, which have shown the greatest growth in recent years, have been basketball and touch rugby – two sports characterized by being less organized, more informal and more controlled by participants and which have actively encouraged participation by both males and females,[11] than the traditional team games of the past.

The new revolutionary world of professional television sport is still young in Australia and New Zealand. Many brought up with the old cultural expectations about sport have not found the revolution easy. The lure of money, the apparent rejection of local and patriotic sentiment, the acceptance of sport as a job and a business, the behaviour of extrovert stars who flaunt their sensational lifestyle rather than accept their responsibility as moral exemplars – all this comes hard to generations brought up in the old order. Hence the anger of the letter-writers and columnists with which these reflections began. The shift to the new assumptions which lie beneath sport will not be easy for these generations. Some of the institutions of the old culture – especially amateur clubs – will not easily survive when sponsorship looks to more visible outlets and drinkers prefer to spend time at inner city bars rather than their local club-rooms.

There can be little doubt that sport as it has emerged in the last 30 years is the shape of the future. The presentation of sport and the sports which people choose to enjoy as either participants or spectators will be determined by the discretionary entertainment dollar. As we move further into this world, so we can begin to see, as this volume has revealed and recorded, that the old sporting world of teams and compulsion and moral character was itself a distinct time-bound culture. The distinctive direction of the future bring into sharp relief the uniqueness of our past.

NOTES

1. E. Dunning and K. Sheard, *Barbarians, Gentlemen and Players: A Sociological Study of the Development of Rugby Football* (Oxford, 1979); D. Newsome, *Godliness and Good learning: Four Studies in a Victorian Ideal* (London, 1961); J.A. Mangan, *Athleticism in the Victorian and Edwardian Public School* (London, 2000).
2. N. Elias, *The Civilizing Process* (Oxford, 1982).
3. See J. Phillips, *A Man's Country? The Image of the Pakeha Male – A History*, 2nd edition (Auckland, 1996), p.114; J.A. Mangan, *The Games Ethic and Imperialism: Aspects of the Diffusion of an Ideal* (London, 1998).
4. In the wider context of imperial culture this has been extensively documented by J.A. Mangan, see, for example, Mangan, *Athleticism*, pp. 179-203, Mangan, *The Games Ethic and Imperialism*, pp. 44-70 and more recently J. A. Mangan, 'Duty unto Death: English Masculinity and Militarism in the Age of the New Imperialism', in J. A. Mangan (ed.), *Tribal Identities: Nationalism, Europe, Sport* (London, 1996), pp.10–38 and J.A. Mangan, 'Regression and Progression: Introduction to the Cass Edition', in Mangan, *Athleticism in The Victorian and Edwardian Public School*, pp. xxxix–xviii. This substantial introduction brings the discussion of militarism, imperialism and sport fully up to date.
5. Phillips, *A Man's Country?*, p. 110.
6. J. Cameron and B. Gidlow, 'Sociology of Leisure and Sport', in H.C. Perkins and G. Cushman (eds.), *Time Out? Leisure, Recreation and Tourism in New Zealand and Australia* (Auckland, 1998), p.140.
7. See C. Obel, 'Local and Global Publics: Shifting Popularity in Rugby Union and Rugby League' in Perkins and Cushman (eds.), *Time Out? ...*, p.156.
8. R. Thomson, 'Physical Activity through Sport and Leisure: Traditional versus Non-Competitive Activities', *Journal of Physical Education New Zealand*, 33, 1 (March 2000), 34.
9. *Sunday Star-Times*, 31 May 1998, p.C4.
10. D. Tait, *New Zealand Recreation Survey 1974-5* (Wellington, 1984), pp.16–17; W. Hopkins *et al.*, *Life in New Zealand Survey*, III (Wellington, 1991), p.32.
11. Thomson, 'Physical Activity', p.34; see also J. Phillips, 'Men, Women and Leisure since the Second World War', in C. Daley and D. Montgomery (eds.), *The Gendered Kiwi* (Auckland, 1999), pp.213–33.

Select Bibliography

Manly and Moral:
The Making of Middle-Class Men in the Australian Public Schools
MARTIN CROTTY

Australian Society for Sports History, *Sport and Colonialism in 19th Century Australasia*, ASSH Studies in Sports History, No.1 (Sydney, 1986)

W. Bate, *Light Blue Down Under: The History of Geelong Grammar School* (Melbourne, 1990)

G. Blainey, J. Morrissey and S.E.K. Hulme, *Wesley College: The First Hundred Years* (Melbourne, 1967)

D. Kirk, *Schooling Bodies: School Practice and Public Discourse 1880-1950* (London, 1998)

J. Kociumbas, *Australian Childhood: A History* (Sydney, 1997)

B. Lewis, *Our War: Australia During World War 1* (Melbourne, 1980)

B. Niall, *Seven Little Billabongs: The World of Ethel Turner and Mary Grant Bruce* (Melbourne, 1979)

B. Niall, *Australia Through the Looking-Glass: Children's Fiction 1830-1980* (Melbourne, 1984)

G. Sherington, 'Athletics in the Antipodes: the AAGPS of New South Wales', *History of Education Review*, 12, 2 (1983)

C. Turney, 'The Advent and Adaptation of the Arnold Public School Tradition in New South Wales', *Australian Journal of Education*, 10, 2 (1966), 11, 1 (1967).

A Pioneer of the Proletariat:
Herbert Milnes and the Games Cult in New Zealand
J.A. MANGAN and COLM HICKEY

G. F. Bartle, *A History of Borough Road College* (Kettering, 1976)

A. Burrell, *Bert Milnes: A Brief Memoir* (Letchworth, 1922)

E.P. Malone, 'The New Zealand Journal and the Imperial Ideology', *New Zealand Journal of History*, 7 (April 1973)

J.A. Mangan, *Athleticism in the Victorian and Edwardian Public School: The Emergence and Consolidation of an Educational Ideology* (Cambridge, 1981)

J.A. Mangan, *The Games Ethic and Imperialism. Aspects of the Diffusion of an Ideal* (London, 1998)

Colin McGeorge, 'The Moral Curriculum. Forging the Kiwi Character', in G. McCulloch (ed.) *The School Curriculum in New Zealand: History. Theory. Policy and Practice* (Palmerston, New Zealand, 1993)

F.H. Spencer, *An Inspector's Testament* (London, 1938)

B. Sutton-Smith, *A History of Children's Play: New Zealand 1840–1950* (Philadelphia, 1981)

Gender Associations: Sport, State Schools and Australian Culture
DAVID KIRK

R. Crawford, 'Sport for young ladies: The Victorian independent schools 1875–1925', *Sporting Traditions – Journal of the Australian Society for Sports History*, 1 (1984)

S. Fletcher, *Women First: The Female Tradition in English Physical Education, 1880–1980* (London, 1984)

M.A. Hall, *Feminism and Sporting Bodies: Essays on Theory and Practice* (Champaign, IL, 1996)

J.A. Hargreaves, *Sporting Females: Critical Issues in the History and Sociology of Women's Sport* (London, 1994)

D. Kirk, 'School Sport and Physical Education in History: An Overview and Discussion of Published English Language Studies, 1986–1998', *International Journal of Physical Education*, 35, 2 (1998)

D. Kirk, *Schooling Bodies: School Practice and Public Discourse, 1880–1950* (London, 1998)

J.A. Mangan (1985) *The Games Ethic and Imperialism: Aspects of the Diffusion of an Ideal* (Harmondsworth, 1985)

J.A. Mangan and R.J. Parks (eds.), *From 'Fair Sex' to Feminism: Sport and the Socialisation of Women in the Industrial and Post-Industrial Eras* (London, 1987)

K.E. McCrone, *Playing the Game: Sport and the Physical Emancipation of English Women, 1870–1914* (London, 1988)

J. Nauright and J. Broomhall, 'A Woman's Game: The Development of Netball and a Female Sporting Culture in New Zealand 1906–1970', *International Journal of the History of Sport*, 11, 3 (1994)

J. Wright, 'Mapping the Discourses in Physical Education', *Journal of Curriculum Studies*, 28, 3 (1996)

The 'Green' and the 'Gold': The Irish-Australians and their Role in the Emergence of the Australian Sports Culture
PETER HORTON

R. Cashman, *The Paradise of Sport: The Rise of Organised Sport in Australia* (Sydney, 1995)

M. Connellan, 'The Ideology of Athleticism, Its Antipodean Impact and its Manifestation in Two Elite Catholic Schools', *ASSH Studies in Sports History Series*, 5 (1988)

D. Headon and L. Marinos, *League of a Nation* (Sydney, 1996)

P. A. Horton, '"Padang or Paddock": A Comparative View of Colonial Sport in Two Imperial Territories', *The International Journal of the History of Sport*, 14, 1 (April 1997)

H. M. Moran, *Viewless Winds* (London, 1939)

P.A. Mosely, R. Cashman, J. O'Hara and H. Wetherburn (eds.), *Sporting Immigrants: Sport and Ethnicity in Australia* (Sydney: Walla Walla Press, 1997)

P. O'Farrell, *The Irish in Australia* (Sydney, 1993)

M. G. Phillips and K. Moore, 'The Champion Boxer Les Darcy: A Victim of Class Conflict and Sectarian Bitterness in Australia during the First World War', *The International Journal of the History of Sport*, 11, 1 (April 1994)

'They Play in Your Home':
Cricket, Media and Modernity in Pre-War Australia
FRAZER ANDREWES

R. Cashman, *'Ave a Go, Yer Mug! Australian Cricket Crowds from Larrikin to Ocker* (Sydney, 1984)

R. Cashman *et al.*, *The Oxford Companion to Australian Cricket* (Melbourne, 1996)

R Cashman and A. Weaver, *Wicket Women: Cricket and Women in Australia* (Sydney, 1991)

K. Inglis, *This is the ABC: The Australian Broadcasting Commission 1933-1983* (Carlton, 1983)

L. Johnson, *The Unseen Voice: A Cultural Study of Early Australian Radio* (London, 1988)

C. Rojek, *Decentring Leisure: Rethinking Leisure Theory* (London, 1995)

R. Simmons and B. Stoddart, *Cricket and Empire: The 1932-33 Bodyline Tour of Australia* (Sydney, 1984)

Brian Stoddart, *Saturday Afternoon Fever: Sport in the Australian Culture* (Sydney, 1986)

B. Stoddart and K.A.P. Sandiford (eds.), *The Imperial Game: Cricket, Culture and Society* (Manchester, 1998)

R. Waterhouse, *Private Pleasures, Public Leisure: A History of Australian Culture since 1788* (South Melbourne, 1995)

'Ladies are Specially Invited':
Women in the Culture of Australian Rules Football
ROB HESS

G. Blainey, *A Game of Our Own: The Origins of Australian Football* (Melbourne, 1990)

R. Hess, 'Women and Australian Rules Football in Colonial Melbourne', *The International Journal of the History of Sport*, 13, 3 (Dec.1996), 356–72

R. Hess and R. Stewart (eds.), *More Than a Game: An Unauthorised History of Australian Rules Football* (Carlton, 1998)

S. Lopez, *Women on the Ball: A Guide to Women's Football* (London, 1997)

J. Nauright and T.J.L. Chandler (eds.), *Making Men: Rugby and Masculine Identity* (London and Portland, OR, 1996)

M. Oriard, *Reading Football: How the Popular Press Created an American Spectacle* (Chapel Hill, 1993)

L. Sandercock and I. Turner, *Up Where, Cazaly? The Great Australian Game* (London, 1981)

R. Stremski, *Kill for Collingwood* (Sydney, 1986)

In Pursuit of Status, Respectability and Idealism:
Pioneers of the Olympic Movement in Australia
IAN JOBLING

P. de Coubertin, 'The Paris Congress and the Revival of the Olympic Games', *Olympic Review* (1981)

H. Gordon, *Australia at the Olympic Games* (Brisbane, 1994)

G. Henniker and I. Jobling, 'Richard Coombes and the Olympic Movement in Australia: Imperialism and Nationalism in Action', *Sporting Traditions – Journal of Australian Society for Sports History*, 6, 1 (1989)

I. Jobling, 'The Making of a Nation through Sport: Australia and the Olympic Games from Athens to Berlin, 1896–1916', *Australian Journal of Politics and History*, 32, 2 (1988)

I. Jobling, 'The Lion, the Eagle and the Kangaroo: Politics and Proposals for a British Empire Team at the 1916 Berlin Olympics', in G. Redmond (ed.), *Sport and Politics* (Champaign, 1985)

M. Letters and I. Jobling, 'Forgotten Links: Leonard Cuff and Olympic Movement in Australasia, 1894–1905', *Olympika – International Journal of Olympic Studies*, 5 (1996)

J.J. MacAloon, *This Great Symbol: Pierre de Coubertin and the Modern Olympic Games* (Chicago, 1981)

K. Moore, 'Strange Bedfellows and Cooperative Partners: The Influence of the Olympic Games on the Establishment of the British Empire Games', in G. Redmond (ed.), *Sport and Politics* (Champaign, 1985)

K. Moore, 'One Voice in the Wilderness: Richard Coombes and the Promotion of the Pan-Britannic Festival Concept in Australia, 1891–1911', *Sporting Traditions*, 5, 2 (1989)

D. Young, 'The Origins of the Modern Olympics: A New Version', *The International Journal of the History of Sport*, 4, 3 (1987)

Surf Lifesaving: The Development of an Australasian 'Sport'
DOUGLAS BOOTH

S. Brawley, *Vigilant and Victorious: A Community History of the Collaroy Surf Life Saving Club 1911–1995* (Sydney, 1995)

S. Brawley, *Beach Beyond: A History of the Palm Beach Surf Club 1921–1996* (Sydney, 1996)

M. Doepel, 'The Emergence of Surf Bathing and Surf Life Saving at the Holiday Resort of Manly, 1850–1920 (unpublished BA Honours, University of New South Wales, 1985)

P. Fryer, *Mrs Grundy: Studies in English Prudery* (London, 1963)

R. Harris, *Heroes of the Surf: Fifty Years' History of Manly Life Saving Club* (Sydney, 1961)

K. Pearson, *Surfing Subcultures of Australia and New Zealand* (Brisbane, 1979)

V. Raszeja, *A Decent and Proper Exertion* (Sydney, 1992)

G. Ryley Scott, *The Story of Baths and Bathing* (London, 1939)

Women's Sports and Embodiment in Australia and New Zealand
ANGELA BURROUGHS and JOHN NAURIGHT

A. Burroughs, L. Seebohm and L. Ashburn, 'A Case Study of Australian Women's Cricket and its Media Experience', *Sporting Traditions*, 12, 1 (1995)

R. Cashman and A. Weaver, *Wicket Women: Cricket and Women in Australia* (Sydney, 1991)

R. Crawford, 'Sport for Young Ladies: The Victorian Independent Schools 1875–1925', *Sporting Traditions*, 1, 1 (1984)

M.A. Hall, *Feminism and Sporting Bodies: Essays on Theory and Practice* (Champaign, 1996)

I.F. Jobling and P. Barham, 'The Development of Netball and the All-Australia Women's Basketball Association (AAWBBA), 1891–1939', *Sporting Traditions*, 8, 1 (1991)

J. McKay, 'Embodying the "New" Sporting Woman', *Hecate*, 20, 1 (1994)

J. Nauright and J. Broomhall, 'The Development of Netball and a Female Sporting Culture in New Zealand 1906–70', *The International Journal of the History of Sport*, 11, 3 (1994)

C. Smith, 'Control of the Female Body: Physical Training at Three New Zealand Girls' High Schools 1880s–1920s', *Sporting Traditions*, 13, 2 (1997)

M. Stell, *Half the Race: A History of Australian Women in Sport* (Sydney, 1991)

I. Young, 'Throwing Like a Girl: A Phenomenology of Feminine Body Comportment, Motility and Spatiality', *Human Studies*, 3 (1980)

Conflict, Tensions and Complexities:
Athletic Training in Australia in the 1950s
MURRAY PHILLIPS and FRANK HICKS

J. Bale, *Landscapes of Modern Sport* (Leicester, 1994)

J. Bale and J. Sang, *Kenyan Running: Movement Culture, Geography and Global Change* (London, 1996)

P.W. Cerutty, *Athletics: How to become a Champion: A Discursive Textbook* (London, 1960)

M. Foucault, *Discipline and Punish: The Birth of the Prison* (London, 1977)

J.M. Hoberman, *Mortal Engines: The Science of Performance and the Dehumanization of Sport* (New York, 1992)

J. McKay, *No Pain, No Gain?: Sport and Australian Culture* (New York, 1991)

M.G. Phillips, *From the Sidelines to Centre Field: A History of Sports Coaching in Australia* (Sydney, 2000)

F. Stampfl, *On Running: Sprint, Middle Distance and Distance Events* (London, 1955)

From a Club to a Corporate Game:
The Changing Face of Australian Football, 1960–1999
IAN ANDREWS

I. Andrews, 'The Transformation of "Community" in the Australian Football League: Part One - Towards a Conceptual Framework for Community in the AFL', *Football Studies*, 1, 2 (1998)

I. Andrews, 'The Transformation of "Community" in the Australian Football League: Part Two - Redrawing "Community" Boundaries in the Post-War AFL', *Football Studies*, 2, 1 (1999)

B. Dabscheck, 'Playing the Team Game: Unions in Australian Professional Team Sports', *The Journal of Industrial Relations*, 38, 4 (1996)

L. Frost, *The Old Dark Navy Blues: A History of the Carlton Football Club* (Sydney, 1998)

A. Gramsci, *Selections from the Prison Notebooks* (London, 1971)

R. Hess and B. Stewart (eds.), *More Than A Game: An Unauthorised History of Australian Rules Football* (Melbourne, 1998)

G. Linnell, *Football Ltd: The Inside Story of the AFL* (Sydney : Ironbark, 1995)

R. Pascoe, *The Winter Game: The Complete History of Australian Football* (Melbourne, 1995)

L. Sandercock and I. Turner, Up Where, Cazaly? The Great Australian Game (London, 1981)

B. Stewart, *The Australian Football Business: A Spectator's Guide to the VFL* (Kenthurst, 1983)

Football as Social Criticism:
Protest Movements, Rugby and History in Aotearoa, New Zealand
MALCOLM MACLEAN

D. Awatere, *Maori Sovereignty* (Auckland, 1984)

G. Chapple, *1981: The Tour* (Auckland, 1984)

C. Dann, *Up From Under: Women and Liberation in New Zealand, 1970–1985* (Wellington, 1985)

G. Marcus, *Lipstick Traces: A Secret History of the Twentieth Century* (Cambridge, MA, 1989)

J. Nauright, 'Reclaiming Old and Forgotten Heroes: Nostalgia, Rugby and Identity in New Zealand', *Sporting Traditions* 10, 2 (1994)

L. Neithammer, *Posthistoire: Has History Come to an End?* (London, 1992)

J.O.C. Phillips, *A Man's Country? The Image of The Pakeha Male: A History* (2nd edition) (Auckland, 1996)

T. Richards, *Dancing On Our Bones: Rugby, New Zealand and South Africa* (Auckland, 1999)

M. Templeton, *Human Rights and Sporting Contacts: New Zealand Attitudes to Race Relations in South Africa 1921–94* (Auckland, 1998)

S. Thompson, 'Challenging the Hegemony: New Zealand Women's Opposition to Rugby', *International Review for the Sociology of Sport* 23, 3 (1988)

R. Walker, Ka Whawhai Tonu Matou/Struggle Without End (Auckland, 1990)

Australian Sport in a Postmodern Age
BOB STEWART and AARON SMITH

P.T. Blyton, and J.A. Morris, *Flexible Future: Prospects for Employment and Organisation*, Walter de Gruyter (New York, 1991)

R. Cashman, *Paradise of Sport: The Rise of Organised Sport in Australia* (Melbourne, 1995)

P. Cerutty, *Athletics: How to become a Champion* (London, 1959)

D. Harvey, *The Condition of Postmodernity* (Oxford, 1989)

F. Jameson, *Postmodernism: The Cultural Logic of Late Capitalism* (London, 1991)

J. Leotard, *The Postmodern Condition: A Report on Knowledge* (Manchester, 1990)

A. McGilvray, *The Game Is Not The Same* (Sydney, 1985)

K. Pearson, *Surfing Subcultures* (Brisbane, 1983)

J. Pine, and J. Gilmore, *The Experience Economy* (Boston, 1999)

B. Rigauer, *Sport and Work* (New York, 1981)

C. Rojek *Decentring Leisure* (London, 1995)

A. Smith, and B. Stewart, *Sports Management: A Guide to Professional Practice* (Sydney, 1999)

Sport 2000 Task Force, *Shaping Up: A Review of Commonwealth Involvement in Sport and Recreation in Australia* (1999)

B. Stewart, *The Australian Football Business* (Kenthurst, 1984)

W. Vamplew *et al.*, *The Oxford Companion to Australian Sport* (Melbourne, 1992)

The Reinvention of Australia for the Sydney 2000 Olympic Games
TARA MAGDALINSKI

D. Booth and C. Tatz, *One-eyed: A View of Australian Sport* (Sydney, 2000)

D. Booth and C. Tatz, 'Swimming with the Big Boys?: The Politics of Sydney's 2000 Olympic Bid', *Sporting Traditions*, 11, 1 (1994)

D. Booth, 'Gifts of Corruption? Ambiguities of Obligation in the Olympic Movement', *Olympika*, 8 (1999)

A. Burroughs, 'Winning the Bid', in R. Cashman and A. Hughes (eds.), *Staging the Olympics: The Event and its Impact* (Sydney, 1999)

E. Herman and R. McChesney, *The Global Media: The New Missionaries of Global Capitalism* (London, 1997)

T. Magdalinski, 'Drugs, Sport and National Identity in Australia', in W. Wilson (ed.), *Doping in Sport* (Champaign, 2000 forthcoming)

J. McKay and D. Rowe, 'Ideology, the Media, and Australian Sport', *Sociology of Sport Journal*, 4 (1987)

J. McKay, *No Pain, No Gain. Sport and Australian Culture* (Sydney, 1991)

J. Nauright and T.J.L. Chandler (eds.), *Making Men: Rugby and Masculine Identity* (London, 1996)

J. Nauright, 'Money, Methods and Medals: The Australian Elite Sports System in the 1990s', in K. Hardman (ed.), *Sport for all: Issues and Perspectives in International Context* (Manchester, 1996)

W. Vamplew and B. Stoddart (eds.), *Sport in Australia: A Social History* (Melbourne, 1994)

Notes on Contributors

Frazer Andrewes graduated with an MA (Hons) from the University of Auckland, New Zealand in 1995. His thesis was a study of the representation of masculinities in post-war New Zealand culture. He is currently a doctoral student in the History Department, University of Melbourne, where he is researching the impact of modernity on the culture of Australia in the 1930s.

Ian Andrews teaches sports sociology and health sociology at the University of Sydney, Australia. Previously, he has published articles on the changing nature of football communities. He is currently completing his doctoral thesis, which examines the relationship between the media, multiculturalism and democracy in Australian society.

Douglas Booth has written extensively on the historical and sociological aspects of sport. He currently teaches history at the University of Otago in New Zealand.

Angela Burroughs works in the planning office at the University of New South Wales and is a doctoral student at Charles Sturt University. She has published on women and sport in Australia and on the winning of the Sydney 2000 Olympic bid.

Martin Crotty is a lecturer in Australian History at the University of Newcastle, Australia. He has published a number of articles in sports history and in the history of masculinity. His doctoral thesis, entitled 'Making the Australian Male: The Construction of Manly Middle-Class Youth in Australia, 1870-1920', is currently being revised for publication by Melbourne University Press.

Rob Hess is a lecturer in the social history of sport and human movement at Victoria University, Australia. He is the founding co-editor of the *Bulletin of Sport and Culture*, and the co-editor of *More Than a Game: An Unauthorised History of Australian Rules Football* (1998).

Colm Hickey studied at the former Borough Road College and is a graduate of the University of London. He completed his MA at the University of London, Institute of Education. He is currently Deputy Headteacher of St Bernard's Catholic School, High Wycombe.

Frank Hicks has taught sociology at the University of Canberra for over 20 years. He has specialized in the sociology of knowledge and education and has contributed in different forums on these topics. In addition, Frank has an interest in the sociology of sport, particularly in the cultures of Australian sport.

Peter Horton is a lecturer in the School of Education at James Cook University in Townsville. He has previously worked in schools and universities in Singapore, Brisbane, NSW, and England. This chapter represents his latest research into the nature sport in culture. He has published widely in the area of sport studies, particularly in the discussion of the nature of sport cultures in post-colonial territories and, upon Olympic issues.

Ian Jobling is a sport and Olympic historian in the School of Human Movement Studies at The University of Queensland, Brisbane, Australia. He is currently Director of the Centre for Olympic Studies at that university, and was an inaugural Editorial Review Board member of Olympika – International Journal of Olympic Studies. Dr Jobling was also inaugural chair of the Education Commission of the Australian Olympic Federation (now the Australian Olympic Committee) and is on the International Advisory Committee of the Greece-based Foundation of Olympic and Sport Education (FOSE).

David Kirk joined Loughborough University in November 1998 as the first Beckwith Professor of Youth Sport and Director of the Institute of Youth Sport. He was formerly Professor of Human Movement Studies at the University of Queensland, Australia. His research interests are in physical education, schooling and social and cultural change. His most recent book is *Schooling Bodies: School Practice and Public Discourse, 1880–1950* (1998).

Stuart Macintyre is the Ernest Scott Professor of History and Dean of Arts at the University of Melbourne. He has published extensively on aspects of Australian history.

Malcolm MacLean is a Pakeha New Zealander with a background in student and trade unions, the Australian and New Zealand public services and several of the political campaigns discussed in his paper. He teaches in the School of Sport at the Cheltenham and Gloucester College of Higher Education, and is exploring the politics of being Pakeha in the Cotswolds.

J.A. Mangan is Director of the International Research Centre for Sport, Socialisation and Society at the University of Strathclyde, Glasgow, and author and editor of many books. He is founder and General Editor of the Cass series Sport in the Global Society and founding and executive academic editor of the Cass journals *The International Journal of the History of Sport, Culture, Sport, Society, Soccer and Society* and *The European Sports History Review*. His internationally acclaimed *Athleticism in the Victorian and Edwardian Public School* and *The Games Ethic and Imperialism* have recently been reprinted by Frank Cass.

John Nauright is Foundation Chair of the Human Movement Studies Unit at Charles Sturt University in Bathurst, Australia. He is the author and editor of many books and articles in sports studies including the Cass books *Making Men: Rugby and Masculine Identity* (1996) and *Making the Rugby World* (1999). He also edited *Sport, Power and Society in New Zealand* (1995). He is the founding editor of *Football Studies* and co-editor of *International Sports Studies*. He is the Vice-President of the Australian Society for Sports History and founder of the Football Studies Group.

Jock Phillips is the Chief Historian for the New Zealand Government. He is the author of ten books in New Zealand history, of which the best known is *A Man's Country? The Image of the Pakeha Male – A History* (1987).

Murray Phillips is Senior Lecturer in Sports Studies in the School of Human Movement Studies at The University of Queensland. He is the author of *From Sidelines to Centrefield: A History of Sports Coaching in Australia* (2000). He has also published extensively on the history of Australian sport. He is the reviews editor of *Sporting Traditions*, the journal of the Australian Society of Sports History.

Aaron Smith is Senior Lecturer in Sport Management at Deakin University, Melbourne, Australia. He has a special interest in professional best practice in sports management and the role of organization culture in shaping sports club performance. He co-authored *Sport Management: A Guide to Professional Practice* and is currently editing a book of readings on sports event and facility management.

Bob Stewart is Associate Professor in Sport Management at Victoria University, Melbourne, Australia. He has written extensively on the commercial development of Australian sport, with an emphasis on cricket and Australian football, and is currently researching the comparative performance of Australian professional sports leagues. His previous publications include *The Australian Football Business*, *Oval Logic* and *High Mark*, which he co-edited with Robert Pascoe and Stephen Alomes respectively, and *More Than a Game: An Unauthorised History of Australian Football*, which he co-edited with Rob Hess. He also contributed to the *Oxford Companion to Australian Sport*, and the *Oxford Companion to Australian Cricket*. His most recent publication is *Sports Management: A Guide to Professional Practice*, which he co-authored with Aaron Smith.

Abstracts

Manly and Moral: The Making of Middle-Class Men in the Australian Public Schools
by Martin Crotty

In the 1870s the ideal of manliness promoted by headmasters, clergymen, the authors of children's books and a range of social commentators was an often effeminate ideal which emphasized the qualities of godliness and good learning. Later in the nineteenth century, fears of racial decline, a growing interest in post-Christian ethics and a militarist nationalism gave rise to an idealized form of manliness which was much more physical, rugged and masculine. Sport was embraced by the public schools as it seemed to hold the potential for the development of qualities which would ensure an ordered society in a post-religious age, and the development of the ability and willingness to defend the nation and empire.

A Pioneer of the Proletariat: Herbert Milnes and the Games Cult in New Zealand
by J.A. Mangan and Colm Hickey

The global influence of Athleticism is slowly but surely being recorded. The chapter deals with a hitherto unrecorded aspect – the transmission of the ideology to Auckland, New Zealand and elementary education there, in the person of Herbert Albert Edwin Milnes, an outstanding exemplar and committed proselytiser. Milnes' career links two significant and influential nineteenth century ideologies – Athleticism and Imperialism. Milnes is important for another reason – he exemplifies the period relationship between sport, imperialism and militarism both in his life and his death.

Gender Associations:
Sport, State Schools and Australian Culture
by David Kirk

Historians have documented uses of physical cultural practices by schools serving the wealthy and privileged in Australian society to construct the gendered identities of girls and boys. However, we know little about how these practices were carried out in government schools serving the masses. The focus of this paper is the construction and constitution of gendered bodies through the practices of school physical education between 1900 and 1950. A brief overview is provided of the concepts of physical culture and the social production of gender. These concepts are then located within a discussion of government schooling and the social regulation of children's bodies through physical training. Following this discussion, a number of syllabuses and texts are analysed. The texts contained for teachers key information on physical training and a narrative on the androgynous child who was to be constructed through a regime of formal physical training. The article concludes with a discussion of the demise of physical training and with it the narrative of the androgynous child, and their replacement with the explicitly gendered practices of sport-based physical education after the Second World War.

The 'Green' and the 'Gold': The Irish-Australians and their Role in the Emergence of the Australian Sports Culture
by Peter Horton

This chapter considers the impact of Catholic Irish-Australians upon the emergence of an Australian sport culture. It discusses the notion that many of what are now considered definitively Australian attitudes and values were in fact the outcome of the conflict between the Catholic Irish-Australians and the Protestant English-Australians. This conflict between the two largest migrant groups, the Irish Catholics and the Protestant English, was critical. Urbanization, education and class were also major influences upon the development of Australian sports culture. In Australia sport became a central feature of the national culture and in many ways now defines Australia and its people.

'They Play in Your Home':
Cricket, Media and Modernity in Pre-War Australia
by Frazer Andrewes

By examining the mechanics of cricket broadcasting and the commercial imperatives that feed it, this essay explores the promises of modernity and the way in which cricket provided a national vehicle for the dissemination of its messages. Drawn by the lure of test match action, Australians purchased wireless sets and licences in ever larger numbers. Cricket became a modern game in the 1930s and helped to disseminate modernity; it became important in the creation of a rhetoric of technological progress, it became a commodity and was 'sold' like so many other things. It also highlighted the gender inequities in Australian society. In a sense the game became a symbol of modern life.

'Ladies are Specially Invited':
Women in the Culture of Australian Rules Football
by Rob Hess

This study traces the history of Australian Rules football by examining the evolving multi-dimensional nature of the game. In particular, the diminution of the once inherent violence of the code is explained in the context of changing relationships between men and women, spectators and players and sport and society. The observation is made that in an age where local cultural practices have been weakened in the face of globalization, it seems that Australian Rules football will continue to promote a strong sense of indigenous identity, a phenomenon that can only be understood within the historical context of the game's distinctive gender relations.

In Pursuit of Status, Respectability and Idealism:
Pioneers of the Olympic Movement in Australia
by Ian Jobling

The efforts of three prominent men, New Zealander Leonard Cuff, and Australians Richard Coombes and Edwin Flack, did much to foster the development of sport as a cultural identity in the Antipodes. Above all, they raised the awareness there of what has since become a paramount sporting festival, the Olympic Games. Richard Coombes, emigrated to Australia in 1886 and became influential as the editor of the Sydney-based weekly sporting periodical, *The Referee*. Leonard Cuff became an inaugural member of the International Olympic Committee (IOC) in 1894 and was a founding member of the New Zealand Amateur Athletic Association (NZAAA). Edwin Flack became known as 'the Lion of Athens' at the Athens Olympics of 1896 and his success there had an significant influence on the Olympic Movement in Australia. These three men epitomize the amateurism, nationalism, imperialism and internationalism in Victorian and Edwardian sport in Australasia.

Surf Lifesaving: The Development of an Australasian 'Sport'
by Douglas Booth

Orthodox histories of surfbathing in Australia and New Zealand typically assume it to be a natural activity, synonymous with sunshine, clear and warm water, golden sands and curling waves. These histories not only tend to play down the local government ordinances that prohibited surfbathing in the nineteenth century, they grossly simplify the circumstances that led to the lifting of bathing bans. This essay argues that complex cultural issues, revolving around particular attitudes towards the presentation of the body in public, underscores the history of surfbathing in Australia and New Zealand

Women's Sports and Embodiment in Australia and New Zealand
by Angela Burroughs and John Nauright

Women have had a long history of participation in sporting activities in Australia and New Zealand. At the élite level many women have performed well in international competitions. Despite this, there has always been resistance from the male-dominated public culture to support and promote female physicality as equally as male physicality. This essay explores the embodiment of women in sport through an historical examination of the construction of ideal femininity in Australasian sport and concludes that expressions of female physicality are still limited by hegemonic notions that confine them to images acceptable for male consumption.

Conflict, Tensions and Complexities:
Athletic Training in Australia in the 1950s
by Murray Phillips and Frank Hicks

This essay examines the coaching of track and field athletes against the broader landscape of Australian culture in the 1950s and 1960s. It details the views of two of Australia's leading professional coaches in the 1950s, Percy Cerutty and Franz Stampfl, and speculates about what framed their approaches to coaching, links their coaching styles with broader social and cultural issues, and briefly summarizes their contributions to contemporary sport. Cerutty and Stampfl espoused different ideas about knowledge, understood embodiment in contrasting ways and, accordingly, designed athletic training programmes that bore little resemblance or similarity. Ultimately, the debates about their training methods were precursors to many features of contemporary sport including the rise of sport science in élite performance, in coach education and in academic institutions.

From a Club to a Corporate Game:
The Changing Face of Australian Football, 1960–1999
by Ian Andrews

Since the Second World War, the elite competition in Australian Rules football has undergone a transformation from a semi-professional, metropolitan concern, into a fully professional and thoroughly commercialized national league. In 1989 this process was reflected in the renaming of the competition from the Victorian Football League (VFL), to the Australian Football League (AFL). This chapter analyses these developments using a social-scientific framework of 'crisis'. Specifically, the League's post-war history is divided into four chronological periods, corresponding to four distinct 'crisis phases' - those of 'origin' (1946-63); 'manifestation' (1964-74); 'high-point' (1975-84); and (partial) 'resolution' (1985-99). The conclusion holds that, as these 'phases' have unfolded, the traditional primacy of the League's cultural role has been lost to economic imperatives and commercial pressures.

Football as Social Critique: Protest Movements, Rugby and History in Aotcaroa, New Zealand
by Malcolm MacLean

During the 1970s and 1980s New Zealand was the site of many social and political struggles centred on colonization, gender politics, economic and social policies, international relations and state power. The biggest protests focused on sporting contact with South Africa and were strongest during the 1981 Springbok rugby tour. This article considers the range of protest during this period and examines the reasons behind the priority given to the campaign against apartheid sport. It examines the significance of rugby in New Zealand and shows how 1981 provided a focal point for social frustrations associated with broader social and political change.

Australian Sport in a Postmodern Age
by Bob Stewart and Aaron Smith

This essay examines the impact of postmodernism on Australian sport. We aim to show that sport has been transformed by the process of postmodernization. The process began in the late 1960s when Australian sport threw away many of its moralistic pretensions and repressive formality and locked itself into the corporate world. By the 1990s a number of professional sport leagues had emerged as amateurism lost its snobbish appeal and sport went about building its commercial value. Corporate signage saturated the major venues and players were marketed as celebrities. Excitement, speed, the 'quick grab', and sensory bombardment became the defining features of the spectator experience. Spectacular and dramatic contests became just as important as skill and aesthetic display. Fans increasingly narrowed their attention span, but were no longer bound by a parochial tribalism. They took on multiple identities that could shift from an elite European soccer team one week, to a suburban Brisbane rugby team the next. At the same time, branding and image making were used to re-position leagues and major events, and attract fans and corporate supporters. Moreover, the television programmer became the final arbiter on how the game should be scheduled and played. The Sydney 2000 Olympic Games convincingly demonstrates that Australian sport has become a chaotic mix of ancient ritual, traditional athletic contests, slickly marketed and customized leisure experiences and ultra-professional sports that combine complex strategy with Hollywood-style showmanship.

The Reinvention of Australia for the Sydney 2000 Olympic Games
by Tara Magdalinski

In the Olympic year, Australia is increasingly positioned as a 'clean' nation, interested more in the 'pure performance' of the amateur ideal than in professionalized sport, sentiments that are embodied in the environmental rhetoric of the bid, the hardline stance on performance enhancing drugs and the promotion of past and present 'wholesome' Aussie sporting heroes. This clean, green image symbolizes more than simply a return to the 'ideals' of Olympism, but rather is part of Australia's quest to 'return' to itself, to a mythical Australia, an idealistic nation caught in the imagined monocultural paradise of 1950s suburbia, exemplified in the memory of the 1956 Melbourne Olympic Games. This chapter explores the links between the 2000 Olympics, sports history and national memory and the reinvention of an "Australia" founded on an idealized national sporting past.

Index

Books of Related Interest

Making the Rugby World
Race, Gender, Commerce
Timothy J L Chandler, *Kent State University* and John Nauright,
University of Queensland (Eds)
This book seeks to understand what has happened to rugby as it has moved from the
private realm of the English public school to the global realm dominated by Rupert
Murdoch and other media entrepreneurs. It explores rugby and issues of race in the
Empire/Commonwealth, rugby in non-British societies, women's rugby, homophobia
and rugby, and nationalism and rugby, before turning to the massive impact that
globalization, professionalization and commercialization have had on the sport.

256 pages 1999 0 7146 4853 1 cloth; 0 7146 4411 0 paper
Sport in the Global Society No. 10

Rugby's Great Split
Class, Culture and the Origins of Rugby League Football
Tony Collins

Winner of the British Sports History Prize for Best Book 1998

'The book is a landmark in the historiography of rugby league and of rugby in general.
... I have little doubt that it will become the standard work on the early development
of rugby itself.'
                                                                        Rugby League Express
304 pages 1998 repr 1999 07146 4867 1 cloth; 07146 4424 2 paper
Sport in the Global Society No. 5

The Nordic World
Sport in Society
Henrik Meinander, *University of Helsinki* and J A Mangan, *University of
Strathclyde* (Eds)

This volume explores the political, social and aesthetic impact of modern sport on
Northern Europe, and the relationship between the Nordic nations and Nordic
cultures, attitudes to the body and the evolution of specific Nordic visions of sport.
The Nordic World shows why sport has played such an important part in both
twentieth-century Nordic society and contemporary European culture.

200 pages 1998 0 7146 4825 6 cloth; 0 7146 4391 2 paper
A special issue of The International Journal of the History of Sport
Sport in the Global Society No. 3

FRANK CASS PUBLISHERS
Newbury House, 900 Eastern Avenue, Ilford, Essex, IG2 7HH
Tel: +44 (0)20 8599 8866 Fax: +44 (0)20 8599 0984 E-mail: info@frankcass.com
NORTH AMERICA
5804 NE Hassalo Street, Portland, OR 97213 3644, USA
Tel: 800 944 6190 Fax: 503 280 8832 E-mail: cass@isbs.com
Website: www.frankcass.com

The First Black Footballer
Arthur Wharton 1865–1930, An Absence of Memory
Phil Vasili, with a Foreword by **Irvine Welsh** and an Introduction by **Tony Whelan,** *Manchester United FC*

'...the most conspicuously absent volume from the library of British Sport...the extraordinary tale of Britain's forgotten all-time sporting great has finally been told.'
Independent on Sunday

272 pages 25 photographs 1998 0 7146 4903 1 cloth; 0 7146 4459 5 paper
Sport in the Global Society No. 11

Scoring for Britain
International Football and International Politics, 1900–1939
Peter J Beck, *Kingston University*
This fascinating book considers the nature and development of linkages between international football and politics between 1900 and 1939, and also provides a history of international football in Britain.

320 pages 15 illus 1999 0 7146 4899 X cloth; 0 7146 4454 4 paper
Sport in the Global Society No. 9

Sporting Nationalisms
Identity, Ethnicity, Immigration and Assimilation
Mike Cronin, *De Montfort University* and **David Mayall,** *Sheffield Hallam University* (Eds)

'Well written, incisive, instructive and thought provoking.'
Culture, Sport, Society

This collection examines the ways in which sport shapes the experiences of various immigrant and minority groups and, in particular, looks at the relationship between sport, ethnic identity and ethnic relations.

240 pages 1998 0 7146 4896 5 cloth; 0 7146 4449 8 paper
A special issue of the journal Immigrants and Minorities
Sport in the Global Society No. 6

FRANK CASS PUBLISHERS
Newbury House, 900 Eastern Avenue, Ilford, Essex, IG2 7HH
Tel: +44 (0)20 8599 8866 Fax: +44 (0)20 8599 0984 E-mail: info@frankcass.com
NORTH AMERICA
5804 NE Hassalo Street, Portland, OR 97213 3644, USA
Tel: 800 944 6190 Fax: 503 280 8832 E-mail: cass@isbs.com
Website: www.frankcass.com
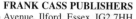

Shaping the Superman: Fascist Body as Political Icon – Aryan Fascism

J A Mangan, *University of Strathclyde* (Ed)

This book is a study of masculinity as a metaphor and especially of the muscular male body as a moral symbol. It explores the Nazis' preoccupation with the male body as an icon of political power, and the ideology and theories which propelled it.

232 pages 15 illus 1999 0 7146 4954 6 cloth; 0 7146 8013 3 paper
A special issue of The International Journal of the History of Sport
Sport in the Global Society No. 14

Superman Supreme: Fascist Body as Political Icon – Global Fascism

J A Mangan, *University of Strathclyde* (Ed)

This sequel to the acclaimed *Shaping the Superman* shows that the idealized image of the Aryan Superman had a wide currency beyond Germany and reveals how Fascist movements in Europe, America and Asia made metaphorical and literal use of the male body for political purposes.

224 pages 38 illus 2000 0 7146 4955 4 cloth; 0 7146 8014 1 paper
A special issue of The International Journal of the History of Sport
Sport in the Global Society No. 15

The Race Game

Sport and Politics in South Africa
Douglas Booth, *University of Otago, New Zealand*

Winner of the North American Society for Sport History Award for Best Book, 1998

'The Race Game is both a scholarly and a readable history of sport ... A major strength of the work is the sharp analysis of the changing relationship between sport and politics from 1948 to the collapse of apartheid, including an excellent reappraisal of the development and contribution of the anti-apartheid international sports boycott.'
African Affairs `

272 pages 2 maps, 10 photographs 1998
0 7146 4799 3 cloth; 0 7146 4354 8 paper
Sport in the Global Society No. 4

FRANK CASS PUBLISHERS
Newbury House, 900 Eastern Avenue, Ilford, Essex, IG2 7HH
Tel: +44 (0)20 8599 8866 Fax: +44 (0)20 8599 0984 E-mail: info@frankcass.com
NORTH AMERICA
5804 NE Hassalo Street, Portland, OR 97213 3644, USA
Tel: 800 944 6190 Fax: 503 280 8832 E-mail: cass@isbs.com
Website: www.frankcass.com

Cricket and England

A Cultural and Social History of the Inter-war Years

Jack Williams, *John Moores University, Liverpool*

'Jack Williams's excellent book ... tightly focused, well written and adept in putting cricket into a broader cultural framework.'

The Guardian

This new study by Jack Williams aims to show that the images of cricket, and how far the world of cricket conformed to them, are essential for understanding English culture and society between the wars.

224 pages illus 1999 0 7146 4861 2 cloth; 0 7146 4418 8 paper
Sport in the Global Society No. 8

The Games Ethic and Imperialism

Aspects of the Diffusion of an Ideal

J A Mangan, *University of Strathclyde*

Now available in paperback for the first time with a new preface and foreword.
This book is far more than a description of the imperial spread of public school games: it is a consideration of hegemony and patronage, ideals and idealism, educational values and aspirations, cultural assimilation and adaptation and, perhaps most fascinating of all, the dissemination throughout the empire of the hugely influential moralistic ideology athleticism.

240 pages 1985; 2nd revised edition 1998 0 7146 4399 8 paper
Sport in the Global Society No. 2

Athleticism in the Victorian and Edwardian Public School

The Emergence and Consolidation of an Educational Ideology

J A Mangan, *University of Strathclyde*
Foreword by **Sheldon Rothblatt** with an introduction by **Jeffrey Richards** and a new introduction by the author

When it appeared in 1981, this book was the first major study of the games ethos which dominated the lives of many Victorian and Edwardian public school boys. Written with Professor Mangan's customary panache, it has become a classic, the seminal work on the social and cultural history of modern sport.

380 pages 2nd revised edition 2000 0 7146 8043 5 paper
Sport in the Global Society No. 13

FRANK CASS PUBLISHERS
Newbury House, 900 Eastern Avenue, Ilford, Essex, IG2 7HH
Tel: +44 (0)20 8599 8866 Fax: +44 (0)20 8599 0984 E-mail: info@frankcass.com
NORTH AMERICA
5804 NE Hassalo Street, Portland, OR 97213 3644, USA
Tel: 800 944 6190 Fax: 503 280 8832 E-mail: cass@isbs.com
Website: www.frankcass.com